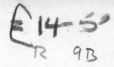

Cambridge Studies in the History and Theory of Politics

EDITORS

Maurice Cowling   J. G. A. Pocock
G. R. Elton   J. R. Pole
E. Kedourie   Walter Ullmann

THE CHRISTIAN POLITY OF
JOHN CALVIN

ÆDES CHRISTI
in Academia Oxoniensi

CWS WE 1904.

THE CHRISTIAN POLITY OF JOHN CALVIN

HARRO HÖPFL

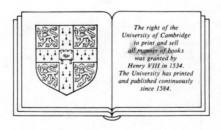

The right of the
University of Cambridge
to print and sell
all manner of books
was granted by
Henry VIII in 1534.
The University has printed
and published continuously
since 1584.

CAMBRIDGE UNIVERSITY PRESS

CAMBRIDGE

LONDON   NEW YORK   NEW ROCHELLE

MELBOURNE   SYDNEY

Published by the Press Syndicate of the University of Cambridge
The Pitt Building, Trumpington Street, Cambridge CB2 1RP
32 East 57th Street, New York, NY 10022, USA
10 Stamford Road, Oakleigh, Melbourne 3166, Australia

First published 1982
Reprinted 1985
First paperback edition 1985

Printed in Great Britain
at the Pitman Press, Bath

Library of Congress catalogue card number: 81–24192

British Library cataloguing in publication data

Höpfl, H. M.
The Christian polity of John Calvin. – (Cambridge
studies in the history and theory of politics)
1. Calvin, Jean 2. Political Science
I. Title
320.5'5   JC145.c/

ISBN 0 521 24417 X hard covers
ISBN 0 521 31638 3 paperback

Contents

Preface

This would be the only part of the work which is an unalloyed pleasure to write, were it not for the fact that in attempting to itemize one's debts, one cannot help but become conscious of the danger of sins of omission. Naming no names, therefore, my list of creditors includes my teachers at the London School of Economics who, a decade and a half ago, inspired me with an enthusiasm for the history of political thought and tried to show me how to study it, and my colleagues in the Department of Politics at Lancaster University, who sustained me during the long period of gestation, even those who regarded my project as an eccentricity to be indulged. *Nominatim,* my thanks go to my head of department, Gordon Hands, who has always seen his way to making the necessary funds available; to Mrs Elizabeth Wetton, who steered the book through Cambridge University Press; and to Mrs Lesley Magowan, who typed the manuscript with accuracy and cheerfulness. The two anonymous reviewers of Cambridge University Press and Professor J. G. A. Pocock in their various ways sought to protect me from myself. And if, in seeking to avoid the gaffes and pitfalls they pointed out, I have fallen into a good many others, the fault will be mine, not theirs.

My final and greatest debt is to Vanessa Elizabeth, Margarethe Anna and last, but first, to Wendy, without all of whom writing this book would have been a more quickly accomplished task, but an altogether more joyless one. The book is dedicated to Wendy, and to the memory of my father.

H. M. HÖPFL
Lancaster, 1981

vii

Note on sources, orthography, notes and translations

For the 1536 *Institution*, I have used P. Barth and W. Niesel (eds), *Joannis Calvini Opera Selecta* (Munich, 1926–36), volume I., compared with the translation of F. L. Battles (*Institution of The Christian Religion*, Atlanta, 1975), the pagination of which work is itself cross-referenced to the *Opera Selecta* (referred to throughout as OS) as well as to the 1559 edition.

For later versions of the *Institution*, I have used the variorum edition in OS, volumes III–V, compared with the translations of H. Beveridge and F. L. Battles (in J. T. McNeill's edition of the *Institutes*). References are by book, chapter and section. All variations between the editions have been carefully noted.

The references to the *Confession de la Foy*, *Articles Concernant l'Organisation de l'Eglise* and the *Catechisme* are to volume I of OS.

For all other writings by Calvin I have used G. Baum, E. Cunitz and E. Reuss (eds), *Joannis Calvini Opera Quae Supersunt Omnia*, 59 vols (Brunswick and Berlin, 1863–1900), referred to throughout as CO. I have compared the Old Testament Commentaries with the translations of the Calvin Translation Society, 47 vols (Edinburgh, 1843–59) and the New Testament Commentaries with the vastly more reliable *Calvin's Commentaries* (Edinburgh and London, 1960–). To facilitate references for those without access to all these massive series, I have noted such references by book, gospel or epistle, and chapter and verse, rather than by page.

Many of Calvin's sermons, both printed in his own life-time and unprinted, appear in CO. For some reason, the edition was brought to an end long before the extant manuscripts were exhausted. Happily, the remaining sermons are now being produced in splendid critical editions as *Supplementa Calviniana* (Neukirchen Kreis Moers, 1961–), referred to throughout as SC.

The responsibility for all translations is of course my own, but I have not lightly departed from the work of better Latinists than myself, except where I felt that they were just wrong, or where Calvin's vigorous French seems to me to have been emasculated by Latinesque translations into stodgy English.

The orthography is as I found it in the sources I have used; on occasion an accent, apostrophe or punctuation mark has been added to facilitate reading. I have not attempted to gild the lily of sixteenth-century French spelling.

Finally, there appears to be no agreed or suitable adjective for the substantive 'reformation'. The Germans have 'reformatorisch' – 'reformational'? Sixteenth-century terminology is unhelpful, as either it is merely abusive, or it operates with categories like 'we' or 'ours' or 'true religion'; terms like 'reformed', 'evangelical' and 'protestant', let alone 'Lutheran' (much used by the opponents of reformation), all have special meanings as well as generic ones. On contextual grounds, I prefer 'evangelical', and use other terms (except 'Lutheran') only for the sake of variety.

Introduction

What follows is an attempt to uncover the relationship between Calvin's practical experience as a political actor and his political theology. My purpose, therefore, is as much to explain how Calvin came to put forward the views he did, as to specify, for each point of his career, what precisely those views were. The guiding thought that informs these pages is that Calvin's practice as a framer of ecclesiastical polity is not a matter of the simple application of principle to practice; this I take to be an impossibility, both in general, for political conduct is always a matter of political judgement as well as principle, and in this particular case, for, as I hope to show, Calvin's theology did not yield any direct injunctions to conduct. Nor is Calvin's political theology a simple rationalization of preceding practice, if for no other reason than that I think his political theology did not adequately assimilate his practice – he wrought better than he knew. Again, I think Calvin's later writings in many respects more satisfactory than his earlier ones, but the reader will find here no echo of that debate of the higher Marxist scholasticism about the 'young' versus the 'mature' Marx; and 'development' seems to me a dispensable concept in intellectual history. There is, in short, no simple account to be given of the relationship between experience and ratiocinative thought, and no such story is told here.

The ground I cover is familiar, the material excellently predigested. Scholars of learning and intelligence have covered every inch of it and a precedent is no doubt discoverable for every assertion I make. I have not attempted to note every assertion which borrows from, depends on, echoes or denies the assertion of some other scholar. In the first place, I have no intention of reworking Calvin's biography; the reader is referred to the many works that already exist. And, more important, scholarship, industry and intelligence have not prevented crimes against history, and even were it the case (and it is not) that the literature on Calvin's political thought were studded with gems, the fact remains that to set oneself to write about any historical topic requires a choice of themes and emphases, the range of which is for practical purposes in-exhaustible. Indeed, this need for an orientation or choice of perspective (to use those visual metaphors so beloved by partisans of the sociology of knowledge), coupled with the desire to be faithful to historical evidence, confronts one with some problems not unlike those faced by the Reformers themselves in their attempts to found their truth on the autonomous authority of a written text. What the interpreter seeks is the whole drift and tenor of a work, but all he can point to as evidence is specific sentences and passages. This not only provides opportunities for arbitrariness in interpretation, but it also poses in an acute form the question of how one resolves disagreements, not about the precise sense of this or that sentence, but about the character of Calvin's thought as a whole.

It may be said that such problems of interpretation have been not avoided, but mostly ignored, in the existing literature, and a good few others have been irrelevantly introduced. The whole literature (for example, Galiffe, Doumergue, Kamp-schulte, Bohatec, Niesel, Pfisterer) is replete with unhistorical orientation. Thus the interpreter's stand about the place of Calvin in history and the contemporary world – a question eminently unhistorical and immaterial – has been taken to be the crux of interpretation. This preliminary orientation – the felt need to take a stand *pro* or *contra* – displays itself in the habit of making verdicts on Calvin's 'guilt' or 'innocence' with regard to various 'accusations', 'charges', 'condemnations' and so forth. Doumergue is perhaps the most notorious public sinner in this respect. In his account of the trial of Servetus, for example, having made several properly historical points, such as that Calvin did not indict, try, condemn or execute Servetus, nor thirst after his blood, he then proceeded to appeal to the 'spirit of the age', in order not to make the historically accept-able point that Calvin's actions are explicable, but to make the quite unhistorical and extraneous point that Calvin should not be 'condemned'.

If the starting-point of scholarly discussion has often been an unacceptable one, methods of validation employed have also left a great deal to be desired. The primary method of validating assertions about Calvin has been by amassing quotations, proof-texts. Such a procedure is incapable of demonstrating anything, and not only when, as so often, the quotations are contextless and random, taken from works of unequal level and from different periods. Rather is the defect in such a procedure one of principle, for the meaning of the lines adduced depends on a particular reading of the context in which they appear, and such a reading must in turn have a reference back to a view of the larger context of Calvin's thought as a whole, and of his times – the celebrated problem of the hermeneutical circle. About such problems the literature is silent.

Given the difficulties in judging between competing interpretations of the master-conceptions of Calvin's thought, precision and sensitivity in the names to be applied to such conceptions is a *sine qua non*. On this ground terms like 'organischer Staatsgedanke' (Bohatec), 'theologia naturalis' (Gloede), 'individualism' (Bohatec), 'true liberalism' (Doumergue), 'anthropologie et sociologie' (Biéler), 'constitutionalism' (Chenevière), 'Romanizing' (Sohm, Seeberg) are all recognizable non-starters, and no purpose is served by continuing to discuss their appropriateness.

It was, of course, as was customary with this style of writing, an assumption of the scholarly tradition that there was a coherence in Calvin's writings, and that the only difficulty was to find it. While this assumption was either gratuitous, or as likely to conceal as to enlighten, it did have one consequence which to some extent mitigated the harm done by the other assumptions. If one looked for coherence, it was only consequent to seek it in the most coherent and comprehensive of Calvin's writings, namely the successive editions of the *Institution* and especially the last, 1559, edition which was taken (again naturally) to be the fruit of the 'development' of Calvin's thought. Now, both Calvin himself and his contemporaries so regarded the *Institution*; indeed, a Genevan edict threatened with punishment anyone who spoke ill of M. Calvin or his *Institution*. But the *Institution* and Calvin's other writings and utterances are not related as text and gloss: the matter is more complex than that.[1] I take it then that there is no justification for treating Calvin as a one-book man, but neither is there any reason to treat everything recorded in the *Corpus Reformatorum* as constituting part of a 'Summa Theologica', equal in all its parts as to authoritativeness, coherence and weight.[2] In this book I have conscientiously attempted to determine the weight to be attached to Calvin's assertions by considering the circumstances in which they were made and the audience to which they were addressed.

The training of a lawgiver

In April 1532, there issued from a Parisian printer a volume entitled *Two Books Concerning Clemency, Written by the Distinguished Roman Senator and Philosopher L. Annaeus Seneca for the Emperor Nero, Elucidated by the Commentaries of Jean Calvin of Noyon*. The volume, which was in Latin and therefore intended solely for the erudite, aroused no interest at the time,[1] and would be of consequence now only to the specialist in humanist Latinity, but for its authorship. The temptation to treat it as the little acorn which contains *in nuce* the mighty oak of the Reformer's later work is to be resisted.[2] It is explored here simply for what light it may shed on the education and political sentiments of a man who, without having any inkling of it then, was to become the teacher of ecclesiastical polity to generations of evangelicals.

In 1532 Calvin was twenty-three years old. He is thought to have begun the work when he was little more than twenty,[3] prior to his graduation as *licencié ès lois* from the University of Orleans (in early 1531). He had long been Master of Arts, proceeding to that degree at the University of Paris in 1525 or 1526.[4] His intention in publishing at such an early age and at his own expense was to make his mark on the world of the humanist literati, and the choice of Seneca for a subject was well thought out, for the most recent edition of the work by Erasmus, the *stupor mundi* of the northern humanists, had contained an invitation to those of greater ability and leisure to do better. Calvin was picking up that gauntlet, but was not to have the success for which he had hoped.[5]

That Seneca should have been chosen as the subject for a commentary by a clever young postgraduate in law requires some explanation. The academic study of law in sixteenth-century France was in the process of bifurcation. Some continued to follow that medieval tradition which, bowing to no one in its admiration for the Civil Law, that is to say, the law of the Roman *civitas*, as opposed to Canon Law, attempted to make that law relevant to current circumstances by way of glosses and glosses upon the glossators.[6] Others were striking out along the path pioneered in France by Guillaume Budé, described by Calvin as the chief glory of good literature,[7] who attempted to return to the pure foundations of Roman law unsullied by glosses, and inclined to see it as a crystallization, so to say, of the mores, institutions and wisdom of the Ancients. The point here was not to find the relevance of Roman law to current circumstances, although such a relevance was taken for granted, but to determine the place of Roman law within what might be known of the Ancients. To describe this as an 'historical approach' is somewhat misleading, for its inspiration was a belief in the superior wisdom and *humanitas*, not to mention elegance, of the Ancients. It is, however, arguable that the approach adopted led eventually, without anyone intending it, to the discovery of a context for Roman law which was so specific as to make that law irrelevant to current circumstances altogether.[8] But in 1530 this was far from apparent: even so celebrated a humanist civilian as Andrea Alciati (attracted to the University of Bourges from Italy at great expense, and in his turn attracting quantities of students there, including Calvin in 1529) was both a humanist and a practical lawyer.[9] The century had in any case no justification available for studies which did not claim religious, moral or practical utility, even though only a pure, disinterested love of Antiquity and all its aspects can explain tomes like Budé's *Annotationes in Pandectas* (1508), *De Asse et Partibus Eius* (1514), *Commentarii Graecae Linguae* (1529), and Alciati's *De Verborum Significatione* (1535), which found not only authors to write them, but also enthusiastic readers. A warm regard for Roman law[10] and an incapacity to ignore the opinions of Greek and Roman philosophers even when it would have made for the streamlining of his theology[11] was to remain with Calvin all his days. When called upon to contribute to the codification of the 'laws and edicts' of Geneva, he turned to the *Corpus Juris Civilis* for models of contract, property law and judicial procedure.[12]

It was the humanist approach to the Roman law which attracted Calvin – it is for this reason that he migrated to Bourges from Orleans – but a career in law seems never to have appealed to him; that he should study law was his father's decision, not his own. It was thus singularly fortunate that Budé should have shown how the study of law and that of 'good literature' (*bonae litterae*, a humanist slogan) could be united. Indeed the *De Clementia Commentary* is, rather circularly, the clearest but not the only evidence that Calvin was in the process of forsaking the law for *humaniores litterae*; witness also his private study of Greek, begun at Orleans under the tuition of his friend Wolmar.

The fact remains, however, that the *De Clementia* is not only a signal instance of 'philosophy' as humanists understood it, but also moral advice lavished by a philosopher upon his imperial pupil (who, alas, proved unteachable), and was a conspicuous example of a 'mirror for princes'. We are therefore left wondering about the significance of this particular choice of subject-matter. An additional problem is that of relating Calvin's 'conversion' to the commentary: was it the work of a man who had already become an evangelical? If so, how would this affect our interpretation of the commentary?

As to the latter question, it does not require discussion at this point,[13] for there is nothing in the work which presupposes evangelical conviction to render it intelligible, nor is there a single point made in it which might be construed as evangelical or as advocacy on behalf of evangelicals. In any case: advocacy to or before whom? Before the abbot to whom it was dedicated? Or before the king? It is true that the *De Clementia* is a 'mirror for princes', but Calvin's work was not aimed at Francis I, nor was it even a bid for royal patronage,[14] and its subject-matter was of secondary interest to Calvin, as will be seen in the sequel. In any case, had Calvin been pleading for evangelicals, he would have asked the king for justice, not clemency which presupposes a crime committed and admitted.[15]

We may say, then, that in 1532 Calvin was a humanist who considered a commentary on Seneca a proper employment of his time, and ambitious for a reputation as a scholar. He had friends, especially Pierre Robert (Olivetanus) and Wolmar, who entertained evangelical views, and he was hostile to the Sorbonne and its works. How much further his thinking had proceeded in an evangelical direction it is impossible to say: there is simply no unambiguous evidence, such as would be afforded by an avowal of the doctrine of *sola fide* or a rejection of the Mass as an 'abomination'. Nor need we stipulate any particular affection for Seneca or interest in the subject-matter of the *De Clementia* to explain why Calvin thought it worthwhile to spend two years of his leisure on the work. Even in the text, Calvin made it clear that he preferred Cicero to Seneca; it happens that there was no room for another commentary on the former. Calvin's description of Seneca as 'the best of authors' and as 'a man of eximious erudition and signal eloquence'[16] are little more than examples of the humanist predilection for superlatives, and his claim that he was defending 'his' author against his many detractors[17] was a mere touting of his wares: no student of rhetoric, such as Calvin, is unaware of the publicity value of claiming to stand against all the world, *Athanasius contra mundum*. Little about Calvin's personal literary predilections and nothing about a desire to teach anything whatever to princes can be inferred from such claims. It seems *prima facie* unlikely that a man should devote two years to the exposition of an author he deems intolerable or fundamentally wrong-headed,[18] but this consideration is of no great moment, as will be seen shortly.

If we are to read the *De Clementia Commentary* for what it tells us about Calvin rather than about Seneca, it is necessary to remind ourselves that the first duty of the commentator (and Calvin all his life was a dutiful man) is to elucidate his text, not to obtrude his own opinions. It is only when we find assertions unwarranted by the text, or when the discussion is skewed in quite another way than the text, that we can be sure we are dealing with Calvin the man, not Calvin the expositor. Explicit dissent from, or criticism of, the text obviously comes in the same category, as does explicit endorsement of opinions expressed there. Both are, in fact, uncommon in this work, and the conventions of the time, as well as the skills of the rhetorician would have permitted a great deal more latitude than Calvin chose to exercise. Somewhat more hazardous as a ground for inference, but not to be disregarded, are those occasions when Calvin failed to comment on some conspicuous part of the text. Arguments from silence are always tendentious, but some of Calvin's silences are altogether too pregnant to be overlooked.

Before we consider what Calvin thought, we may pause to notice what he knew. Even allowing for the compendia of choice sayings he had to hand,[19] Calvin emerges as for his years prodigiously well read in the literature of Antiquity, both historical and 'philosophical'. It may be remarked in passing that neither he nor his preceptors displayed any interest in epistemology, a central concern of what is now understood by 'philosophy', irrespective of school or tradition; as the humanists used the term, 'philosophy' meant discourse about the good life,[20] and even here the issue was not so much to explore the foundations of moral judgements as to set down instructions for conduct in a form deemed particularly high-minded, sage and well turned. In short, philosophy was for Calvin, as for Erasmus and More, a matter of teaching men how to live by exercising the arts of persuasion. Calvin was said to have been a strict censor of the morals of his fellows when still a school-boy;[21] that he should have approved a censorious writer like Seneca is no cause for surprise.

Calvin's learning was Latin; Greek was an accomplishment he was still acquiring; Hebrew he seems to have begun at Basel under Sebastian Münster in 1535. It is not clear how restrictive being confined to Latin actually was; a good many Latin translations of Greek writings were available. The learned editors of the commentary are inclined to attribute much of his Greek material to secondary sources, in which case it would have come to Calvin in a rather contextless form aside from its ordering under general headings, which again would suggest doctrine rather than enquiry. Certainly nothing in the commentary bespeaks any sympathetic and sustained entering into the spirit of Greek philosophical treatises, and especially not treatises on political theory.

It is evident, too, that Calvin knew his way around the history of Antiquity. In the manner of the scholarship of the time he never mentioned a single date according to the Christian calendar; humanists in general tended not to treat history as an ordered, sequential account of transitions, from which point of view attention to chronology might assume great importance.[22] Instead, Calvin would offer isolated and rather disjointed pieces of information drawn from various sources when he felt that the text called for it, with little concern for the reliability of that information. Thus, prompted by the text to display his erudition about the size and organization of a Roman legion, Calvin contented himself with citing several discrepant authorities from various times, and attributing the discrepancies to habits of inexact speech (*De Clem. Comm.*, pp. 98/9). He made no attempt to order the various figures and data into a coherent account of changing circumstances. Again, confronted by the claim that vast numbers of prominent Roman citizens were slain by Sulla, Calvin simply related various figures given by various historians, without any enquiry into their reliability (pp. 206–11). Nor was he embarrassed by the fact that by his reckoning (based mainly on Tacitus), the age of Seneca at death was 115 years (pp. 16/17). In short, 'history' was what it remained to him throughout his life, that is to say, a useful ancillary to other preoccupations, and in particular it was *histories*, the relating of edifying episodes. It cannot be said, then, that 'the chief historical labour in annotating the *De Clementia* was to provide the reader with a grasp of the period of the Civil Wars and the Augustan Age' (p. 118, intro.). On the contrary, the chief historical labour was to clear away obstacles to the understanding of Seneca as rhetorician and philosopher, such as were set up by Seneca's contemporary allusions. The displays of an heterogeneous erudition do not amount to the provision of any sort of grasp of a 'period', and periodicity does not seem to have been a category of Calvin's secular historiography at any point in his career.

If 'history' as he understood it was strictly a secondary concern, what is perhaps rather more striking is the tepid character of Calvin's endorsements of Seneca's moral and religious sentiments. While he dissented emphatically and in a highly patronizing manner from Seneca's stoic view of pity as a disorder of the mind, a violation of the ideal of *apathia* which Calvin also rejected,[23] he never praised Seneca's views on morality and religion with any degree of warmth. Still less did he show any inclination to Christianize Seneca: even the latter's exclamation 'We have all sinned' prompted no adducing of parallels from Christian doctrine.[24] And the lines: 'Now assuredly it were fitting that men, thrusting out desire of another's goods from which springs every evil of the heart, should conspire for righteousness and equity, so that *pietas* and uprightness, along with *fides* and temperance, might arise, and that vice, having misused its long reign, should at length give place to an age of happiness and purity'[25] did not prompt a single word of comment from Calvin. Even Seneca's several references to natural law were treated in an ambiguous manner: one such reference was explained simply as being 'from the teaching of the Stoics who bid us follow nature as the best guide' (*De Clem. Comm.*, pp. 280/1); on the other hand, he claimed that where Seneca invited Nero to consider 'that he should wish to be to his subjects as he would wish the gods to be to himself', he was 'reminding the prince of the natural law' (pp. 122/3). Since it is impossible to argue conclusively from silence we cannot say what was in Calvin's mind, but we have to conclude that Calvin had no disposition towards a syncretism of Christianity and pagan 'philosophy'. And, allowing for humanist habits of hyperbole, Calvin's austerity and taciturnity in the face of Seneca's sentiments reads as much like damning with faint praise as his vague comments in the Preface: 'it is when dealing *en tois ethikois* that he is, so to speak, in his own element,[26] and it is here that he reigns supreme, being conversant with as much of dialectics as was necessary for the cultivation of eloquence'.[27] He then passed immediately to more congenial matters such as Seneca's literary style, where he managed to complain of the 'luxurious verbosity' of the author, and ended by ranking him second to Cicero as a pillar of Roman philosophy and eloquence. None of this suggests that Calvin did not endorse a good deal of what Seneca had written, or that he found him objectionable; it does, however, suggest that his interest in Seneca was of a different sort.

It is, in fact, not at all difficult to discern what that interest was: it was in Seneca as an exemplar of the art and science of rhetoric. This would be entirely apparent, but for the groundless assumption that because Calvin commented on Seneca, his interest must have been in the latter's subject-matter. In fact, comment after comment explains, sometimes simply,[28] but often with a parade of technical terminology,[29] what effect Seneca was trying to achieve, what response he was seeking to elicit, and how he was organizing his argument. The introductory analysis of Seneca's purpose and approach is a masterpiece of rhetorical investigation and it may be noted in passing that Calvin was far from content with Seneca, as one expert discussing the work of another. He deplored particularly

Seneca's failure to offer a definition of *clementia* until the book was almost over, and he did not much care for Seneca's rambling style (*De Clem. Comm.*, pp. 10/11; 352/3). On the other hand he displayed a connoisseur's relish for *bons mots*, well-turned phrases and choice illustrations, for subtleties in approach and elegancies in expression.

Since Calvin was treating the *De Clementia* as a species of the genus Rhetoric, the art and science of persuasion, the fact that the work was addressed to an emperor was relevant only to the extent that this circumstance posed a particular range of difficulties for the practitioner of the art, as does every sort of audience. And in case the use of the term 'rhetoric', malodorous in the nostrils of Anglo-Saxons who have succeeded in persuading themselves that they both can and do dispense with it, has created a false impression, let it be stated at once that a good part of the 'philology' which occupied the affections and attentions of humanists was concerned precisely with this. It is, for example, on the mastery of this art that Thomas More pinned whatever slender hope he held out for humanists at the courts of princes.[30] The *De Clementia Commentary*, therefore, displays and was intended to display its author not so much as a master of philosophy in the then current sense, but rather as fully instructed in the practice and technicalities of the art of the rhetor. And since Calvin's skill at persuasion – it was on persuasion and nothing else (humanly speaking) that his career as Reformer and ecclesiastical politician was founded[31] – has never been denied by friend or foe, it may be said that he had learned his lesson well.

If one pursues this interpretation, Calvin's comparative indifference to the substance of what Seneca was saying at once becomes explicable. For rhetoric is a *techne*, and as such can be used as well for fashioning swords as for fashioning ploughshares; indeed, from the technical point of view, the rhetoric of defending a bad case is more interesting than that of defending a good one, for it calls for more expertise. The moral ambiguity of rhetoric would then, however, come to be the focus of attention, which would in turn distract attention from the technicalities of the practice. But there is nothing to suggest that Calvin offered Seneca as a good defence of an inherently bad case, and the conclusion must be that Calvin was happy enough with the general tenor of Seneca's discussion, and that where he was not, he said so. In general, he was concerned not with content but with expression, and this preoccupation provides the only core of genuine enquiry in a work whose moral substance is dogmatic and derivative. There is precisely no 'grappling with moral questions', nor any 'seeking after the forms of social organization which will insure a life of peace and virtue for the citizenry'.[32] The literary form which corresponds to 'grappling' and 'seeking after' is some kind of dialectic,[33] and dialectic, at any rate in its scholastic form, was a favourite target for humanist abuse, to which Calvin contributed. Throughout his life, Calvin displayed his hostility to 'frivolous' and 'useless' speculation and subtleties;[34] indeed he regarded it as a positive stumbling-block to faith and a vice of the mind. Truth requires no elaborate defence; subtleties and quibbling are the marks of a bad case; and the virtuous life is fostered by the art of rhetoric, not logomachy.[35]

We may take it, then, that Calvin regarded the substance of Seneca as in the main unproblematic. It is hardly subject to doubt that he endorsed Seneca's view that the heads of commonwealths, *principes*, are released from subjection to law, *legibus soluti*.[36] This was not a matter of advocacy for Calvin; it was not even the espousal of a fashionable, and fashionably humanist, doctrine; Calvin was no advocate of centralizing monarchy. Rather, it was a simple entailment of certain other prior assumptions. On the one hand, Roman law pointed unequivocally to the *princeps legibus solutus*. On the other, a distaste for crowds and an acute suspicion of their potentialities suggested the need for a firm hand. Thus Roman law takes it for granted that every law has a determinate author or set of authors, most laws including the name of the proposer in their title, as for example *Lex Cornelia de Parricidiis*. No such assumption was made in customary or common law;[37] but for that Calvin never appears to have had any regard. It is, furthermore, a presupposition of law that there is an ultimate interpreter. It is in the light of this presupposition, and no other, that we must understand Calvin's acceptance of the cliché that the king is *lex animata*, a living law, or indeed, that the king *is* the law (*De Clem. Comm.*, pp. 302/3; 146/7). Equally, it was a commonplace of jurisprudence that a rigid adherence to the letter of the law may itself be injustice, a violation of *aequum et bonum*, and consequently that there must be someone entitled to suspend, or dispense from, the strict operation of the law. 'Budé sufficiently shows in his Annotations [sc. on the *Pandects*] what equity and right are, in contrast to the letter and rigour of the law (*quid esset aequum et bonum, quod iuri summo seu rigori iuris opponitur*).[38] Calvin's term for judging, *jurisdictio*, is ambivalent between declaring a pre-existing law, and making law by a declaration or edict.[39] He did not take issue with Seneca's view that judging was one of the principal duties of the ruler. Factually, of course, judging and ruling were already generally distinct offices, but it was a long time before this distinction attained normative status.

It is not being suggested that we are here dealing with more than assumptions, and very conventional ones at that; nevertheless Calvin's acceptance of the case for a *princeps legibus solutus* was distinctly unenthusiastic, and any speculative flights in its favour are entirely missing. He flatly disregarded the other arguments favoured by the partisans of the New Monarchies, even when the text gave ample opportunity for considering them. In particular the assertion from the *Institutes* of Justinian that 'what has pleased the *princeps* has the force of law' was not reproduced, although Calvin must have known it perfectly well, both because it was commonplace and because he quoted the very next lines that followed it in the *Institutes*: 'for by the *lex regia*, the people transferred all jurisdiction to the emperors'.[40] Neither had he any patience with those cosmological arguments purporting to demonstrate the naturalness and superiority of the monarchical over other governmental forms,[41] even though Seneca paraded all the favourite correspondences: head and members, father and household, soul and body, 'king' bee and bee-hive, God and cosmos. All that Calvin endorsed was the pragmatic view that 'the emperor is the bond whereby the citizens are bound together, that they may not fly apart. If the helmsman and governor (*rector et moderator*) were lacking, by what chains would a factious and seditious mob be bound together?' (*De Clem. Comm.*, pp. 100/1). He also approved the analogy between 'the whole body as the servant of the mind' and the ruler and the body politic, but found nothing whatever to say of Seneca's interpretation of it, namely that 'this vast throng . . . is ruled by [the prince's] mind, guided by his reason, and would crush and cripple itself with its own strength unless it were upheld by his wisdom.'[42] It may be remarked that in an Augustinian view of polity, it is not the mind or the noble purposes of the ruler that sustains the *ordo* of the *civitas terrena*, but, rather more prosaically, his selfish desire to maintain himself in power, which in turn requires that he maintain some kind of order. Calvin merely noted, without comment, the correspondence between the head of a body and the ruler of a commonwealth (pp. 348/9), and the assertion that 'nature itself conceived the idea of kingship', as is shown by the organization of the bee-hive and flocks of cranes, merely prompted the reply: 'one might well wonder why Seneca works out this poetic description in such detail, when it is hardly to the point . . .' (pp. 276/7 ff.) and Calvin went on to discuss bee-hives, citing none but classical sources. Such a comment is inconceivable in a proponent of the Philosophy of Order, who would have regarded arguments of this sort as being the very heart of the matter, and anything other than a 'poetic description'. As for the idea of the king as an earthly god, Calvin simply noted it as a habit of speech among the Romans, but paused to ridicule the Roman custom of apotheosis of their emperors.[43] He did, however, endorse the Christian view of princes as 'ministers of God', quoting Romans 13 in support; of the parallel between good pagans and Christians on this point he made precisely nothing (pp. 30/1).

In short, there is nothing in the entire text to suggest that Calvin thought of monarchy as in any sense particularly natural or divinely ordained by comparison with any other form of government. Also conspicuous by its absence is the idea of the godly prince as the patron of good letters and defender of humanists;[44] but then, Calvin's concern was not with the 'mirror for princes' genre as such. Even the staple of that literature, the problem of how a prince might get good advice and avoid flatterers,[45] received mention only in the context of Calvin's elucidation of the rhetorical task confronting his author (pp. 22/3).

There was, however, one substantive question which forced itself on Calvin's attention, for it concerned Seneca himself and was directly entailed by the acceptance of the *princeps legibus solutus*. The traditional distinction between a king and a tyrant was that the good king rules according to law, whereas the tyrant places himself above the law. What then of the *princeps legibus solutus*? It cannot be demonstrated that Calvin recognized this difficulty, but it is perhaps significant that he used the standard nostrum for escaping from it, carefully qualifying each assertion of *legibus solutus* with something such as 'It is a saying worthy of a ruler's majesty for a prince to confess himself bound to the laws. And surely there is something greater than rule in submitting the principate to the laws . . .'[46] or: 'It is well, then, that princes, freed from laws, yet live by the laws. Nay, they are the very law itself' (pp. 146/7). The last clause, while it does not fit very well with the foregoing one, is not intended to diminish the authority of the law, as is made clear in a later, not significantly more coherent formulation: 'the prince who is the living law, and who must in this matter yield not even a trifle to his feelings, but do all things according to the prescription of the law' (pp. 302/3). Calvin was even happy to adduce the saying from Pliny: 'The prince is not above the laws, but the laws above the prince', which, if taken literally, was diametrically opposed to the idea of the *princeps legibus solutus* (pp. 44/5). Indeed, his own definition of the commonwealth (*civitas*), derived, he tells us, from Aristotle and Cicero, is that it is 'an assembly or society (*concilium coetusve*) of men associated by law (*iure*)'.[47] He then added, as if this were somehow included in this definition, the qualification 'upright morals and fair laws', which makes it clear that he was conflating law and justice. The possibility that laws might be other than equitable was not pursued, and Calvin was enabled to disregard it by the fact that the topic of clemency has nothing to do with whether the laws are equitable or not: it presupposes that they are, but not in every instance of their application.

It looks, therefore, as if Calvin felt himself obliged to admit that the prince must in some sense be above the law, but that he was not particularly comfortable with the admission and was inclined to substitute other sorts of restraint on rulers, in so far as he gave the matter much attention. Having made the congenially philological observation that the distinction between kings and tyrants is one of usage and not of etymology, he remarked that 'now the custom has come to prevail of calling tyrant one who rules against the will of his subjects and exercises power without restraint (*intemperanter*)' (pp. 200–3). Elsewhere, too, the absence of restraint seems to have been of the essence of tyrannical rule for him.[48] His scattered remarks indicate that he attributed the violence which he took to be characteristic of tyrants[49] to an unwillingness to tolerate restraint, and such indiscipline in turn to a delight in evil-doing; at any rate he at one point deliberately took issue with an opinion which he attributed to philosophers, to assert that 'in some way or other, I do not know how, it has become a fact of everyday experience that certain persons are just wicked for no reason at all, and are so frenzied with the pleasure (*libidine*) of sinning, that the very sinning itself delights them for its own sake'.[50] He attributed a delight in slaughter and depredation to Sulla (pp. 206/7), and he used the traditional tag about tyrants drinking greedily of human blood (pp. 210/11). On the other hand, he also asserted that habits of cruelty and violence, once adopted, could not be abandoned: one crime leads to another (pp. 224/5), and a man who is so hated suffers from an insecurity which no quantity of guards can dispel (pp. 220/1). All this despite the fact that he had, and noted in his text, an example to the contrary, namely Augustus, who began cruelly but continued well, and possibly also Dionysius, the tyrant of Syracuse.[51] All this no doubt represents Calvin's opinion, but it is little more than a rehearsal of clichés. Calvin's attention was, as has been said, elsewhere.

Perhaps we may sum up as follows. Calvin was dealing with a work which attempted by anecdote, illustration and argument to drive home the (in itself extremely trite) message that the just ruler tempers justice with mercy. His own chief concern was to examine how, and how well, Seneca had done his work of persuasion. But in commenting he made sufficiently clear his own verdict on certain of Seneca's arguments and sentiments. Thus he evidently concurred with the view of the prince as *praeses legum et custos*, the upholder and guardian of the laws (pp. 220/1). The upholder and enforcer, that is to say, of laws that already exist, rather than the deviser of new ones: if Calvin envisaged an active, interventionist role for the godly prince, he gave no evidence of it.[52] That the prince on occasion makes new laws is peripheral to his main duty of administering extant ones. The supreme governor (whether it be one man or an assembly) is indeed *legibus solutus*, but this is mainly so that he may not be forced into injustice by being bound to carry out the law to the letter. By enforcing laws with the requisite blend of strictness and clemency, the head of the state preserves the body in integrity. That integrity may be destroyed in two ways:

either when the ruler does not accept self-imposed restraints, allowing his passions to 'rage' (already a favourite metaphor of Calvin), and thus becoming a tyrant; or when he is negligent, and allows liberty to degenerate into licence – an all too likely occurrence, given the propensities of the 'fickle crowd'.[53] The well-ordered *civitas* is distinguished from other sorts by 'upright morals [*probis moribus*, which might also be rendered by 'habits of uprightness', since *mores* means both 'customs' and 'morals'] and equitable laws' (pp. 212/3). It is clear that Calvin un-questioningly equated sin and crime; *peccare* is used throughout for committing crimes, and lawbreakers are usually simply termed *mali*, 'wicked men'. It is clear also that he took the business of the *civitas* to be the punishment of vice and the promotion of virtue. Thus he describes the law as having three ends in view in avenging injuries, and that the ruler should also bear them in mind: either 'to reform the person being punished' (*monitio*), in the sense of inhibiting him from becoming 'more unbridled and corrupt' by impunity in sinning (*peccandi*); or 'by punishing him to make the rest better' (*exemplum*); or finally 'by removing the wicked (*malos*) to allow the rest to live in greater safety' (for which he offered no technical term).[54] Which of these purposes ought to have priority Calvin did not say, but he singled out Plato for criticism for having on one occasion omitted to mention the last (pp. 304/5). The just ruler, then, steers a middle course between excessive severity and excessive leniency: he does not punish to avenge injuries done to himself, or because he relishes suffering, but because he is a servant of the 'common good'. Not, one might have supposed, a particularly rich body of insight to equip a man for a career as a Reformer and ecclesiastical politician.

2

The 'Institution': the first version

CALVIN IN 1535

The *De Clementia Commentary* was the beginning and also the end of Calvin's projected career as a humanist scholar. Less than three years after its publication he was an exile living in Basel[1] in straitened circumstances and under the assumed name 'Martianus Lucianus'.[2] His decision to leave France was precipitated by fear of persecution, and by conclusive evidence that Francis I, previously an uncertain and ambivalent defender of humanists, had finally espoused the Sorbonne's interpretation of what was to count as orthodoxy.[3] It is impossible to say what kind of evangelical Calvin was at his arrival in Basel, a place notable for its *de facto* tolerance of a wide diversity of opinions. Nor is it possible to say at what date Calvin conceived or began the execution of the first *Institution*. We do not know either whether Calvin was now putting on record reflections long since habitual with him, or whether it was writing the *Institution* which itself crystallized his thoughts. All that can be said with confidence is that since the *De Clementia Commentary* Calvin had published nothing except two Prefaces to Olivetan's French translation of the New Testament (which were written, it appears, shortly after his arrival at Basel), and had written, but left unpublished, *Psychopannychia*.[4] It is apparent, then, that some time before he left France, Calvin's attentions had been concentrated entirely on theology, and that it was evangelical, and not merely humanist, theology. At any rate, the evangelical Calvin made his appearance in print at Basel in March 1536 with a book bearing the grandiloquent title: *Institution of the Christian Religion, comprising almost the whole sum (summa) of piety and whatever it is necessary to know about the doctrine of salvation: a work most worthy to be read by all persons zealous for piety, and recently published.* (It was not unusual in those days to include advertising copy in book-titles.) The work had, it appears, been completed more than half a year before: the 'Prefatory Letter' is dated '10. Cal. Septembris' (no year given), that is, 23 August 1535. The work seems to have been an immediate success.

Until recently it was the common practice in English-speaking countries to render the title of the book as *Institutes*, on the analogy of the *Institutes* of Justinian, a translation which is eloquent about the posthumous reputation of Calvin,[5] but in fact the work bore no resemblance whatever to a legal codex, either in form or content. Of late, the more ambiguous *Institution* has again come to be preferred. The most current meaning of the term in Calvin's time was 'education', 'instruction', perhaps even 'primer',[6] and the earliest translations of Calvin took that to be Calvin's meaning, or simply reproduced the word.[7] Nonetheless, given the alternative meaning of *instituere*, as well as the meaning of cognate terms like *constituere, constitution*, and the manner in which Calvin used them,[8] given also that the genitive is 'of the Christian religion' rather than 'of Christians', which would have been more congruous, it seems likely that the *Institutio* of the title was an elegant play upon words, the point of which was to indicate that the contents of the work were not only 'instruction' in the commonplaces of the Christian religion, but also an account of that religion as 'instituted' or founded by Christ, as opposed to its current, man-made deformations. To the outside world such an affirmation might be a platitude of fifteen years' standing, but to the newly converted Calvin it would be a significant and hard-won recognition.

In the 'Prefatory Letter' to Francis I with which the book began, Calvin showed himself aware of the proprieties to be observed by a private man addressing his prince, especially when it is in order to criticize his conduct. There were the usual fulsome titles: 'most puissant and most illustrious monarch', 'most Christian king'; there were the conventional pieties about Francis having been badly advised by malicious courtiers, the suggestion that the current persecutions in France were not of the king's doing,[9] the disclaimer of any original intention of writing anything which might be offered to the monarch. There then followed a *defensio* or *apologia* for evangelicals in general, and 'the poor little church' in France in particular, against the charges of schism and sedition, and the pious hope that if Francis would read the appended work, written as it had been primarily with an eye to the needs of Calvin's unlearned countrymen, he would discover the untruth of the charges and the malice of their detractors and calumniators.

Out of all these conventionalities, one thing emerges with great clarity, while all else is deliberately or unintentionally obscured: it is that Calvin was extremely sensitive to the lumping together of evangelicals and Anabaptists, a popular and serviceable weapon of Romanist polemic, particularly in the year after the 'Kingdom of Christ' of Jan of Leyden at Münster had achieved its own apocalypse. It is the attempt to deal with this charge (by a rather subtle indirection, as will be seen) that explains whatever concern with political or institutional matters the book exhibits. As for the rest, it was not true that the work was 'simple' or 'elementary'[10] as Calvin claimed, for it was both detailed and long; moreover, it was written in a rather difficult Latin: on all these counts it was demonstrably unsuitable to be the 'primer' for his countrymen that Calvin described it as being. Nor should the ostensible addressee of the book be taken very seriously; there is no reason to suppose that Calvin thought Francis's ways might be mended simply by a letter or by better information about the beliefs of evangelicals; had he been so minded, Francis might have informed himself about them by consulting another book he had had to hand for more than ten years: Zwingli's *Commentarius de Vera et Falsa Religione.*[11]

As has been made clear enough recently,[12] the specific audience envisaged by Calvin for the 'Prefatory Letter' at its first publication was the Lutheran princes of Germany, for whose benefit Francis I, anxious to secure their alliance against the Emperor, had given out that the current persecutions in France were justifiable severity against Anabaptists and seditious persons, and not savageries against their French co-religionists. It was this particular lie which Calvin was seeking to scotch by giving the appearance of dissociating Francis from it.

But neither the 'Prefatory Letter' nor the book itself depended in their author's eyes for their worth and relevance exclusively on the existence of a Francis I in negotiation with German Lutheran princes, or on persecutions in France.[13] The 'cause'[14] being pleaded here was the cause of all evangelicals, the 'defence' was fidelity to Scripture and the 'court' was Calvin's fellow citizens in the republic of letters. This was ultimately the only public which concerned Calvin; what is more, it was a public which could be consulted over the heads of governors of all sorts, and Calvin had little to say about the bearing of this cause and this defence on matters of governance. He was not offering this public a lesson in how to govern, since for the most part its members were not governors. Nor was he really teaching them obedience, despite the last chapter of the book, for this was advice they had no choice but to follow.

He was in fact offering what the title of the book promised: an evangelical *summa*. For an evangelical, there was of course only one *summa theologica* and that was Scripture itself; nor was the *Institution* intended in any sense as a substitute for reading it. Rather, it was to serve as, so to speak, a set of 'instructions' on how to read it, a digest of its dominant themes, its *loci communes*, addressed to those with eyes to see.[15]

The *Institution* made no attempt to register the intellectual debts Calvin owed. Nevertheless he was manifestly an evangelical of the second generation[16] and he was later to testify several times to his high regard for Luther in particular.[17] In fact the very plan of the *Institution* was taken over from Luther's *Short Catechism* of 1522,[18] although it was not in any way incumbent upon an evangelical to follow that precedent.[19] Since Calvin furthermore retained this order for the *Confession de la Foy* and the *Catechisme* of late 1536 and late 1537 respectively, we must suppose that he adopted it because it permitted a fair presentation of what Calvin at that time regarded as the essentials of faith. And it seems that in inheriting the theology of the first generation of Reformers, especially Luther's, Calvin also inherited Luther's characteristic ways of setting problems, and the difficulties and perplexities which grew out of them. Not the least of these perplexities were those which stemmed from the encounter between the Reformation and the twin ordering institutions of the Christian commonwealth, the church and the magistracy. A word of explanation about the Reformers' attitude to both is perhaps in order so that we may determine more precisely the *terminus a quo* of Calvin's political thinking.

THE POLITICAL THOUGHT OF THE REFORMATION

The evangelical turning away from the current understanding of the Christian life began in a heightening and deepening of the humanist, and especially Erasmian, concern with internality, spirituality, with the inner man, the soul, the quality of the intention. An affirmation of the priority of spirituality over, and at the expense of, 'externals', 'works', the 'outer man', 'the world', 'ceremonies' is on any showing a primary constituent of the evangelical revolt. The evangelical concept of faith both expresses this understanding of spirituality and puts external matters in their proper perspective. Faith (*fides*) is the condition that results from the sinner's experience of the saving action of God, whereby God vouchsafes to the sinner an unshakeable confidence and trust (*fides*) that he, true to his promise, accounts him righteous. And to this justification works contribute nothing at all. All the experiences which convert a sinner into a Christian – travail of conscience, *Anfechtung*, dejection, despair of one's own capacities, searching the Scriptures, certitude of salvation, liberation – were all seen as occurring in an intimate sphere of relations between man and God, and as entirely unmediated by anything except Scripture.[20] 'Externals' – the very term is dismissive[21] – either play no part in this conversion, or worse still, they are a distraction from, or an outright impediment to, faith.

It is not what the Christian does, then, that makes him righteous; rather is it because he is accounted righteous by God on account of his faith that he does good works and that what he does is good. Indeed it is faith which is the judge of what is to count as a good work. In short, what matters is not so much what is done, as the spirit in which it is done. Unqualified, this is antinomianism. The Reformers were not antinomian, for they never doubted that a godly spirit will generally express itself in certain forms of conduct, in a willing conformity to law. All the same, their first concern was to stress the freedom of the Christian from any obligation in conscience to perform anything currently designated as 'good works', his freedom from obligation to obey any man-made laws in spiritual matters, and his freedom to judge for himself what he should and should not do. This freedom is only qualified by the Christian's duty of charity towards weaker brethren.

Since the world and the current practice of piety abounded in man-made laws, deformations and impositions, the assertion of the Christian's freedom of conscience was, it seemed, a far more urgent task than the definition of the 'outward order' of an evangelical church.[22] With respect to the 'outward order' of the church as established, then, the Reformation was in the first instance negative and destructive: a re-forming, a simplifying, a stripping away of deformations, accretions, superfluities, 'masks' (in Luther's expressive word).[23] The criterion to be employed in discriminating between what was acceptable and what was not was Scripture, and it was a constitutive belief of the Reformation that Scripture was self-interpreting and luminously clear, if not immediately in every part, then always by the 'analogy of faith': those who misinterpreted it were either ignorant or malicious or both.[24] Every Christian is therefore competent to judge for himself what is and what is not required of him: even the distinction between a lay and a spiritual estate is specious.

Since what needed to be un-masked (so to speak) and abolished was plain enough, the question of the agents to carry out the work of stripping away corruptions and deformations did not seem of great consequence: let him who can, do. The anarchic consequences of such an attitude seem not to have been apparent to Luther, who began by counselling an 'inner emigration' for those without secular authority,[25] a respect for the susceptibilities of 'weak consciences', and obedience to external authorities, including the papal tyranny,[26] all of which precluded any rebellious or disorderly proceedings.

At this point a distinction must be drawn between Luther and Zwingli, or perhaps more generally between Luther and the Reformers of the free cities of the Empire and the Stände (states) of the Helvetic Confederation. Zwingli's thought (and perhaps also Bucer's)[27] was inherently communal. The 'particular churches' were for Zwingli communities which he without question equated with the secular political unit: its agents were the secular authorities acting on behalf of their citizens/congregations, and reformation was a political activity, with the magistrates acting as 'school-masters'[28] over faith, worship and morals of clergy and laity alike. The long-established practice of magisterial supervision of the church in the Helvetic Confederation made the fact of intervention, though not of course its purpose and direction, unproblematic.[29] This eliminated several of the complications in Luther's attitude to the public realm, although here, too, there was a price to be paid.

Luther's theology was not in this sense inherently communal, and his stance vis à vis the secular authorities was more complex. The experience of faith is personal and private, the (individual) Christian 'is a free lord of all things, and servant of none',[30] the judgement of what is to be believed and done is each individual's right and responsibility,[31] and this applies as much to the laws of particular churches as it does to the commands of secular rulers, or perhaps more so since secular rulers are to be given the benefit of the doubt,[32] whereas the church may impose nothing on the Christian without his consent or against Scripture.[33] This is, of course, not to say that the Christian lives by or for himself: he needs to be baptized, to hear the Word preached, to receive the Lord's Supper, to pray with other Christians and to love his neighbour. He is in that sense a member of a congregation or community (a *Gemeine*) and Luther may even be said to have taken the existence of such a *Gemeine* for granted. But all this yielded no compelling reason why such a *Gemeine* should not be a purely private affair, an association of like-minded private persons; still less did it give a reason why such congregations should be coextensive with existing political units or jurisdictions. In 1523 Luther counselled a private, congregational way of proceeding to reformation in his *De Instituendis Ministris Ecclesiae*, at least as a *faute de mieux*. And certainly the arrangements and blessings of the Roman church were unnecessary for the existence of a 'true' church in the world: anyone can administer baptism, preach, or hear confession, and even the Lord's Supper is not indispensable.[34] What is crucial for salvation is not membership of *a* church, but membership of the *true* church,[35] the communion of saints, which, since it is composed of the dead as well as the living, and, furthermore, contains none but true Christians (a state of soul discernible only by God), can give scant guidance about the ordering of a 'particular' church.

The distinction between faith and externals, and the attendant doctrines of Christian liberty and the priesthood of all believers, were well suited to the work of destroying the legitimations erected to sustain the papal 'tyranny' and the pernicious doctrine of 'work-holiness'. But the question of the ordering of evangelical churches in a predominantly hostile environment does not fit at all well into Luther's conceptual grid of spiritual/temporal, inner/outer, spirit/body, true righteousness/external righteousness; with respect to all these, the worldly order of the church seems to occupy the interstices. And when Luther set out his theology of secular authority in 1523, he added yet another possible source of disorientation and distraction: the distinction between the kingdom of God and the kingdom of the world. All this quite apart from the fact that Luther's teaching about church order, and especially about the authority of secular government in such matters, resembles not the calm and purposive unfolding of the implications of a doctrine, but rather the *ad hoc* responses of a desperately overworked man to a succession of crises crowding in on him, responses governed as much by practical exigencies and inherited assumptions as by theological principle. There were in his thought intimations of quite divergent attitudes to secular authority, and at various times he followed them all.

Despite the fact that the true, invisible church is inherently incapable of being institutionalized, since unlike a 'particular' church in the world it contains only the elect,[36] Luther did make certain inferences of great importance from relationships between true Christians in the universal, invisible church for the order of particular churches or *Gemeine*. His pioneering and paradigmatic analysis of the popish church as a 'tyranny', rapidly extended to a condemnation of it as a *Herrschaft*,[37] a domination like that of any worldly power, depends at least in part on such an inference from the idea of the universal church as an equality under the headship of Christ, excluding all differences of 'degree' or spiritual status, and as a community of mutual love and service, excluding all coercion and imposition of will. So does his doctrine of the 'priesthood of all believers' which he used to legitimate prescriptions about the ordering of a 'particular' church.[38] And so does his assertion of a kind of congregational ideal of ecclesiastical order, according to which it is the community or congregation (*Gemeine*) which has the authority to judge doctrine and appoint and dismiss ministers.[39] It was never made clear why relations appropriate among true Christians, who cannot even recognize each other in this world, should be thought an appropriate model for the order of a worldly church, which was bound to contain a preponderance of Christians in name only. But any worldly church, including a reformed one, was bound to suffer from what had perforce to be an invidious comparison as a result.

A church of a private congregational type was most easily reconciled with the evangelical demand for Christian liberty, Christian witness, unforced consciences and the absence of coercion. However, the entanglement of the institutional church and the secular government of sixteenth-century polities was such that what Luther in fact had to deal with was churches in which magistrates and princes had the upper hand (*Fürstenkirchen*). And the threat from the Anabaptists, as well as the resistance to reformation of the Romanists, lay and clerical, put any thought of private churches *hors de combat*. This left Luther at a loss for models of a well-ordered church. He defined particular 'true' churches by reference to their doctrine,[40] but was extremely loath to make organizational matters into doctrinal ones.

In reflecting about the 'world', a concept as undifferentiated as 'externals',[41] Luther often divided men into two categories, the godly or 'true Christians' and the reprobate.[42] The godly, however, need no external thing, nor can they be harmed by any external thing:[43] being deprived of public opportunities for worship, even undergoing persecution, serves the Christian as well as, or better than, worldly protection and advancement; indeed, it is his lot in life.[44] This ignored what in another context Luther was concerned to stress, namely that even if *coram Deo* there are only elect and reprobate, from the viewpoint of conduct in the world there are any number of 'weak consciences' for whom not only external aids, but also external 'scandals' or stumbling-blocks are of the greatest possible moment, and whose needs and susceptibilities must be regarded by the Christian with compassion.[45] Thus, from the standpoint of the distinction between the elect and the reprobate, the evils that secular and spiritual government do are of no ultimate consequence, for they cannot harm the elect and are adequately combated by Christian witness and martyrdom. From the standpoint of a concern with 'weak consciences', however, secular, and especially spiritual, authority can do incalculable harm; in particular, while Luther never qualified the view that the actions of secular and spiritual authority cannot save the soul, he also thought that they might serve to consign the soul to perdition.[46]

Operating with the sharp contrasts between faith and externals, the kingdom of God and the kingdom of the world, the elect and the reprobate, it was reasonable for Luther to consign matters of 'external order' and 'external righteousness' *en bloc* to the secular authorities. But the implications of this for the public practice and ordering of religion clearly depended on what precisely was to be included under those labels.[47] In *On Secular Authority*, his most comprehensive discussion of the subject, Luther confined the content of 'external matters' and 'external righteousness' to life, property and standing,[48] to the exclusion of anything to do with compelling belief or profession; the reasons given were that it is impossible to compel or to judge belief, and that 'weak consciences' are loaded down with sins by forced professions.[49] And the authority of secular governors is here said not even to extend to what books the subjects shall read,[50] although books might be supposed 'external matters'. The vagueness of the distinction between external and spiritual was such that at times Luther went so far as to disregard altogether his normal, dismissive use of 'external' and to insist on the 'external' as the necessary means whereby faith is mediated.[51] The needs of weak neighbours are here seen to require a very restrictive interpretation of the competence of secular authority. The division of the human race into Christians and not-Christians subject to two different regiments with which Luther had prefaced these reflections also worked in the same direction. Since Christians do not need, and may not use, secular law and the secular sword for themselves, the latter concern the unrighteous, the 'world'. This is not to say that peace and protection from 'the wicked' are of no benefit to the Christian, for they clearly are and it is the duty of the ruler to provide them, but that they are not indispensable or unqualified benefits.[52] And Luther inferred the duty to obey secular authority, and even to act as or on behalf of secular governors, not from any benefits which accrue to the Christian

or the church, but from a direct divine imperative and from the
duty to love one's neighbour, a term Luther did not make more
precise, except that on occasion he added the qualifying 'weak'.
The most intensive investigation and debate in recent years has
failed to demonstrate that Luther regarded the Christian as a
member *of* the civil community (the *weltliches Reich*) rather than
as merely *in* it, a pilgrim passing through.[53] A purchase for the
view of the Christian as in an important sense *of* the world
rather than merely *in* it occurs in *On Secular Authority*, but was
not further used there, or as far as I can see, elsewhere.[54]
Indeed Luther's very terminology for talking about secular
authority served simply to reemphasize its alienness from
Christian modes of conduct, attitudes and relationships. His
term is *weltliche Oberkeit*, and *weltlich* ('worldly') means not
merely secular or temporal, but also 'worldly' in the morally
reprobatory sense; furthermore, the world in Luther's use is
often equivalent to the kingdom of Satan. The emblem of
secular authority is the sword,[55] its characteristic means are
command and violence, and its characteristic relationship is
personal super- and sub-ordination: although the terms *Regiment*
and *Reich* are abstract and impersonal, Luther's paradigm of an
authority is the prince (*Fürst*) or Lord (*Herr*, whence *Herr-schaft*).[56] To this may be added that Luther always had a poor
opinion of the personal qualities of princes and nobles, as
opposed to their office: a godly prince is a rare bird.[57] By
contrast, true Christians do not use commands, nothing is
imposed, no one is forced, and all are subject to each other,
which means that no one is subject; there is only love and
authoritativeness, a function of fidelity to the Word, and
authoritativeness is earned, not imposed.[58] In this context, too,
a very restrictive interpretation of the competence of secular
authority in matters regarding religion was called for.

But, once again, there were other possibilities within the same
conceptual matrix, and at times Luther exploited them. Thus,
as was usual in his time, Luther simply equated crime and sin,
lawbreaking and wickedness, the lawbreakers and the evil,[59]
and thought of the content of laws mainly as more precise
specification of natural laws.[60] (Certainly 'external' and 'true'
righteousness differ entirely *sub specie aeternitatis*, but this
difference generally concerns the intention, rather than the
form of conduct, for there may be no outward difference

between the conduct of the righteous and that of the hypocrites.) The way was therefore open to including under external
righteousness an external piety and worship as well as an
external morality, and Luther took this step when he allowed
rulers, or rather demanded from them, the repression of public
heresy and blasphemy.[61] Both the honour of God and the
protection of weaker brethren might be thought to demand it.
Under these auspices Luther came to advocate the banning of
the Mass and the prevention of heretical preaching, and even
the expulsion of Zwinglians from Lutheran territories,[62] clean
contrary to his earlier views about the futility of persecuting
heresy and enforcing professions of faith.[63] In a sense he, like
the other Reformers, had already taken this step when, in 1520,
he called on the secular authorities to take a lead in legislating
reformation into permanence; his justification then, however,
had been that the secular rulers too were priests, that is,
members of the priesthood of all believers. Sometimes, when he
had sympathetic governors to deal with, Luther went so far as
to ask for active encouragement of godly purposes by the
secular authorities[64] and even to make the previously episcopal
duty of supervising and disciplining the ministry a magisterial
matter.[65] Like all the other Reformers, Luther acquiesced in
magisterial appointment and dismissal of ministers, who in
evangelical states were *de facto* salaried public officials. The
fact that all this, like the evangelical practice of a public
disputation to initiate public reformation,[66] made the secular
authorities the judges of doctrine and determinants of what
might be taught and heard seems to have been suppressed by
the evangelical conviction of the evidentness of truth.

Thus Luther's delimitation of the area of competence of
secular authority expanded and contracted in direct proportion
to the godliness or lack of it of the rulers in question, but Luther
never announced this as a principle; instead he used various
other principles, all consistent with his theology, as the occasion
demanded.[67]

The case of the Reformers of the German and Swiss cities
was not much different, although their attitude to secular
authority was less complicated and less generally negative.
Zwingli at Zurich,[68] Bucer and Capito at Strasbourg,[69]
Oecolampadius at Basel all espoused magisterial assistance in
implementing reformation and thus *de facto* allowed magistrates

a considerable voice in the determination of orthodoxy. When at last the magistrates proved anything but reliable instruments of the Word, various attempts to establish some measure of ecclesiastical autonomy, especially over excommunication, proved a failure everywhere.[70] Magistrates and laity, having at the invitation of evangelicals eliminated clerical autonomy and power, were now quite unprepared to relinquish any part of their new-found independence to an evangelical clergy. In any case, the negotiating position of the Reformers vis à vis their governors was now very weak. In view of the menace to the fledgeling evangelical churches from Anabaptists, from rebellious peasants who articulated their grievances in the language provided by the Reformers themselves, and from the Emperor and the Catholic states and princes, there was little choice but to insist on the duty of obedience to secular authority, and Romans 13 was the most frequently quoted text in political contexts. Nevertheless, none of the others quite matched the extremity of Luther's insistence on passivity and quietism in the face of hostile secular authorities.[71]

Simplifying somewhat, then, we can say that the experience and theology of the first generation of evangelicals confronted their successors with two options about their ecclesiastical polity. They might strive for some kind of delimitation of competences and jurisdictions between the church, which accordingly needed its own agents and representatives, and the secular governors, or they might persist in the old ambition of harnessing secular government in some way to the service of religion. A third conceivable alternative, that of excluding governors altogether from all competence in church matters, was by now too badly compromised by its Anabaptist associations to be entertained. It must be insisted, however, that these are speculative options, open to the theologian without a church to manage; the freedom of choice of pastors with particular churches to defend was often effectively non-existent.

THE ARRANGEMENT OF THE 'INSTITUTION'

In 1535, when he wrote all or most of the *Institution*, Calvin was entirely innocent of any pastoral experience,[72] and *a fortiori* of any experience in matters of ecclesiastical polity or the councils

of princes and magistrates. His entire learning and prudence
in such matters, such as it was, was acquired from books and
from the conversation of those he encountered at Basel. And if
such conversations took an ecclesiastical turn, Calvin left no
record of it.[73] He did not read or speak German.[74] His conversion, what is more, was like Luther's a private matter, unmediated by any organized evangelical church. Not surprisingly
therefore, Luther's conception of faith and the Christian life
met his needs.

Thus the *Institution* left questions of ecclesiastical organization
in abeyance for most of the text. The arrangement of the work,
derived as has been said from Luther's *Short Catechism* of 1529,
was as follows. First: the fallen condition of man, and law (that
is to say, the Ten Commandments) as the measure of the depth
of human depravity. Second: God's mercy, namely the
redemptive work of Christ, experienced in faith. Third: the
doctrinal content of faith, organized around an exposition of
the Apostles' Creed. Fourth: the life of faith, prayer (an exposition of the Lord's prayer) and the sacraments, true and false.
The book concluded with a chapter entitled 'On Christian
liberty, ecclesiastical power and civil administration' which
had no very obvious connection with the chapters that had
gone before.

The first edition of the *Institution*, unlike subsequent ones,
contained no chapter specifically devoted to a discussion of the
church. In chapter 2, the sentence of the Apostles' Creed:
'I believe in one, holy, catholic church, the communion of
saints', called for explication. But what Calvin thought appropriate in this context was to engage in an attempt of a by now
familiar sort at prizing loose the title of 'catholic' from the
institution currently clinging to it, the strategy being to
etherialize the notion of 'church' to such an extent that the
factual multiplicity and disunion of evangelical churches
could no longer derogate from their entitlement to be considered part of the 'communion of saints'. As a result of this,
the transition in Calvin's discussion from 'the communion of
saints' (OS I, 86–9) to 'churches' concrete and determinate
enough to administer excommunication (pp. 89–91) remains
completely unexplained, and Doumergue's contention[75] that
the later introduction of the distinction between the 'visible'
and the 'invisible' churches[76] was merely a change of termin-

ology and not of substance is saved from being utterly laughable only by the fact that, when Calvin first introduced the distinction in the *Institution* of 1539, he did not as yet know exactly what to do with it. In 1535, he apparently took it that he had said enough about 'true churches' in the world when he had referred in an entirely circular and question-begging manner to 'the Word of God purely preached and heard', and 'the sacraments administered according to Christ's institution' (p. 91).[77] Nor did his discussion of the true sacraments in chapter 4 induce him to make any attempt to derive any lessons whatever about the importance or dignity of organized churches in the world from his stress on the necessity of these sacraments, and particularly of 'the Lord's Supper'. And when (in chapter 5, on false sacraments) he returned to the subject of excommunication in the context of a remarkably forced distinction between John 20.22–3 and Matthew 18.17–18 (pp. 187–8), he again left excommunication to 'the church', whereas he had assigned preaching to 'the ministers' (p. 187), before passing on to more congenial matters of anti-papist polemic. The first-generation Reformers had taught their disciples and successors to define the church negatively, by what it was not (it was not papist or Anabaptist) rather than by what it was, and Calvin had learned the lesson all too well.

In short, until the last chapter Calvin's thinking on the church was content to confine itself to what was uncontroversial and commonplace amongst evangelicals. It was of course a mark of the times that Calvin had no sooner mentioned the 'church' than he began to speak of 'excommunication' (pp. 89–91; 187), which had become 'the discipline of excommunication' (p. 187) by the penultimate chapter, and that he took the necessity of such a discipline for granted: controversies about the control of excommunication were a central preoccupation of evangelical churches in the early 1530s.[78] But it must be observed that he introduced the subject with every sign of reluctance, and with many caveats to distinguish what he was discussing from the corresponding popish abomination. Nor did he make excommunication one of the marks of a 'true' church. And as for secular government, Calvin had so far mentioned it precisely once, in a contorted exegesis of the Tenth Commandment (p. 52) which was abandoned in all subsequent editions of the *Institution*, and which said no more than that this commandment tells us to obey superiors of all kinds, including governors and pastors, and tells them to do their duty; the duty of governors as outlined here included no reference to the church or religion.

Chapter 6 was evidently designed to make good some of these omissions. It consisted of three sections: 'On Christian liberty, ecclesiastical power (*potestas*) and civil administration'. Later editions of the *Institution* dissevered these three sections and, apart from expanding the second and third massively, redistributed them in various parts of the book, although Calvin remained dissatisfied with his order of exposition until the last editions (1559/60). This seems to indicate that there had hitherto been a failure to integrate these topics into the main themes of the work, and this indeed proves to be the case. For the rest of the first *Institution* had described the Christian life as if lived in an institutional vacuum; even the church had appeared as a set of uniformly godly and individual free agents, an unspecified 'we', determining doctrine, worship and externals in accordance with an unequivocal and self-interpreting Word; to introduce an external church and secular authorities at the end of the work quite transforms the circumstances and hence the character of the Christian life (a topic about which Calvin from 1539 also felt it necessary to add a very substantial chapter). The discussion of secular authority also necessitated the introduction of the conception of the Christian as subject to a 'two-fold regiment' (OS I, 232–3/3.19.15; 258/4.20.1) which was not thematically integrated into the work until the last edition of the *Institution*. In short, Calvin's theology began almost as apolitically as Luther's.

Nonetheless, Calvin's reason for linking the three topics into one chapter in 1535 is clear, and revealing about the character of his thought. As will be argued in a moment, Calvin regarded the doctrine of Christian liberty as a fertile source of heresies. Equally, it was a serviceable weapon against Romanists which could not well be discarded altogether. Hence the linking of topics in the last chapter: a very guarded exposition of the doctrine which stressed its 'spiritual' nature (against Libertines and Anabaptists), its liberating effects (against Romanists) and its being limited by our duty to God (against evangelical back-sliders and conformists under popery) is followed by an exposition of ecclesiastical power (the first arm of the two-fold regiment), subordinating that power to the Word and thus legitimating the revolt against the Roman tyranny, but preventing disruptive, indecorous and tumultuous proceedings by the duty to regard weaker brethren, the need of the church for order, and the duty of submission to secular authority; and that section in turn is followed by a concluding section on 'civil administration', the other part of the two-fold regiment, where the writ of Christian liberty does not run. Let us now examine the three sections in order.

CHRISTIAN LIBERTY

In contrast to Luther and Melanchthon, and indeed to Zwingli,[79] Calvin clearly did not consider the doctrine of Christian liberty to be central to sound theology, as he understood it. The very first page of the last chapter makes it apparent that he thought of it as a potential menace to ecclesiastical and civil order alike, and the 'we' who are represented as contemplating abandoning the doctrine altogether (OS I, 234), a course Calvin demonstratively rejects, are fictive spokesmen for an inclination of Calvin's own. It was not in fact open to Calvin to dispense with the doctrine altogether, for it was part of the bed-rock of evangelical belief, and freedom from man-made laws, traditions and observances was the very condition of the existence of evangelical churches. But the notion of 'liberty' had connotations which were entirely unacceptable to Calvin. In 1535 Calvin had not as yet formulated his doctrine into the comprehensive ethic of duty it was to become, but he already differed from Luther in his view of the place of God's Law in the life of the elect. The Law is never left behind or transcended for Calvin as it was for Luther; it remains ever relevant as a standard of performance and a perpetual 'spur' to sanctification (OS I, 60: 'We are indeed sanctified . . . our hearts formed to obedience to the Law'; see also pp. 62 and 63). A different accent in the interpretation of Christian liberty was therefore called for, and Calvin was always careful to insist that the freedom in question is a 'spiritual' one (pp. 58–9, the only mention of Christian liberty before chapter 6) and to guard against the possibility that some other sense of 'liberty' might insinuate itself, one which made freedom and duty antithetical. What is more, he discarded altogether Luther's correlative to Christian liberty, namely the doctrine of the priesthood of all believers.[80] Since he rejected the latter doctrine tacitly, no more than a conjecture is possible, but the reason may have been that Calvin's conception of order required a differentiation of stations and duties, which the priesthood of all believers might be thought to impugn. However, in retaining the terminology of Christian liberty Calvin was not playing with words, for by his account the Christian is indeed free: his obedience to God's law is voluntary and unconstrained, and in that (thoroughly Pauline, and it may be added Lutheran) sense, it is free.

Calvin claimed that the doctrine of Christian liberty is of the 'first necessity', and that without it neither Christ nor the truth of the Gospel is rightly understood (OS I, 223–4). He divided the doctrine into three 'parts', that is, three different benefits that flow from it. These are: first, that it teaches the believer to see that his salvation does not depend at all on fulfilling the works of the Law (OS I, 224/3.19.1); second, that in striving to obey the Law, the regenerated heart is so disposed by faith that it willingly obeys God's will (OS I, 225/3.19.3); and finally, that the believer sees that 'as regards our standing in the sight of God, we should have no scruples of conscience about external things, which are of themselves *adiaphora* [sc. morally neutral]' (OS I, 226/3.19.7: 'ut nulla rerum externarum, quae per se sunt adiaphoroi, religione coram Deo teneamur . . .', an extraordinarily difficult sentence). Now, the first part of the doctrine is an aspect of, or gloss upon, the central evangelical doctrine of justification by faith, which had previously been explained with only a single, and extremely guarded, reference to freedom (OS I, 58–9); the second had been explained with no such reference at all (pp. 65–6); and little more was said of these. What concerned Calvin particularly was the third part, barely glanced at before, and to which most of the rest of the discussion of Christian liberty is devoted.

As he put it in a less complicated formulation, the doctrine in this sense means the right 'not to be entangled in snares of observances in those things in which God has wished us to be free' (OS I, 232/3.19.14). Calvin's view seems to be that the Romanist practices of piety fostered a scrupulosity and anguish of conscience which paralyses the will, and is the merest distraction from what true piety actually requires. The imposition of such 'observances' under pain of mortal sin is, further-more, direct evidence that the Roman church is no true church but rather a 'tyranny'. Separation from it is therefore a right and a duty. Christian liberty is thus the right not to practise popery and to separate from popish churches, a right without which evangelical churches would lose their justification and their *raison d'être*.

Now the right not to practise popery and to separate from popish churches in the nature of things could not but be allowed to every *individual*. The danger was that this same individual right of separation from sin, heresy and tyranny might also be claimed as a ground for separating from evangelical churches, or disrupting them, in virtue of some deficiency or defect or other. This Calvin was evidently seeking to prevent. Equally, there seemed to Calvin to be an innate propensity in all mortal flesh to misunderstand and misuse the doctrine of Christian liberty as an excuse for licence and back-sliding. And this too he was determined to preclude. To accomplish both these tasks was no easy matter.

As a result, Calvin seems constantly to be giving with one hand and taking away with the other. Thus his assertion that 'believers' consciences [are] not to be entangled with any snares of observances in those matters in which the Lord has willed them to be free' (OS I, 232/3.19.4) turns out to mean something other than appears at first sight. For what God has left free is not the performance or omission of most things, but the specific arrangements about when and how. Thus men are not left free to pray or not to pray, to hear sermons and receive communion or not to hear or receive, to submit to 'discipline' or not to submit, to fast or not to fast; all that is left free is when and in what form. And it is left free, not to individuals, but to churches.

Christian liberty is further restricted by the need to avoid giving offence to weaker brethren, a concern close to Calvin's heart even before he had assumed any formal pastoral respons-ibilities. 'Offences', or 'scandals' are those acts which, of them-selves indifferent, yet give offence to those weak in faith and thus impede the building up (*aedificatio*) of the church. But whereas Luther's and Zwingli's point had been that there is no sense in upsetting people needlessly,[81] Calvin's was that there is no excuse for letting people be led astray from godly conduct

by allowing such popish practices. The effect of this interpretation is to remove still more matters from the area of 'indifference'. For although an evangelical was free to fast or not to
fast on 'fast-days', to eat meat or not to eat it on Fridays and
days of abstinence, to work or not to work on 'feast-days',
he had now to conduct himself in accordance with his church's
judgement of what was scandalous to the weak, in other words,
what might give aid and comfort to covert or open Romanists.
In effect, this meant that evangelicals *had* (for example) to
work on feast-days, as the Genevan Council was to decree with
Calvin's full approval in 1550.[82] There was to be no room for
conformity in popish practices: 'All that I have taught about
avoiding offences I mean to be referred to things intermediate
and indifferent. For those things that are our duty must not be
omitted out of fear of giving offence' (OS I, 231/4.19.13). And
conversely, those things which it is our duty to omit must not
be done, lest offence be given. Thus hearing Mass, invoking
the saints, praying for the dead, communicating under one
kind, extreme unction, confirmation, pilgrimages, rosaries, in
fact the whole of Romanist piety is understood as falling under
divine interdict and condemnation, indeed as foully polluting,
infesting, desecrating, soiling, spoiling and corrupting the
honour of the Lord.

ECCLESIASTICAL POWER

The topic of scandals brought Calvin to the next part of his
discussion: ecclesiastical power. For his final, and most significant, restriction of Christian liberty, and his most obvious
departure from the precepts of Luther, concerns the moral
standing of the laws (*constitutiones*) and ordinances governing the
'external' worship of the church. And here Calvin was forced
into a hair-splitting distinction, an *argutia* of the sort he
abominated in the scholastics. His overriding assertion, needed
to combat the authority of Rome, is that 'laws by which the
order of the church is shaped' cannot bind the conscience. In
other words, detailed provisions for worship and ecclesiastical
order are not laid down in Scripture, but may and must be
made by men to suit the circumstances. They cannot, however,
claim for themselves the same morally imperative quality
intrinsic to express commandments of the Lord. They do not

'bind the conscience', as Calvin asserted unguardedly. But on further inspection of Calvin's account, that seems to be precisely what they do: 'Many unlettered persons, when they hear that believers' consciences are impiously bound by human traditions [which are in fact to be regarded as null and void], apply the same deletion to all the laws by which the order of the church is shaped' (OS I, 255/4.10.27). And Calvin proceeded to disabuse such 'unlettered persons': 'We are so far from condemning the laws that conduce [to good order and concord in churches] that we contend that churches, when deprived of them, are wholly deformed and scattered, their very sinews torn' (OS I, 255/4.10.27). Now the true Christian can hardly view the disintegration, deformation and scattering of godly churches with indifference; on the contrary, his duty is to participate in building up such churches according to his station and capacities (OS I, 231/3.19.12). It is, therefore, also his duty to preserve and adhere to those arrangements which aid *aedificatio* and prevent disintegration; in a word, it is his moral duty to obey the laws that order the church. Calvin did not specify how, or by whom, laws were to be made, but in as far as they are properly laws, and godly ones to boot, they do oblige in conscience, they do 'bind the conscience', even if they do so in a more circuitous and indirect manner than express commands of God. The profound difference which Calvin claimed to discern between evangelical and 'impious' (that is popish) laws therefore reduces itself to a difference of content and to a difference in the manner in which they acquire their obligatory character. And even the latter contention depends on an account of what Romanists claimed about the duty to conform to their observances which had become as ritualized and remote from any Roman primary sources as all the rest of the evangelicals' sheet of charges against popery (e.g. OS I, 237–9).

What led Calvin to emphasize this distinction without a difference is not far to seek. Calvin was utilizing the first generation of Reformers' conceptualization of the difference between themselves and the Romanists. That conceptualization, as we have seen, was primarily destructive and rather unguarded, in the sense that it could also underwrite assaults on evangelical churches from the 'radical Reformation'. It was Calvin's purpose, as a second-generation Reformer, to prevent

such disruption and to assist *aedificatio*. And his preoccupation
with good order in churches did not harmonize perfectly with
the original idea of the free conscience; it required a different
emphasis.

As far as scriptural validation is concerned, the whole edifice
of ecclesiastical laws and obedience constructed by Calvin
rests on the slender foundation of St Paul's informal admonition
that 'all things be done decently and in order' (1 Corinthians
14.40; cited at OS 1, 255/4.10.27), an injunction which any
Anabaptist church might fairly claim to have obeyed in letter
and spirit without any formal arrangements (of the kind Calvin
had in mind) whatever. This, however, was not the primary
legitimation which Calvin adduced for his insistence on laws and
obedience. Instead we read lines which come straight from
'philosophy'. 'We see that some form of organization[83] is
necessary in all human societies to foster the common peace
and maintain concord. We further see that in human trans-
actions, some set form must always be observed for the sake of
public decorum, and even for *humanitas* itself. If so, it ought
especially to be observed in churches, which are best sustained
by an arrangement in all respects well ordered, and which
without concord become no churches at all' (OS 1, 255/4.10.27).
As will appear shortly, Calvin was far from having offered any
principle of concordance to reconcile human reason and
revelation, and the absence of such a principle here is somewhat
striking, even if partially concealed by the appeal to St Paul
quoted above. What seems to have happened is that Calvin
had simply introduced some of the essentials of his pre-
evangelical political attitudes into his thinking about the
church, at some cost to the homogeneity of his argument. Thus
concord is made constitutive of the very being of churches,
and concord is held to be the fruit of law, for 'such diversity
exists in the habits of men, such variety in their minds, that no
polity is sufficiently strong unless constituted by definite
laws . . .' (OS 1, 256/4.20.27). And these laws are accounted
the 'sinews' (*ibid.*) of the church, in a fashion identical with the
discussion of the role of laws in civil society which follows and
with that which Calvin had offered in the *De Clementia Commentary*. The parallelism between political and ecclesiological
thought is already striking. Unless the context were indicated
it would, for example, surely be impossible to tell from the

following quotation whether church or civil society was meant: 'confusion in such details [of arrangements] would become the seed of great contentions, if every man were allowed to change matters affecting public order according to his fancy' (OS 1, 257/4.10.31). (It was in fact church order of which Calvin was speaking.) What is more, Calvin said very little about what sort of 'laws' he had in mind, and nothing about whether they were to be civil laws and who was to make, interpret and enforce them. All he ever does say is that he has committed to civil government 'the duty to establish religion rightly' (OS 1, 260/4.20.3) – which, considering the times, was begging not a few questions.

There are some further surprises in store for anyone expecting to find what has come to be thought of as Calvinism in the first *Institution*. One is that Calvin had little, and nothing new, to say about the reformed pastorate. Nothing was more character-istic of Calvin's later ministry than attention to the standing, authority and organization of the pastorate: it was the hinge on which his whole enterprise, and that of his followers, turned. And certainly Calvin's account of the Christian life gave him considerable scope for holding before evangelicals the image of a revitalized, but unmistakably evangelical ministry. The Christian life is one dedicated to the building of the church, which is the kingdom of God in the world, that *aedificatio* to which Calvin so often referred.[84] A substantial aspect of *aedificatio* is orderly and zealous public worship, especially the fervent preaching of the Word and frequent communion – Calvin resisted vigorously what he took to be Zwingli's attempt to diminish the significance of the Lord's Supper.[85] And a zealous and prestigious ministry is indispensable for both. But much of the section on 'ecclesiastical power' is taken up instead by a contrast between evangelical ministry and the 'tyranny' and 'oppression' of Romish popes and bishops, concentrating on the latter. Again Calvin was defining evangelical truth by reference to what it is not – it is almost as if he could see no threats to evangelical ministry from within the reformed camp: *pas d'ennemi à gauche*. It is only here and there that one can detect a glimmering of what was to come in later years (OS 1, 90, 187, 237).

In fact, not even the subject of excommunication and the power of the keys (OS 1, 89–91 and 165–89) moved Calvin to any more extensive reflections about the role of the ministry in an evangelical church. The discussion of excommunication, like that of the organization of the ministry, did not even appear in the section on 'ecclesiastical power'; instead Calvin said most of what he had to say about these matters – again as part of an anti-Romanist polemic – in the section of chapter 5 ('On false sacraments') devoted to 'ecclesiastical orders'. And there Calvin went out of his way to deny that the power of excommunication implied any peculiar prerogative or authority on the part of the ministry. Indeed he did not even say precisely *who* was to excommunicate, contenting himself with the vague 'we' or 'the church' (OS 1, 187/4.11.2) and emphasizing, in a manner quite alien to his later discussions, the uncertain and tentative nature of excommunication: 'In so far as one is permitted to discern. . .' and 'the elect cannot be recognized by us with assurance of faith'; 'although, while we are as yet uncertain of God's judgement, we are not permitted to distinguish individually those who belong to the church or not': these are his typical formulations (OS 1, 89–91/4.1.8; 4.12.10; 4.11.2). At one point, outlining a desirable form of communion service, he did indeed remark that the minister 'should excommunicate all who are debarred from [communion] by the Lord's prohibition' (OS 1, 161/4.17.43), but even here it is not clear whether a general or a specific excommunication was intended; and the former seems the more likely. And although he did not minimize the significance of excommunication – 'The Lord testifies that the judgement of believers is nothing other than the proclamation of his own sentence' (OS 1, 187/4.11.2) – one would be inclined to describe his terminology as studiously vague, were there the slightest indication that he recognized any obscurity in what he was saying.

In orthodox evangelical fashion he denied the Romanist distinctions within the ministerial order – 'I call presbyters or bishops indiscriminately "ministers of the church" ' (OS 1, 212/4.3.4 and 4.3.8) – and he also called them 'elders' (*ibid.*)[86] and 'pastors'.[87] As for their appointment, we find something familiar in one sense, unfamiliar in another: 'Whether it is enough for the bishop [sc. minister] to be created by the meeting of the whole church, or by the vote of a few . . . or by the magistrate's decision, no definite law can be determined.' 'But because it scarcely ever happens that so many heads can unanimously settle any matter, and it is generally true that "the fickle crowd is divided into contrary interests", it seems better to me that either the magistrates or the senate or the elders (*seniores*) perform this office of choosing, always (as I have said) with some ministers (*episcopis*) as advisers, of whose good faith and probity they are assured' (OS 1, 214/4.4.15). Those who like to regard Calvin's thought as encompassing 'development', but no contradictions, may of course reconcile this with his later practice and doctrine; to my mind nothing more remote from it than the sense of this passage can be imagined. Nor is anything said of 'elders' in the later sense, and the order of 'deacons' is mentioned solely, it seems, with a view to denying the Romanists the right to use that title; nothing is said of the corporate ministry, nothing of its recruitment or discipline. All that is held out is an ideal of evangelical ministry (OS 1, 237/4.8.9–10) which might have come straight from Luther.

CIVIL ADMINISTRATION

The first arm of the 'two-fold regiment' to which man is subject, then, is a government of the Word, to which the ministers of the Word (as their title indicates) are strictly subordinated. Calvin's stress on its nature as a 'spiritual' government, as pertaining to the life of the soul, the inner man, residing in the mind (OS 1, 232/3.19.15) served, as it had done in Luther, to differentiate it from civil government and also to minimize its capacity to inform the government of visible churches. With these implications Calvin was content in 1535. He now turned to civil administration, pausing only to recall his earlier warning that in virtue of their different jurisdictions, aims and methods, the 'spiritual kingdom' and the 'political kingdom' 'must be examined separately, and while one is being treated, we must call away and turn aside the mind from thinking about the other' (OS 1, 233, referred back to at OS 1, 258).

Calvin was, and in subsequent editions remained, particularly pleased with this section, subsequently to become book 4, ch. 20: 'My readers, assisted by the very clarity of the arrangement. . .' (OS 1, 260/4.20.3). The arrangement was a division into (1) the divine institution of the magisterial office, (2) the nature and extent of its functions, and (3) the duties of citizens with respect to it. This manner of presentation well suited his

ostensible message, which was the Christian duty of obedience.
But this was artful, for it was not Calvin's purpose to belabour
French evangelicals with advice they had no choice but to
follow; rather was it to offer, under the guise of a presentation
of the evangelical doctrine of obedience, an implicit exoneration
of his co-religionists from the charge of subversiveness. But this
was not Calvin's only purpose, for it appears that he thought
that his co-religionists actually did need to be taught not
obedience, but a proper regard for the magistracy and civil
order. Both purposes could be served by a concentration on the
duty of obedience.

Calvin commenced his exposition of 'the magistracy or
government' by saying that its office 'pertains only to the
establishment and maintenance (*ad instituendam*) of civil justice
and outward morality' (OS I, 258/4.20.1). This is verbatim
Luther's 'two-fold regiment' conception of politics, which (as
we have seen) had been a source of some ambiguity and
disorientation in Luther's political thought, and which turns
out not to meet Calvin's requirements precisely either.

The first topic to be considered was 'what is the office of the
magistrate and whether . . . it is a lawful calling approved by
God'. Judging by the supercilious tone which Calvin adopted,
as well as by the close verbal parallels with the Schleitheim
Articles,[88] Calvin thought that only Anabaptists denied
something so obvious. But since they supported their denial of
the rightfulness of worldly authority (or at any rate its relevance
to the elect) by some scriptural arguments sufficiently impressive to unsettle the unlearned, a refutation was necessary. Its
purpose was, as always, not to convince those wedded to
pernicious beliefs, but to reassure the converted and to sway the
undecided. To accomplish his task, Calvin employed the only
method clearly in keeping with his theology, but one which
was at the same time only of use in preaching to the converted:
the assembling and exegesis of proof-texts, coupled with a
line-by-line refutation of the proof-texts and exegesis of the
opposition. Calvin's conclusion was as emphatic as could be,
although the formulation was somewhat casual: 'No one ought
to doubt that civil authority is a vocation not only sacred and
lawful in the sight of God, but also the most sacred and by far
the most honourable of all callings in the whole of mortal life'
(OS I, 261/4.20.4). More honourable than the ministry? Or is

that not a calling 'in mortal life' in the relevant sense? Calvin
did not say.

The 'use' of government,[89] then, 'is not less than that of
bread and water; indeed its dignity is far more excellent'
(OS I, 260/4.20.3). And there follows a statement for which
Calvin's initial distinction (which echoed an earlier point
about 'constrained and forced righteousness', OS I, 62) between
two sorts of government and two sorts of righteousness had ill
prepared his readers. For now he told them that 'not only does
government provide for men's living together', but it 'also
prevents idolatry, sacrilege against God's name, blasphemies
against his truth and other public offences against religion from
arising and spreading among the people. . .' (*ibid.*). Calvin was
evidently aware that this was an unannounced new arrival in
his thought – 'Let no one be disturbed that I now commit to
civil government the duty of rightly establishing religion'
(*ibid.*) – but he tried to reassure his readers by saying that 'I do
not here, any more than before, allow men to make laws
according to their own pleasure about religion and the worship
of God.' But what was new and unsettling was that he had
hitherto confined the office of magistrate to the maintenance of
a merely civil, external order, and a merely civil or external
righteousness (e.g. OS I, 232–3/3.19.15; 258–9/4.20.1–3),
whereas he was now introducing a set of functions for government which had *prima facie* nothing whatever to do with worldly
considerations of this sort. The whole matter seems to require
more careful investigation.

As Calvin presented his whole theology, there were two
enemies to evangelical truth: Romanists and Anabaptists.[90]
And since Romanists did not deny the legitimacy of civil
authority, it appears that only Anabaptists needed to be dealt
with in this connection.[91] But in fact outright denial or emphatic
affirmation of the legitimacy of civil government were not the
only possible options. A third possible position was to affirm
the legitimacy and necessity of government in the world, and
yet to regard it as essentially peripheral to the main concerns
of the evangelical good life, a position to which Luther inclined
throughout his career as a Reformer, as we have seen.[92]
Calvin evidently recognized the existence of such an attitude
amongst evangelicals when he asserted that 'You will find many
who very respectfully yield themselves to their magistrates,

and are not unwilling to obey them, because they know that to
do so is expedient for the public welfare; nevertheless they
regard magistrates only as a kind of necessary evil' (OS 1,
372/4.20.22). That Calvin here had evangelicals in mind is
clear from the gentle tone in which his criticism is advanced.
But the *Institution* made no secret of Calvin's opposition to this
view. What is less clear is what view he proposed to place in
its stead. In outline, it seems that Calvin intended to re-
sacralize the magistracy by investing it with functions central to
evangelical preoccupations, and with a dignity commensurate
with so elevated a position in the divine economy. Nevertheless,
this was not the only moment in his thought: the inherited
'two-regimes' conception of magistracy which he had also
espoused served constantly to reawaken the memory of the
conception of government as an external and a necessary evil.

Calvin's very choice of language and proof-texts points to the
conclusion that he recognized himself as engaged on a labour of
diminishing the distance between the office of magistracy and
the minds and hearts of the godly. Thus he adopted the term
administratio to designate what magistrates do. As a humanist
and stylist, Calvin knew how to deploy language. *Administratio*
was certainly a familiar synonym for government; but so far
from using it in a neutral fashion, Calvin meant, it seems,
to exploit the connotation of 'ministry' implicit in the term;[93]
indeed, 'ministry' (*ministerium*) is a term he frequently employed
in the text to refer to the magistrates' office. Thus he designated
them as having been 'ordained *ministers* of divine justice'
(OS 1, 261/4.20.6; my italics); he referred to the Lord putting
the sword into the hands of his 'ministers' (OS 1, 264/4.20.10);
and he told them to apply themselves to their 'ministry' (*ibid.*).
Later he quoted Paul (Romans 13.4) to the effect that magistracy is a 'ministry' of God for our good; and the quotation
struck him as so apposite that he repeated it twice more
(OS 1, 270/4.20.17; OS 1, 272/4.20.19). And most conclusively,
he spoke of the magistracy as a *sacrum ministerium* (OS 1, 262/
4.20.7). This terminology, judging by the consistency with
which Calvin used it, was carefully chosen; it is the same as
that which he employed to designate the pastorate, and it was
evidently intended to raise the standing of the magistracy in
evangelical eyes. In speaking of the magistracy's office as
administratio, Calvin meant precisely to speak of it as a 'ministra-

tion', in other words a service, to all men, including Christians.

The ground thus prepared by the choice of terms, Calvin offered an array of choice quotations from Scripture which would invest the office with every honour and majesty. Its holders, he told his readers, are described by God himself as 'gods', as his 'vicars', 'vicegerents' and 'regents'. And unlike Luther, Calvin nowhere gave any room even to a suspicion that the office of magistracy has regard purely or primarily to the unrighteous. Civil government does indeed have 'as its appointed end, so long as we live amongst men, to accommodate our life to human fellowship, to reconcile us one with another and to promote and foster general tranquillity' (OS 1, 259/4.20.2). And these goods (we may note, although Calvin did not explicitly say so) are certainly of benefit to the reprobate, but Calvin immediately insists that while 'we' go as pilgrims, our 'pilgrimage' requires such 'aids'. The 'we' here can only refer to the righteous; civil government, therefore, is unequivocally a boon to the righteous.

It was with the same end in view that Calvin rejected as firmly as was consistent with evangelical solidarity the idea that 'the office of magistrate is superfluous, as far as Christians are concerned, because they . . . are forbidden to take revenge, cite before a judge, or go to law' (OS 1, 270/4.20.17). While this was certainly the view of Anabaptists, it was also that of Luther, who, while he insisted that it was the duty of Christians if called upon to take part as officials in judicial proceedings, also insisted that the duty to turn the other cheek prevented Christians from going to court in their own defence.[94] In Calvin's view of magistracy, 'the magistrate was ordained by God, so that, being defended by his hand and aid against the dishonesty and injustice of wicked men, we may live in peace and tranquillity' (*ibid.*). It therefore made no sense to deny to Christians the right to invoke his aid. It was of course necessary to distinguish between the spirit of litigiousness and revenge which Calvin admitted to be prevalent in judicial proceedings in these times (OS 1, 271/4.20.18) and the 'proper use' of such proceedings.[95] Christians are bound to abstain from the former, and to be ready to yield to others as well as forgive, but this 'will not prevent them from using the help of the magistrate in preserving their own possessions, while maintaining friendliness toward their enemies, or, out of zeal for the public good, from demanding the punishment of guilty and pestilential men, who, they know, can be reformed only by death' (OS I, 272/4.20.20).

This being the office of the magistrate, and its specific relevance to the Christian's life, the duty of the Christian subject is clear. And Calvin relentlessly spells out what is involved: 'The first duty of the subjects towards magistrates is to think most honourably of their office, which indeed they should recognize as a jurisdiction bestowed by God, and on that account to esteem and reverence them as ministers and representatives of God' (OS I, 273/4.20.22). Calvin's first injunction to the reader, then, concerns not what he is to *do*, but what he is to *think*, what attitude he is to have towards magistracy. For in true humanist style Calvin thinks that from a correct disposition will flow correct conduct. We are to 'honour' and 'reverence' rulers, not out of some tepid calculation about the 'public welfare', but for conscience's sake, in that obeying rulers we obey God, disobeying them we disobey him. Thus disposed we will readily act rightly, obeying their laws, paying taxes, undertaking public offices and burdens, and executing any other commands. Our sincere subjection, springing from the heart, will also show itself in prayers for the safety and prosperity of rulers (OS I, 273/4.20.23).

What Calvin had to say on the obedience of subjects is in many ways pure St Paul, although all his more detailed material on the godly prince (a term he curiously never used) is taken from the Old Testament, for next to nothing about godly princes is to be found in the New. But he now proceeded to assert some things which, while coherent enough with the rigorously apolitical attitude of the New Testament, are not illustrated with proof-texts and seem to derive from another source. For under 'obedience' Calvin includes 'the restraint which private citizens ought to bid themselves keep in public, that they may not deliberately intrude upon public affairs . . . or undertake anything at all of a public nature'[96] (OS I, 274/4.20.23 and cf. OS I, 263/4.20.8). Such a veto on political activism is plainly not dictated by the New Testament, but rather by Calvin's distaste for tumult, disorderliness, commotion, turbulence or sedition, all of which terms he was disposed to construe in the most inclusive fashion.[97] Only activity by properly constituted authorities was justifiable.

Although these injunctions to obedience are massive enough as they stand, Calvin proceeded to elaborate on the full extent of Christian duty in this area. Our duty, in his view, is quite independent of the goodness or badness of a particular prince. Indeed we now learn that we are not even permitted to inspect the prince's claim to be entitled to hold his office: 'We are subject not only to the authority of princes who perform their office uprightly and faithfully as they ought, but also to the authority of all who, by whatever means, have got control of affairs' (OS I, 275/4.20.25). Not even the familiar medieval distinction between the tyrant by title and the tyrant by practice, if Calvin was aware of it, is allowed to stand: 'even the most worthless kings are appointed by the same decree by which all kings are established' (OS I, 277/4.20.27). And here the popular quotation from 1 Samuel 8.11–18, concerning what is to be expected by those subject to kings, was pressed into service.

In insisting on the duty of obedience, Calvin had of course no more intention than Luther had of denying that there are occasions when we must obey God rather than men. But on his view, as on Luther's, these cannot entitle private men to take up arms against their rulers. All they may do is pray for deliverance, petition and remonstrate, or take flight. At best, there may be magistrates who happen to be appointed to restrain wicked rulers; ephors, tribunes and 'perhaps, as things now stand, such power as the three estates exercise in every realm when they hold their chief assemblies' (OS I, 279/4.20.31). This exception, pregnant with momentous possibilities for later Calvinism, was all that Calvin would allow.[98] But this left evangelicals almost defenceless where the tyranny of the ruler takes the form of denying his subjects the right to advance evangelical truth and piety. As Calvin stated the position here, Christians could be rendered as private and as devoid of institutional and congregational resources as an ungodly ruler cared to make them. Now the martyr's witness and the submissive insubmission of the godly are not negligible weapons with which to fight God's battles. But the devising of institutional (as opposed to doctrinal and private) means of furthering reformation even when governors are recalcitrant or hostile had evidently not yet been thought of. It seems that in 1535/6 the institutional autonomy of the church was not as yet a matter of any consequence to Calvin.

We have so far omitted what Calvin regarded as another significant part of his subject, namely the place of law in the *Christiana politia* (OS I, 267/4.20.14). For whenever he was to speak of magistrates, his mind turned naturally to the function of the ruler in administering the law (e.g. OS I, 267/4.20.14; 270/4.20.17), just as it had done in the *De Clementia Commentary*. His very definition of the parts of civil government was with respect to 'the laws' (OS I, 260/4.20.14). Laws, Calvin told his readers, are the sinews of the commonwealth, the soul without which the magistracy cannot survive, a silent magistrate, just as the magistrate is a speaking law, at least ideally (OS I, 267/4.20.14). His reading for the *De Clementia Commentary*, where most of these Ciceronian tags had also been cited, had evidently not gone to waste. He amplified his thought in dealing briefly with the Anabaptist assertion that the Mosaic law in its entirety ought to govern Christian polities.[99] Here Calvin introduced the distinction between the ceremonial, judicial and moral parts of the Mosaic law, which he acknowledged to have been borrowed from ancient (he might have added medieval) writers, but which was in any case an evangelical commonplace (OS I, 268/4.20.14).[100] Only the moral law, summarized in the Decalogue, is still binding. Concerning it Calvin recurred to the distinction between the *aequitas* of the law and the *constitutio*.[101] The latter is a general term for statute law, so the distinction is that between the moral purpose of the law and its specific positive formulation. The latter's content is said by Calvin to 'depend in part on circumstances' (OS I, 260/4.20.16). There is thus nothing to prevent diversity of laws, provided they all have 'equity' as their *scopus*, their end in view, the mark they aim at. Calvin illustrated the point by the claim – already contradicted a few lines earlier – that laws all forbid theft, false witness, adultery, murder, but differ in the severity and kind of punishment they assign for these crimes.

Now this is not excessively subtle. For example, it ignores the fact that law also, and necessarily, *defines* what is to count as a crime, as murder, theft and so forth. More to the point, however, Calvin's discussion here is conspicuously devoid of scriptural buttressing, and seems to depend on appeals to 'conscience', 'nature' and 'equity' which sit oddly with Calvin's more usual conceptual equipment.

Calvin's inclinations, his intended audience and the task in hand all conspired to make Scripture the final court of appeal, the *ultima ratio* of his account. And it was certainly not his intention to abandon Scripture for 'reason' or 'philosophy' when it came to discussing politics. Indeed, his treatment of the staples of humanist thought, that is, the thought of contemporary representatives of 'philosophy', is dismissive and supercilious. He declined to enter into a discussion concerning the best kind of laws in a Christian polity, on the singularly unconvincing grounds that it would 'be endless and would not pertain to the present purpose' (OS I, 267/4.20.14). But he was never a man to be deterred from lengthiness if the subject seemed to warrant it, and he had given no reason for thinking it did not. He also rejected the opportunity to present a mirror for magistrates, although it would have cost nothing to permit himself a brief reference to the *De Clementia*. And his treatment of the topic of forms of government seems almost deliberately designed to deny the capacity of unaided reason to deliver anything conclusive for the Christian. The question of political forms, more precisely the relative merits of aristocracy, monarchy and democracy, was one which touched an exposed nerve among humanists: it related to their interpretation of their public place. Calvin's brief survey of the topic, notable chiefly for its derivativeness and superficiality, was prefaced by a prohibition (subtly modified in later editions) of discussion of this topic by private men,[102] and by the remark that 'this question permits of no absolute solution, unless one were to be lacking in circumspection, for the *ratio* of the discussion depends on circumstances' (OS I, 263/4.20.8). All forms of government have their attendant evils (a classical platitude) but a view of the world as a whole, or at least of widely separated regions, testifies to the wisdom of Providence in equipping various countries with different forms of government. (The whole section was drastically altered in later editions.) And, anxious to get on to something more congenial, Calvin concluded by saying that 'all this is superfluous speech to those for whom the will of the Lord is sufficient reason' (*ibid.*). Amongst them Calvin surely meant to include both himself and all right-thinking people. Finally, Calvin expressly took issue, and then not once but twice, with the verdict of 'heroic and nobler natures' in ancient times about the rule of one man (OS I,

263/4.20.7), and later widened this dissent to include the 'inborn feelings which have always been in the minds of almost all men, [namely] to hate and curse tyrants as much as to love and venerate lawful kings' (OS I, 275/4.20.24).

It seems, then, that Calvin regarded what he had to say about governance as simple reporting from Scripture, and that it was no part of his intention to allot to natural reason any power over the minds of the righteous.[103] He did not consider exactly what magistrates needed to know in order to perform their office, or who might acquire such knowledge and how: the whole area of political wisdom or 'prudence' did not concern him, for it was not his purpose to provide guidance for magistrates, even if he did feel that he had some uplifting things to say to them. His business was to teach obedience to private men, but even this we have seen to be a rhetorical device, for the task on which he was engaged was, by preaching obedience, to tell those magistrates who needed reassurance that the godly *were* obedient, even unto death. The references to 'reason', 'conscience' and 'equity' are not, therefore, an attempt to adduce an additional source of politically relevant knowledge apart from the will of the Lord, nor are they evidence of a *theologia naturalis*.[104] Instead, what had happened was that the weapons he was using against the Anabaptists – for this was the context in which these concepts make their appearance (OS I, 296–70/4.20.6) – presupposed the validity of scholastic and humanist styles of thought which Calvin now denigrated, but which he had once entertained. That this is the case is clear not only from the absence of scriptural support, but also from Calvin's own direct and indirect quoting of Cicero, and the echoes of Budé.

All that we have encountered so far served Calvin's intention of diminishing the distance between magistrates and the godly. What is conspicuous by its absence, however, is any conception which would bring together the various functions allotted to the magistracy under a common umbrella. But at this point in his career, the conception of 'the honour and glory of God' was still so far from being the directive thought in his political theology that it did not even appear in his 'political' chapter.[105] (Indeed, throughout his subsequent revisions of this chapter he never integrated into it any reference to the glory of God.) Instead, the Lutheran[106] distinction between 'external' or 'civil' righteousness and 'true' righteousness so far dominated his thought that he on occasion even forgot that he had allocated to magistrates the care of *both* 'the public manifestation of religion amongst Christians, and humanity amongst men' (OS I, 260/4.20.9). For in a later section he claimed that 'it should be [the magistrates'] only study to provide for the common peace and well-being' (OS I, 264/4.20.9), just as early on, after beginning the discussion with an allusion to the 'two-fold regiment' (OS I, 258/4.20.1), he had claimed that 'government has as its appointed end, so long as we live among men, to adapt our conduct to human fellowship, to form our manners to civil righteousness, to reconcile us one with another, and to promote the common peace and tranquillity' (OS I, 259/4.20.2).

There was nothing specifically evangelical about regarding it as part of the ruler's office to maintain the public form of religion: all the rulers of Europe subscribed to this view. What was specifically evangelical was that Luther's thought gave Christians grounds for uneasiness about it. Calvin on the contrary refastened the bonds which Luther had, perhaps inadvertently, begun to loosen, despite the fact that in order to do so he had to resort to the Old Testament, for the New did not yield a single unequivocal word in support. The justification for treating the Old Testament as authoritative in this manner he was not to provide until years later. The conclusion once again appears to be that Calvin presented as a principle of scriptural political thought what was in fact a residue of his pre-evangelical inheritance, whose non-evangelical nature he did not apparently recognize.

To sum up, what we have seen so far of Calvin's political thinking was not in any way novel or particularly profound, nor can it be said to have faced squarely all the issues that confronted evangelical ecclesiastical polity in the 1530s. His marking out of the place of civil government in the providential economy is, however, unequivocal as compared to Luther's, except where the two-regimes conception supervened, and in this sense Calvin may be said to have played his part from the start in stemming that evangelical 'flight from civility' to which Wolin refers.[107] But his discussion of civil government was not all of a piece with the rest of his theology, either in its mode of argument or in its substance. For although Calvin seems to have understood his discussion of things political as simply a summary or report of gospel teaching on the matter, he had in fact appealed to 'philosophical' considerations without explaining what business these had appearing in a 'tota fere pietatis summa'. And since he had not worked out a clear conception of the 'visible' church, except in so far as was necessary to conduct an anti-Romanist polemic, he was in no position to explain clearly the relationship between such a church and the temporal kingdom. Nor is his conception of the Christian life as dedicated to the building up of the church entirely harmonious with his denial to Christians, either as churches, or, still more, as individuals, of any right to take initiatives towards *aedificatio*. In 1535/6 Calvin spoke as a defender of evangelical truth and a scourge of Romanist and Anabaptist heresy, not as an architect of ecclesiastical polity.

We are left, then, with a puzzle. There is nothing in Calvin's first theology to explain why, once he was at Geneva, his conduct was sure and confident from the start. He had defined the church negatively for the most part, and it is only with the benefit of a great deal of hindsight that one can point to a certain homology in his political and ecclesiological thought. It is true that, whether he was speaking of ecclesiastical or political organization, his master-concepts were the same: order, or harmony, is the *sine qua non;* order requires law, and laws need enforcement; there must be a differentiation of functions commensurate with the diversity of gifts, and these functions must be adjusted to the common purpose; each must adhere to his station and perform its duties willingly: 'Just as members of one body share amongst themselves by a sort of community, each nonetheless has his particular gifts and distinct ministry' (OS 1, 92/4.1.3); 'Let each man consider what, in his rank and station, he owes his neighbour, and pay what he owes' (OS 1, 53/2.8.46). But Calvin had not elaborated this underlying parallelism in ecclesiastical and civil *politia*; his concern to differentiate between evangelicals and Romanists had in fact made an unequivocal statement of the need for ecclesiastical discipline (to correspond with the acknowledged need for civil discipline) impossible; and he had offered no detail whatever about ecclesiastical order, except to submit the appointment of pastors to the secular governors! Consequently there can be no question of an interpretation of Calvin's later public ministry as the 'application' of previously formulated general principles,[108] even if such a thing were imaginable. All we are per-mitted to suppose is that the case of his thought was not inimical to practical activity, that it perhaps provided some points of orientation to steer by, and that it allowed extrapolations congruent with Genevan circumstances. This proves to have been the case.

3

The first public ministry

At Farel's urging, Calvin went to Geneva in August 1536 to become 'reader in Holy Scripture', not being selected for the pastorate, it seems, until some months later.[1] But within little more than a year he, with Farel, was recognized as the leading spokesman of reformation at Geneva. By November 1537 he had produced, either wholly or for the most part, three substantial pieces bearing on the public form of an evangelical church: the *Confession de la Foy* for the inhabitants of Geneva, presented to the Petit Conseil on 10 November 1536, the *Articles sur le Gouvernement de l'Eglise*, presented on 16 January 1537, and the *Catechisme* (originally entitled *Instruction et Confession de Foy*) of November 1537. Of these, the *Articles*[2] were the most specifically organizational. The *Catechisme* and the *Confession de la Foy*, first published in French, were subsequently (in 1538) translated into Latin, equipped with a preface enjoining solidarity and mutual tolerance on evangelicals, and despatched for consideration by that wider audience which was never far from Calvin's mind.

The *Confession* and the *Catechisme* are Calvin's attempts to instruct an unlearned public about the essentials of faith, and the brevity this entailed meant that Calvin was constrained to concentrate on what he really did consider essential, for he had not the space to cover everything that he might have classed as 'essential' from some point of view or other. Interpretations of Calvin's thought may therefore be measured for fit against these two works. Moreover, all three works represent Calvin's first reorientation of his thought in the light of the experience of pastoral practice. Any change in accent, any departure from what he had said before, any innovation, may therefore serve to illuminate how Calvin attempted to organize that experience.

Although Calvin never, as far as I am aware, sufficiently recognized the importance of specifically Genevan circumstances and specifically Genevan politics to the character and success of his enterprise, he was in fact exceedingly fortunate in his 'choice' of locale for his ecclesiastical polity: his belief in Providence here receives eloquent confirmation. One must single out especially the compactness of Geneva as a political and social unit. In Wolin's terms,[3] the 'political space' in which Calvin moved was unusually supervisable; it was possible to keep an eye on things in a city-state of around 13,000 inhabitants enclosed within high walls. Some evidence for this view is afforded by the fact that the rural parishes under Genevan control were always troublesome and generally inferior in discipline. What is more, Geneva enjoyed a social order of unusual homogeneity, without overlord or aristocracy, without guilds or proletariat or strong corporations of clergy, and while reformation had already been proclaimed by public authority a few months before Calvin's arrival,[4] no evangelical practices or traditions had yet hardened.

Calvin, it is true, never had anything remotely comparable to *carte blanche* for his ecclesiastico-political activities. But given the compactness of Geneva's political space, he was not compelled to blunt the edge of his activities and dissipate his energies in devising and administering an organization of the complexity that would have been required by a larger, less homogeneous state. More intangibly, it was possible for him to bring his personal authority, his presence, to bear: he was always where he was most needed, for everywhere was within a short walk. Elsewhere this would have been impossible. And it would not do to minimize the importance of this. As Rousseau remarked of 'the lawgiver' for which Calvin provided one of the models: 'As the lawgiver can . . . employ neither force nor argument, he must have recourse to an authority of another order, one which can compel without violence and persuade without convincing.'[5]

THE 'CONFESSION' AND THE 'ORDONNANCES'

The fact that Calvin's Christian polity was located at Geneva was of critical importance, but there was nothing in Calvin's political theology which would dispose him to attach importance either to the size of a church or to the particular arrangements or circumstances of the government of the territory in which it was located. Calvin had said nothing whatever about what ought to determine the territorial, demographic and political limits of a church; indeed he did not directly address himself to this question even in later years.

For all that, Calvin was advantageously placed from the point of view of practice by having a magistracy sympathetic to reformation, and he exhibited from the start a very clear idea of what reformation required. The very first document he placed before 'Messieurs' (as the syndics and the so-called 'Small' or 'Narrow' – *estroict* – Council were known) was a *Confession of Faith*, intended to be administered to all the inhabitants of Geneva, citizens or not. The twenty-one articles into which it is divided summarize the main tenets of the evangelical faith, contrasting them with the 'superstitions' and 'blasphemies' of the 'churches governed by the pope's ordinances', churches which are described as 'rather synagogues of the devil than Christian churches' (OS 1, 424, section 18). What exactly the purpose of this *Confession* was is discussed below, but part of the intention was presumably to force the more fervent partisans of the old faith to declare themselves. Some of the articles which the inhabitants of Geneva were to affirm seem also to have been specifically designed to smoke out Anabaptists: for example, the assertion of the legitimacy of infant baptism (OS 1, 423, section 15), the claim that a true church can exist even when 'there are some imperfections and faults, as there always are amongst men' (OS 1, 424, section 18), and the section on 'Magistratz' (OS 1, 425, section 21): all of these would have had the assent of papists. For the rest, the *Confession* simply restates the familiar Lutheran themes of the helplessness, ignorance and corruption of fallen man, redemption in Christ through faith, prayer and the sacraments as outward testimonies to men as well as inward exercises of faith. Christian liberty is mentioned once, in passing, and refers to absolutely nothing apart from the freedom not to be submitted to papal authority. There is again not a single word about the 'priesthood of all believers'.

It is only at the end of the *Confession* that something new attracts our attention. In the first place the organization collapses entirely. Thus a description of the church, which ought logically to have preceded the sections on prayer and sacraments, in fact follows them. It is itself preceded by a section on 'traditions humaines', which ought to have followed, or been amalgamated with it. The section on the church is followed by one on excommunication, the latter in turn by one on 'Ministres de la Parolle', and the whole concludes with a homily on 'Magistratz' which has no thematic connection at all with the rest of the *Confession*.

Calvin was neither indifferent to, nor incompetent in, matters of elegance and presentation. A collapse in the organization of his material tends therefore to suggest that he had not yet found his bearings in the tangle of problems now crowding in upon him. The content of these sections however suggests that he had already seen that new emphases in his doctrines were called for.

A special section (OS 1, 423, section 17) was devoted to 'human traditions'. In substance it is merely a denunciation of Romanist practices such as 'pilgrimages, monkeries, choice of meats, prohibitions of marriage, confessions and such like' (OS, 1, 423-4). But in pursuance of the *Institution*'s polemical distinction between popish ordinances made to bind the conscience and evangelical ordinances, which also bind the conscience, Calvin now added another polemical point which was to be fruitful later on: 'We do not at all take for human traditions the ordinances which are necessary to the external good order (*police exterieure*) of the Church . . . in as much as they are comprehended under the general commandment of St Paul that he wants all things amongst us to be done decently and in good order.' Here Calvin was ignoring entirely the need for human agency in the devising of such ordinances governing *police exterieure*; the authority of St Paul covered them all. Such a bald assertion was only possible because 'human traditions' had come to be absolutely nothing more than an abusive term for 'Romanist practices'; in that sense evangelical ordinances were indeed not 'human traditions'. All that we have here, therefore, is the pleonasm that popery is impious and tyrannical, but that the good order of an evangelical church is not.

The new section on the church adds nothing to the account of the *Institution*. But excommunication has a new prominence; it is now held to deserve more comment than, say, baptism, and Calvin's formulations are much sharper. He now stressed the 'discipline of excommunication' as a 'punishment' for those who 'despise God's sacred Word', as a means to 'avoid the corruption of the good' and 'dishonour of our Lord', and as a way of shaming people into penitence '(*ayans honte ilz se retournent a la penitence*)' (OS 1, 424, section 19). The whole account is punctuated with references to the divine institution of the discipline. No echo remains of the reservations and caveats about the celestial meaning of terrestrial acts by a terrestrial body; instead Calvin treated his public to the first of those many lists of miscreants which flowed so easily from his pen. This time he saw fit to mention: 'manifest idolators, blasphemers, murderers, robbers, lechers (*paillars*), false witnesses, the seditious, the quarrelsome (*noiseulx*), detractors, brawlers, drunkards, dissipators of their wealth' (OS 1, 424–5, section 19) as suitable subjects for excommunication.

There follows a section on 'Ministers of the Word'. It is well to remind ourselves that to each section Calvin required the public assent of all residents of Geneva. He now required them to affirm that 'we do not attribute to [the ministers] any other power or authority[6] than to *guide, rule and govern* the people of God committed to them by that same Word through which they have power (*puissance*) to command, forbid, promise and threaten . . .' (OS 1, 425, section 20; my italics). We are to receive them as 'messengers and ambassadors of God, who must be heard as we would hear God himself, and we are to hold their ministry to be a commission from God necessary to the Church . . .' (*ibid.*). This is a much more positive and un-qualified affirmation of the dignity and importance of the ministry in a reformed church than anything which may be found in the *Institution*, and it constitutes Calvin's first assessment of the dangers to the Reformation from ostensibly reformed quarters, rather than from papists or Anabaptists. The anti-papist flourishes, and the well-worn antitheses between the godly minister and the 'ravenous wolves' who pass for pastors among the Romanists which Calvin appended are now quite secondary in importance.

The final section on *magistratz* adds nothing to the doctrines of the *Institution*, but simply repeats the most forceful assertions of 'passive obedience' to be found there. It makes no mention at all of any role for magistrates in the external order of the church, but on the other hand it does not mention obeying God rather than men either. It seems, therefore, that this section was included simply to reassure 'Messieurs' without giving them any hostages.

On 16 January 1537, the ministers placed before the Seigneurs certain 'admonitions and exhortations' (*advertissemans et exhortations*) which are in fact an informal draft of a set of church ordinances. In view of their ingratiating tone (OS 1, 370), these seem to have been the initiative of the pastors; had the latter been acting on instruction, they would hardly have failed to mention the fact. Although evasive at critical points, these *Ordonnances* are full of suggestive lines of thought. What is more, they betray no uncertainty about what is to be done; although suitably deferential, they are firm, and the implications are clearly drawn.

Wasting no time on preambles, the ministers (which I think means Calvin, writing for the rest) began at once with five desiderata: frequent communion, celebrated in a reverent and godly manner (*sainctement*); the 'discipline of excommunication'; the singing of psalms; the instruction of the young, and new *ordonnances* concerning marriage. The very first line of the address spells out the preoccupation of the authors: 'une eglise .. bien ordonnee et reiglee' (OS 1, 369).

The desiderata set down, the ministers went on to amplify and justify them. After the 'trouble and confusion' of the time before the Gospel was 'received with one accord', and granted that 'it was not possible to reduce everything to good order at a single stroke' (p. 370), the ministers now judged the reign of the Lord to be better established and that it was time to consider what order (*police*) there should be. The ministers based their right to suggest anything in this area on their *cognoissance* of the Word, but seem to allow an independent judgement of what the Word contains to the magistrates: 'If you see our advice to be part of the holy word of the Gospel . . .' (*ibid.*).

The *Ordonnances* then proceed with firmness and economy. And one is struck at once by the salience of the 'Lord's Supper'.[7] The frequent and reverent celebration of the Lord's Supper is interpreted as essential in a well-ordered church, and it is only because of the 'infirmity of the people' that the ministers are prepared to settle for monthly communion. (The Genevan Councils eventually concluded that four times a year was sufficient.) The Lord's Supper is said to be ideally the frequent 'exercise' of our faith and charity, a source of consolation and exhortation to praises of God and to Christian living, but it is unmistakably communion and not preaching alone that is taken to be the focus of public worship. While this is no departure from what Calvin had said in the *Institution*, such an attitude was nonetheless somewhat idiosyncratic in an evangelical context,[8] and is one of the few matters in which Calvin's followers did not follow him. But the purpose of this evaluation of the significance of communion is visible just below the surface of the text. The reformed Lord's Supper is intended as a corrected alternative to the 'abomination of masses'; as so often, Calvin was defining evangelical faith by negation, and it is perhaps for this reason, rather than because of any momentum generated by the evangelical life, that the Lord's Supper is given such prominence. As Calvinists ceased to define themselves as not-papists, so the reason for the emphasis on sacraments as opposed to preaching disappeared.

But it is not, I think, far-fetched to suggest another reason for the salience of the Lord's Supper. Calvin now described it as 'this sacred and excellent mystery' (OS i, 371) and went on to say that this 'high mystery', which was to be 'treated with the greatest possible dignity', is the province of the ministers of the Word, whose 'proper office it is to administer all that pertains to the mysteries of God' (*ibid.*). Calvin could hardly have been more explicit about his intention to emphasize the dignity and standing of the evangelical pastorate which flowed from this association between ministry and mystery. It required no alteration in Calvin's theology to put it like this, and indeed the precepts for the dignified administration of the sacrament closely resemble those of the first *Institution* (OS i, 161); but in his theology of the Eucharist in that place, the only references to a 'mystery' in connection with the sacraments had been a general one to the 'three witnesses to the redemptive work of Christ, water (baptism), blood (the Eucharist) and the Spirit', 'the primary witness' (OS i, 126); and a sarcastic reference to the 'very great mysteries' of the Mass (OS i, 157). The emphasis on the 'mystery' of the Lord's Supper is thus altogether new.

The locating of the Lord's Supper as the central act of evangelical worship is connected with another feature of the *Ordonnances* and the *Catechisme*. It is not clear whose insight it was, and it was not much in evidence in the *Institution*, but both pieces betray a sensitivity to the capacity of public forms and ceremonies (all those things that Luther had somewhat dismissively labelled 'externals')[9] to reach the heart and jolt the affections of congregations out of their habitual 'coldness': 'Truly, as we do now, the prayers of the faithful are so cold, that it must turn to great shame and confusion' (OS 1, 375). And what distracts the attention and cools the hearts is a lack of 'dignity', 'order' and 'decorum' (*honnesteté*), as well as lack of involvement on the part of the congregation. The twin dangers are seen to be disorderliness and irreverence on the one hand, and passivity on the other; and the better management of 'externals' is reckoned crucial to the building up (*l'edification*) of the church. It is for the same reason that the ministers urged the public singing of psalms during services, and the public examination of children about the content of a *catechisme* yet to be produced.

The sacrosanctity and the mystery of the Lord's Supper were taken by Calvin to demand and justify the most energetic measures to prevent its profanation. Calvin here ransacked the French language for terms expressing pollution: he wrote of the sacrament being 'pollué', 'contaminé', 'profané' (OS 1, 371), and followed this with talk of cutting off 'membres punais et pourriz . . . corrompus . . . gastez' (pp. 372, 415). The gravity of the matter established, Calvin adduced 1 Timothy 1 and 1 Corinthians 5 to support the contention that it is to avoid such dishonouring of God that 'the Lord has placed in his church the corrective and discipline of excommunication'. The practice of excommunication is ascribed to the early church (Calvin had evidently not yet 'discovered' it to be scriptural); its discontinuance to wicked bishops and the consequence of failing to observe it was said to be punishment 'by a great vengeance of God' (pp. 372–3). He was careful to add, however, that excommunication does not mean exclusion from sermons: there is to be no relief from sermons in this life, not even (or rather, especially not) for the most conspicuously reprobate.

As an instrument of this discipline which has excommunication as its last resort, the ministers proposed a committee of persons of good life and repute, to be selected from the magistrates' own number so that all the quarters of the town would be covered, who were to keep an eye on ('ayant l'oeil sur') the life and conduct of everyone, in cooperation with ministers (p. 373). No more precise details of the arrangement envisaged were provided, nor a legitimation for it. There was, however, one ominous addition. The church could not go beyond excommunication. But although this had been enough for St Paul, the ministers expressed themselves dissatisfied: if there was someone abandoned enough in perversity to scoff at excommunication, the magistrates were urged to consider 'whether [they] shall long suffer and leave unpunished such a contempt and mockery of God and the Gospel' (p. 374). The peroration twice more took up this theme: the magistrates were to reflect on 'the consequence and importance [of these admonitions and exhortations] to the maintaining of the honour of God in its *estat* and to keeping the church one and undivided'. And in the very last lines, the magistrates and the ministers become a 'we', linked in the hope that God 'will bring *our enterprise* to a good end' (p. 377; my italics), the enterprise being to 'chercher sa gloyre'.

Assisted, perhaps, by hindsight, it does seem possible to identify certain shifts of emphasis distinguishing the *Confession* and the *Ordonnances* from the first *Institution*, and also certain imperfectly articulated assumptions of the former which had not appeared in the latter. Thus it is apparent that Calvin was now interpreting the church for all practical purposes as a 'congregation' or 'assembly' of the 'faithful', ordered by common 'laws' or 'ordinances' governing the worship and morality of its members, and discriminating between those entitled to belong to its fellowship and those not. Indispensable to its existence are pure teaching, rightly administered sacraments and 'the discipline of excommunication'. And all of this is seen to require a prestigious and vigorous ministry. The business of the church, its enterprise, is *aedificatio* and the upholding of the honour and glory of God, and in this enterprise ministers and magistrates are implied to be partners, in a rough equality. On the other hand, Calvin was clearly assuming that magistrates, *qua* magistrates, are not the holders of an ecclesiastical office, for without this assumption it would have made no sense to say, as Calvin did, that in punishing, 'the church' cannot go beyond excommunication, or for him to request the magistrates to designate some of their number as participants in disciplinary arrangements. Calvin had not, however, explained why the profanation and defilement of the sacrament should be a specific concern of the magistracy.

Now since excommunication and discipline had as their province not simply the religious belief and observance, but also the morals, of the community; since, furthermore, the distinction between sin and crime was of little practical significance in early modern Europe; and finally, since the congregation liable to ecclesiastical discipline was identical with the subjects of the civil government of a particular territory, there were bound to be problems of jurisdiction the moment Calvin specified (as he had done in the *Ordonnances*), that the church was to have its own set of governors to 'govern' it. Calvin, furthermore, was already describing the church in a terminology which might equally well be used of the polity. It did not require much political expertise to recognize that this began to look like the establishment of a state within a state, and that excommunication was liable to prove a serious irritant lodged in the sensitive area of magisterial–ministerial relations. Calvin evidently judged the matter important enough to risk making enemies over.

The *Ordonnances* further asked 'for this time only' – in other words, Calvin recognized that there would be hostility to this proposal, and was trying to head it off by saying that this was to be a once and for all measure – that all the inhabitants of Geneva should be made to subscribe to the *Confession de la Foy* (p. 375) which had been in the hands of the magistrates since 10 November 1536.[10] The ministers now also urged the magistrates to set a good example by themselves subscribing speedily, and then enforcing subscription on others.

Neither the purpose nor the presuppositions of such a confession as a public act are entirely clear, and the ministers did not explain their intention. It was obviously not merely a tactic to gain an idea of the strength of the disaffected party, as some apologists pretend, for pressure was to be brought to bear on people to make it. Nor was it merely an outward profession, an act of civic loyalty, that was being required; the ministers expressly rejected that as insufficient.[11] Nor was it a question of eligibility for civic office in what was after all a reformed city. For subscription was demanded of mere *habitants*,[12] that is to say alien residents, who were ineligible for any civic office and did not even have the franchise. Public demonstrations of evangelical civic solidarity were not unheard of, and this was perhaps all that the ministers intended, even though there appears to be no precedent for a test administered to every inhabitant. Whatever the purpose, it is legitimate to ask what assumptions are required for such a course to appear a reasonable thing to propose. And what was assumed was that every inhabitant of Geneva, a unit defined by political and not religious criteria, must be willing to accept (in conscience, since he was on oath) the main tenets of reformed religion. No more complete fusion of civic and religious allegiance could be imagined; even residence at Geneva was to be impossible for all but professing evangelicals. No connection between this public act and evangelical theology was established: it concerns the character of a visible church, a topic on which Calvin had not yet formulated a clear position and which in the meanwhile was governed by inherited, medieval assumptions about the necessary identity of civic and religious allegiance. An indirect theological justification for this assumption, and for the related beliefs about the proper way to deal with the irreconcilably sinful or heretical, was not developed by Calvin until the war of pamphlets over Servetus in 1553. In 1537 he had other more pressing things to worry about. His problem was not that of dealing with isolated heretics; magistrates and population alike proved exceedingly reluctant to subscribe to the *Confession*.[13]

On the basis of these documents, then, it does not appear that Calvin had worked out a clearer theological position on the relationship between the 'universal church, the communion of saints' and 'churches' particularized by location and organization, or on the relationship of the latter to the magistracy or to the civil polity. What we do find is a marked shift away from the outward–inward, spiritual–civil, two-fold regiment distinctions of the *Institution*, and a movement towards the idea that civil society comprises not only a civil but also an ecclesiastical *police*, so that upholding the public honour of God is a task both for magistrates and for ministers, and that obedience to ministers is also a civic duty, just as obedience to magistrates is also a religious duty.

THE 'INSTRUCTION ET CONFESSION DE FOY' ('CATECHISME')

In the *Ordonnances* the ministers had referred to the need for a 'short and easy summary (*somme*) of the Christian faith' for the instruction and public examination of children by the ministers. And in 1537 Calvin did indeed write and publish an *Instruction et Confession de Foy*.[14] It was, however, neither short nor easy enough to be of use for children. And if, as McNeill says, it was a 'masterpiece', it was certainly more than a 'masterpiece of condensation'[15] of the *Institution*. Nor is it correct to assert, as Wendel does,[16] that the *Confession de la Foy* was an abstract of the *Catechisme*, for the former was written earlier.

It was not Calvin's habit to retract what he had written – I am not aware that he ever did so over any matter of substance. This has been used by Doumergue to say, and by others (Bohatec, Chenevière, Baur *et al.*) to imply, that there were no changes in his thought, only development. But the same sentence can take on an entirely different meaning when it is transposed into a new context; again, it is one thing to assert something in passing, quite another to make the same assertion the mainstay of a paragraph or chapter; and finally, 'development' carries (to my mind uneliminable) connotations of the autonomous unfolding of potentialities, a process requiring only thought and time for its realization. My argument is flatly against this: Calvin's own experience seems to me to be crucial. The inner momentum in his thought that does seem to me demonstrable throughout is a striving for orderliness and coherence in the flow of ideas and presentation: 'All things decently and in good order' was a passion with him.

With these considerations in mind, one may characterize the changes that took place in Calvin's thought in the two years or so between the *Institution* and the *Catechisme*. As before, Calvin's theology concerns us only in so far as it has a direct bearing on his political thought, and hitherto we have found cause to question Calvin's more or less explicit assumption that his general theology and his political thought were all of a piece. In the *Catechisme* the discontinuity is much less evident, especially since no mention whatever is made of merely 'civil righteousness', the 'merely constrained and enforced righteousness' said to be adequate for civil relations in the *Institution*, or of 'conscience' and natural 'equity'. Instead the reader is given a stiff dose of scriptural imperatives to obedience to the 'ministers and lieutenants of God'. The magistrates in turn are enjoined 'to conserve in its true purity the public form of religion, to arrange (*instituer*) the lives of the people by good laws and to procure the well-being and tranquillity of their subjects in public as well as private matters' (p. 416). Since subsequent editions of the *Institution* returned to all the themes and concepts which the *Catechisme* omitted, we must conclude that it was not a change of heart which prompted their omission; but it remains of consequence that Calvin felt able to dispense with them in a *Catechisme* which spelt out many other things at great length: they were obviously not the heart of the matter for him.

Apart from the rather adventitious homogeneity of style which resulted from the exclusion of non-scriptural categories, the explicitly political doctrine (i.e. the section on *magistrats*) remains as much of an appendix to the theology as ever, for although Calvin had amassed scriptural proof-texts calculated to inspire awe before magistrates, the only way of linking the magistracy to the main lines of the account of the providential economy that he had yet devised was the assertion that it was God's good will and pleasure that we should obey all magistrates. This was no negligible connection: Calvin's God is always a God who expects punctilious obedience, and whose ways are ultimately inscrutable. But Calvin tended as a rule to find more intelligibility in God's workings than a divine *sic volo sic jubeo: stet pro ratione voluntas*. And he once again did not attempt to become more specific about the magistrates' office in the extremely sensitive area of pastoral–magisterial relations. It is to anticipate only a little to say that the next (1539) edition of the *Institution* was no clearer on the point, and one must conclude that Calvin had simply not thought the matter through.

If we allow, then, that despite the incongruousness of such an attitude in the light of his experience as a minister, Calvin persisted in regarding questions of *respublica* as marginal to his concerns as a theologian, it is still an occasion for some surprise

that Calvin's ecclesiology was not more fully worked out than
we find it to be. My view is that Calvin was in the process of
rethinking the general lines of his theology, but had not as
yet come to its ecclesiological implications. (It will be recalled
that ecclesiology is here treated as part of political theology, in
view of Calvin's unaltering conviction that the church is a
public entity, and that the magistracy has ecclesiastical
functions.)

The impression must not be allowed to arise that Calvin had
learnt nothing from his pastoral experience.[17] On the contrary
he had learnt a great deal even since the *Confession* and had
incorporated it into his thought. Thus the sections of the
Catechisme dealing with ecclesiastical matters now have a
somewhat more coherent structure, and judicious omissions,
new emphases and rearrangements of the subject-matter make
their appearance. The *Catechisme* now proceeds logically from a
discussion of the sacraments to a new section entitled 'Of the
pastors of the church and of their power (*puissance*)', and then
to human traditions, excommunication and finally the magistrates. This order is still imperfect: the section on 'excommunication', for example, occupies a no-man's-land between
'pastors' and 'magistrates', which is no doubt symbolically very
apt, but was presumably unintentional, and the section on
'human traditions' is free-floating. Even so, there is now firmness in the choice and designation of leading themes. Christian
liberty has been eliminated entirely; a single use of the phrase,
and that in an uncharacteristically polemical context, recalls its
former prominence in the *Institution* (OS 1, 415). The already-
mentioned sections on pastors, human traditions and excommunication contain all that Calvin had to say about the visible
church. It is surely not excessive to conclude from this that
Calvin was beginning to allot to 'pastors' and 'laws' an overriding dignity and status in the church for which the *Institution*
certainly did not prepare us. Nor does this high estimation
stand dissociated from the rest of the argument; it flows
directly from the prominence given to the 'mystery' (p. 413) of
the Lord's Supper, and the preaching and prayer that must
attend it: all these call for order, and therefore, in Calvin's
view, law and the 'ministry of men'.

The discussion of 'excommunication', not to mince words,
was more contradictory than before. By its nature, excom-

munication can be no other than a solemn and public act, and as such cannot possibly emanate from the 'church' as the invisible communion of saints. This, however, is the only 'church' that Calvin explicitly identified, its connection with 'assemblies of the faithful' or the manner in which such assemblies can be said to act being left as obscure as ever. Indeed, in legitimating this 'discipline', Calvin argued that 'seeing that the church is the body of Christ, she must not be polluted and contaminated by such foetid (*punais*) and putrid (*pourriz*) members, who turn into a dishonour of the head [sc. Christ]; and further, that the saints may not be corrupted and spoilt, as is wont to happen, by the conversation of the wicked' (p. 415). But the 'church' which is the body of Christ is the universal invisible church, and it cannot possibly be polluted or contaminated by putrid members, since, by definition, it does not contain any.

But if Calvin left it opaque what agencies were to be responsible for excommunication,[18] and if his rationale for it was confused, there is no mistaking the prominence he was now disposed to give to it. His assertion that 'outside this church and communion of saints there is no salvation' (p. 402),[19] and that 'such a judgement [of excommunication] of the faithful is nothing else than the pronouncement of [the Lord's] sentence' (p. 416), now create quite the opposite impression to that conveyed by the *Institution* (OS 1, 89–91) where his point had been to assert the contingent and tenuous connection between the verdict of any earthly body and the judgement of God. No echo of former caveats and distinctions now remains. In exactly the same way, whereas the *Institution* was concerned to insist that ministers of the Word had authority *only through*, and *in so far as* they limited themselves to, the Word of God (OS 1, 234–5, 237), the *Catechisme* now says that ministers have authority *unless* they proceed to their own dreams and inventions (p. 414); the words may be the same, but the implication is very different.

The section on 'human traditions' adds nothing to Calvin's previous discussion. It merely repeats the assertion that those practices which conduce to decency and order, peace and concord, in the assemblies of Christians must not be numbered amongst 'human traditions', and persists in contrasting them with laws made to bind consciences (OS 1, 415).

On the other hand, the discussion of the sacraments and the explicit demand for respect for the 'ministry' (*ministère;* it is the office rather than the incumbents Calvin has in mind), founded on the 'will of the Lord' that 'his word and his sacraments be dispensed by the ministry of men' (OS i, 413–4), establishes a much closer connection between the bulk of the *Catechisme* and the ecclesiological sections than ever existed in the *Institution*. What is somewhat less obvious, but possibly of greater moment, is that the general tenor of Calvin's theology has changed. For within the confines of an outline which Calvin had not recast, a rather different, and clearer, choice of themes emerges. Calvin's theology now appears as a meditation on knowledge, law and duty, and zeal.

These themes were certainly not absent from the *Institution*, but what is new is their emergence as leitmotifs in Calvin's theology. The account of the human predicament that Calvin now offered (and which subsequent editions of the *Institution* were to utilize for a gradual recasting of the entire work) suggests that Calvin's theology now ran as follows.

In the first place, the Christian life is seen by Calvin as a life of service, of endeavour, of zeal, and all for the honour and glory of God. The first paragraph of the *Catechisme* sets out the theme of the whole work: 'We are all created to this end, that we may know the majesty of our Creator; and having come to know it, that we might venerate it above all else, and honour it with all fear, love and reverence' (OS i, 378).

What we owe to God, then, is a 'true and pure zeal', a zeal which seeks knowledge of God from God himself, embraces his justice and has a horror of offending him. This is seen to entail that we love God with all our hearts and that we love our neighbour as ourselves (p. 388). The statement of what this implies is the Law, the Ten Commandments, which set before us 'the exemplar of a just and holy life, and even the perfect image of justice: so that, if someone expressed in his life the Law of God, he would lack nothing before the Lord of what is required for perfection' (p. 389).

Now, although Calvin did not say so, his thought assumes what is true enough, namely that performance of any duty requires two things: first, a knowledge of our duty, and second, the means to perform it. Man as we find him, however, is deficient in both respects. He lacks clear knowledge of what is required of him, has not the strength and resources to perform his duty even when he does perceive it, and indeed has a positive inclination to do the opposite: he takes a positive delight in wrong-doing (a fact on which Calvin had already remarked in the *De Clementia Commentary*). 'Man's spirit is so alienated (*aliené*) from the justice of God that he neither conceives nor undertakes anything which is not wicked, perverse, iniquitous and soiled' (p. 381).

This, of course, is not how God created man. On the contrary, man was created in the image and likeness of God, but instead of finding reasons to admire the author of the 'gifts', the 'ornaments' with which he found himself endowed, man stupidly took a pride in them and forgot from where they came. Stripped of his divine attributes, but not of his duties, man can only deserve the harsh judgement of God, and the punishment is death. But while this deprivation consequent to the Fall of Adam is certainly a punishment (indeed, it means the death-penalty), that is not all it is, nor even, from the point of view of the elect, is it mainly a punishment. Rather is it a necessary precondition for the recovery of the *cognoissance* of God and duty.

The manner in which this saving *cognoissance* is recovered, according to Calvin, seems to be this. Consciousness, knowledge that there is a God is never lost, even by fallen man. But the corruption of his understanding (*entendement*) and the vitiated affects of his heart (*concupiscences, cupiditez*) (p. 362) conspire to prevent man finding the truth about God and about what his service requires, causing him rather to lose himself in his own vain imaginings. Thus the physical universe, which ought to reveal to us God's immortality, power, goodness, justice and mercy, in fact teaches us nothing (p. 380). For that reason man needs direct assistance from the self-revelation of God in the written Word, 'the true knowledge of God' (p. 382), vouchsafed in 'figures' to the prophets, and in its fullness through Christ.

The Word (if this is the right interpretation of Calvin's not entirely orderly account) both prepares us for salvation and teaches us that we are saved. The preparation is the recognition (*intelligence, recognoissance*) of our own helplessness, ignominy and perdition, and it arises out of the contemplation of our sins. The Law of the Lord (in other words the Ten Commandments) here provides the correct yardstick against which to measure ourselves, a set of external rules constituting an external 'exemplar of a just and holy life' (p. 389). Its author is God: the Ten Commandments begin with the declaration of God that it is he who has the right to command. But knowledge of what is required of us, especially a knowledge that God demands not only external acts but also rightness of intention, cannot alone save us: it rather reduces us to despair.

What is required before we can even begin to comply with the 'exemplar' is a knowledge of God's mercy, and a change of heart. This too can only come through the direct action of God. And thus, while God appears as perfect justice in his Law, as Christ his face shines full of grace and benignity towards us (p. 390). Christ is offered in Scripture, and is 'apprehended' by faith. Faith, however, is not a simple matter of *intelligence* or *cognoissances*, something that 'flutters about (*voltige*) in our skulls without touching our *hearts*' (p. 391; my italics), but rather is a 'firm and solid confidence of the *heart*' (*ibid.*; my italics.)[20] As with Luther, whose account this greatly resembles, faith is understood to be a matter of emotion and feelings, of *confiance* and *persuasion* (p. 392); the problems entailed by such subjectivism are simply disregarded. Such faith is an unmerited gift of God: it is an 'enlightening of our understanding', a 'confirming of our hearts in a certain persuasion'. And by this faith, whose object is Christ, we are justified, or more precisely, God chooses to regard us as justified; he 'attributes' or 'imputes' (p. 393) to us the justice which is only Christ's. But such justification does not come by itself; rather is it accompanied by sanctification, the imparting of a power (*vertu*) whereby we are made able to obey the Law, which henceforth is not simply the measure of our helplessness, but rather 'a lamp to guide our feet', 'our wisdom' and our 'discipline' (p. 394). This is the first instance I can find in Calvin of the notion of 'discipline' spreading its range of reference beyond excommunication. Another instance occurs later in the same work, where the 'ministry of men' in the dispensation of the Word and the sacraments, that is, the pastorate, is described as exercising a 'discipline and order' (p. 414).

Despite the concision which a catechism demands, Calvin now[21] devoted two sections, one of them entitled 'Concerning election and predestination' (pp. 390–1), the other in the exposition of the Creed's 'resurrection of the flesh, eternal life' (pp. 402–3), to spelling out that election, which is experienced as faith, is by no means for everyone; rather does God's mercy predestine some for salvation, while the rigour of his justice is exercised against others; the reason why he distinguishes individuals in this way is unfathomable to human minds (p. 390). This is that 'great secret of the counsels of the Lord'[22] not to be enquired into or speculated about, but simply to be accepted: 'let us not, in order to confirm the certitude of our salvation, seek to penetrate the very heavens and to enquire into what God from all eternity has determined to do with us . . . rather let us rest content with the testimony by which God has sufficiently and amply confirmed our certainty' (p. 391), and we are to be assured that in possessing Christ we also possess eternal life (*ibid.*). The passage on the resurrection contrasts the joy of the celestial kingdom with the 'perpetual darkness and eternal torments awaiting the reprobate' (pp. 402–3). And Calvin urges his readers to find in both election and reprobation argument and material for 'exalting the glory of God' (p. 391).

Now predestination was a necessary entailment of the evangelical and Pauline doctrine of justification, and in particular of its rejection of the 'semi-Pelagian' doctrine of the cooperation of man and God in salvation, and Luther had made no bones about describing it as the *res ipsa*, the *cardo rerum* of theology.[23] The choice for evangelicals was not whether to accept or reject predestination, but whether or not to emphasize this aspect of justification by faith alone. Some thought it best to be silent, particularly Melanchthon;[24] Calvin chose to stress it. His reasons for doing so do not, however, appear at this point. That pastoral considerations were important to him is apparent from his attempt to reassure those anxious about their salvation, but these do nothing whatever to explain his insistence on reprobation, or his putting of election and reprobation on a par. Nor did Calvin explain in what way reprobation is a matter for glorifying God, even if it is plain enough why election is. But Calvin was always a whole-Gospel man: if the Scriptures taught both election and reprobation, then that was what he must teach, no more, but also no less.

The lives of the elect, then, are a matter of becoming sanctified, of zeal, of striving to realize in our thoughts and outward conduct that righteousness which God in his mercy already imputes to us. And this 'sanctification' is realized in a better knowledge of God, as summarized in the Apostles' Creed, love of our neighbour, prayer and sacraments (pp. 410–11).

What has emerged here as the centre of Calvin's theology is an account of the Christian life as first a matter of 'knowledge'. Faith indeed is a kind of knowledge. But the kind of knowledge in question is not in essence a knowledge of propositions, a knowledge *that*. The point of Calvin's constantly repeated contrast between the 'heart' and the *intelligence* is that the understanding of God and of ourselves that is at issue is a matter of the emotions, dispositions, inclinations (in scholastic language, the *habitus*), as well as of the intellect. And this sort of knowledge bears fruit in a zeal for God's honour, a willing obedience to his Law. Christ's redemptive work itself is seen as consisting in perfect obedience (p. 398). This insistence on obedience is coupled with a strong depreciation of 'speculation', 'inquisitiveness' and questioning generally: given the ultimate unintelligibility of Calvin's God, nothing but unquestioning obedience makes much sense. It is scarcely surprising, therefore, that the notion of discipline should have spread outwards: the whole of Christian life is now conceived as a kind of training, under supervision and command, for immortality. The impetus towards the conversion of the evangelical understanding of the Christian life into an ethic of duty is apparent, and as a consequence the gap between the general and the political theology narrows perceptibly: both deal in duties, owed in both cases to God. Finally an ethic of duty is an ethic of obedience, and obedience presupposes command. It cannot surprise, therefore, that Calvin should have begun to assume the need for ecclesiastical as well as civil commanders.

To summarize: the writings of 1536 and 1537 intimate emphases and changes for which the *Institution* had not prepared us. First: a preoccupation with the visible church now all but excludes a concern with the invisible church. Second: the visible church is characterized by laws, discipline and a potent ministry.[25] Third: the ministers are seen as ideally cooperating with the magistrates in a common enterprise of *aedificatio*, now quite a salient concept in Calvin's thinking. *Aedificatio* is an instilling of habits of piety and discipline in the citizenry – congregation. And finally, what is aimed for is zeal, for faith is not a matter of assent to propositions; it engages the heart, the passions: it fires with a zeal to do God's work.

It should be apparent from this account that Calvin had not been intellectually idle since writing the *Institution*. And while it is no part of my reading of his thought to interpret it all as a response to the political circumstances in which he found himself, some of the changes and new emphases can be seen as called for by Genevan circumstances, or at any rate circumstances which Geneva shared with other evangelical polities. For the reformation at Geneva had not converted a backsliding, religiously indifferent or merely habitually observant and anticlerical population into a pious and godly nation, nor had it diverted governors from their traditional preoccupations and inclinations. In his farewell address to the Genevans shortly before his death Calvin claimed that almost nothing had been done when he first arrived. This was no doubt an exaggeration, but the marked lack of zeal, the profound ignorance of evangelical doctrine in young and old alike, and the hostility of magistrates and citizens to any more vigorous direction to piety and righteousness by the ministers are all plain enough: they surfaced in open hostility to the ministers and eventually resulted in the latter's expulsion at Easter 1538. Calvin and Farel were considering the moral qualities and fashioning the institutional implements whereby reformation might be made a reality. But the Genevans had no stomach for the enterprise.

4

Reconstruction

All four syndics[1] elected in February 1538 were hostile to Farel and Calvin. The final confrontation came before Easter; the immediate issues were the magistrates' demand that all be admitted to communion who would present themselves[2] and the adoption of the Bernese rite, which was somewhat less aggressively anti-Roman and anti-traditional than what Calvin had in mind. Although Wendel is right to say that the Bernese rite *per se* was not an essential of faith for Calvin,[3] the fact that its adoption was being pressed by the magistrates made it something to be resisted. Nor had excommunication been identified by Calvin as one of the marks of a true church, even though there is no mistaking the importance which he had come to attach to it. In any case, both parties understood clearly that what was at issue was who should be master in what the ministers, but not the magistrates, regarded as their own house. The last straw, the prohibition of preaching (which followed attacks by the ministers on the new officials, delivered from the pulpit), was an attack on one of the marks of a true church. It was followed rapidly by the ministers' refusal to administer communion, their ignoring of the order to refrain from preaching, and the summary dismissal of Calvin, Farel and Courrault, an intransigent and blind old minister.

It appears that the ministers were shaken by their expulsion and at first did not regard it as final.[4] But their attempts to secure reinstatement with Bernese assistance proved unavailing. The Genevans were glad to be rid of them, and Calvin and Farel offered no concessions on ecclesiastical discipline. Of the *Articles Proposed by Calvin and Farel*,[5] three concerned the 'permanent establishment of discipline', 'otherwise whatever is established for the time being will soon collapse'. In particular, they insisted on the clear division of the city into parishes with a minister responsible for each, and harked back to the 1536 proposals for the selection by the Petit Conseil of certain upright and stout-hearted men from each neighbourhood, to cooperate with the ministers in the discipline. Discipline, it appears, had become non-negotiable in Calvin's and Farel's mind.

Calvin's endeavours to retire into the life of a private scholar, once he had accepted his expulsion as final, were once more frustrated, this time by Bucer's pressing him to come to Strasbourg. Calvin gave in in September 1538. Contrary to his expectation, life at Strasbourg was to prove in most respects satisfactory and rewarding. Aside from his establishment and management of the French refugee church, he was also required to lecture on theology in Johann Sturm's newly founded academy, to preach at the Cathedral, and to assist Bucer, Capito and Hedio at the various colloquia amongst evangelicals and between evangelicals, Romanists and the Emperor, between 1538 and 1541. At the same time he managed to produce a new version of the *Institution* (in August 1539) and a French translation (in 1541); the *Reply to Sadoleto* (September/October 1539), which apparently took less than a week to write (a credible claim, for it was in most respects a rather mechanical anti-Roman tract of a sort which came all too easily to Calvin); the *Short Treatise of the Lord's Supper* (written in 1540 and published in 1541); and the first of his *Commentaries*, characteristically on Romans (finished by October 1539 and published in 1540).[6] By October 1540 the composition of the syndics and the Petit Conseil had changed so drastically that the first requests were made for his return.[7] This had not figured in his calculations: his taking of Strasbourg citizenship and his marriage in August 1540 were hardly the actions of a man who regarded himself as of no fixed abode, and his reluctance to return to Geneva was only marginally greater than that of the Strasbourgeois to allow him to do so.[8] Geneva had nothing of Strasbourg's evangelical or political standing, and the comparatively obedient and zealous congregation of French refugees at Strasbourg was not to be readily exchanged for the recalcitrant and indifferent indigenous population of Geneva. It was only considerations of duty and the prospect of a chastened magistracy and congregation that finally clinched the decision to return.

In September 1541, the very day of his return according to his pious biographer Beza, Calvin presented himself before the Seigneurie and 'asked that the church be set in order'.[9] With the other ministers, none of whom can have contributed much except Pierre Viret (on temporary loan from Lausanne and soon recalled, to Calvin's chagrin), and six councillors to assist him, a draft of a set of ecclesiastical ordinances was completed within twenty of Calvin's fully occupied days. Calvin himself referred to these ordinances as 'ecclesiastical laws' (*loix ecclesiastiques*) in a letter of the time.[10]

Immediately on his return, then, Calvin was in a position to submit a comprehensive church ordinance, far surpassing in clarity of direction and precision of detail anything he had produced so far. It seems not unreasonable to attribute this new-found clarity to his learning at Strasbourg.[11] At any rate, the *Institution*, published in August 1539 but completed early that year,[12] and the *Commentary on Romans* of October of the same year do not reveal Calvin as having adapted his theology in order to incorporate the lessons we have seen him to have learnt about civil and ecclesiastical polity at Geneva. In particular (as will be seen) he had no new thoughts to offer on magistracy. As we saw, the only political doctrines which did not require to be extorted from him were the doctrines of political obedience and of the civil enforcement of piety and godliness. And in the Strasbourg which now occupied his attentions, and engaged his affections in a way in which Geneva never did, the magistracy must have appeared to him (by comparison with Geneva) as the very embodiment of that reformed magistracy which had been merely a speculative desideratum in the first *Institution*. He was also now concerned mainly with the instruction of private men. He could thus leave thorny political questions in abeyance and devote himself to his favoured kind of theology.

THE 'INSTITUTION' OF 1539[13]

'My object in this work' (he wrote in the Preface to the revised *Institution*), 'has been so to prepare and train students of sacred theology for the study of the divine Word that they might have an easy access into it, and be able to proceed in it without hindrance' (CO 1, 255).[14] And the work was now well on its way to the status of an evangelical *summa:* it had swollen to thrice its former volume, and there were now seventeen chapters instead of six. One consequence of this was that the organization of the work after the first few chapters quite disintegrated, and indeed Calvin said in the Preface to the 1559 edition that he had never previously been satisfied with it.

The work was completed too early to bear much of an imprint of Strasbourg. Echoes of his experience there are, however, conspicuous in several places, where additions or amendments were prompted by polemic against Anabaptists. Now Geneva was not much troubled by Anabaptists; its way with them had always been rather short. Strasbourg on the other hand was still reaping the rewards of a greater tolerance: it had been a sort of sanctuary for Anabaptists, much to the chagrin of Bucer and eventually even of Capito, who had always inclined to indulgence. On his arrival, and especially in the tailors' guild in which he enrolled, Calvin was at once confronted with the need to argue against Anabaptists. It will be recalled that he had already composed, but not published, a substantial piece against the widespread, though not salient, Anabaptist heresy of psychopannychism or soul-sleep.[15] He now took up the cudgels again in the revision of the *Institution.* The minimal changes in the section 'De Politica Administratione', now made into a separate chapter but reproducing the content of the 1536 version almost verbatim, were all directed to immunizing some of the assertions made there against Anabaptist challenges. The same considerations account for much of the expanded treatment of the 'one, holy, catholic church' in the otherwise familiar chapter 'De Fide' and for the expanded section on oaths in 'De Lege'. Another chapter, 'Concerning the similarity and difference between the Old and the New Covenant', tried to fill what Calvin had evidently discerned as a considerable lacuna in the first edition, but here too it was the exigencies of dealing with Anabaptists and not the tranquil concerns of the study that moved Calvin: he was contending against the view, which he attributed to the Anabaptists, that in the Old Testament, unlike the New, the promise of the covenant was simply earthly felicity. It may be remarked in passing that Calvin is said to have enjoyed

conspicuous success in converting Anabaptists;[16] his personal
manner in dealing with them will have differed from that
which he adopted in writing against them, which consisted of
convicting them of scriptural errors and ignorance. Calvin in
person seems to have been much less harsh and supercilious
than his writings.

The polemic against the Anabaptists was, however, only one
aspect of Calvin's wider preoccupation with the integrity of
evangelical churches and with the prospects of evangelical
ecumenism – of any more inclusive ecumenism there is scarcely
a hint in the length and breadth of Calvin's work. For what was
at issue in his discussion of Anabaptist arguments was not
merely disputes over specific doctrines, but a whole structure of
considerations all of which served to demonstrate that there
were no grounds for separation from an evangelical church,
however imperfect, provided such a church exhibited certain
elementary *notae*, 'marks'. This topic will occupy us again
somewhat later.

In the main, however, the new *Institution* was concerned to
provide an exposition of the essence of evangelical doctrine,
and it contained little that bore directly on Calvin's
ecclesiastico-political experience. In substance, its theology
may be regarded as a consolidation of the changes already
signalled in the *Confession de la Foy* of 1536/7 and the *Catechisme*
of 1537. The main changes (emphasized *inter alia* by two new
chapters which begin the book and precede the old chapter
'De Lege') are an increased emphasis on Scripture as the source
for the *cognitio* (*cognoissance*) of God and Man, a knowledge
which, taking possession of the heart and affections through
faith, finds its fruits in a life of the progressive evacuation of the
self and its replacement by the will of God and a regard to his
glory. This is the great theme of the longest addition of all: a
very substantial chapter (reproduced in all later editions with
minimal additions, and also published separately), 'Concerning
the life of a Christian man', which terminated this and all
subsequent editions until 1559. The chapter has a homilectic
and hortatory quality which is somewhat out of keeping with
the alternately expository and polemical character of the rest.

Another new chapter (chapter 7) concerned the evangelical
bed-rock, 'De Justificatione Fidei', previously more or less
taken for granted, which was now fully exposed to view in a

long chapter entirely devoid of theological novelty, but taut and orderly, and which did not omit a fling at the papists, even if it failed to do even elementary justice to the sources cited, presumably in order to maintain the comfortable notion of the abyss which separates papist 'Pelagians' from evangelical truth. And yet another quite new chapter (chapter 8) dealt with 'Predestination and the providence of God', which, as we have seen, had barely rated a mention (and then in the context of excommunication and the uncertainties thereof) in the first edition. Calvin was well aware that this was a topic on which many evangelicals, especially Melanchthon and the Zurichers, considered silence golden, but the doctrine was now important enough to him to warrant a separate chapter, even at the risk of open disagreement amongst evangelicals. The place of this doctrine within Calvin's theology will be examined elsewhere;[17] suffice it to say here that Calvin drew neither ecclesiastical nor political inferences from it.

While Calvin thus indulged himself in terms of printed pages over theological issues of the most general sort, we find nothing whatever corresponding to such an indulgence in more earthly matters concerning ecclesiastical order or the polity. The old catch-all chapter 6 was, indeed, now broken into three chapters, and these were inserted (incongruously enough) between the sections on true sacraments (chapters 10–12) and false ones (chapter 16) of the new work. 'Christian liberty', once thought worthy of one third of a chapter in a book of six, became one chapter in a book of seventeen, some of them very substantial, and remained as one chapter (unchanged from 1536) in all subsequent editions, becoming at last one chapter in a book of eighty-seven. Given the general character of Calvin's theology, this is not greatly surprising. As for explicitly political doctrine, only two changes are worth signalling. In the chapter on 'Political administration', where the 1536 edition had simply asserted that Paul 'lists "ruling" among God's gifts [Romans 12.8]' (OS I, 61), Calvin now added: 'In that place, he is indeed properly speaking of the senate of grave men who were established in the primitive church to take charge of public discipline. This office in the Epistle to the Corinthians he calls *kyberneseis*, "government" [1 Corinthians 12.28]. Still, as we see that the civil authority has the same end in view, there can be no doubt that he is commending every kind of just precedence (*praefecturae*)' (CO 1, 1103). In his first New Testament commentary on Romans, at the appropriate place, Calvin was even more specific about the matter. He now took Paul to be referring to 'those who rule', 'those to whom the government of the church was committed. These were the elders (*seniores*) who presided over and ruled the other members and exercised discipline.' And he made clear that these must be officials of the church who were 'censors of morals', there being at that time no godly magistrates.[18] Of this more anon. It is worth noting, at any rate, that the very general reference in the first *Ordonnance* to some sort of lay supervisors[19] had now crystallized into something approximating to a scriptural desideratum. The other change to be noted is that in the chapter 'De Lege' the Fifth Commandment, comment on which was much extended from one modest paragraph to four, was now taken to refer not simply to parents, but to 'those whom God has placed above us', and this is later amplified (CO 1, 408) to be understood as 'princes, lords and every sort of superior'. To all of them we are said to owe 'reverence, obedience and gratitude' (p. 407), however objectionable this may be to the human mind, in view of the fact 'that every individual is set over us by his [God's] appointment' (p. 406). There is of course nothing new in this, but the authoritarian tone is remarkable. The gratuitous remarks to the same effect previously included in the commentary on the Tenth Commandment were now omitted.

If the addenda to the explicitly political doctrine are quite insubstantial, it must be said of the ecclesiology of the 1539 *Institutio* that the changes were numerous and substantial, but that what results is far from being a well-rounded doctrine. The section on the authority of the church was retained verbatim; in other words, Calvin was still arguing as if the main enemy to be dealt with was the papacy, and he still persisted as if it were part of his theology, as it was of Luther's, to insist on the derivative and inferior status of 'external' matters, and as if his theology had any significant place for the 'things indifferent'. The notable changes are in the exposition of the section of the Creed (chapter 4) dealing with the 'one, holy, catholic church'.

The first *Institution*, it will be recalled, had been completed when Calvin was quite innocent of ecclesiastical experience or responsibility. A relative abstractness in matters of detail and practice was therefore only to be expected. What borders on the inexplicable is Calvin's obscurity in such matters in 1539. And yet the chapter on the Christian life, where Calvin surely had space in which to unfold his ideas, left the concrete implications of the life of self-denial and obedience to God untreated, and on the ecclesiastical, let alone the political dimension of this life there was hardly a word.[20] Or rather, what there was simply serves to intensity perplexity. Discoursing on the requirement that we treat all good things as merely entrusted to our steward-ship, Calvin said that they were to be used 'for the common good of the church' (CO 1, 1130), and that the pious man's mind is set on the common building up of the church, so that whatever he can do for his brothers, he ought to do. Is the duty of the Christian, then, confined to other members of the church? Clearly not, but it is interesting that Calvin, who was anything but a careless writer, should have seen fit to express himself in this way.

His thought had come to be more and more centred on the visible church, or rather churches. Indeed the distinction between the 'visible' and the 'universal' church had now entered his writing, though he was as yet far from knowing what to do with it. The universal church, the communion of saints, continued to recede inexorably from view, becoming at last no more than a device for dealing with the Creed's assertion of the one-ness of the church in such a way as to wrest this weapon from the Romanists, or, on a more charitable reading, a theological datum capable of sustaining Calvin's evangelical ecumenism. Having dealt with the papists, Calvin passed to the more substantial matter of 'the visible church, the one which falls within our knowledge' (CO 1, 542). Now a true visible church is not to be identified by the character of its members, for the state of election or reprobation is not discern-ible by man. Here Calvin repeated much of what he had said in 1536,[21] but what is instructive for Calvin's thought is how, in what context, he repeated it. Previously his remarks had been directed at minimizing the significance of excommunication. Now the same words were used simply to deny Anabaptists and sectarians any ground for separating from imperfect evangelical churches, and not at all to minimize the significance of excommunication. Rather is the face of an evangelical visible church to be identified by the familiar marks (OS 1, 91).

And evidently Calvin had recognized that the first *Institution* had failed to link the church in the world with the church of the Creed. For he now introduced, albeit obscurely, a distinction between the 'universal church', visible churches, and the communion of saints. The last is the theological entity composed of all the elect, living and dead. The 'universal church' is described as 'a multitude gathered out of all peoples whatsoever, which, albeit dispersed and separated by distance of place, nonetheless consents in the truth of one divine doctrine and is bound together by the chains of the same doctrine' (CO 1, 543). Visible churches are 'comprehended' in this universal church; by reason of human necessity, they are disposed by town and village, and each receives by right the name and authority of a church; also 'comprehended' are individuals, 'who, in virtue of their profession of piety, are deemed to belong to the church in some manner, even if they are in truth strangers to it, until they are expelled (*exterminati*) by public judgement' (*ibid.*). And Calvin added that a 'slight' distinction was to be made in judging individuals and churches. Individuals whom churches tolerate in their midst even though we think them unworthy of fellowship we are only required to bear with and tolerate; this does not imply approval. Whole churches, on the other hand, provided they have the marks, are to be regarded as true churches.

Although it had not penetrated the chapter on the authority of the church, Calvin's overriding concern here (as opposed to the 1536 *Institution*) was to prevent schism in and separation from evangelical churches, however seamy. Calvin made it quite explicit that his intention was to ward off the attacks on evangelical churches which came from Anabaptist quarters: they are the only conceivable targets of his contention that the Lord wishes us to cultivate his communion in such external societies of the church (p. 548). And he tried once more to utilize the distinction between essentials and inessentials of faith (p. 545): while some doctrines are necessary to be known, there are others 'which although controverted between churches, do not, however, tear apart the unity of faith'. It will be noticed in the first place that Calvin had insisted that ideally there should be agreement in everything, and that disagreement arose out of 'remnants of ignorance' (*ibid.*). Secondly, although the matter at issue was disagreements *within* churches, Calvin referred (as if it made no difference) to disagreements *between*

churches ('sunt alia, quae *inter ecclesias* controversas', *ibid.*);
the former were apparently too much for him to take. Finally,
it is notable that when he came to giving an example of a
matter which might safely remain controverted, the only
example that Calvin saw fit to bring forward was one of
breath-taking obscurity and triviality. 'Why,' he said, 'should
it be regarded as a ground of dissension between churches, if
one, without any spirit of contention or perverseness in dog-
matizing, holds that the soul on quitting the body flies to
heaven, and another, without venturing to speak positively as
to the abode, holds it for certain that it lives with the Lord?'
(CO 1, 545).[22] Why indeed? But the controverted doctrines
between and within churches bore no resemblance either to
this topic or to this manner of conducting disputes. The fact
that he could not find anything more contentious which might
safely be left unresolved gives the lie to the general assertion,
which we have already seen to be implausible in the context
of the 1536 discussion of *adiaphora*. If Calvin's theology had left
any real room for adiaphorism, there were infinitely more
immediate and contentious matters amongst which to choose
illustrations of things which might safely be left in dispute
amongst evangelical friends.

In working out his conception of the visible church, there
were in fact a number of pitfalls which Calvin had to avoid,
and a number of different concerns to be attended to. Thus, it
was all too easy for a thorough-going anti-separatist argument,
such as Calvin's evangelical ecumenism and his perception of
the sectarian menace required, to prove too much. That is to
say, such an argument might end up by demonstrating that
evangelicals ought not to have separated from the Roman
church, a point on which Calvin showed himself acutely
sensitive in his exchanges with his erstwhile friend Jean du
Tillet.[23] The latter had argued that since evangelicals refused to
rebaptize those already baptized by the Romanists, they must
ipso facto admit the legitimacy of the Roman church. The
Anabaptists were of course not vulnerable to any such argument.
To deal with both Romanists and hyper-critical contemporary
Donatists and Catharists (that is, Anabaptists), Calvin specified
the qualifications for the status of 'true church' in a minimalist
manner: all that was required was that the Word be truly
preached and that the sacraments (that is, baptism and the

Lord's Supper) be rightly administered. Since the Roman churches were deficient in both respects, separation from them was righteous; but the same pretext could not possibly be pleaded as a ground for separating from an even minimally reformed evangelical church. And Calvin went on to say that our tolerance of imperfections in the members of visible churches ought to be even greater than our tolerance of doctrinal and sacramental imperfections.

While this position was cogent in that it surrendered nothing that was absolutely indispensable and dealt with what Calvin regarded as the gravest threats to the being and solidarity of evangelical churches, it was not altogether free from difficulties. By not anathematizing the Roman churches outright, Calvin was able to escape du Tillet's strictures, but he could offer no very convincing reason for not anathematizing; he certainly had no doubt that Roman churches were not true Christian churches and that salvation within them was not possible, at any rate not for those who had been vouchsafed a glimmer of the truth. Perhaps he was sounding as irenic a note as he could manage at a time when negotiations between papists and evangelicals were still proceeding, but it is still not clear how being baptized into a Romanist church could count as baptism into the church of Christ.

Furthermore, a minimalist specification of the conditions for status as a true church required Calvin to exclude from the marks of a true church certain features which he was coming (along with other Reformers) to regard as vital to the well-being of a visible church. Indeed, having asserted against the Anabaptists the need for tolerance in the face of imperfections of life, doctrine and worship in evangelical churches, Calvin at once went on to proclaim it as his conviction that visibly corrupt members ('criminals', *sceleratos*) would not be tolerated in the bosom of well-conducted churches, for from such, as putrid members, corruption spreads to the whole body. To obviate this, excommunication has been instituted by God. And launching into one of his lists of miscreants, Calvin went on to assert that their expulsion was simply the exercise of an authority delegated by God. Matthew 18.18 was adduced to support the view that such a judgement on the part of the (visible) church was nothing other than the promulgation of God's sentence. He concluded this section (subsequently suppressed, but substantially incorporated elsewhere) by asserting that 'they are deceived in their opinion who think that churches can long stand without this bond of discipline. Unless perhaps it were possible for us to do without that support (*adminiculo*) which God has provided for us, as being necessary' (CO 1, 550). There then followed the 1536 qualifications about the meaning and efficacy of excommunication, now, however, located in a context of the indispensability of excommunication in particular and discipline in general, so that they threw doubt only on its *ultimate* significance (and even that was illogical in the light of what has just been quoted) and left its *immediate* seriousness and importance untouched.

What is more, slightly earlier in the same section, Calvin had asserted that it was the current endeavour of Satan 'to overthrow the ministry, which, however, Christ has so ordained in the church, that when it is taken away, its building (*aedificatio*) must fall' (p. 544).

If excommunication, and more broadly discipline, was essential to the well-being of visible churches, if it had been instituted by God and was a doctrinal matter, it is not immediately apparent why discipline was not included amongst the marks whereby a true church may be recognized. It seems that, without saying so, Calvin was distinguishing between the mere existence of a tolerable church, and the well-being of a truly evangelical church. Such a distinction would be a way of dealing with the demands of his campaign against separatism and sectarianism on the one hand, and with his insight into what the progress of reformation ideally required on the other. Nonetheless he did not make it explicit.

If, as I take it, the 1539 *Institution* may be taken as an index of the state of Calvin's theology after Geneva but prior to any extensive experience of Strasbourg, it is fair to say that while his interests had now shifted decisively to the 'visible' church, he had not as yet worked out any clear ecclesiology, nor any precise ideas about the institutions and arrangements of a well-ordered church. The unfinished state of his thinking on the subject would perhaps explain why, although he was unwilling to dispense with the quotation (now attributed to Scripture) that 'outside the unity of the church there is no salvation' (p. 539), he now transposed it to a context in which it became the merest tautology. As Doumergue rightly observes,[24] for

Calvin the church outside which there is no salvation is (here) the universal church; Doumergue omitted to observe that the sense of this assertion is now that outside the totality of the elect there are no elect. The last edition of the *Institution* returned to the more meaningful, if more menacing, assertion that no salvation was to be hoped for outside the visible church.[25] His concentration on the minimum specifications for a true visible church as a congregation identified by true preaching and the sacraments also deprived him of any incentive to consider more carefully the relationship of a well-ordered evangelical church to the polity, which he continued blandly to take for granted as the territorial and organizational basis of a church. A church exhibiting only the minimum requisites for the status of a true church is unlikely to encounter the hostility or obstruction of any but those magistrates who forbid reformation altogether.

If we contrast the 1539 *Institution* with the wealth and precision of institutional detail in the draft *Ordonnances* for the Genevan church of 1541, and the elaboration of the ecclesiology in the 1543 *Institution*, it becomes difficult to escape the conclusion that Calvin had learnt a great deal at Strasbourg. Equally it is difficult to say precisely what his debt to Strasbourg was. We have already seen Calvin's thought and practice moving, perhaps independently, in the same direction as Bucer's and Capito's on the subject of ecclesiastical discipline. It is nonetheless the case that at Strasbourg there was much for him to learn and nothing to teach on this matter. If, as I suspect, Calvin learnt more easily from those he regarded as authoritative than from experience, his respect for Bucer in particular (who had persuaded him to come to Strasbourg) would have made him open to learning from Strasbourg, quite apart from the fact that he obviously felt at home there. Bucer was regarded as perhaps the most efficient ecclesiastical organizer in Europe; such was his prestige that he was employed as consultant (so to say) by evangelical magistrates in their ecclesiastical reordering of Ulm, Münster (after the Anabaptist holocaust), Kassel and Hesse. Thanks to his endeavours and those of Capito, Johann Sturm, Hedio and Zell, and the sympathy of the magistrates, preeminently Jakob Sturm, Strasbourg had been a solidly evangelical city since the mid-twenties. Thanks to the firmness, skill and solidarity of the ministers, Strasbourg exhibited not only exemplary provisions for schooling and the poor, but had also managed to avoid some of the worst excesses of the Caesaropapism to which the Reformation was prone. The battle over excommunication which Calvin had fought had already been fought by Oecolampadius at Basel and by the ministers (among whom Bucer was the foremost, without violation of collegiality) at Strasbourg, and while the ministers had nowhere won, they had derived from the battle, and from mutual advice, clear intimations about the kind of arrangement needful if the purity of evangelical doctrine was to be preserved.[26]

THE 'ORDONNANCES' OF 1541

The draft *Ordonnances* are obviously not the place in which to look for an explicit articulation of the state of Calvin's ecclesiology in September 1541. Their style was explicitly juridical, terse and laconic; for the most part they consisted of bare regulations, the rationale for which was merely hinted at in occasional phrases; indeed, the style of legal documents of the day would have permitted rather greater expansiveness in this respect. And there must be a doubt in principle about comparing an organizational document such as this with a theological document such as the *Institution*. But that doubt lacks force in this instance. The caveat to be entered is that what Calvin presented to the Genevan Councils was, of course, contingent on what he thought stood some chance of acceptance, or in his words, what he thought 'the infirmity of the times would bear'.[27] That being said, it appears that in Calvin's view, a theology of the church is not to be distinguished from an account of the quite specific, albeit ideal arrangement which Calvin deemed stored up in Scripture and in the practice of the early church, to be reproduced in a particular place with the greatest possible fidelity. The *Ordonnances* were such an implementation.

Although what was advanced was in intention and effect a legal code, Calvin managed to begin with the affirmation that the ministry was the *sine qua non* of good order and even of survival of a reformed church. What is more, the contours of that order are thought of as scripturally derived.[28] It is because 'there are four orders of offices instituted by our Lord for the government of the church' that 'if we will have a church *well ordered* and *maintained whole* (*en son entier*), we ought to observe this form of government' (OS, II, 328; my italics). The equation of 'order' and 'government' and the use of such language in an ecclesiastical context hardly calls for comment in the light of our previous account: it may, however, be observed that not all evangelicals shared such habits of speech.[29] What is striking is the intensity and single-mindedness of Calvin's concern with the ministry. More was involved here than simply consideration of the matter at hand; it was not self-evident that an evangelical should talk as if *ecclesia* meant *clerus*, and Calvin continued to protest against that equation when it was perpetrated by papists. He was simply putting first things first.

The *Ordonnances*, then, evidence a determination to leave unturned no stone that might contribute to the work of ordering things in such a way as to ensure the autonomy and authority of the ministry. Thus they begin with the recruitment, training and examination of candidates for the ministry, the manner of their appointment, the devices for resolving differences between them for 'the preservation of purity and concord of doctrine', the proper way of correcting misconduct and maintaining discipline, and the duties of ministers. And Calvin's purpose throughout was not only to arm the ministry with formal rights, but also and more important to secure a ministry which, by its own high standards, self-discipline and corporate solidarity, would have the kind of moral authority that is worth more than any quantity of formal rights. As he said in the context of the (self) discipline of the clergy, its purpose was that 'the ministry may retain respect and that the Word of God [may] be neither dishonoured nor scorned because of the ill regulation of the ministers' (OS II, 333). And what lies behind this is not difficult to detect. The end of the church is the honour and glory of God; to honour God is to preserve purity of doctrine and good order; and the ministry is the key-stone in the edifice of pure doctrine and good order.

Now magisterial 'policing' of the ministry (the felicitous term is Wolin's) was inescapable in evangelical churches, if for no other reason than that evangelical bed-rock belief required the abolition of benefit of clergy and clerical immunity, and Calvin did not touch this. What he did do, however, was to attempt to ensure that such intervention was a last resort. Thus the appointment of ministers proposed would, if properly carried out, make the acceptance of candidates for the ministry a formality, and indeed no candidate was ever rejected by the magistrates in Calvin's time, though the ministers frequently resisted magisterial recommendations successfully. The matter was not made entirely unequivocal, but the 'order' envisaged here, and attributed to the early church, began with an examination ('in private') of the candidate's doctrine and morals; it must be assumed that such examination was the business of the ministers. For the next step was for the ministers to *choose* suitable candidates.[30] Once selected, such candidates are to be presented to the Council ('estant premierement appres l'examen fayct presenté a la seigneurie').[31] The congregation's part in all this was that of a cypher: it was required to receive a candidate 'by common consent' after presentation and certification by the magistracy, the latter presumably acting *in loco populi* (OS II, 329). The possibility of a candidate being found unworthy, and hence of the need for a new election, was indeed mentioned, but no arrangements were provided for such an eventuality (p. 330). On the other hand, the ceremony of the imposition of hands in the ordination of new ministers was approved, but reluctantly laid aside because of the unfortunate associations it had acquired (*ibid.*). Since this ceremony was recognizably scriptural, one sees why Calvin was never able to dispense altogether with the distinction between externals and essentials; the scriptural warrant for imposition of hands, and the untenability of the assertion that ordination was not, on evangelical criteria, a sacrament, continued to trouble him until he eventually grasped the nettle in 1543; he never went so far as to admit in the structure of the *Institutio* that there were three, not two, evangelical sacraments. It may be remarked, however, that what Calvin found to approve in imposition of hands was clearly its effect in signalling the distinction between ministers and laymen.

Once appointed, the next thing needful was of course 'to have a sound arrangement (*bonne police*) for maintaining [the ministers] in their duty' (p. 332) and a variety of devices to that end were articulated. First: weekly meetings to discuss Scripture, the so-called *congrégations*, from which not even the country clergy were exempted, were provided for. These had been held during Calvin's first stay at Geneva and were also the practice at Strasbourg. The point of this arrangement was plainly to maintain the zeal and increase the learning of the ministry. Next, differences of doctrine were first to be discussed amongst the ministers themselves; then amongst ministers and elders (together forming the clerical corpus); differences were to be submitted to the magistrates only if the disputants were still irreconcilable (pp. 332–3). It may perhaps be thought surprising that Calvin should have allowed any magisterial intervention at all in a matter so central to ministerial solidarity and collegiality, but, as a comment in passing makes clear, the kind of dispute Calvin had in mind here was one in which one of the ministers was becoming intolerable to the rest ('because of the obstinacy of one of the parties', p. 333); under Genevan circumstances, ministers were not competent to dismiss a minister unilaterally.

Next, exacting standards of ministerial conduct were set: 'There are crimes which are quite intolerable in a minister' and prominent among them are 'heresy, rebellion against ecclesiastical order, blasphemy . . . simony and all corruptions in presentations [to parishes] . . . leaving one's church without lawful permission or just calling', in short, all breaches of corporate discipline as well as criminal offences (p. 333). All these were held to merit instant dismissal; in addition there were a host of lesser 'crimes' which might be corrected by simple admonition: these included contentiousness, negligence, loose speech, quarrelling and conduct unbecoming a minister (p. 334). The two lists were not very precisely drawn, for 'duplicity', 'drunkenness', 'gaming forbidden by law and scandalous', 'dances and similar dissoluteness' were ranked as unforgiveable, but 'lying', 'slander', 'quarrels and contentions' and 'laxity of manners' were not. Since the crimes mentioned as unpardonable were all criminal offences, Calvin was conceding nothing to the magistrates which they did not have already; even here, however, the first investigation of accusations and complaints was to be by 'the assembly of ministers and elders' (*ibid.*), an arrangement evidently designed to shield ministers from malicious charges. In the case of lesser crimes, 'one is to proceed according to the command of our Lord', that is to say, by way of admonition by the Venerable Company and the elders. As we shall see, the Company was to meet weekly in a Consistory, but three-monthly meetings of the ministers and elders were also provided for with a view to bringing such lesser delinquencies to the surface and remedying them: what was intended was sessions of mutual and fraternal self-criticism (p. 335). The possibilities of such an arrangement for consolidating collegiality, solidarity and the maintenance of high standards are apparent.

Having provided the place of honour for the clerical *estat*, the *Ordonnances* moved on to doctors, elders and deacons. Of these only the elders were contentious; the status of teachers as clerics and their subjection to ecclesiastical discipline were explicitly asserted (p. 339) in case there should be any doubt. As for deacons, their office was to do what the pre-Reformation regular clergy had done in the way of care of the sick, helpless and poor; the evangelical status of this office had been explicitly recognized in the *Institution* of 1536. The arrangements at Strasbourg both for education and for the care of the helpless were much better developed than those of Geneva, but Calvin had already shown preoccupations in this direction during his first stay at Geneva.

This left the office of elders. Enough has already been said about the importance which the office had come to assume for Calvin; what Calvin seems to have derived from Bucer, judging by the *Commentary on Romans* and the 1539 *Institution*, was doctrinal legitimation.[32] Calvin now proposed a legal formulation of the office's organization and functions. The office of elders 'is to superintend the life of everyone', and 'they should be chosen in such a way that there will be some in every quarter of the city to keep an eye on everyone' (p. 339). This is a direct echo of the *Ordonnances* of 1537. There were to be twelve elders, chosen from the Councils[33] after conference with the ministers, and although elections to magisterial offices were annual at Geneva, Calvin as ever did not much approve of a rapid turn-over in personnel: 'It is inexpedient that they be changed often without cause' (p. 340). These elders and the ministers, the *Ordonnances* continued, 'are to assemble once a week, on Thursday morning, to see that there is no disorder in the church and to discuss together such remedies as are required' (p. 358). They are to be provided with officers by the Seigneurie to ensure that offenders attend the meetings of the Consistory. (That word appeared only once in Calvin's draft, and then in its traditional meaning of a matrimonial court, which would

be a lay affair, with ministers as technical experts, p. 345.)[34]
The whole paragraph is rather curious in that such a consistory
had already been established during Calvin's absence;[35] the
Seigneurie in one of its amendments to the passage in question
followed that use of the term, but in another referred to the
weekly meetings of elders and pastors as 'the Consistory', and
later in the same paragraph still more confusingly speaks of
'the ministers with the Consistory' (p. 361, fn.a). Evidently the
terminology was still very fluid.

Calvin's draft already affirmed that 'the elders have no
coercive authority or jurisdiction' (p. 358), but to this the
Seigneurie saw fit to add: 'all this is to take place in such a way
that the ministers have no civil jurisdiction, nor use anything
but the spiritual sword of the Word of God, as Paul commands
them, nor is the Consistory to derogate from the authority of
the Seigneurie or ordinary justice. The civil power is to remain
unimpaired' (p. 361, fn.a). This presumably reflects a determination to ensure their supremacy over the ministers, even
when their bargaining position was rather weak. All the same,
it was a rather inept gesture; while they were affirming their
authority in ringing tones, the substance of *auctoritas* was
slipping away to the ministers.

Now Calvin at no time saw anything objectionable in
double jeopardy; on the contrary, his ideal of harmonious
cooperation of magistrates and ministers in the disciplining of
the people–congregation may be said to have institutionalized
it at every point. Nonetheless, he was extremely careful to
specify the manner of proceeding of the Consistory in such a
way that jurisdictional disputes would be avoided. Thus the
Consistory was to be the agency of the first instance in dealing
with those who 'dogmatize' against the received doctrine. If
such admonitions fail, the miscreant is to be first excommunicated and then reported to the magistrates. The same
procedure was to apply to back-sliders in matters of church
attendance and to those who showed themselves contemptuous
of the ecclesiastical order. Secret vices, on the other hand,
were to be secretly admonished; only if that failed did there
follow admonition by the 'church' (pp. 358–9). The clericalist
interpretation of 'church' here is noteworthy.

Finally, no special article was devoted to excommunication.
In view of the contentiousness of the matter, this is a curious

omission, and the Petit Conseil was later to pretend a lack of clarity in the *Ordonnances* as ground for arrogating this right to itself. In fact, however, the *Ordonnances* were plain enough: in each and every case of 'discipline' the procedure is private reprimand, public reprimand and finally excommunication followed by a report to the magistrates. And 'if anyone in contumacy or rebellion wish to intrude [into communion] against the prohibition, the duty of the minister is to turn him back, since it is not permissible for him to be received' (p. 360). There is no mention of any magisterial part in the procedure at all.[36]

This account of the office of the elders was in general clear enough, though it might perhaps have specified more clearly that elders are ecclesiastical officials and not representatives of the civil authority. But as for working the office into the structure of his theology, Calvin had barely begun. The obvious place to insert the elders in the providential economy of Christian polity was in the context of the partnership of ministers and magistrates for the maintenance of the public honour of God. But this idea remained undeveloped, and, more mundanely, the cooperation desired remained an abstract desideratum, the concrete implications of which had not been explored. For even the discussion of Romans 12.8[37] raised more questions than it settled. Paul was understood there to be referring to *seniores* who were 'the censors of morals (*morum censores*)'. The context of the passage was a dilation on Calvin's favourite theme of a diversity of gifts and offices, with no one arrogating to himself the rights of another or usurping another's office (on Romans 12.4–6). The obvious inference would be that just as there are offices of ministering and teaching, so there is an office of governing, which like the former should be vested in specifically designated office-holders who, like the former, should stick to their lasts. But the reference to the absence in Paul's time of any Christian magistrates left it obscure whether, once there were such Christian magistrates, these might legitimately assume the function of elders.

We may now hazard some conclusions about the tendency of Calvin's thinking between 1538 and the end of 1541. Such conclusions could not, of course, be warranted by referring only to what is after all a set of ecclesiastical laws, confined strictly to the public arrangements of the church. Fortunately there is adequate supporting evidence from various letters of the time, most of them in some sense (and some explicitly) public documents, and from the comprehensively rewritten 1543 *Institution*, which was substantially complete by January 1542[38] and which constitutes the last major reworking of the *magnum opus* before the definitive editions of 1559/60. There are also certain other writings of the period which shed some light. Between them, these sources allow us to say that whereas Calvin had given no further consideration to political theology, his ecclesiology had hardened in a clericalist direction and his notion of discipline had expanded its compass to include much of *police* and the censorship of morals.

Calvin had clearly concluded that the ministry was the only reliable guardian of the honour of God and of the safety of his church, a conclusion not very surprising in that most of the German and Swiss Reformers had reached it long before. But despite Calvin's inveterate identification of order and rule, he had not at all opted for some ecclesiastical version of monarchy; on the contrary, he clearly valued an aristocratic arrangement, where the ecclesiastical collectivity is governed by an aristocracy of merit, and the latter's own conduct is vouched for by external and internal policing, but primarily by self-discipline. In its control of the congregation, the ministry's main weapon remained excommunication; secular reinforcement was not to be relied on. But excommunication, since it was exclusion from communion, and not from sermons or all contact with the faithful, presupposes the centrality of the Lord's Supper in the life of the church, despite the fact that a drift towards making the sermon rather than communion central to the life of the church had been discernible even in the early stages of the Reformation. Calvin's emphasis on the mystery and grandeur of the sacrament was therefore in a sense demanded by his stress on discipline, although there is nothing whatever to suggest that this was Calvin's design, or that he adopted his position in the sacramentarian controversy in order to reinforce the discipline: there is no evidence that he ever entertained any other view.

Given his position, the sacramentarian controversy (that is, the controversy amongst evangelicals concerning the view to be taken of the words of institution, *hoc est corpus meum*) could not but be a matter of extreme regret to Calvin. Not only was every division amongst evangelicals itself a scandal according to the opinion of the time, but each party claimed authentication for its view from *sola scriptura*, with the result that the controversy threatened the evangelical fundament itself. Indeed, not even Calvin's minimalist specification of the marks of a true church could cope with the matter, for the dispute was precisely about what (to quote the marks of a true church specified in the *Augsburg Confession*) should count as 'the sacrament rightly administered' and 'the Word of God truly preached'. Calvin did not regard, and could not regard, the dispute as irresolvable, but pending its resolution the thing needful was that the division of the churches and the multiplication of sects and factions should be resisted at all cost. And only sacrosanctity of the ministerial estate, whatever the shortcomings of its personnel, could be of avail here, although in the long term the discipline was the only safeguard.

With perfect consequentiality Calvin had, therefore, insisted throughout his absence that his partisans at Geneva submit to their ministers, compromised as these were. No matter: as he said in an open letter to the Genevans of 25 June 1539, the Genevans were to treat their ministers with the obedience and reverence due to the Lord's messengers, *suos etiam angelos*, and to maintain communion.[39] 'Nor, furthermore, should you regard it as of little moment that schisms and sects arise and ferment in the church, a thing no Christian breast could even hear about without horror.'[40] The mixed metaphor is Calvin's, emotion for once getting the better of his Latin. In a private letter[41] to Farel of the previous year, Calvin had said the same thing, even more forcefully:

So great must be their [the people's] reverence for the ministry and the sacraments, that wherever they see them to be extant, they must believe that there is a church. It is sufficient for us if the doctrine on which the church of Christ is founded has place and obtains. Nor must it hinder us that that pastor is not to be regarded as legitimate who has not only fraudulently insinuated himself, but indeed criminally burst into the place of the true minister. This is not a reason for the private person to entangle himself in scruples.[42]

A heightened estimation of the importance of the ministry also presumably accounts for Calvin's practice of distinguishing sharply, and terminologically as well as in terms of duties, between ministers and laymen. Referring to the hostile reception accorded to the open letter mentioned above, Calvin recounted that in a dispute with one of the Genevan protagonists, 'I begin with the distinction between ministers and the people' and shortly after referred to 'the private members of the church (*privatis ecclesiae membris*)'.[43] Another (private) letter of the same year asserted that Calvin's antagonists in some dispute 'involve themselves and the whole business in miserable confusion, as long as they do not distinguish between the minister and the private member [of the church]'.[44] And slightly later, in another letter to Farel recounting some discussions at Frankfurt, Calvin said that 'the first thing that made them angry was that I was distinguishing between the minister and the people, and was asserting the former to be a steward, in whom prudence and fidelity are required. From private persons less is asked, I said...'[45] Long before the theological exposition of the distinction in the 1543 *Institution* and its legal formulation in the *Ordonnances*, Calvin had returned to the old distinction between layman and cleric, and expected more from the latter than from the former.

We may, I think, treat as part of the same reading of the place and importance of the ministerial estate Calvin's recovered appreciation of the value of a kind of evangelical auricular confession.[46] This, it seems, proved rather too much for some of his French congregation at Strasbourg, but Calvin persisted, as he explained in yet another letter to Farel: 'I have often told you of my view that it is not prudent to abolish confession in churches, without putting in its place what I have lately instituted [*institui*, sc. here at Strasbourg] ... When the day of the Lord's Supper approaches, I announce that all who wish to communicate are first to present themselves to me. At the same time I explain my purpose, namely that those who are still rude and inexperienced in religion might be better instructed; next, that those who need some special admonition should hear it; and finally, that if anyone is tortured by some unquietness of conscience, he might receive consolation.'[47] Somewhat defensively, Calvin added that 'there is a danger lest the people, who do not sufficiently distinguish between the yoke of Christ and anti-Christian tyranny ...' and affirmed that his practice 'in no way derogates from our liberty' since he was enjoining 'nothing which Christ himself has not prescribed'. He did not say where. Elsewhere he recorded that a certain 'pest' had tried to burst in on 'that sacrosanct mystery' without first purging himself before Calvin or even promising amendment,[48] saying in derision that 'he left confession to papists. I replied that there is also a Christian sort of confession.'[49]

The status of the ministry, communion, confession and discipline had now evidently become closely intertwined in Calvin's mind. We have seen that by August 1539 he had found scriptural warrant for the censorship of morals, and that he was coming more and more to regard discipline as crucial in a well-ordered evangelical church, even if he did not count discipline as one of the constitutive marks of a true church. In the *Reply to Sadoleto* he went so far as to say that 'there are three things on which the safety and well-being (*salus*) of the church is founded; viz. doctrine, discipline and the sacraments . . .'[50] How near discipline now was to his heart, and how far the compass of the notion had spread, is revealed in his exclamation: 'with what fairness is the charge of subverting discipline brought against us?'[51] and the subsequent affirmation that 'the body of the church, to cohere well, must be bound together by discipline as by sinews',[52] an expression he had used in the *De Clementia Commentary* for the function of laws in the body politic. Sadoleto had not brought any such charge; he had not in fact mentioned discipline at all, but had referred to the Reformers' 'trampling on the laws enacted by the church'[53] and had remarked that 'since these men [sc. the evangelicals] began, how many sects have torn the church? Sects not agreeing with them yet disagreeing with each other – a manifest indication of falsehood.'[54] Calvin, not usually short of rejoinders, had no answer to this palpable hit, and lamely evaded it by pretending that Sadoleto was referring to disputes between the Reformers and the Romanists.[55] He did not, however, in that work link together discipline and 'the zeal to make the glory of God shine forth'[56] which ought to be the 'principal motive in [the Christian's] existence'. But it is clear that the notion of discipline has here become coextensive with 'order', or 'government'. The same is true of the *Ordonnances's* expression, *maintenir ceste discipline en son estat.*[57] Such a use of the term in fact becomes more and more commonplace between 1538 and 1542. In the April 1538 *Articles* cited earlier, the expression *disciplina stabilienda* refers to the parochial organization of the church.[58] The 1539 *Institutio* has several such references: for example, zeal for the *publica aedificatio* is said to be demanded of individual (private) members of the church, but decently and in good order (*secundum ordinem*), 'lest we disturb *politiam et disciplinae compositionem*'.[59] And in one passage *ecclesiastica disciplina* twice refers to the designation of ministers (*in designandis per homines ministris*).[60] Similarly, in an open letter to the Bohemian Brethren of 1540 Calvin remarked on the Brethren being 'indeed fortunate in possessing such ministers to govern and organize them, such good morals, such order and discipline. We have long known the value of these things, but in no way succeed in achieving them here [sc. in these western parts].'[61]

In none of these passages is there any reference to the former meaning of discipline as 'excommunication', even though, as we have seen, that remained the church's chief weapon in the attainment of discipline (rather than being synonymous with discipline). It seems indeed that apart from the Zwinglians, all orthodox evangelicals were coming to the same view. We have already commented on the markedly clericalist and disciplinary conception of the church which Bucer and Capito had adopted; I presume that Calvin was alluding to their struggles as well as his in the letter to the Bohemian Brethren. And Calvin recounted (in yet another letter to Farel) how he and Philip Melanchthon had lamented the state of discipline together. 'When it came to discipline, he [Melanchthon] lamented at the manners of others. Indeed it is easier to lament the miserable condition of the church in this regard than to correct it . . .' And having commented on some bad news from Ulm and Augsburg about what had happened to censors of morals there he remarked: 'Indeed after this it will be considered a triviality to disturb pastors in their ministry and to throw them into exile.' And he concluded with the comment: 'Nor can this evil be mended, because neither the people nor the princes distinguish between the yoke of Christ and the tyranny of the pope.'[62]

Discipline, then, in the sense of a comprehensive censorship of morals, was now being considered as 'the yoke of Christ' (a somewhat curious idea; the original New Testament quotation alluded to refers to discipleship of Christ in a very general sense) and evangelical laymen were evidently finding that yoke anything but sweet; indeed, they were inclined (as Calvin also remarked with regard to confession) to view it as a restriction of their liberty indistinguishable from popery. The reason was simple enough: what was being contemplated was unmistakably a new clericalism distinguished from the old mainly by the greater thoroughness and probity of the new executors.

In sum, then, 'discipline' was now a term encapsulating a diagnosis of the current condition and salient requirements of evangelical churches. All that remained to be done from the theological point of view was to articulate the view of the Christian life it implied and to integrate it with the main lines of Calvin's theology. And on that task Calvin was already engaged. The penultimate recasting of the *Institution* was not published until March 1543, but it seems to have been completed by January 1542; in other words within a few months of the *Ordonnances*.

5

The 'Institution' of 1543

The new edition of the *Institution* was now a large volume of twenty-one chapters; some of the chapters, not as yet divided into sections, had become very unwieldy. Wendel has said of this edition that 'the alterations and additions [made in it] are of much less importance than those of the edition of 1539'.[1] Certainly many of the changes and additions were simply amplificatory, or designed to ward off past or potential criticism; the host of quotations from Augustine was in the main of this sort. Others again simply used up material which Calvin presumably prepared for the various colloquia he attended. But the most amplified, changed and reworked section was that on ecclesiology, concentrated almost entirely into the exposition of the Creed's *Credo unam sanctam catholicam ecclesiam*, which now formed one chapter of enormous length.[2] Here, as well as much material reproduced verbatim from previous editions, there were substantial and important novelties, and given that Calvin regarded ecclesiology as part of theology, it will hardly do to leave the matter at the comment that the new edition now 'contained a somewhat detailed exposition of Calvin's ideas about ecclesiastical organization'.[3] What it contained was the image of a godly church, defined not merely by exclusion (as non-papist) but positively, and with a decisiveness and clarity of outline without precedent elsewhere.

In this respect, the general tendency of the discussion to consolidate and make doctrinal the conclusions reached in public and private between 1538 and 1541 is indeed impressive. Two cognate features now dominate in Calvin's portrayal of a true church. The first is its aggressive clericalism. The second is the centrality of 'discipline' to the whole ecclesiastical order, complementing the explicit reading of this aspect of the church's work as *jurisdictio*. The parallel between these features and the *Ordonnances* is obvious and confirms our interpretation of the latter as reflecting a judgement about the place of the clerical estate in the providential economy.

THE VISIBLE CHURCH

The discussion began with a more deliberate exploitation of the visible/invisible church distinction, although Calvin was still not entirely satisfied with it, as is shown by the fact that he began twice (4.1.7 and 4.1.9).[4] The Scriptures, he now asserted, gave two readings of the term 'church'. In one sense it was the totality of the elect, living and dead. In another sense (the only sense which interested Calvin throughout the book), the 'visible' or 'external' church was the 'multitude' of those united in the worship of the true God, the profession of true doctrine, and the celebration of the sacraments, both as spread out over the whole world ('the universal church') and as distributed by towns and villages according to human necessity ('particular churches'), each of which also had the name and authority of a church by right (4.1.9). The specification of the marks which identify a true (visible) church was as formal and circular as before, except that (as a foretaste of what was to follow) Calvin inserted 'the ministry instituted by Christ for preaching the Word (4.1.7) and 'the ministry of the Word' (4.1.9) as if these were obviously comprehended within the uncontentious marks of rightly administered sacraments and the preaching of true doctrine. For the rest Calvin remained preoccupied with the need to avoid schism and separation from even minimally reformed churches, and repeated his 1539 assertions on the subject, with the result that discipline still did not figure among the marks of a true church.[5] Given the character of the discussion that followed, in which discipline now appeared not as the incidental to other concerns that it had been in the first edition, but in the interpretation of the Creed, and thus as in every sense 'De Fide' (chapter 8), this reticence is not easy to explain. Even the distinction between essentials and desiderata, which we have imputed to

Calvin in order to explain his non-inclusion of discipline under the marks of a true church, scarcely serves here.[6] For in so far as Calvin now argued that there are scriptural directives concerning the right order of the ministry, ecclesiastical order itself becomes an item of doctrine, and thus falls under the mark of 'the gospel purely preached',[7] however unfortunate this might be from the point of view of evangelical ecumenism and Calvin's campaign against separatism.

There followed an entirely new discussion, occupying 170 sections,[8] the entire concern of which was the organization of the church, the 'order by which God has wished his church to be governed' (4.3.1). It began with an argument to commend the 'ministry of men', which so far had been asserted only as a matter of scriptural dogma. Both the phrase and the argument are curious, but characteristic. For Calvin had now to contend with the abiding evangelical distrust of clerical authority. The argument which he deployed was that for God to subject us to ministers who in every respect but their office are men like ourselves is the 'best and most useful training in humility', an opportunity to demonstrate our piety and reverence which any more direct exercise of divine omnipotence would not have afforded, and a most apt means of fostering mutual charity and making us aware of our mutual dependence and lack of self-sufficiency (4.3.1). Ephesians 4.4–16 was adduced in support, but it had scarcely any bearing; the view advanced derived its force and weight from Calvin's conception of the Christian life as one long training in humility, self-denial and service.

The terms which Calvin was using to refer to a visible church were 'multitude' and, in less conspicuous places, 'society'. These are nerveless descriptions for an evangelical to employ: one misses Luther's, Zwingli's and Bucer's emphasis on the congregation or assembly. In any case, the choice cannot have been due to inattention on Calvin's part. As a 'multitude', and thus by implication inherently shapeless, or a *corpus*, or *societas*, and hence in need of headship, the church obviously required a *regimen*, a *gubernatio* and an *ordo*, just as secular polities do; Calvin explicitly made the comparison several times (e.g. 4.11.1, 4.12.1). Of course, it has a head, Christ, but this does not preclude the ministry of men (*administratio*; the political parallel is obvious);[9] on the contrary, that is exactly what Christ has instituted. On the other hand, the overriding authority of Christ qualifies what kind of governance could be legitimate in the church. And the gravamen of Calvin's accusations against the papacy is that it is an unacceptable sort of *gubernatio*, involving both ecclesiastical monarchy and (according to Calvin) an absolutist claim to make laws other than those commanded by God. On this count, separation from the temple of Antichrist is not only legitimate, but a duty. Calvin followed this with a predictable 'Comparison between a false and a true church', which, while it licensed separation from Rome, yet managed not to require the rebaptism of former papists. The virtuosity of this performance shows how well Calvin deserves the title of 'master of equivocation'.[10]

THE MINISTRY

The ministry of men, then, is part of the divinely ordained manner of government of the church (4.3.2), and Calvin went on to find in Scripture and the early church – the 'visible image of the divine institution' (4.4.1)[11] – a comprehensive ecclesiology bearing marked resemblances to the order already established at Geneva. And if it should be thought extraordinary that an evangelical should treat Scripture as a body of laws governing the arrangement and practices (the 'externals') of a Christian church, Calvin's language is plain enough: 'the order by which the Lord willed his church to be governed' (4.3.1); 'the one and only pattern of God's Word (*unicam illam verbi Dei normam*)' (4.4.1); 'God is the sole lawgiver' (4.10.8); 'I approve only those human laws (*constitutiones*) which are both founded upon God's authority and drawn from Scripture, and are thus wholly divine' (4.10.30).

The account which Calvin gave of the office of ministers in the church now positively bristled with terminology originally employed to designate the relationship between a Roman emperor and his agents. This source of metaphors had become open for exploitation because on the view Calvin now held, the subordination of ministers to their 'Sovereign' and his law by no means excluded the former's *vicarious* and delegated exercise of the latter's *imperium*; on the contrary, that is precisely the correct interpretation of the ministerial office, which we now find described as exercising God's *imperium*, a commission (*mandatum*), the task of a representative (*vicariam operam*), interpretation of God's secret will *(arcanae suae voluntatis)*,[12] acting as delegates *(legatione fungantur)*, representing God's person. It is in this sense too that we should understand Calvin's application of the terminology of civil government to the office of ministry: presiding over, governing, ruling, God's use of the ministry for the government of his church, the order of the church, the regime of the church according to Christ's institution, the type of regime *(genus regiminis)*, administration, dignity, honour, maintaining the peace of the church, the Apostles who were to reduce the world from its defection to true obedience to God, well-ordered churches, a holy, inviolable and perpetual law.[13] It is now entirely proper to speak in this way, provided it is understood that what is meant is a conditional and delegated exercise of *potestas*.

Nonetheless, such a way of speaking about the evangelical ministry, especially when it included a clerically administered discipline, was bound to grate on evangelicals and therefore stood in need of justification. The most promising material for such a justification was provided by the Imperial church, stripped of papal excrescences, especially in its ideal refraction in the writings of the Church Fathers. And indeed Calvin had always been prepared to allow a considerable measure of authoritativeness to the early church, the Fathers, the Councils, and on occasion to reason and common experience. But on Calvin's interpretation none of these could be represented as independently authoritative, independent (that is to say) of Scripture.[14] Their status in validating any doctrine was therefore that of a gloss upon the adamantine verities of Scripture. The more contentious the matter at issue – and Calvin's conception of the power of the ministry was highly contentious – the greater the urgency of finding scriptural legitimation. Thus an ecclesiastical order which could easily have been shown to accord with the practice of the early church, the teachings of the Church Fathers (fields in which Calvin had quite astonishing knowledge) and the necessities of evangelical churches in current circumstances, had also and first to be found in Scripture.[15] As a result, Calvin's interpretation of Scripture is often rather strained.[16] This is not, of course, to say that Calvin was consciously distorting Scripture to make it fit a preconceived pattern, or that Calvin's view of the church owed nothing to Scripture. It *is*, however, to say that Calvin's reading of the ecclesiastical polity of Scripture itself owes a great deal to a theology and ecclesiology which are by no means exclusively scriptural, contrary to Calvin's own view. On occasion Calvin was indeed prepared to allow some scope to prudence and necessity, in short to practical judgement in the affairs of the church, but whenever any arrangement of which he approved became controversial, his habit was to make his own position doctrinal and scriptural. There would, for example, have been less necessity to press the New Testament proof-texts so hard, had Calvin allowed more matters to fall within the area of things external and *adiaphora*.

On Calvin's account, then, ministerial government of the church is divinely ordained, and the subordination of laity to clergy inevitably follows. Indeed that distinction (which, as we have seen, had become a commonplace in his letters) now appears in the *Institution* (4.12.1).[17] More usually, he spoke of ministers and *plebs* or *populus*, and sometimes called members of the latter 'private individuals' (e.g. at 4.3.10). The basis of the distinction is the occupancy of an ecclesiastical office, function or charge (*munus, functio*) which Calvin sometimes explicitly described as 'public' (e.g. 4.3.9 and 10, 4.12.1). Compared to this distinction, the further classifications and subdivisions of ecclesiastical offices into separate degrees (*gradus distinctos*) are rather secondary in importance.

There then followed a description of the minister's office which was as honorific as Calvin could make it. Ministers are the main 'sinews' by which the faithful are held together as one body, the 'defences' without which the church cannot be preserved unharmed; the gifts of Christ are distributed through their ministry; theirs is the building up of the body of Christ; mere undervaluing of their dignity and their importance, let alone any attempt to abolish this government, is a plotting of the devastation, ruin and destruction of the church (4.3.2). In short, 'there is nothing in the church more noble and glorious than the ministry' (4.3.3; cf. also 4.11.1). At one point Calvin even tried out a somewhat speculative identification of the office of ministers and that of apostles (4.3.5). And already he slipped in 'private admonitions' and 'discipline' as if these were uncontentiously entailed in the teaching and sacramental office. In sum, their business was 'to train the people in true piety by the doctrine of Christ, to administer the sacred mysteries, and to preserve and exercise true discipline' (4.3.6).

The ministry of the Word is not the only office in the church: by judicious selection Calvin extracted from 1 Corinthians 14 and Romans 12 not only 'bishops, presbyters, pastors and ministers' (all originally synonymous, 4.3.8), but also elders and deacons, the latter plainly inferior in status and ancillary in function to the others. The various lists of offices he drew up do not harmonize (compare 4.3.4, 4.3.8 and 4.4.1) and, what is more, they leave the status of elders in some doubt. In one place, elders are described as 'part of the order of presbyters' (4.4.1); in another, only those who had the office of teaching are called presbyters (4.4.2). I cannot explain this incoherence: perhaps the matter was not central once it had been un-equivocally established (as it had been) that elders were ecclesiastical not civil officials, that their office was apostolic and scriptural (even if only on the flimsy evidence of Romans 12.7 and 1 Corinthians 12.28) and that they were to work in intimate liaison with the ministers: 'to unite with the bishops [i.e. ministers] in pronouncing censures and exercising dis-cipline' (4.3.8), or 'the censorship of morals and discipline' (4.4.1). Together ministers and elders formed a 'senate' (*senatus, conseil ou consistoire*), and such a senate had been in the church from the beginning (4.11.6). This 'senate' is not to be confused with the 'governing common council of presbyters', which excluded elders, and included only 'pastors and doctors', and was also accounted an institution of the apostolic church (4.4.2). Without making a point of it, then, Calvin was dis-covering in Scripture the Genevan distinction between the 'Consistoire' and the 'Venerable Compagnie'. He had also made it explicit that ministerial government was collegial.

So far the discussion had casually assumed that the territorial compass of the 'church' is the town or city, this being the unit of concern both in the New Testament and at Strasbourg and Geneva.[18] But speculatively Calvin went much beyond this: he allowed that the early church (but not, apparently the apostolic church, although he did not make the distinction in these terms) had, by human arrangement, introduced 'bishops' in a different sense, namely 'presidents' of the *coetus presby-terorum* (4.4.2), analogous in their office to consuls in the senate, 'merely to preserve order and peace' (*ibid.*) and to see the decisions of the council of pastors executed.[19] This arrangement enjoyed Calvin's entire approval. Indeed, he agreed that the 'early church' had in fact instituted archbishops and even patriarchs. Calvin queried the term 'hierarchy' for this arrangement of offices (4.4.4) as implying *dominatio* and *primatus* of one over many, presumably because of the way in which the term was commonly used; etymologically, hierarchy (as he would have known) means a 'government *of* priests' not a 'government *over* priests', and a government of priests was precisely what Calvin had in mind as being of divine ordinance. At any rate, the unit beyond the town or city is the province, its rulers are synods of presbyters, and its president is an archbishop. Beyond this Calvin did not make himself explicit, but the drift of his thought is clear. He specifically dissociated himself from any idea of impugning the institution or authority of Councils of the church as a whole: on the contrary, he explicitly approved 'Nice, Constantinople, the first Council at Ephesus, Chalcedon and the like' (4.9.8, this being, incidentally, the correct chronological order) and added: 'We readily admit that when any doctrine falls to be decided, there is not a better or more certain remedy than that a synod of true bishops should convene, at which the controverted doctrine might be examined' (*excutiator*, which might also mean 'settled', 4.9.13). Indeed such an arrangement not only conduces to authoritative decisions, but is actually Pauline. Whether 'bishops' was intended here in the apostolic or post-apostolic sense is unclear: Calvin was not dealing with an immediately envisaged arrangement, but with demolishing Romanist pretensions; but one sees which way his thought was tending. He positively approved hierarchy as a means to decency and good order in the church; his sole concern was with excluding *primatus* and *dominium* of one minister over others. The ministry must be collegial. And the history of the Roman church, which Calvin proceeded to narrate at considerable length,[20] was precisely a melancholy and lamentable story of the deterioration of the intrinsically sound arrangement of a presidency ultimately subject to the ministerial college, into a corrupt anti-Christian tyranny of one over all the rest.

Calvin's legitimation of the *Ordonnances'* procedure for the selection, training and appointment of ministers (4.3.11–16) need not detain us: it amounted to the assertion that what the *Ordonnances* provided (they were of course not mentioned) was, in fact, either scriptural or at the very least in harmony with the uncorrupt practice of the early church. Thus (for instance) the examination of candidates for the ministry by the college of ministers was held to be Pauline, apostolic and ancient, although no scriptural evidence was cited to support the view (4.4.10). Calvin's practical insight is apparent throughout: he was, for example, extremely sensitive to the possibility that a bad occupant of the ministerial office can discredit not only himself but also his office, however divinely ordained, though he preferred to ascribe this insight to St Paul. Paul was thus called on to support the view that 'none is to be chosen [for any ecclesiastical office including that of elder and deacon] save those who are of sound doctrine and holy lives, and not notorious for any defect which might destroy their authority [*auctoritas*, meaning more precisely 'authoritativeness'] and bring disgrace on the ministry', nor must they be 'unequal to the burdens imposed on them' (4.3.12). Apart from the imposition of burdens, Calvin also now strongly approved the imposition of hands in ordination (4.4.14, 4.3.16), a practice uniformly observed by the Apostles and therefore to be regarded as a 'precept'. Although this might be thought a classic instance of an external ceremony with respect to which the church was – according to Calvin – free, he did not choose to allow any latitude. And the reasoning which moved him was explicit: 'it is certainly useful that by such a symbol the dignity of the ministry should be commended to the people and he who is ordained reminded that he is no longer a free agent (*sui ius*), but is bound to the service of God and the church' (4.3.16). Furthermore, only pastors are to lay on hands. All of this betrays an ecclesiastic's sensitivity to symbolism. His reason for not admitting ordination as a third sacrament was that it is not 'ordinary, or common to all the faithful, but a special rite for a particular function' (4.19.28).[21]

There are also few surprises in Calvin's discussion of *who* was to choose (that is, select and appoint) ministers. Here, of course, he had to tread carefully in order not to allow too little or too much to the congregation or to magistrates, and his words are nicely judged. Presbyters were to be chosen not *by* 'the people' (Calvin usually used *plebs* or *populus*, rarely 'the church') but 'in the presence of the people' or 'with the consent and approbation of the people' (4.3.15 and 4.4.10). About the part to be played by the magistrates in the selection Calvin was a little vague, I suspect deliberately. But he had formulated the question in a leading way, which did not even mention magistrates: 'Whether a minister should be chosen by the whole church, or only by colleagues and elders who have charge of discipline, or by the authority of one?' (4.3.15). The last was obviously excluded; the first and second were deemed conciliated in a procedure where the initiative in selection and nomination lay with the ministers, and consent with the people, which included the magistrates. What Calvin was in fact supposing, though his term 'choose' did not differentiate between initiative and consent, was that the initiative in designating candidates would lie entirely with the ministry: thus he insisted on the desirability of a long and intensive training for the ministry, beginning in boyhood and passing through various minor ecclesiastical functions. As a consequence, eligibility for the ministry would be severely restricted and the character of candidates known in advance. Speaking of the selection of bishops, Calvin again approved the kind of procedure which would curb the crowd's natural tendency to tumult, and his general sentiment is perhaps best summed up in a passage where, admittedly, he was discoursing specifically about the selection and appointment of bishops in the early church: 'It was not lawful for the clergy to appoint whomever they liked, nor were they bound to submit to the foolish desires of the people' (4.4.12). Calvin's antipathy to the mob had in no way abated, but he was not about to institute tyranny in place of ochlocracy: the people, the magistrates and the ministers were to constrain one another to right conduct. There was nothing Calvin detested more than anyone or any group in a position to exercise a *sic volo sic iubeo*.

Having rendered questions of training, recruitment and appointment for the ministry matters of theology, Calvin passed on to the *potestas* of the church in relation to doctrine, legislation and jurisdiction. This was, as we have seen, a minefield: Calvin had to maintain his evangelical credentials, distinguish the true church from the papacy without excommunicating evangelical churches, distinguish ministry and magistracy, and equip the church with the implements Calvin judged essential for its mission of 'building up' (4.8.1), all at the same time.

ECCLESIASTICAL POWER

Here one must attend carefully to Calvin's terminology, as he evidently did. The word usually translated as 'power' was *potestas*, meaning a right or rights vested in an institution or office. This he distinguished carefully from *imperium*, the comprehensive set of rights enjoyed by a Roman emperor and claimed by current absolutizing princes, and thus connoting might and even sovereignty (*maiestas*).[22] *Imperium* and *maiestas* in the ecclesiastical sphere belong to God alone. He distinguished both from *potentia*, 'might' or 'force', but the distinction is to some extent lost in the French, where, for reasons not clear to me, Calvin translated both *potentia* and *potestas* as *puissance*, a term often used in connection with sovereignty.[23] Ecclesiastical *potestas* is distinguished by Calvin from force (*ius gladii, vis*), coercion (*coactio, coercitio*)[24] and domination (*dominatio, dominium*, the power of a *dominus* or lord: there could be only one Lord in the Christian church). The *potestas* of the church is that of a *gubernatio, regimen* or *politia*, and by the force of these terms, which Calvin had selected with care, such power extends to the issuing, interpreting and enforcing of laws and commands. And again, this was not an accustomed language among evangelicals.

We must not allow ourselves to be misled by anachronistic notions of lawmaking and sovereignty. Calvin was of course familiar with the idea of a *princeps legibus solutus*,[25] but it did not fire him with any enthusiasm even as a young humanist commenting on Seneca's *De Clementia*, and in the context of the church the very idea of anyone *legibus solutus* was abhorrent and absurd: 'God being the only lawgiver, it is not permitted to men to assume that honour to themselves' (4.10.8, where the target is of course the papacy). What is more, 'everything relating to the perfect rule of life the Lord has so comprehended in his Law, that he has left nothing for men to add to the summary given there' (4.10.7). We first encountered this contention in the *Catechisme* of 1537; it now made its appearance in the *Institution*, where it comprehended church organization and worship: '[The Lord] wishes to be regarded as the sole legislator of worship' (4.10.23). It follows that the *potestas* of the church cannot include the power to make laws at its discretion, whatever else it may include.

In the main, therefore, the church's power is one of *jurisdictio*, used in its etymological sense (corresponding to the German *Rechtssprechung*) of declaring laws not of its own making: 'Properly speaking, Christ did not give this power [of binding and loosing] to men, but to his Word, of which he made men the ministers' (4.11.1). Such a distinction between making and interpreting or declaring law seems suspect, but its contentiousness did not obtrude itself greatly on the sixteenth-century mind. The way in which Calvin was thinking is relatively clear. Church and church order he now understood as direct objects of divine volition. God is a God of order, not of chaos; his will is the source of order in the world wherever order appears. God's will is law; indeed God was the only absolute lawmaker Calvin was prepared to tolerate in the whole universe. God's law, mediated imperfectly and darkly by the prophets and perfectly by Christ, finds its expression in Scripture, and the church is the divinely appointed interpreter of that law. But in speaking the law, the church is in every respect subordinated to the divine lawgiver, whose will is unequivocally revealed in Scripture. In thinking Scripture self-interpreting, Calvin was, of course, simply adhering to a constitutive belief of the evangelical revolt. But it was now the ministry's interpretation of Scripture that was, humanly speaking, final, and no extraministerial appeal was anywhere considered, let alone tolerated. Whether Calvin recognized this implication of his thought is not clear. It seems unlikely, given that he took himself to be doing no more than giving utterance to the words of his Master.

The analogy which all this suggests is that of a judge, but this analogy is not adequate. For a limited lawmaking capacity was included in *jurisdictio*: 'In external discipline and ceremonies, the Lord has not been pleased to prescribe every particular we ought to observe; . . . in them we must have recourse to the general rules he has given' (4.10.30). This implies authority to make further laws (*constitutiones*, *leges*) of an administrative, procedural or amplificatory sort. The criterion to be used in all such cases is what makes for the *aedificatio* of the church (4.10.30 and 32), and the ecclesiastical governors were explicitly given a certain leeway,[26] although as usual Calvin was not prepared to give any examples of even the slightest degree of contentiousness of what he had in mind (4.10.30 and 31). And any matter that did become contentious, as we have noted before, had a way of falling within the sphere of what God had authoritatively determined. All of this was no more than a *carte blanche* for the godly to make such laws and orders of worship as Calvin approved,[27] and it also allowed Calvin to rehearse once more the old confusions about externals not binding the conscience (when on his own account they clearly do),[28] confident in the knowledge that nothing that *his* church demanded was merely the traditions of men, or at any rate that what was admitted to be of human devising was for the sake of decency and order (4.10.28).

To summarize our account so far: the visible or external church is divided into 'the people' on the one hand and a corporation of office-holders of various 'degrees' and functions, the 'ministry' or 'clergy', on the other. The task of the latter is 'governance', that is to say, control and animation, without which there can be no order either in secular or in spiritual society. The *potestas* of the ministry is strictly subordinate to the *maiestas* of God, and consists in declaring the Word and Law of God and settling contentions about it, but also in making administrative and amplificatory regulations within the framework of the divinely ordained Law, and enforcing it. And it is here that Calvin turned to the discussion of 'discipline', which is either simply a synonym for *jurisdictio*, or more usually, its exercise with respect to the morals and orthodoxy of the congregation.

THE PURPOSES OF THE DISCIPLINE

'As no city or village can exist without magistracy and *politia*, so the church of God (as I have already stated but am now obliged to repeat) also requires its spiritual *politia*, so to speak' (4.11.1).[29] The reason Calvin felt obliged to repeat himself was that, as we have already learned from his letters, evangelical laymen displayed a lack of enthusiasm for the clerical discipline envisaged.[30] What they disapproved of was perhaps not a censorship of morals as such, but a clerical censorship.[31] Calvin had therefore to demonstrate not only that a *jurisdictio* and discipline were necessary, but also that this ought to be a ministerially enforced discipline, and that such a ministerial discipline was compatible with the authority of the magistrate. His discussion was restarted several times (4.11.3 and 5,

4.12.1 and 4.12.5), beginning each time with a new list of 'ends'
served by the discipline. These ends were stated in various
ways which do not quite tally. He began by talking about the
ends of *jurisdictio*, which are in fact exactly the same thing as the
ends of discipline (an aspect of *jurisdictio*), and here he listed
(1) getting the sinner to avow penitence by chastisement
voluntarily undergone (4.11.3) and (2) the prevention and
eradication of 'scandals' (4.11.5). He then returned to the
subject, this time listing the functions of discipline as (3) a curb
to repress those who rage against Christ's doctrine, (4) a spur to
those lacking in zeal, and (5) a 'fatherly rod to chastise those
who have lapsed' (4.12.1). Finally, using verbatim material
from 1536 and 1539, 'the ends in correcting and excommunicating' were deemed to be (6) to prevent God, his church
and especially the Lord's Supper being dishonoured by the
presence in his church of those of base and outrageous lives,
(7) to preserve the good from contagion, and (8) to bring
sinners to repentance (4.12.5). In the meanwhile he had
asserted (quoting the 1539 formulation) that the 'judgement of
the church' is 'nothing other than the promulgation of [the
Lord's] own sentence' (4.12.4, reinforced by a 1543 addition,
4.11.1), and he had further asserted that discipline is the
'sinews of the church, for it is by virtue of discipline that the
members of the body cohere together, while each maintains his
own place' (4.12.1).[32]

It was Calvin's habit to compose with scissors and paste (so
to speak), interpolating additions and rearranging sections in an
existing text rather than beginning with a new sheet. The
untidiness of the discussion here is therefore no more than
evidence of Calvin's method of working. In any case, it is easy
to reduce these various purposes to three headings.

The first purpose of discipline is to maintain order, but order
of a rather peculiar sort. Like civil laws and magistrates,
ecclesiastical discipline serves to keep everyone in his own
'place' or 'station', but in the church a place is not defined
simply in terms of external performance. On the contrary, all
Christians are engaged in an endeavour or striving, associated
with the building-up of Christ's church.[33] Such an endeavour
goes against the grain of fallen man, and therefore requires a
spur or stimulus against sluggishness and indifference (4.12.1–2)
and chastisement for lapses. Hence, of course, the reason why

such chastisement should be fatherly, why Calvin insisted on its administration in a spirit of gentleness and leniency, why great care must be taken not to alienate the sinner rather than bringing him to reformation, and why such chastisement must be undergone voluntarily. Hence, also, excommunication is not a sentence of death on the soul, but an assurance 'that perpetual damnation *will* follow if the sinner does not repent' (4.12.10; my italics). 'If this moderation is not carefully and religiously preserved, the danger is that we should soon degenerate from discipline into butchery' (4.12.10).[34] Hence, finally, Calvin was quite happy to repeat even here the 1536 caveats about the *ultimate* significance of excommunication, even though he had insisted on its being the sentence of the Lord on the sinner. This might be termed the corrective view of discipline,[35] and its connection with Calvin's view of salvation history as a constant 'building up' of a church prone to lapses is evident.

But this by no means covers all of Calvin's thinking about discipline. It has little to do, for example, with his distinction between manifest, or public, and private sins, which according to Calvin called for different modes of treatment. If the sinner's state of soul were the only consideration, that distinction would be irrelevant: a sin is a sin, whether committed before a few ('private') or many ('public'). Yet Calvin went on to say (4.12.6, repeating and amplifying 4.12.3) that unless there is open defiance and bravado in private sinning, such sins do not come before the church. The distinction seems vacuous. At any rate, the Genevan Consistory subsequently dealt with numerous cases of a markedly private nature: a woman praying at the grave of her dead husband; a man lighting a candle at the bedside of his dying child (both of them peculiarly abominable intrusions on private grief); a woman wishing to marry *in partibus infidelium*. Where everything is properly the subject of regulation and control, there can be no such thing as private sin, and Calvin was on far safer ground when he distinguished between the crimes of public and private persons in the church: that distinction remained with a vengeance. At any rate, Calvin's willingness to make the distinction indicates that he was moved by a consideration animating discipline quite different from the one previously adduced. What was at issue here was not so much the soul of the sinner himself as the encouragement of the others, potential sinners all. Calvin did not explain his notion of a 'scandal' (4.11.5), but his term for serious sin, *flagitium*, meant an outrage, and scripturally a 'scandal' is a stumbling-block. The point of discipline in this sense, then, is to isolate the sinner in order to prevent contagion (4.12.5). Where this purpose was concerned, what was crucial was not whether the sinner submitted to punishment voluntarily and repented, but whether the faithful were edified and protected by the example made of him. (The best state of affairs would, of course, be the notorious sinner brought to repentance and amendment of life by the exercise of discipline.) This might be termed the 'antiseptic' view of discipline.[36]

Even now, however, Calvin's thinking about discipline is not exhausted. He did not, perhaps, link together in express words discipline and the glory of God. But he did repeat and expand the 1536 *Institutio*'s view that the first end in 'correcting and excommunicating' ('correcting' being a 1543 addition) is to prevent dishonour, infamy and insult to the name of God, such as must occur if the church tolerates those of 'shameful and flagitious lives' (4.12.5), and in a paragraph subsequently suppressed he spoke of the outrageousness of tolerating 'dogs and swine' at the Lord's table. We noted that in the *Confession de la Foy* and the *Catechisme* of 1536/7, Calvin's language was a text-book example of Durkheim's distinction between the sacred and the profane, and that he was free with the terminology of profanation, soiling, pollution, defilement, corruption, debasement and so on. In the 1543 *Institution* such preoccupations are not absent: a passage was specifically appended to the 1536 version to emphasize that the Church and the Lord's Supper must be preserved from profanation, sacrilege, pollution and so on (4.12.5).

It seems, therefore, that discipline is not simply concerned with the offence given by flagrant sinning to the faithful, but with the insult offered to God, which must be repressed in order to avert his wrath. This perhaps explains, at least in part, Calvin's inclusion under the heading of 'discipline' of public fasts, prayers and other exercises of humiliation, repentance and faith (4.12.14). For when the Lord makes danger (of pestilence, famine or other disasters) appear, 'he declares that he is prepared and, so to speak, armed for vengeance' (4.12.17). That Calvin had only Old Testament proof-texts to offer in support of this, aside from one irrelevant one from the New Testament (Matthew 9.15; Luke 5.34) is hardly surprising; he indeed anticipated that there would be objections to 'passages which are adduced from the Old Testament, as being less applicable to the Christian church' (4.12.14), but rejected them in advance and asserted, quite without evidence, that 'it is clear that the Apostles acted thus' (*ibid.*). Why God should be more dishonoured by public than by private, or for that matter secret, sins Calvin did not explain. We might term this the 'wrath-averting' view of discipline.[37]

It is hardly surprising that Calvin should have assigned several purposes to an institution as important as the discipline, particularly in view of the fact that all of them can be seen as inferences from a view of the Christian life as one lived in association with others in a visible, that is to say public, church, where the actions of each are of possible consequence to all. The various purposes of the discipline do, however, suggest different considerations to be emphasized in different cases; they are in complete harmony only in the optimum case of a notorious sinner brought to repentance and amendment of life by a charitable yet strict exercise of the discipline. But this was not to be expected nor, in certain notorious cases (Bolsec, Castellio, Servetus, Gentilis), did it even remotely resemble what took place. Furthermore, the *Institution* remained silent in 1543 and subsequently about the civil implications of the last resort of the discipline, excommunication; what it stressed was the difference between ecclesiastical and civil power (4.11.3), whereas Calvin was always much concerned that the two should work in harmony.[38] Thus, for example, the death-penalty as the civil complement to excommunication for grave and impenitent heresy (which Calvin espoused and adhered to despite a storm of protest) is cogent in terms of the wrath-averting and antiseptic purposes of the discipline, but not in any obvious way in terms of correction. Moderation, mildness and clemency in the exercise of the discipline, again, can be easily reconciled with correction, but may or may not be compatible with antisepsis or wrath-aversion.[39] Calvin might, of course, reasonably have argued that which consideration was to dominate in a particular case was a matter of practical judgement which might be left to a Consistory. But the corrective purpose of discipline, which seems to predominate both in the

Institution and in the activities of the Genevan Consistory, is itself liable to internal difficulties. For, as Calvin insisted, if there is to be charge, trial and condemnation, there must be some formal judicial procedure (4.11.1, 4.12.2–4).[40] But the church, like any secular tribunal, can judge only of outward action and profession, not of the secrets of the heart, still less of election or the secret working of God: it has to take the deed for the will (4.1.8).[41] The demands of discipline are therefore satisfied by outward conformity, which may be mere hypocrisy. Nonetheless, it does not seem to have been Calvin's opinion that hypocrites, who await a favourable moment to break into open sin and meanwhile work their evil in secret, are less dangerous to the church than open sinners.[42] The possibly inquisitorial implications of this line of thought are apparent, and the distinction between secret and private sins is of no avail here: once a sin has come to light it is no longer secret.

Why then should a church be judged godly in proportion to its efficiency in producing hypocrites, seeing that the relative numbers of elect and reprobate do not change because of the employment of such means? The correction of sinners does not automatically require an elaborate set of judicial institutions, still less secular reinforcement. And why should a fugitive and cloistered virtue, shelter in an aseptic environment, be what the church aims for? Calvin was clear that discipline and excommunication can be applied only to those who profess themselves to be of the household of the church (4.11.5); he omitted to mention that since 1536 he had demanded such a profession as a condition of merely residing in an evangelical commonwealth.

The idea that flagrant iniquity provokes the wrath of God was entirely conventional in sixteenth-century Christendom, and this, taken together with Calvin's concern for having all public matters dealt with in an orderly fashion, is perhaps enough to account for Calvin's neglect of this sort of consideration: there are occasions enough left even in the best-ordered church for the Christian to be exercised in virtue. Nonetheless, since the conventionality of the view is scarcely an adequate explanation of why Calvin held it, it seems legitimate to adduce a more general consideration from Calvin's ecclesiology, even if he did not mention it in this connection. Calvin's view of the church is of an embattled community; its ecclesiastical order is

designed to preserve and defend.[43] And while this would be the
case universally until the Second Coming, it was particularly
and visibly the case in his own time. A godly church, beset by
enemies on all sides, cannot afford internal division, disorder
and indiscipline; neither can it afford to be less than exemplary.
Calvin's Genevan church was intended by Calvin to be
exemplary (Geneva for its own sake did not matter to Calvin –
his heart was in Strasbourg and with the Brethren in France);[44]
hence the diffusion abroad of the documents relating to the
Genevan ecclesiastical order.[45] But in this respect Geneva was
no more than what *any* evangelical church ought to be. Anything that was an occasion for scandal or mockery outside
evangelical churches was therefore to be scrupulously avoided.
Hence part of Calvin's concern for the 'face' of a reformed
church.

As far as the status and office of the ministry were concerned,
it did not matter which purpose of the discipline was emphasized: in every case, it was the ministry which exercised it,
and exercised it collegially in order to prevent arbitrariness
(4.11.6). And Calvin now entered a refinement which is
exactly what the *Ordonnances* and the rest of the discussion in the
Institution would have led us to expect. He now differentiated
in express words between the application of the discipline to
the clergy (*clerus*) and to the people (4.12.1). Discipline over
the clergy (according to Calvin) was in post-apostolic times
exercised by bishops, who had framed many canons and
appointed annual visitations and synods for the purpose, these
bishops being in turn subject to the college of presbyters
(4.12.22). 'It is fitting that the people (*plebs*) be ruled by a
more humane and, if I may so put it, a laxer discipline; that
the clergy should exercise a sharper censorship amongst
themselves, and show less indulgence to their own members
than to others' (*ibid.*). Calvin did not trouble to explain why
this should be so, but in the light of what he had already said
there was no need. *Quis custodiet ipsos custodes?* The *custodes*
themselves, which can only be if they themselves are above
reproach and are required to act in all things collegially and in
the sight of magistrates and people. And there Calvin left the
matter.

ECCLESIOLOGY AND POLITICAL THEOLOGY

It remains for us to consider what progress Calvin had made in integrating his ecclesiology and his view of secular government. For the City of God and the *civitas terrena* are inevitably in tension, but nowhere more so than when the former is understood as the visible church represented by a spiritual regime, organized in every detail for authoritativeness and autonomy, confronting a secular regime which on Calvin's account owes neither being, form nor legitimacy to the church. What is more, there was now even less question than before of avoiding conflicts by delimiting respective spheres of competence. The *jurisdictio* of the church was not primarily concerned with preaching or worship, with educating the young or succouring the poor – all areas where a degree of magisterial indulgence or at least indifference might be presupposed – but with the repression of vice and heresy. Now Calvin, like most of his contemporaries, assumed that the law concerned itself precisely with the repression of vice; indeed crime was not infrequently understood as merely the sort of sin of which a court of law can take cognizance. It followed that the subject of civil and clerical jurisdiction was, or might be, the same crime and the same culprit, especially given the still largely unshaken assumption that it was the business of the magistrate to enforce doctrinal orthodoxy, an assumption with which Calvin enthusiastically concurred. An evangelical magistrate sensible of his duty might, therefore, well wonder why a specifically ecclesiastical tribunal independent of the magistracy was necessary at all. And as Calvin well knew, it was not enough to point to the example of the apostolic church, even if Calvin's interpretation of it was admitted: there were then no Christian magistrates.

In reply to this difficulty, Calvin began by begging the question: 'Ecclesiastical and civil power are widely different because neither does the church assume to herself anything which belongs to the magistrates, nor is the magistrate competent to do what the church does' (4.11.3). He gave as the reason that the church has neither the right to the sword with which to punish or coerce, nor *imperium*, nor prisons, nor other penalties which magistrates are in the habit of inflicting. Nor, it seems, are the concerns of the magistrates and ministers the same, although we have seen that Calvin elsewhere denied this. For the magistrates are satisfied when punishment has been undergone, however unrepentantly; the church, however, is not: it requires a solemn declaration of penitence[46] before readmitting to communion (*ibid.*). What is more, the magistrate himself sometimes requires to be chastised, or he may be negligent. Rather ought the magistrate to purge the church of scandals (*offendicula*) by punishment and coercion, and the ministers ought to assist the magistrates, presumably by training the congregation in moral rectitude, 'so that not so many sin'. ('Sinning' here is characteristically used for both sins and crimes.)

Further, the pious magistrate 'will have no wish to exempt himself from the common subjection of the children of God' (4.11.4). This was repeated elsewhere (4.12.7) with increased emphasis. Thus while ministers, following the example of the ancient bishops (4.11.15), must not 'think it any injury to themselves and their order to conduct themselves as subjects', there are (as pious emperors admitted) such things as 'ecclesiastical causes', for example offences against ecclesiastical canons, and 'questions of faith' or 'matters pertaining to religion'. Some limitation of the competence of secular tribunals is therefore necessary. But here Calvin trailed off into a vagueness not characteristic of him except in this context. The Church Fathers 'did not disapprove when princes interposed their authority in ecclesiastical affairs, provided this was done to preserve, and not to disturb, the order of the church; to establish, not to destroy, discipline'. And then he uttered a most revealing statement: 'Seeing that the church has not, and ought not to seek, the power to coerce (*cogendi potestatem*) – I speak of civil coercion (*civili coercitione*) – it is the part of pious kings and princes to uphold religion by laws, edicts and judgements' (4.11.16). In short, the church required to be sustained by a power it could not itself exercise, and which had correspondingly to be exercised by secular magistrates acting ideally as tame instruments of the clergy. Calvin did not, of course, say so; indeed, he did not even trouble to clarify the bounds of 'matters pertaining to religion' or 'questions of faith' which might in principle include anything whatever.

All this amounts to no more than the assertion of a pious velleity or desideratum: magistrates and ministers should cooperate (4.11.3). The idea of a modern magistrate as an obedient son of the church was itself somewhat optimistic. More technical and theoretical matters were simply not discussed. Thus Calvin had not even clarified whether ministers were to be regarded as public or as private persons, or (conversely) whether magistrates were also officials of the church in virtue of their civil office. The problem arises because Calvin shared the conventional assumption that the distinction between private and public was to be made in terms of persons rather than matters: as a result, ministers both were and were not public persons. Similarly Calvin's assertion (reminiscent of the most sweeping claims of medieval papalism) that magistrates are sons of the church supposes that they are private persons with respect to the clergy, while his concession of a *ius reformandi*, somewhat unwillingly exorted both by the history of Protestantism and by his own needs, and his admission of a magisterial part in the appointment and dismissal of all types of 'ministers', supposes that they have a right, and therefore an office, within the church.

As for the activities and duties of magistrates in matters which do not directly regard the order of the church, the chapter on the 'political ministry' remained virtually unchanged, except in one important respect. Where previous editions denied to private men any right even to speculate about the best form of a polity, Calvin now inserted the important qualification 'in the place where they live' (4.20.8), and went on not only to admit the legitimacy of speculation about this topic in the abstract, but also to offer his own opinion. For where he had previously asserted the equal susceptibility to abuse of all political forms, he now completely, albeit subtly, changed his view by inserting the contention that considered in itself and abstractly (*in se*), 'the form which greatly surpasses the others is aristocracy, either pure or modified by popular government' (4.20.8). This was taken by Calvin to be the lesson of experience, confirmed by the authority of the Lord himself, in the form of government, 'an aristocracy bordering on popular government (*politia*)[47] which he established in Israel before the kingship of David' (*ibid.*).[48] 'There is no more felicitous kind of government than one in which liberty and that decorum which is fitting are reconciled, and which is framed in such a way as to be durable' (*ibid.*). And he went on to insist that citizens and magistrates fortunate enough to enjoy such a polity had not only a right but also a duty to do their utmost to preserve it (*ibid.*). Since the only other addition to this chapter was a more explicit justification of the right of magistrates to fight wars, it seems that what Calvin had in mind here was the defence of such a polity against external enemies, and that he was perhaps thinking particularly of Strasbourg (menaced by the Emperor) and of Geneva (threatened from Bern and Savoy). But internal enemies were not specifically excluded. Calvin was evidently conscious of a certain *risqué* aspect to what he had said, for he then issued a stern warning to private men to be content with the form of government which the Lord had assigned to them, before reverting to his 1536 text about the wisdom of Providence in giving different forms of polity to different regions (*ibid.*).

All of this remained without amplification. Calvin had briefly joined a debate of 'philosophers' (*ibid.*) and had therefore strayed beyond his self-appointed boundaries. He had not even explained what he understood by 'liberty'.[49] He continued to express himself elsewhere in a supercilious and derogatory manner about 'the wisdom of philosophers', and even the passage in question shows him unprepared to allow experience to be independently authoritative in political matters without confirmation by the Word. Neither had he said anything about how, and by whom, questions of this kind might properly be handled. Nonetheless, and indeed precisely because its broader ramifications had not been explored, the addition is suggestive.

Throughout his ecclesiology, Calvin had been careful to insist that the evangelical ministry must act collegially, especially in *jurisdictio* (4.3.8; 4.11.5–6), but also in the choice of ministers (4.3.15; 4.4.13), and the resolution of doctrinal difficulties (4.9.13). At the only point at which he had considered the organization of the church beyond the territorial compass of the city-state which was his normal focus of concern, he had envisaged a synodial (4.9.13), that is to say a collegial, arrangement. He had also allotted to the people a right of participation, even if in a controlling and consensual and not an initiatory capacity (4.4.2; 4.4.10–12; 4.12.7); perhaps this was mainly a polemical point to damn the papacy, and certainly nothing like this was realized in Geneva, but these are not reasons for treating his assertions about the 'common right' of the people as mere window-dressing. He had been careful to exclude from the Christian church any primacy which bore the slightest resemblance to *imperium* or *dominium* or the rule of one (4.4.2; 4.6.7; 4.6.10; 4.7.19; 4.11.8); arguments by correspondence taken from the animal kingdom (4.6.8) to demonstrate the naturalness of monarchy had received the same short shrift as in the *De Clementia Commentary*, and angelic hierarchies, indeed any hierarchies, had met with the same response (4.4.4; 4.6.10). His point was explicitly not to exclude an orderly precedence, an organizational *primus inter pares*; on the contrary, it was his view that nature itself demanded that sort of primacy (4.6.8; 4.11.6), but Calvin's statement of the relationship between Peter and the Apostles was paradigmatic.[50] And although Calvin had nowhere given an extensive reasoning for excluding monarchy and lordship from the order of the church, contenting himself with the precepts of Scripture and the practice and doctrine of the early church, his reason for wishing to see all exercise of power controlled in these ways is plainly that ecclesiastical power can bear no resemblance to the power of one man to do as he pleases.[51]

At several points, Calvin reinforced his teaching with the comparison between ecclesiastical primacy of an acceptable sort and the role of the consul in the senate (4.4.2; 4.6.8; 4.11.6). The fact that this comparison, as well as the allusion in 4.20.8 to the opinion of the philosophers, sprang so readily to Calvin's mind, makes it appear that his reasons for espousing aristocracy (whether pure or modified by democracy) in the church, were independently available in philosophy as far as civil government is concerned. That they should have proved applicable to civil government is, therefore, scarcely surprising.

We have already discerned a fairly detailed homology between Calvin's reflections about ecclesiastical and civil polity. The 1543 *Institution* makes the homology almost as explicit as Calvin ever made it. When in 1559 Calvin added to the much-amended 4.20.8 the contention that 'men's fault or failing makes it safer and more tolerable for several persons (*plures*) to exercise government, so that they may help one another, teach and admonish one another; and so that if one pushes himself forward more than is reasonable, there should be a number (*plures*) of censors and teachers to restrain his lawlessness (*libido*)', he was not saying anything which had not informed both his ecclesiastical and political thinking in 1542. But whereas he had by 1542 reflected extensively about the law, organization and practice of ecclesiastical polity, nothing approaching such comprehensiveness had yet appeared on the political side. The first edition of the *Institution* had expressly disavowed any intention of teaching magistrates their duty – presumably Calvin was here alluding to the 'mirror for magistrates' or 'de regimine principum' genre of which the *De Clementia* was a conspicuous exemplar. Subsequent editions of the work all repeated this self-denying limitation. The business at hand was the instruction of private men. This, however, became progressively less appropriate as the *Institution* came more and more to instruct everyone, magistrates included, in the principles of ecclesiastical polity. But the *Institution* was not the only piece of writing which Calvin laid before the learned public. Rather was it the *vade mecum* to accompany the massy tomes of his scriptural exposition which henceforth preoccupied Calvin. His *Institution* received only one more substantial recomposition; for amplification of Calvin's political thought, as well as specific content to flesh out the generalities of the ecclesiology, we must look elsewhere.

6

Geneva and Calvin, 1541–64

By the beginning of 1542 Calvin had formulated a rounded scheme of ecclesiastical polity, the digest of his pastoral experience at Geneva and Strasbourg as mediated by reflection upon Scripture and discussion with the leading evangelical theologians and organizers of his day; had buttressed it by scriptural legitimation; and had rendered it more or less coherent with the guiding themes of his theology (though here much remained to be done). But it is one thing to meditate a political scheme, another to have it received for law (and this had been accomplished by 20 November 1541, by which time all the Genevan Councils had accepted the draft), and yet another to transform scheme and law into a living reality – especially when the scheme was conspicuously vague at crucial points about the relations between a church as there outlined and the secular authorities, whose good-will and cooperation it required. More important, nothing specific had been said about what exactly these two *potestates* or *regimines* were actually to do, whether severally or in tandem. For the ends of both had so far only been set out in very general terms with little substantive content, and the same can be said about the character and conditions of their 'cooperation'.

Our purpose now is to investigate what clarification in matters hitherto left problematic or very general is to be found in the writings of the twenty or so years that remained to Calvin, and in particular whether, how, and to what extent his own experience and conduct in matters of ecclesiastical and civil polity are either sedimented in these writings, or are in turn informed by ideas expounded in these and earlier writings. In order to accomplish this purpose it is necessary to make certain general observations about sixteenth-century Geneva, about Calvin's place in the Genevan polity, and about the form and character of his literary activities.

THE GENEVAN POLITICAL ORDER[1]

It is to be remarked that the Geneva to which Calvin returned in 1541 had never been one of the Imperial free cities, nor was it one of the cantons of the Helvetic Confederation. It was not on the great trade routes, it no longer had its own fair, it had neither imposing civic buildings nor a university. It had neither great wealth, nor great manufactures, nor guilds of artisans; Genevan watch-making and printing are the consequences of French immigration.[2] Economically and culturally it was not to be compared (unless invidiously) with Basel, Bern or Strasbourg. Politically, too, Geneva was a city of no great consequence. It had never been a supplier of mercenaries on any scale, nor did it now have soldiers to offer: its militia, such as it was, was needed at home. For not even its autonomy was assured. By the time of Calvin's first arrival the city had thrown off the domination of the dukes of Savoy, its technical status as a city of the Holy Roman Empire was the merest form, although the Emperor's armies could make it a threat, and it had espoused the Reformation. But even reformation and political autonomy were not at Geneva straightforwardly civic enterprises, expressions and affirmations of civic virility; on the contrary, Bern's protection was crucial for both. Such protection was not however animated by pure philanthropy or evangelical zeal: Bern nursed persistent ambitions to reduce Geneva to the status of a dependency, a reliable buffer between its territories and Savoy. And it was Bern which controlled most of Geneva's hinterland, on which the city depended for its provisioning and trade, in which Genevan citizens owned land, and whence it derived a great deal of money in the form of dues, tithes, legal fees, fines and even taxes.[3] Thus Geneva confronted on the one side a belligerent Savoy anxious to reduce it once more to subjection, and on the other a Bern linked with it until 1556 in an alliance (a so-called *combourgeoisie*), but aiming at hegemony, and ready to exploit all divisions and conflicts within the republic, to harbour Genevans expelled from their city,[4] and to countenance the harassment and vilification of Geneva-inclined ministers in its dependencies. And the Bernese alliance and reformation had in turn cost Geneva the enmity of the Catholic city and canton of Freiburg (Fribourg), its nearest neighbour to the north: in the drawn-out wars between the Emperor and his Catholic allies and the evangelical cities and princes, on the fortunes of which Genevan autonomy to some extent depend, no help was forthcoming from there.

In a very real sense, therefore, Geneva was a city in a permanent state of siege. Its walls were always guarded; the suburbs outside the walls were razed in 1534 and the walls restored. Its citizens were required to keep arms in their houses according to their station, and to practice with the militia if of military age. These weapons were regularly inspected. At elections, citizens wore their swords as a kind of insignia of citizenship. The supervision of the guards was a duty of one of the four burgomasters or 'syndics'; detailed regulations concerning this matter were provided for in the revised civic ordinances of 1543. A curfew at 9 p.m., after which time everyone had to carry a lantern, was in force during the whole of Calvin's stay.[5]

The military and political exigencies of Geneva's position need to be borne in mind when we come to investigate the morals-police of Geneva. Quite simply, reformation, autonomy, morals and morale were interdependent, not only in the obvious sense in which morale and religion are always connected, but also by virtue of the fact that the common sense of the sixteenth century made no attempt to disentangle them and confidently anticipated that celestial vengeance would be visited *en gros* and *en detail* upon conspicuous immorality. In any case, partisans of reformation did not distinguish sharply between a reformation of worship and a reformation of morals: a toughening of the traditional *Zucht* (surveillance of morals, previously exercised by ecclesiastical courts, often called 'consistories') was usually taken in hand by the civil authorities in the reformed cities.[6] To this Geneva was no exception: it had attempted to tighten civic discipline during Calvin's absence,[7] and a consistory of sorts, to which we have already alluded, was restored before his return.[8]

Nothing, then, could be remoter from the truth than to imagine Geneva as an old-established free city, enjoying a traditional autonomy and secure in possession of long-established governing institutions, ancient laws and privileges.

This however is precisely the impression Geneva liked to convey: the political mind of the time could not countenance innovation, and as to revolution, of that it had not even the concept. And yet a 'revolution' (of the pre-1789 sort) was precisely what was enacted between 1526 and 1536. What is more, the leaders of that revolution were not an old urban aristocracy, used to governance and comfortable in its old dignities. The revolutionary elite of merchants supported by artisans was itself divided between Bernese and French sympathizers,[9] and the latter, whose temporary eclipse coincided with Calvin's and Farel's expulsion and whose restoration was the precondition for Calvin's return, itself subsequently broke up. The most bitter enemies of Calvin in the later forties and early fifties, the Favres, Bertheliers and Perrins, had been the agents of his restoration in 1541, but their idea of a free Geneva proved not to be Calvin's.[10] The political leadership of Geneva, therefore, was neither old-established nor united. Nor did it have to hand a set of traditional political institutions to compensate for the failings of the personnel. Its constitution, legal arrangements and institutions after 1536 were all somewhat new and experimental, even if it must be admitted that a continuity of forms with the medieval past was admirably preserved. And the citizen population at large had got into habits of political activism which in no way facilitated the business of governance.

The Genevan polity may perhaps be best described as a city-state of classical dimensions: it described itself as a *cité* or *civitas* or *république* (although the last-mentioned term was not used in official documents),[11] and boasted of pre-Roman origins: it was mentioned in Caesar's *Gallic Wars*. As it was a *civitas* or republic, ultimate authority was vested in a 'Conseil General' of all the citizens; this, however, was usually summoned only twice a year, for the elections of the syndics and some senior officials in February, and for fixing the price of wine and corn in November. And like republics throughout the ages Geneva already displayed marked oligarchical tendencies, which were reinforced with Calvin's approbation, though not at his initiative or instance, throughout the period under consideration. For most purposes, the governance of the city was conducted by the so-called 'Petit Conseil' (PC), also referred to as the 'Conseil Estroicte', 'Conseil Ordinaire' or simply the 'Conseil', a

significant abbreviation in that there were strictly speaking
four 'conseils'. Its Latin title 'Senatus' was not only gratifyingly
august; it was also singularly appropriate in that, like those of
the Roman prototype, the PC's members were all magistrates
or ex-magistrates, were self-censoring and self-selecting. Its
members collectively were formally the 'Magnifiques Seigneurs',
'Messieurs de Genève', 'la Seigneurie', or 'Syndiques et
Conseil', or some combination of these honorifics, the apparent
bumptiousness of which is somewhat attenuated when we
realize that they exercised the power of life and death and
admitted no appeal beyond their jurisdiction. As was the case
generally in republics, although the PC was composed of
laymen, it judged criminal as well as civil cases; even its chief
legal officials, the 'Procureur General' and the 'Lieutenant de la
Justice', who acted as examining magistrate, attorney general
and public prosecutor, were not necessarily lawyers. The
members of the PC were, of course, unpaid, except that they
received some sort of attendance fee, and those who exercised
specific offices collected some commission.

The PC itself comprised twenty-five members, as well as
the four so-called 'Syndics'. The latter were elected annually
by the 'Conseil General' of all the citizens from a list of eight
drawn up by the out-going syndics, the PC and the 'Conseil des
Deux Cents', an institution established in 1527 in imitation of
Bern's as a more viable alternative to the Conseil General.[12]
The members of the PC were themselves chosen by the Deux
Cents and the out-going and new syndics;[13] like the syndics, the
members of the PC were elected annually, but unlike them, they
were eligible for re-election every year. The members of the
Deux Cents were in turn chosen by the PC, which 'peruse[s] the
roule of the yere past'.[14] Such proliferation of councils and
interdependence amongst them is not at all unusual in republics.
It is unclear why there were *four* syndics; Strasbourg and Basel
each had only one burgomaster. It may have had something
to do with a fear of autocracy, which certainly in part accounts
for the fact that four years had to elapse between occupancies of
the syndical office, and that the senior syndic (who presided
at meetings of the PC) was only *primus inter pares* of the syndics.
Proposals for changes in the law required the approval of the
Deux Cents, which was also a court of appeal in criminal
cases, and on occasion that of the Conseil General.

There was, furthermore, a 'Conseil des Soixants', a relic of the fifteenth century, which continued a notional existence, though I do not find it to have done anything in Calvin's time.[15] The PC met three times a week (on Monday, Tuesday and Friday),[16] and at all hours when the need arose; the syndics met daily.[17]

What needs to be stressed in this connection is that all Genevan public offices and councils were in some manner and measure elective. While a persistent drift in an oligarchical direction is discernible,[18] habits of popular activism, or at any rate assembly-politics, had been contracted by the citizenry. These centred as often as not on the taverns, and drunken and noisy demonstrations in the streets were by no means unknown. But however much choice at elections might be guided and constrained, it was real choice. It follows that opinion for or against Calvin was convertible into political power, and Calvin owed both his expulsion in 1538 and his return in 1541, his harassments at the hands of the PC from the late forties until 1555 (the *annus mirabilis* of his triumph) and his ascendancy thereafter, to precisely such changes in opinion reflected at elections. This is to be borne in mind when we come to consider Calvin's ambiguous utterances concerning 'liberty'.

The Genevan population was divided into *citoyens*, *bourgeois* and *habitants*. The distinction between *citoyens* and *bourgeois* seems to be uniquely Genevan; it made its appearance in the 1520s[19] and was based on whether or not a man was born and baptized in Geneva of *citoyen* parents. The humbler status of *bourgeois* was purchasable by long-standing residents; since it usually cost a fair sum, it was used as a way of raising funds; no *bourgeois* was eligible for membership of the PC, although his Genevan-born sons were. A *bourgeois* might, however, participate in elections, and was eligible for the Conseil des Soixants and the Deux Cents. *Habitants* were simply registered aliens resident at Geneva whose names were recorded in the *Livre des Habitants*, kept from 1549;[20] they had the right to sue in civil cases, and were subject to the same laws and duties as everyone else, but had no right to carry swords,[21] to participate in elections, or to hold any public post, except pastor or lecturer at the school;[22] and the latter only because there was absolutely no indigenous Genevan talent to fill such posts, for apart from that there was no reason why a mere *habitant* should occupy such a well-paid, official post. Calvin was technically a *habitant* until he was given the citizenship, free of charge, in 1559. This meant (for example) that until 1559 he was liable to summary expulsion.

The main business of sixteenth-century governors, aside from the conduct of foreign affairs and the devising of expedients to raise revenue, was the administration of a system of civil and criminal law. As has been noted, the conflation of judicial and political business was characteristic of Geneva. A civil court, presided by the 'Lieutenant de la Justice' and four Assessors, all elected by the General Assembly for two-year terms, heard civil cases. Criminal justice was in the hands of the PC, sitting as the supreme judicial authority of Geneva. Here the Lieutenant acted as examining magistrate, required to present preliminary findings and a case to answer within a very short time after the apprehension of a *criminel*. The Genevan judicial process was occasionally accused of excessive haste – similar accusations were also levelled against the practice of the cities of the Empire – and Geneva prided itself on the expedition of its proceedings. The senior legal official of the republic, the 'Procureur General', a member of the PC, acted as prosecutor and was assisted in these functions by the Lieutenant. There was no public defender, and, at any rate in the cases familiar to me, no right to counsel. The magistrates, here in complete accord with Calvin's innermost sentiments, displayed a marked distaste for legal technicalities and prevarication; as far as knowledge of the law was concerned they were for the most part laymen, or at best notaries. This was by no means unusual: the *Carolina* itself (explained below) was written in lay terms for laymen; legal advice might be sought at specific points, and Calvin was on occasion called to give such technical advice.

What laws governed procedure, types of cases and penalties is unclear, despite the fact that procedure was perhaps the foremost concern of sixteenth-century legal thought. In 1532 the Holy Roman Empire received a new criminal code, the *Peinliche Gerichtsordnung Kaiser Karls V*, the so-called *Carolina* (*Constitutio Criminalis Carolina*) but I am unable to discover whether it was accepted in Geneva;[23] neither defendants nor verdicts, nor laws make any reference to it in Calvin's time, and it is not even clear that it was available in a French translation. The official language of Geneva was French, and a general drift in the direction of Savoyard and French legal practice is said to be discernible throughout the century.[24] But since both the Empire and France inclined towards Roman law, there may not have been any great difficulty.[25] It may be noted in passing that the spoken language of the Genevans was a Savoyard patois, containing substantial admixtures of German. How well ordinary Genevans understood the entirely French and francophone ministry is unclear: Calvin certainly did not preach in patois, and there is no evidence that he understood more than a few words of it. The French of the official Registres display a spelling and grammar which are extraordinary even by the undemanding standards of sixteenth-century orthography. Be that as it may, the *Carolina* was certainly not adhered to as regards 'confessions' made under torture, which according to article 58[26] were inadmissible in court; witness, for example, the trial of Battonat in September 1552,[27] or the case of the *hereges* ('heretics', the Genevan word for witches and sorcerers) of Peney,[28] or the case of Gruet or the Comparet brothers.[29]

To enforce its laws, regulations and moral norms, Genevan justice had at its disposal the normal sixteenth-century range of punishments. In this array, one item (from our point of view) is conspicuous by its absence: Geneva had only a holding-prison, capable at most of accommodating a few miscreants on bread and water for a few days, and mostly used to hold those awaiting or undergoing trial. There was consequently no option of long-term imprisonment as a possible penalty for serious crimes.[30] The choice of penalties was therefore either death, simple (by decapitation) or with torments (maiming, burning on a slow fire and so on), exile and confiscation of property (a most unsatisfactory punishment for political offences, given Bern's readiness to welcome certain sorts of exiles), or exile for some period, like 'ten years' or 'a year and a day', heavy fines (difficult to collect), whipping (unsuitable for gentlemen), or most leniently, public humiliation (usually described as a sentence to 'crier mercie à Dieu et la justice'), which meant some or all of the following: appearing in public in a garment of humiliation, carrying a torch, crying pardon at one or more specified places in the city. Since exile and heavy fines were often inappropriate penalties, we may perhaps understand the relatively high number of executions in Geneva in Calvin's time, but also before and after: after the overthrow of the Perrinist faction in 1555, it averaged nine a year, although at the height of a panic about plague-spreaders in 1545, thirty-five people were executed in the space of four months, the women after having one hand cut off.

Accurate population figures are impossible to come by. Pfisterer, following Doumergue, gives 13,000 natives and 2000 *habitants* for the city and 5000 for the country population in Calvin's time;[31] Monter gives 10,300 in all for 1537, and about 5000 *habitants* between 1549 and 1560, a great many of whom moved on.[32] In the 17 years for which there are records between 1542 and 1564 there were 139 executions at Geneva; this may be compared to the 572 executions in the canton of Zurich, which had a population of 73,000, in the whole sixteenth century.[33] It may be that Geneva punished where other states only threatened, and certainly Calvin inclined towards severity. As elsewhere, torture was frequently employed – and this too had Calvin's approval – but the Genevan method of the strappado was not calculated to delight sadists; and the more ingenious ways of prolonging death devised elsewhere were used in Geneva only for witches. There is nothing whatever to suggest that Calvin at any time favoured anything except quick and efficient executions.[34]

While the citizenry was, as we have seen, armed and accustomed to political activity, there was only a civic militia, which as far as I am aware was not used for domestic policing, was of course amateur, and was in any case composed of precisely those who might be involved in civil disturbances. To police the city, and run errands for the PC, there was an exiguous watch (*guets*); heads of households of military age had to take their turn at policing the city and guarding the walls at night-time.[35] It is, in fact, a wonder that there was so little bloodshed throughout the period. For the detection and prevention of crimes, the Seigneurie had to rely on its own knowledge of the population and on information laid by the citizens: there was a legal duty (at Geneva as throughout Europe) to denounce malefactors; denunciation is in any case one of the less lovable typical features of the classical republic.[36] The keepers of the two dozen or so inns and hostelries of Geneva were under strict instruction to report on the conversations of foreigners;[37] the story, related by Galiffe and, following him, by the normally scrupulous Kampschulte, that ecclesiastical spies were instituted in 1544, has been convincingly refuted.[38] Geneva was, however, divided into a number of districts called *dizaines* (although there were probably twenty of them), each with its own supervisor (*capitaine*) to keep an eye on things; and for the purposes of the discipline, the twelve lay elders of the Consistory were selected by the PC with a view to the supervision by each of a particular district. These lay elders were rarely changed (although their term was technically for a year); this allowed a building up of expertise and was in line with Calvin's preferences expressed in the *Ordonnances*. They were headed by one of the syndics, the other three having respectively the duty to preside over the PC, the Chambre des Comptes (the Genevan treasury and municipal bank) and the watch. The Consistory's charter has already been described. It should perhaps be added here that one of its specific concerns, namely matrimonial causes, had not been settled: a proposed *ordonnance* of Calvin of November 1545 was not made law until the overall consolidation of the ecclesiastical and disciplinary ordinances of 1561,[39] and that the supervision of discipline in the rural parishes was (and remained under the *Ordonnances* finally established for them in 1546) in the hands of the secular magistrate, the *châtelain*, albeit with the assistance of the minister for the area in question. Discipline there continued to be enforced by fines and short periods of imprisonment, despite Calvin's insistence that the church had none of the punishments usual with secular authorities. But then, the supervision of the rural parishes was always difficult, and no pastor wanted to go there, with the result that the misfits and incompetents of the pastorate were dumped there as an alternative to outright dismissal. Jacques Bernard (who had remained at Geneva after Calvin's dismissal) was retired to Peney, Henri de la Mare went to Jussy, and a similar fate was contemplated for the frightful[40] Philippe de l'Eglise (Ecclesia) before his eventual outright dismissal for criminal offences.

To sum up, Geneva was a recently established republic, governed by elected magistrates and councils. Its strategic position, autonomy and reformation were recognized to be interdependent; as was in any case typical of early modern states generally, and of republics throughout the ages, the religion and morals of its subjects were deemed the proper concern of governors, and 'privacy' was not a good or right admitted, even if burghers *de facto* knew very well how to prize it.[41] Furthermore, Geneva was a compact city-state surrounded by walls and the lake, and thus was supervisable, unlike the sprawling new monarchies. And it may be said immediately that no part of Genevan law or civic order owed its existence, form or legitimacy to Calvin except the Consistory and the Venerable Company. The *esprit des lois* is another question.

CALVIN AS MASTER AND SERVANT

This, then, was the context and locus of Calvin's activities. And there is certainly every reason to look to Genevan (amongst other) circumstances and events for enlightenment about the character and implications of Calvin's political thought. On Calvin's own terms political thought and conduct may be taken to illuminate each other, for, as he insisted, thought is to be subservient to action and godly practice is the 'fruit' of a godly disposition. And again, what Calvin's view on paper left vague and general (for example, the way in which he envisaged the cooperation of magistrates and ministers, or the political ideal of a 'pure aristocracy, or a rightly proportioned compound of aristocracy and popular elements', or the relationship between ecclesiastical disciplinary institutions and the processes of the criminal law) may be given substance and detail by reference to how such matters were managed at Geneva. Now it happens, thanks to the piety of disciples, the labours of scholars and the zeal of propagandists *pro et contra*, that we are massively well informed about Calvin's views, public and private, about almost any matter civil or ecclesiastical. We know what he thought about the place of women in God's scheme of things and about acceptable style in the trousering of a Christian, about a reasonable level of interest on loans and about condign punishment for witches. We know too about the political institutions and practices of Geneva, though here our information is somewhat more sketchy. And we have great quantities of information about Calvin's public activities. And from this springs a most dangerous temptation, which is that of finding in all this a system of ideas with the rigour and consistency which it is usual to predicate of ideology. But there are two considerations which militate against any such way of proceeding. In the first place, some measure of congruence is to be expected only between *Calvin's* thought and *Calvin's* activities, and not everything that was done at Geneva was Calvin's doing. In the second place, the systematic character of Calvin's thought, and the nature of the relationship between his theology and his public conduct, are matters for enquiry, and not things to be presupposed in enquiry.

The first problem, then, is to discern what may be counted as *Calvin's* activities. Here the literature is, alas, replete with *niaiseries* and naivities. One absurdity, not much touted since Stefan Zweig's nonsense in a good cause (although the egregious Pfister still sustained this view) is that of Calvin as the Genevan Dictator, ruling a cowed population with a rod of iron. On the account of the Genevan polity just advanced, it is unintelligible how a Genevan pastor, who for most of his life was not even a *bourgeois*, might be supposed to have dictated to the 'Magnifiques Seigneurs' of the PC and to the Deux Cents. The fantasy has a long pedigree: it was begotten in Calvin's own time by people such as Bolsec and Castellio who should have known better. Calvin himself protested in 1554 against the habit of 'ignoramuses' (*ignorans*) of ascribing everything done by 'our *senatus*' to him.[42]

A currently more popular image, which recognizes the weakness of the idea of Calvin as autocrat, has him as a humble pastor of the church,[43] a loyal servitor of a very independent and, at least until 1555, not very sympathetic magistracy. But whereas the former view is merely crass, the latter is naive instead, in that it fails to distinguish what Calvin distinguished very well, namely *auctoritas*, the capacity to inspire respect, *potestas*, *imperium*, the 'right to do' that goes with a particular office, and finally *potentia*, the resources with which to coerce.[44] The formal *potestas* of Calvin was that of a salaried official, one eventually protected by law from insult;[45] he was entitled to make representations on behalf of the ministry before the councils; he was also a member of the Consistory, enjoying the legal powers of that anomalous body; finally he was entitled to preach and thus to exploit the most important public medium of the day. But he had no right to act independently of the ministry, and in any case valued collegiality. And he was also dismissible by the authorities. But to concentrate on his formal legal standing is to miss the whole point, which is Calvin's personal authoritativeness, his capacity to inspire respect and awe, to initiate, suggest, urge, warn, rebuke, embarrass, spur on, remind, condemn, all of them certainly powers, even if not *potestates*. It was this that enabled him to resist not only his colleagues, but also the magistrates: his wrath must have been a fearsome thing, and there was simply no one else in Geneva, layman or cleric, who could speak as he could, as an equal with the leading evangelicals of his day, one whose addresses were not beneath the notice of some of Europe's crowned heads and highest dignitaries. He was probably better informed about the religious and political affairs of his time than anyone else in all Switzerland, with the exception of Bullinger. Such a man was not to be trifled with, even if his official title was only 'Minister of the Word'.

We must conclude, therefore, that things done at Geneva can be taken to illuminate Calvin's thought only in so far as they were either initiated by him or received his endorsement. Even then, it remains to be asked what kind of correspondence we may legitimately expect between his theology and his conduct, and what kind of internal coherence we are to look for in the reflections on things political that are to be encountered throughout his writings.

An historical understanding of Calvin's thought presupposes that an intelligible connection between Calvin's various views is to be found, whether these views were expressed on paper or revealed in conduct. But it does not follow from this that the connection is that of a tight and fully articulated system of thought, nor does it follow that his conduct must be regarded as so many practical inferences, still less deductions, from his theology. Nonetheless, a reflective man such as Calvin, and one who was frequently called upon to justify his thoughts and actions before a public in varying degrees hostile to him, may be expected to have been concerned that his views should be consistent, and that his conduct should be in keeping with the general views he professed. This does not preclude the possibility that Calvin made assumptions which were perfectly conventional in his time and place, and which he would therefore see no need to justify, regardless of their importance for the cogency of his thought. Such assumptions would not of course be ones of which Calvin was totally unaware; but he would not regard them as *assumptions*. As for the presence of entirely unrecognized assumptions, the demonstration of their presence would only be possible in a fully articulated system of ideas (if then),[46] and Calvin's various political reflections were certainly not offered in that form. And before any questions of this sort are tackled, one must first ask about the form in which Calvin's political reflections were offered, the status he thought them to have and the standards he thought appropriate to apply to them: in short, we must ask what he took himself to be doing when he thought about matters political.

THE POLITICAL CONTENT OF CALVIN'S WRITINGS, 1541–64

The first thing to be noted about Calvin's political thought is that he never drew together his various reflections on godly polity into a single treatise, in contrast to his ecclesiology, which he organized into an orderly exposition in the *Institution*, or to his conception of the legal and institutional order of a godly church, which was not only made into written law at Geneva, but also published for the world to see. Nor did he ever pen a model civil ordinance to correspond to such a model ecclesiastical ordinance: there is no sign that he ever contemplated any such thing, not even a draft, fragment or hint. And whatever may have been Calvin's contribution to the 'revision' of the Genevan civic ordinances of 1543 (whatever it was, it certainly does not amount to that of a lawgiver, *pace* Rousseau), the mere fact that he did not publish these ordinances is conclusive evidence that he regarded his work in this field (unlike the ecclesiastical or schools ordinances, the order of services, or the Genevan catechisms) as of parochial rather than universal significance.[47]

What is more, he did not even compose a comprehensive treatise on morality, which would have encompassed much of his political thought, given the character of his thinking on morality. The nearest approximations are the publication in 1562 of the transcript of some weekday sermons on Deuteronomy (part of a *catena* delivered in 1555), and a much fuller exposition of the Decalogue which formed part of his *Harmony of the Last Four Books of Moses*, published within a year of the death which Calvin had had reason to expect much earlier. He had made time for interminable writings against Westphal, Castellio and others, so the matter cannot have been of very great significance for him. That comprehensive casuistry of the evangelical life, which his Puritan descendants Ames, Perkins and Preston provided for their contemporaries in the next century, is no part of the Calvinian corpus.

We may take it, therefore (unless we wish to regard Calvin as negligent in his duty), that he thought he was providing what it was his duty to provide in his commentaries (for the more scholarly), his sermons (*homiliae, sermons*, for the Genevans) his lectures (*praelectiones, leçons*, to the Academy) and the *congregations* (expositions of the Bible, given by the ministers in turn, and open to the public). In addition, he frequently addressed himself to specific doctrinal or moral issues as they arose, drawing some general inference from a particular episode or contention and setting down his views in a pamphlet or book.

There is no very marked difference in approach or content between Calvin's sermons and his commentaries. Indeed, the latter were invariably preceded by courses of sermons, and in some cases the commentaries were the verbatim record of such sermons.[48] Considerations of concordance, textual and translating problems, the defence of Scripture against (usually unnamed) detractors, all these are more prominent in the commentaries, and the message, moral lesson or exhortation to be taken away by the hearers of the Word tends to be more heavily underscored in the sermons. The sermons are also somewhat less guarded and circumspect than the commentaries, and a little more direct and more vigorous in exposition, in part because they were delivered in French, a medium which always gave Calvin more scope for muscular expression than the stylized, outworn vocabulary of humanist Latinity.[49] But in both cases Calvin tended to treat the scriptural texts as literally true if factual assertions were involved, and usually as the *ipsissima verba* of whomever he supposed to be their author.[50] But his concern was with the 'use' and 'edification' to be derived from the texts. And the exhortations or lessons he found in the various texts are much the same in both sermons and commentaries: they are always the uplifting themes of God's providence and mercy, especially towards the church, of justification despite conspicuous lack of merit, of the promises of God, the prefiguration of Christ and his mediacy, of the depravity of man, of the need to curb passions both *en gros* and *en détail*, to be vigilant and zealous, and so on and so forth. There are indeed a few asides about specifically Genevan concerns, especially in the *Sermons on Deuteronomy*,[51] and Calvin was not averse to pointing out the analogy between scriptural and Genevan circumstances, but he was far from using the pulpit for political speeches to the Genevans, at least in the sermons that have come down to us.[52] And neither commentaries nor sermons deal in casuistry: their morality is the morality of precept and exhortation.

It might be supposed that some inferences can be made not only from what Calvin actually said, but from what he chose for comment. A predilection for the Old Testament has often been attributed to Calvin, and this used to support the thesis that this was because the jealous, vengeful God of the Old Testament, and the materials for theocracy and hierocracy to be found there, were much more congenial to him that the New Testament. Certainly too the Old Testament offers more scope to the legalistically inclined moralist than the New. But in fact only very guarded assertions of this sort are permitted by the evidence. The churches of the New Testament are not state-churches, and magistrates appear there mostly in the character of antagonists and enemies of the godly; for something more analogous to the situation of the state-churches of the Reformation – still more for something corresponding to the cooperation of magistrates and ministers that Calvin considered ideal – the Old Testament is much more fruitful, and many of Calvin's proof-texts in political matters in the *Institution* and the polemical writings are, in fact, drawn from there. But if priority in time means priority in importance, and it well might, for Calvin was often very ill and had reason to expect an early demise, New Testament theology must have had pride of place in Calvin's estimation, for it was only after completing a set of commentaries on all the Pauline Epistles[53] and almost all the other Epistles that Calvin turned to the Old Testament. He did not comment on Revelation.[54] It is the case that he had intended to by-pass the Gospels and Acts completely, and to go straight on to Genesis (on which he was already working in 1550), and that the commentary on Isaiah appeared before any Gospel commentary.[55] But this does not reflect any judgement of relative worth as between the Old

Testament and the Gospels; it merely means that from his point of view, the essential content of the Synoptic Gospels was to be found in the doctrine and in the 'birth, death and resurrection of Christ . . . [in which] is contained the whole sum of our salvation',[56] and that he could deal with all of this in the context of an exposition of the Pauline Epistles, the 'canon within the canon' and the key to the whole of Scripture. In any case, he changed his programme: his commentary on Acts was already well advanced in 1550 and it eventually appeared in two stately volumes in 1552 and 1554; a commentary on the Synoptic Gospels appeared in 1555 in the form of a 'harmony' or 'concordance'; John was accorded a separate volume in 1553.

For the Old Testament Calvin offered commentaries on Isaiah (1551),[57] Genesis (1554), Psalms (1557), the Twelve Minor Prophets (1557–9), Daniel (1561), Joshua (1562) and Jeremiah (1564). Had the legal–moral aspects of the Old Testament been his chief concern, it would be unintelligible why he left Exodus, Leviticus, Numbers and Deuteronomy to the very end of his life.[58] He published no commentary at all on the historical books (Judges, Ruth, Samuel, Kings, Chronicles); his sermons on Samuel (1561–3) remained unpublished in his lifetime,[59] and those on Kings were interrupted by his final illness.

If we turn to the texts chosen for the sermons, in so far as we know what they were,[60] our conception of Calvin's choice of texts is somewhat altered. Again, Calvin devoted far more time to the exposition of the Old than the New Testament, and again there is a clear predilection for the prophetic books of the Old Testament. But this is counterbalanced by the fact that in the period for which our information is fullest,[61] the Old Testament provided the material for the weekday sermons, at which attendance was not compulsory, but the New was explicated at the Sunday morning sermons, at which attendance was compulsory.[62] Having preached on the Pauline Epistles in the thirties and forties,[63] Calvin preached on Acts; he also preached sixty-five sermons on the 'Harmony of the Gospels' between 1559 and 1564. It is the case that he sometimes chose for his sermons texts appropriate for the particular circumstances of Geneva. Thus, during his most embattled period (1549–55) he preached one hundred and eighty-nine sermons on Acts, which is full of material on the hardships and detractions suffered by the servants of Christ, and on Jeremiah and various other prophets who recall the people to their duty; and with the consolidation of his position in Geneva in 1555–6 he chose Deuteronomy. But in these sermons, Calvin was exceedingly sparing in direct comment on the domestic issues of the day, and his allusions to his own times are somewhat general and not very revealing. In his sermons on 1 and 2 Samuel, and on Deuteronomy (1555–6), however, he several times explicitly referred to Genevan affairs and extended himself on political matters. A concern for the sufferings of the godly *in partibus infidelium* is not infrequently displayed throughout Calvin's sermons.

Certain conclusions suggest themselves from this survey. Calvin obviously did not select for comment those books of the Old Testament which were the most clearly suitable either for political lessons or for a casuistry of morals, nor can he be said to have preferred the Old Testament to the New. Like the other Reformers, he was much more interested in *doctrina* than in *historia*,[64] and this accounts for the obvious preference for the Pauline Epistles and John among the books of the New Testament, as well as for the neglect of the historical books of the Old. For Calvin (as for evangelicals of his time) history serves to exemplify, illustrate and make concrete and vivid what is already known and knowable in a general form as doctrine.[65] And his understanding of true doctrine in turn treats Paul as far and away the most authoritative expositor of Christ; it is Paul, too, and for the same reason, who furnishes the key to the interpretation of the Old Testament.[66] In these terms, what most calls for comment in Scripture is the great themes of God's eternal and endless mercy and care for his church and his promise of salvation through Christ, apprehended in faith, as contrasted with the inveterate ingratitude and disobedience of men, beginning with Adam. Consequently men need to 'have their ears beaten'[67] in season and out of season with this doctrine and with the calls to repentance, obedience and zeal for the glory of God which follow from it. For a mind informed by this conception of God and the world, the most congenial and edifying material in the Scriptures is the prophets, and both the weekday sermons and the commentaries are heavily weighted in favour of the prophetical books. Now the office of the prophet is described by Calvin in a way which assimilates it to that of the pastor and theologian: it is 'to bring forth nothing new, but only to explain the parts of the Law misunderstood before'.[68] The 'Law' in turn has 'three principal parts. First, the doctrine of life; second, threatenings and promises; and third, the covenant of grace (*foedus gratiae*)'.[69] The Law, therefore, is not understood simply as a codex of regulations, although he did say that it is 'prescribed as a perpetual rule for the church (*perpetuam regulam ecclesiae*) . . . to be followed by all posterity',[70] and there is no mistaking the place of obedience as the foundation of every virtue for Calvin. Like Calvin, the prophets were given to inveighing against the faults and back-slidings of their contemporaries and calling them to repentance. And finally, lest this account of Calvin's themes and preoccupations be thought to undervalue the centrality of Christ in Calvin's theology, it is to be remembered that Calvin read the prophets as proclaiming Christ, as does the rest of the Old Testament; so that the Old Testament and the New are not distinct in *scopus*. It may be remarked, however, that Calvin's preference for a literal reading meant that the proclamation of Christ which was Calvin's 'official' and programmatic statement about the interpretation of the Old Testament was far from being what occupied most of the space in his commentaries.

As for the polemical writings, Calvin was usually moved to write them in order to support or defend some teachings of the *Institution* which had become controversial. They tend merely to restate, at greater length and with more arguments and additional defensive scriptural exegesis, what had already been said in the *Institution*. Much of their content in turn found its way into the last edition of the *Institution* in the same way that the *Catechisme, Confession de la Foy* and *Ordonnances* were used to rewrite the editions of 1539 and 1543. What concerned Calvin in such pieces was usually the same issues of high theology which were also treated in the commentaries, lectures and sermons; in other words, not questions of a political nature. The sole exception to this, and it is a very important one, is the discussion of the duty of magistrates with respect to heretics, on which the *Institution* remained elusive and equivocal. For the rest, the main targets of Calvin's attacks remained the Anabaptists and the papists; the latter's efforts at putting their house in order at the Council of Trent, political and military successes in the late forties[71] and persecution of the French brethren made a continuance of that kind of writing necessary. It may be seen as the literary complement to Calvin's intense diplomatic activity on behalf of the godly, and to his battle to keep the evangelical churches united, and free of any taint or pollution by contact with the ungodly. In that context Calvin had nothing new to teach, and he was certainly quite unwilling to learn: any show of an irenic spirit, especially by Melanchthon, provoked his wrath.[72] To these were added in the course of the fifties various writings to defend Geneva and Calvin against their detractors abroad[73] and the voluminous contributions to the sacramentarian controversy, all of which played their own part in the undoing of that very evangelical unity which was one of Calvin's main concerns throughout his ministry, and in the embittering of his temperament. The list is completed by pamphlets warning the faithful against some particular evil, like conformity to Romish practices,[74] relics, Anabaptism and Libertinism,[75] and judicial astrology.[76] In the fifties and sixties, such writings are comparatively rare.[77] And for some reason no political event or issue, not even the persecution of the French brethren from the late fifties or their taking up arms in the early sixties, elicited from Calvin's pen a volume devoted to the elaboration of his political theology; even the defence of the execution of heresiarchs (the justifiability of which had previously been taken for granted) was incidental to a defence of trinitarian doctrine. The deposits of political material in these writings, again with the exception of the matter of public and impenitent heretics, prove on inspection to be exiguous.

In sum, then, Calvin's literary activities, as well as his sermons and *leçons*, had as their primary subject the most general themes of evangelical theology, and as their purpose instruction in the doctrine of life and exhortation to godliness and zeal. The commentary-format and Calvin's choice of texts on which to comment only rarely permitted any sustained or discursive treatment of matters of civil polity, given Calvin's habits of restraint in comment and attention to the text. And when Calvin did depart from his text, it was likely to be with a view to offering sententious verdicts on conduct narrated in the text, elucidating the justice of God where it was not immediately apparent from the text, or explaining the point of some sentence, repetition or apparent anomaly; these sorts of comments are most frequently called for in the commentaries on historical texts.[78] If the matter under consideration was doctrinal, Calvin was likely to link the text to the great themes of justification, election, the mercy of God and the mediatorship of Christ, the dignity of the ministry and the duty of obedience in its every facet and aspect, or to show that there was no contradiction between the text and those doctrines. In neither case is there any sign of a disposition to systematize his political reflections more than had been done in the *Institution*. And given the character of Calvin's mind and purposes, it is obviously out of place to look for any pursuit of speculative, epistemological or philosophical questions. 'Speculation' is uniformly a term of abuse in Calvin's vocabulary, and while he was careful to dissociate himself from the (usually Anabaptist) devaluation of secular learning, his work and pursuits are set by Scripture and the demands of *aedificatio*. It remains to be determined whether his refraining from speculative questions on political matters was because he thought that such things do not pertain to the office of an evangelical theologian, or because he thought no one had any business occupying himself with such things. A general discussion of whether political thinking is to be regarded as a colloquium at which evangelical theology is an honoured partner along with other independently authoritative sources of knowledge relevant to the understanding and conduct of the business of government, or as a monologue in which evangelical theology speaks and the godly listen and obey, is not to be found in Calvin's writings.[79]

This is not, of course, to say that the commentaries, sermons and polemical writings between 1542 and Calvin's death in 1564 do not amplify or modify what Calvin had already written or that they do not more fully reveal the workings of Calvin's mind on matters of civil polity. On the contrary, Calvin had a great many things to say on a very wide range of political topics. It nonetheless remains a question, precisely in view of the quantity of this material, why he should never have drawn it all together in a more comprehensive fashion than book 4, chapter 20 of the *Institution*. For quite apart from the generality and allusiveness of the discussion there (on which we have already remarked), certain topics of considerable concern both to Calvin and to his contemporaries are scarcely discussed in that place at all. In the first place, the whole question of the relationship between the church and the polity (denoting by those terms two corporations with overlapping membership but independent apexes) was handled only in pieties about cooperation; hardly any consideration was given to the kind of political order which would be most compatible with the (scripturally determined and unalterable) ecclesiastical order. In this connection, and given Calvin's unceasing attention to the activities of the Genevan Consistory and its capacity to provoke irritation and contention both at home and abroad, the whole question of the relationship between the ecclesiastical and the civil discipline, and between civil (criminal) and ecclesiastical law, also remained to be considered. Finally, much of Calvin's activities, especially in the fifties, may be described as diplomacy. But whereas experience of diplomacy had spurred Machiavelli to the formulation of views on the relationship between politics and morality which proved highly disturbing to Christians (and not least Calvin's own followers),[80] Calvin himself nowhere deigned to notice that work or to formulate a reply to it; it is not apparent that he had ever heard of it.[81]

Various suggestions to account for Calvin's not assembling his political ideas in one place may be dismissed out of hand. Calvin did not believe that political and religious matters are ultimately separable, any more than any other Reformer did. Again, he could not possibly be thought to have regarded civil laws and institutions as matters remote from theology, given his view of the content of Scripture and the quite unqualified dominance of the moral element in his conception of law. His understandable anxiety to discourage private men from any political thoughts other than thoughts of obedience was not an impediment to offering at least a general account of the 'condition of a well-ordered commonwealth'.[82] And even if he regarded Scripture as varying in the degree of detail with which it specifies the laws of a godly polity, this did not prevent Calvin setting down, in *ad hoc* fashion, a great number of laws which he thought he had derived from Scripture. Finally, the idea of a model civic ordinance, or at any rate an outline of the main laws and institutions of a godly polity, was certainly not beyond the conceptual resources of a reader of Plato, a draftsman of several ecclesiastical ordinances and part-drafter of a civil one, and an admirer, if a qualified one, of Roman law.

It was therefore not inherently inconceivable that Calvin should have assembled his moral and political ideas into a single treatise. The fact remains, however, that he did not conceive of any such project. And part of the reason for this is, of course, that Calvin regarded what he had to say on moral matters (and to that extent on political and legal ones) as obvious to all godly men, and in many cases to ungodly and even pagan ones as well. Even care of religion as the principal concern of a commonwealth was reckoned by Calvin as a thing understood by natural men. Right conduct was never for him a realm of ambiguity and perplexity in which the services of a problem-solver are called for. His 'office' as a theologian and a minister was to remind men of what they knew already and to urge them on to better performance, and he was certainly doing that day after day, even if not in the form of a single treatise.

It nonetheless remains curious that Calvin did not see fit to publish to the world at least the sumptuary and disciplinary laws of Geneva which he and the ministers had always urged on the magistrates, and which bear the unmistakable imprint of his teaching, and possibly of his own drafting. Indeed, in 1562 an Englishman recently returned from Genevan exile produced for the contemplation of the more godly of his countrymen a translation not only of the ecclesiastical *Ordonnances* of 1560, but also of the *Edicts* of 1543 (that is, the civil constitution) and of various sumptuary and disciplinary laws, complete with their sermonizing preambles: *The Lawes and Statutes of Geneva, as well concerning ecclesiasticall Discipline, as civill regiment . . . Translated out of Frenche into Englische by Robert Fills* was published in London in 1562.[83] The author claimed that his 'booke conteineth lawes and statutes, without which a common weale can no more be ruled, than the body lyve w[ith]out the soule . . . and they are ye statutes of Geneva, a Citie cou[n]ted of all godly men singularly well ordered, as well for good policie, as also for the gouvernement of the church in all estates and vocations . . .'[84] Presumably because he was aware of an accusation which might be levelled against him, the translator then proceeded to disclaim any intention of being a 'new lawe maker, or author of any innouacion, or that his industrie and diligence is in any wyse preiudiciall to the lawes of this our realme, which are laudable, good and godlye. . .'[85] In short, the 'lawes and statutes' of Geneva, both ecclesiastical and civil, were already between them seen as the very model of a godly commonwealth in Calvin's own life-time.

But this is Fills's view of Geneva; it is not one Calvin himself urged upon the world. He did regard the ecclesiastical order of Geneva as exemplary, at least as far as its constitution went – the practice was obviously far from perfect. But he was not the propagator of the Genevan example in its civil aspect, and he never made any particular civil order into a part of evangelical doctrine as the counterpart of scriptural ecclesiastical polity. Our next task is that of piecing together from his writings an outline of a godly polity. But the fact that it is possible to do so, and that a fairly clear and comprehensive picture of such a polity emerges, ought not to lead us to forget that it is we who are constructing it, not Calvin.

7

The civil order of a Christian commonwealth

Our account of Calvin's conception of a Christian common-wealth must begin where he did in any matter of *politia*, at the top. The apex is the two-fold regime of magistrates and ministers. The 'form' of the latter, both as ecclesiology and as the ecclesiastical constitution of Geneva, has already been described. What remained to be done in this connection was to attend to the detail which makes the difference between the letter of the law and a working set of arrangements. Thus Calvin unceasingly badgered the PC for competent ecclesiastical personnel in adequate numbers, attempted and eventually secured (by the later forties) the elimination of the remaining unfit ministers, prevented the imposition of objectionable candidates on the Venerable Company by the magistrates, extracted not ungenerous remuneration and lodgings for at least the urban ministers and doctors, tried to secure official protection for ministers against abuse and recalcitrance, and in 1559 saw through the establishment of the Genevan 'Academy' for the training of future pastors and magistrates. To the same end he fought a running battle to ensure the Consistory's mastery over the 'discipline', a battle not effectively won until 1555; his success was symbolized in 1560 by the ending of the practice whereby the syndic who presided at the Consistory came bearing his staff of office: without it, he was now clearly designated as an ecclesiastical and not a civil official.[1] This did not, however, prevent the Consistory being furnished with a beadle to ensure the attendance of culprits. In all these battles Calvin enjoyed the support of the lay majority[2] of the Consistory, appointees, it will be recalled, of the Councils. All this is exactly how we would have expected

Calvin to behave in virtue of his interpretation of the ministry, and since the history of Calvin at Geneva has been described many times in the literature, it need not be repeated here.

By contrast, the ideal form envisaged for the other head of the two-headed regime was nowhere clearly laid down. And as far as Calvin's 'official doctrine' (as opposed to his actual preference) is concerned, there was never any deviation from the position of the 1536 *Institution* that any form of government whatever, be it monarchy, aristocracy, polity or some mixed form, is equally legitimate and equally competent to perform its divinely appointed office, and that any tyrannous government is to be endured without rebellion.

ARISTOCRACY AND LIBERTY

Calvin, then, remained committed to the view that a scripturally determined 'form' of ecclesiastical polity might and ought to cooperate with whatever form of civil government it happens to find established. But Calvin had taken up this 'official' position when his practical knowledge of any sort of government (civil or ecclesiastical) did not extend beyond what was derivable from the bookish diet of a humanist, when he had very little to say about the external order of a godly church, and when his teaching on the relation between Christians and civil order was largely confined to the doctrine of obedience. His opinions on civil government, especially in its monarchical form, underwent considerable modification in the course of the rest of his life. But it is not possible to be totally confident that there is a single, anti-monarchical direction in these modifications.[3] And the views that Calvin expressed elsewhere were never quite taken up in the *Institution*, which, in any case, given the successive qualifications and additions interpolated into a residue of unchanged formulations, presents a confusing picture.

The clearest and most substantial change in Calvin's political thinking, as has already been noted, occurred in 1543, when, without prior warning, he suddenly proclaimed the superiority of aristocracy, whether pure or modified in the direction of polity, over other political forms.[4] It is hard to see this general preference as the upshot of reflection on specifically civil matters: Calvin's contentment with the well-ordered evangelical polity of Strasbourg and the repentance of Geneva hardly made inescapable a general preference for aristocracy over monarchy. And whatever we are disposed to conjecture about Calvin's part in the revision of the Genevan civil ordinances, there is nothing whatever to suggest a conversion to aristocratic principles, rather than Calvin's endorsement of aristocratic tendencies in the Genevan order on the basis of an already existing set of aristocratic preferences. There is, however, abundant evidence that Calvin engaged in sustained reflection about good order in the church, and the mixed form of government which he advocated there bears a striking resemblance to what he was now advocating for civil polity.

Calvin's repeated use of civil analogies to explain what sort of headship was necessary and tolerable in the church presupposes that he was aware that what he had said about the desirable order of ecclesiastical government could also be said about the good order of a civil government. But his justification for his conception of ecclesiastical polity had been primarily scriptural, whereas his allusion to 'experience' and the arguments of philosophers, which is all he then offered to support his espousal of aristocracy, suggests a prudential sort of argument, traditional in political theory; and he had not in 1543 devised, nor did he devise subsequently, any clear account of the place of prudence in matters of ecclesiastical government.[5] And on occasion Calvin insisted that the spiritual and the political *regnum* 'are always to be viewed on their own and separately. When one is being considered, we should carefully avert our minds from considering the other.'[6] Thus philosophical and prudential thinking about political forms would be one thing, and determination of the will of God about right order in the church would be quite another. However, such an extreme assertion of the intransitivity, so to speak, of civil and ecclesiastical reflection is perhaps due to Calvin's terror of misinterpretations of the doctrine of Christian liberty, which he was trying to defuse in that place.[7] It is also at variance with the marked parallelism of his ecclesiastical and civil thought throughout. And even if he did not ever clarify the place of prudence in the organizing and governing of churches, neither did he ever deny its importance; indeed, quite the contrary.[8] The fact that Calvin considered scriptural legitimation more authoritative and convincing than any merely prudential argument does not of itself demonstrate that the latter did not weigh more heavily with him or possibly even govern his interpretation of the ecclesiastical polity to be found in Scripture; those more inclined to the monarchical form of government in general had found, and continued to find, scriptural support for ecclesiastical monarchy. *Mutatis mutandis*, therefore, what Calvin had said about the government of the church might equally well be applied to the government of the civil polity.

A clear preference for an aristocratic, or better still a mixed, form of civil polity was therefore on record by 1543. But this preference, which was subsequently restated and reinforced, had always to compete with a theological *parti pris* to the effect that in forms of polity, whatever is, is right. And although Calvin had enlisted 'experience' in support of the mixed polity, the reflections of the philosophers which he had just adduced did not argue unequivocally in favour of aristocracy against monarchy,[9] for each form has its characteristic defects. Nor did Calvin's own experience give grounds for an unambiguous commitment against monarchy as such. Perhaps no good ever seemed to be coming to the brethren from the French monarchy,[10] but Calvin at one time or another entertained hopes about Duke Christopher of Würtemberg, Protector Somerset, Edward VI and Elizabeth I of England, King Sigismund of Poland, King Christopher III of Denmark and his son and designated successor Prince Frederick, John Frederick, Duke of Saxony, Gustavus Vasa, King of Sweden, the Elector Palatine Frederick, Radzivil, Duke Palatine of Vilna, and Henry of Navarre, all of them sometime dedicatees of Calvin's works. With rather less hope, and perhaps by way of a gesture only, Calvin also addressed himself publicly to successive French kings and even to the Emperor Charles V.[11] His final disillusionment with Anthony of Navarre did not come until 1561, although Calvin had privately been both despondent and derogatory about his character for years; even then, all hope was not lost for Louis de Condé, the other prince of the blood, or for the Admiral of France, Coligny, with whom Calvin remained on the most cordial terms.[12] Thus it was never entirely clear that 'princes' or 'kings', most of them actual or would-be autocrats, were unsuitable instruments of the Gospel and Reformation. Indeed, a concentration of power and knowledge, which would be at its speculative optimum in a godly monarch, the more absolute the better, had its attractions for humanists.[13] But there is no unequivocal expression of this point in Calvin. Conversely, republics (that is to say, city-states, especially the Imperial free cities) were not reliable, let alone distinguished, servants of the Cause as Calvin understood it. The republic of Bern sheltered Bolsec and permitted ceaseless insults to Geneva and its ministry throughout the forties and fifties,[14] while harassing Calvin's close friends and partisans Pierre Viret and Guillaume Farel in Lausanne and Neuchâtel respectively, especially as regards their attempts to establish *congregations* and ecclesiastical discipline. The city of Basel not only would not tolerate an independent ecclesiastical discipline, but provided a haven for the heresiarch Castellio and a nest of other heretics, including the infamous David Joris, who lived out his days there, tranquil and protected by powerful friends.[15] Calvin's beloved Strasbourg was too weak to resist the *Interim* and was forced to watch the departure of Bucer (who died in exile in England) and Peter Martyr Vermiglio, while the Hanseatic city of Hamburg became the home of Westphal. Experience, therefore, did not argue for the republic as the uniquely suitable agency for reformation, even if some sort (a Caesaropapist sort) of reformation was characteristic of republics, that is, cities, and not generally characteristic of the New Monarchies.

Nor were Genevan politics after Calvin's return conducive to an unequivocal endorsement of republics, even supposing that Calvin had been minded to draw a universal lesson from a single instance. Faction, disorder and sedition had traditionally been associated with the republican form of polity, and Calvin had alluded to these defects in the 1543 *Institution*. Geneva exhibited them all. Thus his own difficulties at Geneva were directly proportional to the successes of his opponents in the elections for syndics and the PC. He was not unfamiliar with tumultous assemblies, and one or twice had to take his life in his hands. On occasion the sermons burst out into condemnation of the *canaille*, the 'meschans [qui] s'assemblent pour faire leurs complots'.[16] And in the second of the *Commentaries on Acts*, he referred on numerous occasions to the 'vehemence', 'rage', 'seething' of the 'people', their propensity to be aroused by self-seeking men and to sweep all before them, even the magistrates.[17] The theme of the propensity of magistrates and judges to 'howl with the wolves',[18] to be swept away by popular tumults, the habit of 'politic men'[19] to do whatever will quiet the crowds, irrespective of whether it is right or not, also occurs in other places in his writings.[20] Their business, he once declared in his *Sermons on Deuteronomy*, is 'to go to war against the whole world'.[21] The writing and publication of the Acts commentaries coincides with growing opposition to the French immigrants, a hostility on which the Perrin–Favre–Sept connection capitalized at their electoral triumph of 1553, when they not only secured the election of syndics hostile to the French *habitants* and their ministers, but also changed the rules about the selection for the PC[22] and increased their support there. One of their partisans, Philibert Bonna, was the only Consistory member favourable to Servetus.

Under the circumstances, a generous warmth in Calvin's discourse about crowds is understandable, and it would not be surprising to have found a general equating of 'the people' and 'the mob'; Calvin's education had after all left him well provided with a stock of clichés about unruly mobs and giddy multitudes. Republican 'liberty' could also have fallen victim to such an attitude, which would then have issued in a preference for a narrow aristocracy. In fact, however, hostility to 'the people' and all its works is far from being the most conspicuous motif in Calvin's political reflections; some golden opportunities for its expression were quite ignored in the commentaries.[23] On the contrary, the 1543 *Institution*'s addition about the happiness of a government which combines liberty and *moderatio* was reasserted elsewhere with greater vigour, especially in sermons for Genevan consumption, although some of these found their way to publication. We are therefore dealing with a consistent sentiment. Thus the *Sermons on Deuteronomy* of 1555 refer to the 'privilege, which is by no means common to all peoples, of choosing those who are to govern', and went on: 'And here's the reason why tyrannies have come into the world, why people everywhere have lost their liberty, why there are no longer any elections . . . What other cause for it is there but that those people who had elections abused the privilege?'[24] 'To be in a free *estat*' he described as 'much better than being under a prince',[25] and as a 'singular gift' of God to his people, whereby he demonstrated 'that he wanted their condition to be better and more excellent than that of their neighbours, where there were kings and princes, and no liberty'.[26] Even here, however, he reminded his readers that speculative arguments (*disputs*) are not very profitable, for those under a prince are not to 'vex their minds with plans for innovation'.[27] In the *Sermons on 1 Samuel* (1562–3) he referred to 'liberty' as an 'inestimable boon';[28] he explained away the text where Samuel is said to have made his sons judges over Israel as meaning, not that he wanted 'the charge committed to him to be transmitted like a hereditary right to his posterity', but rather that his sons were to act simply as his delegates, thus leaving the liberty of the people intact;[29] and he drew from the celebrated verses on the institution of Israelitic kingship (1 Samuel 8.11–18) the lesson 'how great a benefit liberty is, when God has bestowed it on someone'.[30] And in a passage hidden away in the latter part of the *Harmony of the Last Four Books of Moses* Calvin indicated an awareness of one of the more prominent tenets of the classical republican tradition, though of course he made it out to be a piece of divine wisdom: 'in as much as God had given them [sc. the Israelites] the use of the franchise, the best way to preserve their liberty for ever was by maintaining a condition of rough equality,[31] lest a few persons of immense wealth should oppress the general body. Since, therefore, the rich, if they had been permitted constantly to increase their wealth, would have tyrannized over the rest, God put a restraint on immoderate power by means of this law'.[32] There are many places from which Calvin could have derived this, and he was certainly familiar with Polybius and Aristotle; the point, however, is that he did not think this reflection, or the law to which he was referring, appropriate for his times.

Calvin had not said precisely what he understood by 'liberty'. But many of these comments come in sermons to Genevans, and in that context one meaning of the term is plain enough: a people is at liberty if, like the citizens of Geneva and republics generally, it has a right to choose its governors. A broader meaning of liberty, usual in the sixteenth century, is that of the secure enjoyment of legal rights ('liberties'); and republicans were likely to see the right of electing their governors as being a crucial safeguard for 'liberties' in general. Nor did Calvin make precise how 'the people' is to be understood in this context. But he will have taken for granted the distinction between citizens and resident aliens, especially since the condition of a resident alien is not one of rightlessness, but only of being debarred from electing or being elected to civic office. It may furthermore be recalled that it was a commonplace of ancient and medieval republicanism to identify 'the people' with the *valentior pars* of the citizenry.[33] It would be entirely in keeping with the character of Calvin's political thought to read him as favouring a guided and controlled kind of popular participation, such as was practised at Geneva, where the Deux Cents normally represented the popular element in the polity (the General Assembly of all the citizens meeting only rarely) and where the PC, although itself elected by the citizenry, nevertheless vetted the membership of the Deux Cents which in turn vetted the PC's membership. We may remind ourselves that such a system of reciprocal controls was advanced by Calvin as the ideal order for appointing members of the ministry, even if the role of the congregation at Geneva was even more passive than this.[34] And if this is the kind of popular participation Calvin had in mind, the somewhat opaque lines of the 1543 *Institution* – 'I freely admit that there is no kind of government more happy than one in which liberty is reconciled (*composita*) with that *moderatio* which is seemly, and which is properly constituted so as to be durable' – become clearer. *Moderatio* is a term Calvin not infrequently employed to mean 'government'; its connotations are those of containment and regulation rather than direction. Calvin is therefore saying here that the best form of government is one permitting a controlled and regulated kind of popular participation, as well as a secure enjoyment of legal rights, and the duty of magistrates to defend liberty where it is established (to which he referred in the next line) must be read to include the defence of electoral liberty against its misuse by the citizenry, as well as defence of the free *estat* against outside attack.

Finally, it would be prudent not to bring the term 'democracy' into this discussion at all, since in its modern use it is entirely ambiguous as between the legitimacy of a whole system of rule and the authorization of particular persons to occupy positions within a pre-existent system. Calvin nowhere qualified, but rather reinforced, the position of the first

Institution that divine authorization for a system of rule is to be inferred from events and the *status quo*, and not from the *vox populi*.[35] His concern was exclusively with the authorization of persons to occupy offices within a divinely legitimated system of rule, and in that context (depending on the positive laws of the polity in question) a controlled and qualified participation of 'the people' is desirable.

OF KINGS, COURTS AND TYRANTS

The complement and obverse to this espousal of aristocracy and elections is an impressive range of hostile references to kings and courts. These tended to be more overt and forceful in sermons that remained unpublished, but there is quite enough evidence in the published writings to make it clear that this was a fixed attitude, at least after 1543, which perhaps he thought it prudent not to state too loudly; he had after all good reason for not biting royal hands which he hoped might feed various flocks of Christ's sheep.[36] It is unclear whether Calvin changed his views substantially after 1543. We do not have the texts of sermons before 1549, and the writings before the mid-fifties deal for the most part with the New Testament, where the church had to deal with provincial governors, high priests and city councils rather than with kings. Nor would it be sensible to make too much in this connection of any growing familiarity on Calvin's part with kings and their courts; his personal contact with monarchs was entirely by letter and report, and much of what he said, especially about the 'courts of princes', could have come from books, and probably did. It might even have been extrapolated from traditional evangelical stories about that 'sink of iniquity', the court of the papal monarchy. No doubt disgust at the conduct of certain princes accounts for the warmth of his sermons, especially in 1562 and 1563, but he had long been out-spoken enough. And we have already discovered a plausible reason, independent of this, why his ecclesiastical and political thought should have moved in the same direction.

Calvin's condemnations were directed against the persons and conduct of princes rather than against monarchy as such; an explicit distinction to that effect was added to the *Institution* of 1559.[37] In any case, all forms of government for Calvin are of divine institution; to condemn monarchy rather than monarchs would have been to condemn the divine handiwork. He may even have read the Old Testament as expressing a direct endorsement of monarchy as the form selected by God for the Chosen People,[38] although that form is a rather 'mixed' monarchy. The fault, then, is not in the form, but in the personnel, and 'human depravity is no reason for rejecting a divine institution'.[39] However, since monarchy is vulnerable to failings endemic in fallen human nature, Calvin's approval of monarchy in its uncorrupted form would have been perfectly compatible with a universal disapprobation of monarchy in this fallen world. In fact, a godly monarch would precisely not conduct himself like a monarch, and especially not an absolute one. But God's will had been announced, and all the arguments whose validity Calvin elsewhere recognized had therefore to founder on the rock of the duty of obedience.

Calvin had always (as we have seen) been unimpressed by the pretensions of absolutizing monarchs and their advocates. Furthermore, certain remarks of his indicate that he believed that rule by one was, strictly speaking, impossible.[40] All rulers, however much they might resent having peers or companions in power, perforce depend on counsellors, administrators and delegates as their 'eyes and hands',[41] and the trappings of autocracy can hardly conceal the reality that such dependence conveys power to the 'dependents'. In an aside of 1562 Calvin once remarked that 'rulers are check-mated (*mattez*) by their own officers'.[42] And again: 'All princes, good and bad, must have their "satellites" and administrators.'[43] And the condition of the people depends as much or more on the conduct of the subordinates as on that of their master. Why he described Nerva as a good king in this connection, when he failed to exercise proper control over his officers, is unclear.[44]

Literally, therefore, there is no such thing as rule by one man. But equally all forms of association were held by Calvin to demand a certain primacy, ideally that of a *primus inter pares*.[45] We have already seen that Calvin was prepared to allow considerable independence and authority to bishops (in the modern sense), provided they were ultimately answerable to the college or company of pastors, and there was once again no reason for not thinking the same about a civil *princeps*. Thus, in another aside which incidentally exhibits the familiar and extemporary style of Calvin's sermons, he contended that 'where there are kings, there must be officials as well; kings must have their council.[46] And even in republics there have to be *chefz*. Wherever there is a *compagnie* of people, there must be a council, for one man could not have power and breadth of vision enough to govern [sc. by himself]' – and it is for this reason that the devil attempts to 'pollute' councils by sowing envy and ambition.[47]

It should be understood here that the 'problem of counsel' – to adopt Hexter's terminology[48] – was a standard topic of humanist discourse.[49] In a nut-shell, the problem was that since humanists were disposed to favour princely rule, and since they were in no position to appoint princes themselves but had to make do with what they had, those princes who most needed good advice would not get it, or heed it if they did. Since Calvin at no time displayed any enthusiasm for princely rule, still less for centralizing monarchy, this was not strictly speaking his problem. But on the view we have attributed to him, all government must contain a monarchical as well as an aristocratic (and perhaps also a popular) component; what distinguishes monarchy from tyranny must therefore be some particular relationship between the *princeps* and his advisers. Thus, discoursing on the state of Israelite government under the tribe of Judah, he remarked off-handedly: 'In order to make the distinction between a legitimate government and tyranny, I acknowledge that counsellors were joined with the king, who should administer public affairs in a just and orderly manner.'[50] In another place, he asserted that nowadays things are quite different; instead of having 'upright ministers and counsellors' and taking notice of the advice of Jethro to Moses ('Thou shalt provide out of all the people able men such as fear God, men of truth hating covetousness; and place such over them to be rulers', Exodus 18.21), 'those who aid or pander to their lusts and who court and flatter them, are promoted by kings to honours and high rank. . .'[51] And it seems that when he meant to speak of monarchy, he referred to 'councils' and 'advisers', but when his subject was tyranny, he spoke of 'courts', 'courtiers' and 'flatterers'.

The courts of princes, then, were represented by Calvin as nests of ambition, hypocrisy, flattery and servility.[52] He singled out particularly the corruption of judges[53] and the venality of judicial office, as well as the advancement of the unworthy, as being the order of the day there. Advancement, if it is achieved, is no more than 'fetters of gold', and the sensible man is content with a private station, for 'there will be, I say, more liberty in many a poor man's house, than in those great pits, the courts of princes'.[54] He noted also a 'theology of the court', which prostitutes itself to the service of the powerful.[55] And in an addition to the *Institution* of 1559, he identified 'flatterers of princes' as one of the main threats to the *sinceritas fidei* in his time, the other being presumably Anabaptists and Libertines.[56]

Calvin does not appear to have seen any problem in ascertaining why courts of princes were as he supposed them to be. There was, at any rate in England, a tradition of explaining evils which went beyond (though it presupposed) moral condemnation, and More's *Utopia* is a fine product of this tradition, but if Calvin had any access to it, he did not reveal it.[57] His was rather the style of Erasmus,[58] where the preacher's work has been done once corruptions have been assigned to various vices. Consequently corruption at court would appear as simply a further instance of the ubiquity of depravity, more specifically of pride and ambition. There was then no reason to draw up a balance of culpability between courts and kings; but on the whole Calvin expressed himself at much greater length, and with much greater vehemence, about the latter, especially in the sermons, where one constraint on free speaking – the presence of kings in his audience – was absent.

There too, however, he did not get very far with the rhetorical question he once posed: 'Why is it,' he asked dramatically in 1555, 'that kings and princes seem to want to put their foot on the whole world's throat?' The answer followed at once and predictably: 'It's because of that pride which has poisoned their hearts.'[59] But he did not trouble himself further to trace the source of this poison. Sometimes he seemed inclined to attribute it to the education in vice received by children in royal families.[60] Sometimes he attributed it to lack of self-restraint in kings, a dangerously simplistic notion for a moralizer to employ in that it implied that the evils which bedevilled kingdoms might be repaired by a royal change of heart: 'Let kings rather learn from this history to bridle their own power (*potentia*) and to use their *imperium* with restraint; in short, to impose a voluntary law of moderation upon themselves.'[61]

It was unnecessary for him to go beyond condemnation of kings for their vices, for no obvious difficulties resulted from such a position. Calvin supposed that by far the greater part of men were reprobates and that the apparent civility of much human conduct is the product of hypocrisy. There was therefore little cause for surprise if princes too were mostly reprobates, and since in their case there was less reason for hypocrisy and more opportunities for sinning, it was only to be expected that they would openly avail themselves of them.[62]

What might have been expected in the light of what Calvin had said about ecclesiastical monarchy is some parallel discussion of civil monarchy. And fortunately for the case being advanced here, that is precisely what we find, and we find it, what is more, not hidden away at the back of a commentary, or in an unpublished sermon, but in an alteration to the already much-altered section 8 of book 4, ch. 20 of the *Institution* of 1559/60. For there, to the addition of 1543 already noted[63] Calvin added the explanation that the defect of monarchy was not in the form as such (*in se*), but rather because 'it rarely happens [and here the French version of 1560 added: 'and is almost a miracle (*quasi miracle*)'] that kings exercise such self-control[64] that their will never deviates from what is just and right, or that they are so equipped with sharpness of mind and prudence that they can discern by themselves all that is needful. On account of the vices and defects of men, therefore, it is safer and more tolerable that many should rule, so that each might be a help-mate to the others, each teaching and warning the others; and if anyone pushes himself forward unduly, there should be other censors and magistrates to repress his licentiousness.'[65] Much the same thing had been said in 1543 about the advantages of the collegial ministry: the use of the term *censores* about civil magistrates in this connection is particularly revealing.[66]

If we now turn from this formulation to the commentaries and sermons, it is perhaps not forced to see there a line of thought which is a little more rewarding than just another sermon on pride. The terms of the indictments persistently return to the theme of kings' unwillingness to be constrained; the charge of promoting flatterers of course tends in the same direction, since flatterers are the least constraining and molestatious species of advisers; they merely tell kings what they wish to hear. Thus Calvin insisted in public and private that the authority of the Old Testament kings was circumscribed within certain limits, but even the best kings did not keep to them: 'We know, of course, how insatiable are the desires (*cupiditates*) of kings: they imagine they can do what they like.' 'The wilfulness and pride of kings could scarcely be repressed by any constraint.'[67] As for kings in Calvin's own time, 'even subjection to the reign of Christ they deem an intolerable diminution of their rightful authority (*auctoritas*)'.[68] But all this is somewhat tame compared to the outbursts of the sermons. There he defined tyrants precisely in terms of an unwillingness to tolerate restraint: 'Tyrannus sola voluntate et libidine sua imperat.'[69] And he harked back to what he had already described as an opinion fit for tyrants thirty years before, the proverb *sit pro ratione voluntas*.[70] Kings act as if there were no law or rule that bound them.[71] 'They are so swollen up with pride, they think the world was made for no one but them.'[72] 'They want to be privileged beyond other men. They would like to be outside the ranks of mortals altogether.'[73] He compared them to mighty rivers, by whom subjects are more likely to be drowned than benefited.[74] He accused them of negligence and indifference where their duties were concerned,[75] of being anxious only for the extension of their power, of being 'vast, bottomless pits of extravagance'.[76] Their wars fill the land with widows and orphans, but to all that they are indifferent. When told of how many men have perished in a battle, their reply is 'let us have some more, then!'.[77] If reproached for their conduct, their reply is that 'they are princes and have *puissance* to act like this'.[78]

Perhaps because he attributed the desire for large states to the 'ambition', 'arrogance' and general intolerance of legitimate restraint of princes, or because of his attachment to the idea of a closely supervised, and therefore city-state sized polity combining *moderatio* with liberty, Calvin on occasion voiced marked hostility to large states, at that time monarchies almost by definition. Thus, in a long digression in the *Commentary on Isaiah* on the verse: 'Et rex fortis dominabitur eis' he wrote: 'We may also understand the meaning to be that the princes of smaller nations deal more humanely (*humaniores sunt, sont plus humains*) with their subjects than those who are more powerful. The latter, relying on their greatness, allow themselves to do what they please; for, reckoning their power (*potentia, puissance*) to be without limit (*nullum esse modum, infinie*), they set no bounds to their freedom of action, and rush on, without restraint, wherever their passions drive them.'[79] He went on to condemn the 'folly' of those who wish for a powerful king, dominating many countries (*dominant sur beaucoup de pays, multis ditionibus imperantem*), and cited the experience of those living in France and Spain to show how little profit the subjects derived from this 'honour'.[80] In the *Sermons on 1 Samuel*, he compared the wholesome restraint of 'princes with more restricted authority', and the consequent wealth of their subjects, with 'monarchs' (*monarchae*), devastating lands far and wide, wanting their will to count for a reason.[81] Finally, in a revealing misquotation of Augustine in the *Commentary on Genesis*, Calvin referred to 'the old proverb: great kingdoms are great robberies'.[82] Augustine's celebrated saying had made no mention of 'great' kingdoms: 'Remota Justitia, quid sunt regna nisi magna latrocinia?' and had gone on to say: 'Quia et latrocinia quid sunt nisi parva regna?'[83] but Calvin did not care to follow him. Great kingdoms, it seems, were for Calvin both a consequence of, and an opportunity for, wrong-doing by kings.

A 'CIVIL MANNER' OF RULING

Calvin, then, was disposed to see kings as typically intolerant of restraint. We must now seek to determine a little more narrowly what sort of restraints Calvin had in mind. The most simple answer would seem to be 'laws', and there are a number of passages were he sounds as if he were simply echoing the familiar tag: 'Rex debet esse sub Deo et sub lege'. Thus in the unpublished section of the *Sermons on Deuteronomy* of 1555 he asserted that 'the best state and the one to be desired most would be to have judges; that is to say, to be at liberty, and yet to have the laws to govern'.[84] In the (also unpublished) *Sermons on 1 Samuel*, he cited it as a particular mark of divine favour to the Chosen People that 'the magistrates themselves were subject to the laws.'[85] Elsewhere in the same catena, continuing the passage already quoted about the tyrannical saying, he said that even among kings 'those spoke a little more decently who admitted that they should live under the laws. And certainly it is arrogant beyond measure to say that one is subject to no laws; nonetheless that opinion was received by custom (*usu*) in the laws (*institutis*) of the Roman emperors.'[86] Similar sayings are common in writings published in Calvin's life-time which began as lectures (*leçons, praelectiones*). Thus in the *Lectures on the Prophet Jeremiah* of 1563 (delivered the previous year) Calvin asserted that kings 'want to be exempt from all law'.[87] And all of this is simply an echo of what he had said a score or more years before in his *De Clementia Commentary* about Roman law, the *princeps legibus solutus* and the *digna vox*.

Despite all this, Calvin's position is far from straight-forward. For one thing, Calvin's was not a 'common-law mind'[88] but that of a man brought up on Roman law, where the mutability of law is simply taken for granted,[89] and where consequently kings and magistrates cannot be said unequivocally to be subject to law, whatever the attraction of a 'government of laws, not of men'. In the second place, Calvin's use of the term 'law', despite his vaunted legal training, was not very much clearer than Luther's.[90] He did not, for example, always make it clear whether he was speaking of positive law (for which *statuta, constitutiones* would be contemporary equivalents) or of what Hooker called 'divine positive law', that is to say the Decalogue, or even of natural law (of which more in due course).

As to positive law, Calvin was in something of a quandary, as his musings of 1555 show.[91] There were in civil as in ecclesiastical matters those who believed 'that one must keep always and in all things to what is old: it even seems to them that one should be governed according to the laws and statutes of one's ancestors, and that nothing should be changed which has previously been thought good'. And to this Calvin offered the standard response of the humanist[92] with an alternative to the good old law to propose: 'if a thing is old and not good, being old simply augments the evil'. He then went on to narrow down considerably the scope of the radicalism implied in that assertion: 'But as for human laws, antiquity must be respected, so that nothing should be changed lightly or for the sake of change; otherwise everything would constantly have to be started all over again. One ought therefore to keep to the old laws as much as is possible, but when necessity demands a change, the Lord wishes us to use the means he has shown and delivered to us.'[93]

What Calvin in fact needed from the law was both mutability and fixity. The godly magistrate must be left room to eliminate relics of popery, and this may require legislative activity. Nor is he to be inhibited from making such new regulations as the Christian polity is seen to require from time to time. And contrary to Calvin's inclination to keep laws few and general, there seemed always to be some reason why Messieurs de Genève needed to be prompted to make more and more detailed ones, so as (in Calvin's favoured phrase) to 'mettre ordre a cela'. On the other hand, Calvin had a rooted aversion to all casual changing of laws, and his entirely conventional assumption was that *ceteris paribus*, the old laws are the best laws.[94] In any case, much of his work was to consolidate and defend such gains as the Reformation had already made. The position he actually adopted on the question quite lacked the relative clarity and economy of the distinction later made by Beza and Gentillet between *loix fondamentales* (immutable) and other sorts of law (mutable),[95] but it did illustrate the polemical advantages of leaving well alone. He simply relied on an undifferentiated 'Law of God' to shelter and preserve from change such laws as he considered desirable, and could thus quite comfortably speak about subjection of magistrates to law when the occasion demanded it. This left godly magistrates free to change objectionable laws, in such a manner as was compatible with prudence. And prudence dictated caution: 'les changements sont toujours a craindre'.[96] A certain ambiguity in his attitude to 'custom' was however inescapable. He could neither quite endorse a respect for *ancienneté*[97] nor quite reject it. In a revealing passage in the *Gospel Harmony* of 1555 he wrote: 'If a rule of a holy and pious life is *not always and in all places* to be sought from civil laws, much less ought we to seek it in custom.'[98] But in the *Commentary on Acts* of 1552, he had cited the proverb that 'custom is the father of prudence',[99] and he was prepared to accept both slavery and the succession of women to royal office because they were customary, although they violated natural law.[100] Sometimes and in some places, for example in godly Geneva, political laws could be looked to for a rule of conduct. Custom, on the other hand, is in principle unreliable. The reason for this attitude may ultimately be that since custom is made by people in general, and is therefore the product of vitiated human nature, it cannot have the authority of positive law, which is made by determinate individuals who may be identifiable as righteous. Or perhaps 'custom' was just an innocent bystander injured in the heavy evangelical shelling of *traditions humaines*.

Thus, when he made the distinction between tyrants and lawful magistrates, it was by no means always in terms of the insubordination of the former to the law and the subordination of the latter. Commenting on Nimrod, traditionally as well as for Calvin the prototype of tyrants, Calvin did not mention law at all. Rather, on his account, Nimrod (driven, need it be said, by ambition) replaced by tyranny a mode of governing which Calvin described in some enlightening terms: 'The condition of men at that time was one of rough equality (*mediocrem statum*), so that while some ranked higher than others, they nonetheless did not lord it over them (*dominarentur*)[101] or claim a regal *imperium* for themselves, but instead remained content with a certain measure of *dignitas*, ruled the rest in a citizen-like manner (*civilem modum*), and had more personal authority than might (*plus auctoritatis haberent quam potentiae*).'[102] The exegesis of these lines is made easier by the fact that the same terms recurred in the *Harmony of the Last Four Books of Moses*, where commenting on the celebrated words of institution of kingship (Deuteronomy 17.14–17), Calvin wrote that 'here the *potestas* of kings is circumscribed within certain[103] limits lest [the king], relying on the glory of *imperium*, should exalt himself beyond measure.' He continued: 'However splendid the dignity of kingship might be, God does not wish it to be a pretext for unlimited might (*immensae potentiae*), but restricts and restrains it *ad civilem modum*.'[104]

In both cases, as of course elsewhere,[105] *potentia*, which unequivocally means 'might', whether or not accompanied by right, is linked with *imperium*, the extensive power of an *imperator*, and contrasted with *potestas* and *civilis modus* of governance, greatly to the former's disadvantage. Calvin did not explain what he meant by a 'civil manner' of governing, but the allusion must be to *civis*, 'a citizen', and *civitas*, 'a republic', or 'citizenry'. Calvin's predilection for the republican form is once again at work. His meaning becomes even more apparent when we notice his marked, if qualified, distaste for the pomp and extravagance characteristic of monarchs. Genesis recounts the ornaments bestowed on Joseph by

Pharaoh, and this prompted in Calvin the characteristic question 'whether it was lawful for the holy man to appear with such great pomp?' He answered: 'Although such ostentation can scarcely ever be free from blame, and frugality in external ornaments is best, yet not every kind of magnificence in kings and other princes of the world is to be condemned . . .'[106] Councillors who have no choice in the matter he specifically excused: where the 'servants of God have a choice, nothing is safer for them than to eliminate whatever they can of outward splendour. And where they must accommodate themselves to public usage, let them beware of all ostentation and vanity.'[107] This seems to be an instance of that tendency in Calvin's thought whereby all distinctions of rank are flattened into insignificance by comparison with the awesome *maiestas* of God: whatever the importance of distinctions of rank in society, magistracy is an *officium* and *vocatio*, not generically different from any other.[108] All necessary distinctions are therefore ruthlessly functionalized, and pomp and circumstance have only a very restricted utility in this context, although it is impossible to exclude them altogether. They tend to be a derogation from God's *imperium*, and a citizen-like bearing, dignified yet modest, much better becomes a godly magistrate. The constraints to which Calvin wished magistrates to be subject, then, were religious and moral, and only secondarily legal.

He did not, however, deliberately reject law as a possible and desirable constraint on arbitrary activity by rulers, in exchange for the unsecured goodwill of magistrates (a genus which includes the species king)´ and to have done so would be incomprehensible in terms of the position which has here been attributed to him by 1542 at the latest. Rather, leaving monarchs free of law was an unlooked-for consequence of Calvin's concern to free godly magistrates, but not ungodly princes, to enact justice. It was simply that law, even when it was ancient law, was not an entirely reliable indicator of righteousness. But in some circumstances, that is to say when it suited him, Calvin could assume that certain sorts of laws ought to be considered immutable. A critical case in point is his argument for the rights of 'popular magistrates'.[109] Now why should resistance, including armed resistance and therefore civil war (in the case, for example, of the Holy Roman Empire), be considered tolerable, and indeed a duty? Because it is the action of magistrates and not of private men. But what makes the distinction between a private man and a magistrate? Here Calvin's thought trails off into obscurity, for on occasion he wrote as if anyone who had somehow got his hands on *potentia* became *ipso facto* a public man and entitled to obedience, for all is in the hands of God.[110] But clearly this is an instance where, pushed by his fear of private political initiatives, Calvin's doctrine of divine sovereignty and omnipotence tilted over into a kind of fatalism. His normal assumption was that a public man was one occupying an office and exercising powers (*potestates*) defined by a legal order; it is not the Law of God that defines a person as a prince of the blood, a popular magistrate or a member of an Estates General. And it is in virtue of the conformity of resistance by magistrates of this kind, public men, with the positive law, that such resistance is acceptable. The point was articulated in a much more sophisticated and clear manner by French disciples in the 1570s.[111] In the circumstances, the attribution of a 'constitutionalist' doctrine to Calvin himself is unwarranted but explicable.[112]

To sum up: Calvin's thought from 1542 onwards demonstrates a very clear but imperfect homology between the order of ecclesiastical and of civil polity, both as to what was clearly stated and what was left uncertain. There is an unmistakable preference for an aristocratic form with popular admixtures of sorts, and for small territorial units. Monarchy is explicitly rejected for ecclesiastical polity on scriptural grounds; in civil polity no such outright rejection was possible because of the earlier *parti pris* in favour of the divine authorization of all forms of government and Calvin's almost inflexible opposition to political resistance. Nonetheless, the animus against monarchs is clear enough, and civil monarchy remains a discrepant and disturbing element in an otherwise carefully synchronized arrangement of mutual constraints. Nowhere else in his thinking about organization did Calvin rely only on self-restraint, not even in the case of ministers, who, unlike princes (especially hereditary ones),[113] had at least been carefully selected and trained for their job.

8

Political morality in the thought of Calvin

We now know how Calvin wished the magistracy to be organized. But we are still left asking what exactly he wished magistrates to do. The first *Institution* described the office of magistrates in such a bland and abstract way that no fault would have been found with Calvin's account by Servetus, Castellio and most Anabaptists, let alone by papists and other evangelicals: 'to accommodate our lives to human fellowship, to shape our morals and conduct so that they may accord with civil justice,[1] to reconcile us one with another and to promote the common peace and tranquillity'.[2] But this formulation relies upon Lutheran external/internal, religious/civil distinctions which (as we have seen) had ceased to be adequate to Calvin's thought by 1542 at the latest. And at last, in the 1559 *Institution*, Calvin made additions which clarified what had long since been explicit in other writings. He prefaced the account of the 'appointed end' of magistracy just cited with: 'to cherish and protect the outward worship of God, to defend the sound doctrine of godliness (*pietas*) and the order and standing (*status*) of the church'.[3] In that edition he also went on to insist that the competence of magistrates extends to both tables of the Ten Commandments, that is, to the enforcement of *pietas* as well as *aequitas* and external righteousness.[4] And all this, too, would have been capable of a relatively uncontentious interpretation, but for the fact that Calvin was known to mean that persistent heretics and blasphemers should be punished by death.

It is, however, by no means the case that Calvin confined himself to such generalities, still less that he thought a theologian has nothing more than this to say about the life of a Christian polity. On the contrary, he thought that his descriptions of the business of governors (taken seriously) would commit the man of faith and piety to support for a whole range of very specific practices and arrangements, and that failure to subscribe to these was at the very least evidence of ignorance or deficiency in godliness. This disposition of his to link general moral maxims or pious slogans with highly specific modes of conduct presupposed a relationship between principle and practice, or slogan and practice, which Calvin never explained. As preacher and prophet, he did not concern himself with so abstruse a matter as the correct form of moral argument. As Chenevière says, he was no metaphysician. But no account of the laws and mores of the Calvinian Christian commonwealth is possible unless we consider what assumptions Calvin made about the proper form of moral, and therefore political, argument. For Calvin viewed the whole of *respublica* under the aspect of morality: what is crucial to governance is knowledge of what is right. That other sorts of knowledge and skill might also be requisite was a consideration which did not preoccupy Calvin, as will be seen.

The derivation of practical guidance from general maxims and principles, or conversely, the legitimation or condemnation of specific actions in terms of such general maxims and principles, is of course the substance of casuistry, an art and discipline prized equally by lawyers and scholastic theologians. On these counts alone, casuistry stood condemned before any evangelical with blood in his veins: it promotes distinctions such as those between venial and mortal sin, and between duties and works of supererogation, which to an evangelical appeared as a mere indulging of the inveterate human propensity to back-slide and to prefer one's own will to God's. Calvin (as has been seen) construed Christianity as an ethic of duty and obedience which demanded strenuousness; it was therefore no part of the office of a Christian pastor or prophet to make the moral life easy, which casuistry was all too likely to do. He was a most reluctant casuist.[5]

Instead, his exposition of morality moved upon two distinct planes. On one plane, what is at issue is the *ex post facto* identification of the universal characteristics of righteousness and piety as aspects of human conduct. It was here that Calvin was most at home. He would instance a tendency to promote the honour of God and his glory, *aedificatio* and *aequitas*, and would elucidate Christ's distillations of piety and righteousness: to love God and one's neighbour. These are, however, postscripts to morality: they enjoin no specific action, and no action or course of conduct can be derived from them even by inference, let alone deductively, without a great deal of additional and precise information.

As well as working on this plane, Calvin addressed himself to what may be termed practical moral questions, where the concern is with the conduct of the Christian in his specific circumstances, the choices to be made, the alternatives to be espoused or rejected, approved or reprobated. Evidently these two planes require to be linked in some way. But Calvin never identified them as distinct: he simply made connections without considering the abstract question of how such connections ought to be effected.

The simplest way for an evangelical to link the two planes of grand theological principle and the detail and circumstance of moral choices in actual life was to claim that Scripture itself teaches what is to be done in all the circumstances which the Christian encounters on his pilgrimage. And it is not implausible to regard Calvinian morality as supposing precisely this. We have seen that from his earliest writings as an evangelical onwards, Calvin regarded Scripture as containing a 'complete rule of life'.[6] Nor can there be any question that Calvinian morality is emphatically a morality of obedience, so much so that perfect obedience would obtain salvation;[7] such a possibility of course remains purely speculative in the condition of fallen man, but is actualized in Christ. And since the most straight-forward morality of obedience is one which demands simple adherence to a set of precise and detailed rules, it might be supposed that Calvinian morality was of this sort, with Scripture serving as the relevant legal code or book of rules.[8]

In fact, any simple legalistic morality of this sort was ruled out for Calvin in principle. His Lutheran tenets militated against it, for it was precisely Luther's, and before him Erasmus's complaint against the current understanding of the Christian life that is saw 'merit' in the performance of 'external' actions (so-called 'good works'), when goodness was really a matter of the spirit or intention which informed conduct. Indeed, the only reason why Calvin was capable of asserting that Scripture contains a 'complete rule of life' was that he never supposed scriptural morality to be, or to be no more than, a set of rules to do or to forbear. For one thing, Scripture contains a large number of rules which Calvin *did not* regard as binding, namely those consigned to the capacious receptacle of the *passé* which Calvin termed 'ceremonies'.[9] For another, Scripture, as Calvin interpreted it, yielded copious condemnations of luxury, intemperance, ambition, concupiscence, selfishness and other vices, but left the referents of these condemnations somewhat unspecific. The Decalogue, furthermore, contains no explicit prohibition of drunkenness, lying, rebellion, sodomy, cruelty to humans or animals, or even fornication. (This did not, of course, inhibit Calvin from finding a location for such prohibitions even within the Decalogue – by implication – let alone in the surrounding pasturage of amplificatory moral legislation.) But the most significant injunctions to be found in Scripture, as far as Calvin was concerned, were precisely those at the 'theological' level: imperatives to 'avoir la gloire [or 'l'honneur'] de Dieu en recommandation', to love God and one's neighbour, and so forth. A rule of life need not be a lawbook, and if Calvin's thinking did tend in the direction of reading Scripture in that way, it was not that Calvin wished to go down that road, but that he was drawn.

To elaborate a little: there were two dangers to be avoided, and Calvin's thought was, as it were, an attempt to steer between them. On the one side there is legalism, where what is prized is simple conformity to rules. As serious, or more serious, is the antinomian alternative, where rules are considered altogether irrelevant, provided the spirit which animates conduct is right. This was one of the current Anabaptist heresies against which Calvin fought to the end of his days.[10] And the whole evangelical inheritance, especially as regards 'ceremonies', 'forms' and 'externals', made this something to be reckoned with: its foundations in the evangelical tradition were laid very deep.

Since there was no controversy with anyone except papists concerning the requirement of a godly spirit as a *sine qua non* of righteous conduct,[11] Calvin's problem was to demonstrate that such a spirit habitually (though not invariably) expresses itself in a righteous man's conforming to strict rules. Why this was

Calvin's problem has been set out elsewhere, but the reasons may be summarized briefly here. First, Calvin was committed to the view that the 'external' laws of the church do not 'bind the conscience', but that they impose a moral obligation nonetheless. Secondly, it was his profound conviction that no church can stand without laws, and arrangements to enforce them. Conversely, the disciplinary proceedings of the church must be of a quasi-judicial sort, which presupposes that there are specific rules to be enforced. Where there is no rule, there can be no offence. Later, he added the view that affronts to the honour of God must be repressed and punished in order to avert the wrath of God. This too required judicial, or quasi-judicial proceedings, and therefore rules. By contrast, the spirit which animates conduct is only to a very limited degree open to the inspection of the civil authorities, although Calvin's writings equivocate about whether the church has any greater competence in the inspection of souls than have magistrates.[12] Public proceedings must therefore be concerned with the external characteristics of actions, in other words, with their conformity or non-conformity to rules. Finally, the wafer-thin argument that 'ceremonies' do not bind the conscience vanishes altogether when the ceremonies themselves were what was at issue in religious controversy.[13] Ceremonies, after all, both presuppose and reinforce belief.

On each of these counts, the Christian's duty must be proved to lie in a conformity to rules; a willing conformity certainly, but a conformity nevertheless. Now such rules may be many and detailed, or alternatively they may be few and general, with their interpretation left to a body of censors. The latter alternative was vastly preferable to Calvin, both because he saw the content of morality as unproblematic and because nothing was more antipathetic to him than legal wranglings, niceties and chicaneries, all of which perforce increase in direct proportion to the complexity of the legal code in force. But much as he might have preferred simple blanket rules, interpreted by a reliable and austere body of censors, it became necessary to defend proceedings and verdicts whenever these were called into question, and in so doing to specify more precisely what was being defended. The punishment of heretics, permitted Christian names, laws governing dress, ornament and consumption, the law and discipline of marriage, all illustrate this tendency for the regulations of the godly polity to become ever more detailed.

How then did Calvin habitually link theological maxims and detailed regulation? It seems that his moral and therefore also his political arguments are variations on the familiar Aristotelian 'practical syllogism'.[14] The first has the form:

Major Premise: A general imperative demanding a certain disposition in conduct: to honour God, love our neighbour, build up the church, etc.

Minor Premise: A statement that in specific circumstances, a certain kind of conduct (C) is harmonious with, or demanded by, the general imperative.

Conclusion: In the circumstances specified, do C.

The second has the form:

Major Premise: In all circumstances of type A, the Christian's duty is to do X.

Minor Premise: This is a circumstance of type A.

Conclusion: Do X.

Only the second of these types of argument is at all promising for the moral rigorist. A syllogism of the first sort offers little hope of a precise instruction for conduct (or of legitimation of things already done, for the reasoning is the same). In the first place, the number of minor premises which Scripture may be deemed to yield is limited only by the ingenuity of the exegete, leaving the practical inference an open one. What is more, the major premise enjoins a disposition, not a determinate sort of conduct. But the same disposition may be conjoined with the most diverse and contradictory range of actions: mercy-killing may be killing out of love; obedience to God may entail either cherishing a wife or child, or slaying them, as in the case when they prove false prophets and dreamers of dreams,[15] or in the case of Abraham and Isaac.[16] Finally, various descriptions of the circumstances in which one finds oneself are in principle always possible: for example, 'I may get myself killed here, and then who'll look after my wife and children?'; or: 'This is the threshold of immortality'; or: 'My condition now is precisely like that of the three young men in the fiery furnace', and so on *ad infinitum*. Various courses of conduct may therefore legitimately count as appropriate in the same set of circumstances.

In the second type of argument, by contrast, if the major premise is made inclusive (or alternatively, precise) enough (for example, 'Thou shalt not suffer a witch – or heretic – to live'), the only difficulties that remain are those of determining the appropriateness of the specified crime (witchcraft, heresy) as a description of the matter at hand, and of excluding other possible descriptions. The problems of arriving at rock-hard imperatives (or, equally, iron-clad legitimations for duty performed) seem to be sensibly diminished, especially given evangelical polemical techniques such as alluding to the 'analogy of faith' or the *germanus* (or *genuinus*) *sensus* of the whole of Scripture, and making *ad hominem* references to the dissentient's state of soul. Calvin's personal refinement of these techniques, or contribution to the staple, was to exclude a whole range of minor premises which might be offered by counterposing merely human opinion and sentiment[17] with the inflexible requirements of the 'glory of God' or the Christian duty of obedience regardless of cost. If an evangelical was moved to offer resistance to those imprisoning or tormenting or threatening with death himself, his family and his fellows, he was told that the eternal command of God is that 'we must possess our souls in patience'.[18] If it was claimed that matters of faith and doctrine were not proper subjects for civil punishments, the retort was that the glory of God required it.[19]

Given controversy and the need to defend his precepts and conduct, Calvin was constantly pushed into arguments of the second form, which alone promised to establish the incontestable righteousness of what was done or advocated. The need to choke off any movement in an antinomian direction worked in the same way.[20] And Calvin's life was beset by controversy, opposition, hostility and reproach. Even when the leading faction hostile to him at Geneva, the 'Perrinists', had been suppressed in 1555, Calvin still had to contend with the hostility of the Bernese, of anti-trinitarians and anti-predestinarians,[21] of Lutherans,[22] of exiles, papists, 'Libertines' and 'Nicodemites' (i.e. evangelicals inclined to conformity under papism). It was the need to cope with such opposition and hostility which fuelled the movement towards legalism.

The propensity to minimize the significance of the gap between general imperative and specific conduct, by insisting that it was bridged by Scripture itself, ran riot in Calvin's ecclesiology, where ever more precise detail of ecclesiastical organization was discovered in Scripture. But in questions of *respublica*, in so far as the legal or magisterial ordering of the church was not at issue, Calvin explicitly announced in all editions of the *Institution* that while the general duty of magistrates to secure *aequitas* and *humanitas* was invariable, the laws and arrangements needed to secure them varied with the circumstances of particular commonwealths.[23]

It is therefore tempting, and not altogether without support in Calvin's own writings, to tidy up Calvin's thought by constructing out of it a neat parallelism or homology to the following effect: in virtue of Calvin's explicit and repeated description of both pastorate and magistracy as *ministerium*, it follows that both pastors and magistrates are agents acting under instructions from their principal, who is, of course, God and not 'the people', whether as the *vox Dei* or in any other authorizing capacity. In Old Testament times, God's agents sometimes received his Word directly from his lips, but today neither ministers nor magistrates have any such privileged access: the terms of their commission may be found only in Scripture and in the natural law respectively, the magistrates' duty being identified by Calvin as that of enforcing *aequitas* and *humanitas*, both recognizably natural law concepts. Of course Scripture also has much to offer magistrates. But Scripture leaves to magistrates rather more freedom than it does to the church, which is subject to divinely revealed laws governing its organization and conduct in very considerable detail.[24] By contrast, magistrates are left free to devise such laws and arrangements as they judge expedient within the limits of natural law, except of course *in sacris*, where they are bound as much as ministers by divine law.

There is a pleasing symmetry about this image of God's governance by way of agents constrained respectively by divine law and natural law. It receives further support from other analogies between the constitution of civil and ecclesiastical polity which have already been noticed. And certainly Calvin's references to natural law are not occasional or peripheral; on the contrary, they occur in most of the places where moral questions are treated. Although lists are tiresome, it is necessary to offer some illustration of the range of moral questions on which Calvin took natural law to deliver rules of conduct, and the sometimes surprisingly specific character of those deliver-

ances. Thus Calvin thought that 'nature' or 'natural sense'
or 'reason' teaches the authority of fathers over wives and
children,[25] the sanctity of monogamous marriage,[26] the duty
to care for families,[27] breast-feeding,[28] primogeniture (albeit
with qualifications)[29] the sacrosanctity of envoys and ambassadors,[30] the obligation of promises,[31] degrees of marriage,[32]
the need for witnesses in murder trials,[33] the need for a distinction of ranks in society;[34] and natural law prohibits incest,[35]
murder,[36] adultery,[37] slavery,[38] and even the rule of one man.[39]
And again, nature itself teaches the duty to award honours
only to those qualified,[40] respect for the old,[41] equity in
commercial dealings[42] and that religion must be the first
concern of governors.

Apart from such specific provisions, Calvin also in various
places committed himself to more general assertions. Thus in a
sermon in 1555 he wrote: 'seeing that that which is naturally
followed in all the world is approved by the mouth of God';[43]
he described 'nature' as the 'ordinary law of God';[44] he
asserted that 'what is natural cannot be abrogated by either
consent or custom'[45] and again that 'the law of nature cannot
be abolished by men's vices'.[46] He conceded a natural knowledge of good and evil[47] which is 'imprinted by nature on men'[48]
or 'inscribed', 'engraven'.[49] And the general assertions of the
1536 *Institution*, as bolstered and extended in 1539, were
allowed to stand in the last edition. It is there that we find
perhaps the most unguarded of all Calvin's pronouncements
on the subject: 'since it is evident that the Law of God which
we call moral is nothing else than the testimony of natural law
and of the conscience which God has engraved on the minds of
men, the whole of this *aequitas* of which we are now speaking
is prescribed in it. Hence it alone ought to be the aim, the rule,
and the end of all laws' (4.20.15). The *lex moralis* mentioned
had just been explained as part of the whole law of God,
delivered to Moses (4.20.14). Nor was this an isolated aberra-
tion: Calvin also referred elsewhere to an 'internal law'
(2.8.1), and particularly mentions that men have a 'somewhat
better [natural] understanding of the contents of the second
table of the Decalogue, as being more closely connected with
the preservation of civil society among men' (2.2.24).

References to natural law, then, are not confined to any one
part of Calvin's life or work or to any one issue, nor are they

peripheral or casual, even if deficient in precision. It can therefore hardly be denied that Calvin believed that there was a natural order of moral laws to be discerned, and that men did discern it, at least when it did not cross their interests. What is controversial is not this, but the force he attached to assertions of this sort, the weight he was prepared to rest on them. And what diminishes the impressiveness of this array of allusions (which might have been extended) is that Calvin never allowed to natural knowledge of the moral law any independent adequacy as a guide to moral conduct for Christians; it was always treated as an inferior adjunct to the written divine law,[50] and as unreliable (2.2.24–6). The polemical intent of references to natural law was also often only too obtrusive: it was to hammer Anabaptists for their literalism, or to account for the undeniable elements of soundness in the morality of the pagans[51] (whose philosophers, and especially Plato, Calvin continued to read and quote). But perhaps the main purpose served by such assertions in the *Institution* was as a way of defending the justice of God's reprobating and punishing those who have no access to Scripture: they are condemned in their own consciences in that, knowing what is good, they do what is evil.[52] A weakness of such arguments was that they could not account for the reprobation and 'punishment' of children, especially that entailed by the vengeance upon whole cities and peoples to which the God of the Old Testament was much given.[53]

But even apart from this, natural law was systematically being ground into insignificance between the upper millstone of divine law and the nether millstone of positive law. The authoritativeness of the latter was assured in ordinary circumstances, if somewhat indirectly, by the assumption that rulers will operate by laws, and by the insistence that rulers are to be obeyed. In so far as any more reliable touchstone for the authenticity of their laws was required, this was to be found in divine law, which Calvin understood as unequivocal. Having set to work, Calvin found himself able to extract from Scripture more and more detail about the form and content of positive law. By 1555 he had found (at least for the purposes of sermons to the Genevans) not only scriptural warrant for his and Messieurs' predilection for expedition in legal proceedings, but also a scriptural requirement that there be an appeals procedure.[54] In 1562 and for the same audience, he found biblical support for the institution of circuit-judges and for the requirement that every subject have easy and proximate access to justice.[55] It is related that in one of the endemic disputes between ministers and magistrates about the Consistory, the scriptural verse 'Go and announce it to my People, go into the house of the King' was deemed to invalidate the demand of Messieurs that before any sensitive matter was treated in the pulpit, it should first be cleared with Messieurs, since this would violate the scriptural order.[56] However, natural law said nothing about ecclesiastical tribunals or condign punishment for persistent heretics, or about women wearing their hair loose, or about embroidered shirts, gold and silver chains and bracelets, or about the number of courses to be served at banquets. Conversely, those matters on which it was unambiguous were not contentious. It was not disputed at Geneva, or amongst evangelicals, or even between the latter and papists, that theft, murder, breach of contract, incest, fornication, false witness and sedition were moral enormities liable to civil punishment.

Perhaps the only contentious issues on which Calvin was prepared to call upon the oracle of natural law and *naturalis sensus* were the suppression of blasphemy and heresy, and the death-penalty for adultery. Calvin first made use of the former to justify the execution of Servetus; he was plainly on the defensive for adopting a policy which he condemned in papists, indeed for doing the papists' work for them,[57] and had no New Testament support except of the most forced and laboured kind. Under these circumstances he was prepared to adduce the *sensus naturae* as dictating 'that in every well-ordered polity, religion must have pride of place and is to be preserved intact under the supervision of the laws, as even unbelievers confess'.[58] An assertion to the same effect found its way into the 1559 *Institution* (4.20.9). But this was fairly feeble stuff with which to justify the death-penalty among Christians, and it was quite peripheral to the main theme of the 'glory of God'.

As to the death-penalty for adultery, Calvin's position was both ambiguous and curious. Pfisterer,[59] citing Beza's *Vita*, is probably correct in his assertion that there was no execution for simple adultery in Geneva in Calvin's time, but this says much about the attitude of Messieurs and nothing about

Calvin's. He repeatedly urged the PC to greater severity against adultery and fornication and made much of the so-called *estuves*, a kind of public bath frequented, it would appear, by members of both sexes. Even his interdiction of all dancing was because he saw it as 'nothing but preambles to fornication'.[60] In all matters of sexuality Calvin's statements suggest a basic contempt and loathing for a business invariably pollutant and shameful, the grossness of which could be decently 'covered over', but not effaced, by the remedy of matrimony.[61] Adultery, as the voluntary espousal of such pollution in its least pardonable form, merited the utmost severity. Accordingly, commenting on the Seventh Command-ment, Calvin said: 'By the universal law of the Gentiles, the punishment for adultery was always death; wherefore it is all the more base and shameful in Christians not to imitate at least the heathens. Adultery is punished no less severely by the *lex Julia* than by the Law of God.'[62] And in similar vein, but more opaquely, he wrote in the *Commentary on Genesis*:

The law of God commands adulterers to be stoned. Before this punishment was set down in written law, the adulterous woman was, by the consent of all, committed to the flames. It is established that this was done by a divine instinct, under the direction and teaching of nature, so that the sanctity of marriage might be defended as by a strong guard . . . How much more vile and how much less excusable is our negligence nowadays, which cherishes adulteries by allowing them to go unpunished. Capital punishment, indeed, is considered too severe for the measure of the offence. Why then do we punish lighter faults with greater rigour? Truly the world was bewitched by Satan when it suffered a law implanted in all by nature to become obsolete.[63]

What is curious about this is that the penalties for sins/crimes in the Old Testament are classed by Calvin under 'political supplements', that is to say, provisions expressly intended for God's Chosen People, and in principle abrogated. What is more, natural law in the form of *aequitas* regards the end which law is to aim at, and not the level of punishment, which Calvin had expressly left to the discretion of governors in the *Institution* (4.20.15). He was of course also immediately in difficulty with John 8.7 and 11: 'He that is without sin amongst you, let him cast the first stone', and 'Neither do I condemn you', and his attempts to explain away these sayings of Jesus to the woman taken in adultery are amongst the most tortuous pieces of exegesis in the whole Calvinian corpus. [64] In other words, since the New Testament here gave no support to Calvin's case at all, but rather the contrary, and since his case was plainly out of harmony with the opinion of most of his contemporaries, any assistance was welcome.

In sum, references to natural law served Calvin as partial justification for God's reprobation of those who had no access to Scripture; it was incidental confirmation of what was more adequately stated in divine law; and it served as a polemical weapon against those who appealed to reason against Calvin's interpretation of Scripture, or to Scripture against Calvin's notions of what was reasonable. There is no question of any serious examination of the idea of natural law: Calvin never clearly specified the manner in which it is apprehended, but merely referred to the 'heart' or the 'intellect' or the 'conscience', and on occasion to 'natural sense' and 'reason'. His appeal to the consent of the ages, or of the Gentiles, to specific articles of the natural law was equally unconcerned with the difficulties of this type of argument. All of which points to the entirely secondary importance of natural law within his thought; he had, in any case, sound theological reasons for doubting the capacity of fallen man for any worthwhile knowledge about God or about the 'rule of righteousness' out of his own unaided resources.

In the light of these remarks, we may perhaps dispose of the outworn issue of whether Calvin was or was not a proponent of theocracy. [65] If we are to make any sense of a term which in any case was not Calvin's or his century's, we must suppose it to mean the ideal of a commonwealth governed in accordance with the will of God. In that sense there are few sixteenth-century writers, and no evangelicals at all, who cannot be described as theocrats. Again, if by 'theocracy' we mean the belief that the authority of governors derives from God rather than (say) the consent of the governed [66] or the antiquity of the established order, then Calvin was a particularly extreme theocrat, who did not even allow that the authority of governors comes from God mediately; more precisely, he was indifferent about the manner in which political power was obtained, and saw the hand of God in the establishment and fall of princes and politics. [67] The only relevant question is whether Calvin's theocratic view of polity was of a biblicist sort; in other words, whether he abandoned the respect for antiquity, for prudence in governors, and for the capacity of reason and experience which normally qualified theocratic doctrines of polity, in favour of Scripture as the only means of access to the will of God, in accordance with which the commonwealth is to be governed. And no unequivocal answer to this question emerges from Calvin's writings. Since experience, conscience, natural law and custom are reliable guides to the will of God only when tutored by Scripture, they are all capable of being construed as redundant for the Christian; on the other hand, they provide enough moral knowledge to enable pagans to sustain a semblance of civility and to condemn them in their own consciences, and may also be treated as supplementary political resources for the Christian.

Since natural law is thus neither a necessary nor a sufficient guide for magistrates in their performance of their duty, the parallelism suggested earlier between a ministry subject to scriptural law and enforcing it upon their congregations, and a magistracy subject to natural law and enforcing that by positive law, must be abandoned as too neat and unequivocal a statement of Calvin's views. But equally, the strictly clerocratic view of the magistracy as ideally a mere agency of a divine will authoritatively expounded to it by the ministry was never explicitly announced by Calvin, even though it seems to follow from two doctrines he certainly did entertain: namely, that divine *lex scripta* is the only infallible guide to the will of God, and that the ministers are the authorized expositors of its contents. Indeed, while Calvin claimed to derive a great deal that was specific and detailed in the way of arrangements and policies from Scripture, he felt no need to demonstrate the scriptural provenance of every item in the Genevan polity of which he approved, and (as we have already seen) he offered no image of an ideal commonwealth to the world. And on at least two matters of consequence to him, he went so far as to deny that there was any certain rule to be derived from Scripture: concerning who was to be involved in the appointment of ministers[68] and concerning ornaments.[69] This harmonizes nicely with our previous references to Calvin's distaste for detail in legislation.

A tentative suggestion may be ventured to account for

Calvin's unwillingness to close the gap between general moral and spiritual imperatives and the detailed implementation of a *Sittenpolizei*. An extrapolation from various asides and incidental remarks suggests a practical recognition on Calvin's part that the bare Word is by no means all that the statesman needs for the performance of his duty.[70] Having granted himself a licence for not concerning himself with matters of this kind,[71] Calvin preferred to moralize about the duty of magistrates to have Christ rule over them,[72] to be indeed *patres patriae*,[73] rather than to inventorize the equipment they needed for their office. But he did make some interesting remarks in passing. Thus he considered that civil government was a skill or craft, an *ars; ex vi termini* he had to concede that it was comparable to, and part of, the 'liberal arts and sciences', an aptitude for which was a gift of God serving 'the common use and convenience of life', and which, moreover, 'have come down to us from the pagans'.[74] In several places, where his subject was St Paul's apparent condemnation of 'human wisdom', Calvin went out of his way to qualify such condemnations and to exempt from them a number of skills which are of interest to us: 'Who will not extol with the highest praises that civic prudence by which republics, principalities and kingdoms are sustained?'[75] Paul does not condemn (he insisted) 'that natural perspicacity . . . or prudence, gathered by practice (*usu*) and experience, or the cultivation of the mind which is furnished by letters. Let us note, therefore, that we must restrict what Paul here teaches about the vanity of worldly wisdom to the circumstances of the particular matter at hand.'[76] And elsewhere in the same commentary he said vaguely that 'prudence is sometimes given a kind of intermediate status between knowledge (*scientia*) and wisdom (*sapientia*): [it is] skill at turning knowledge to some practical use'.[77] Painting with a somewhat broader brush in the *Institution* (from 1539 onwards), he asserted that 'we have one kind of understanding (*intelligentiam*) of earthly things, but another of heavenly things . . . Of the former sort are governance (*politia*), the management of households (*oeconomia*), all the mechanical arts and the academic disciplines (*disciplinae liberales*; 2.2.13 ff.). His point here, however, was not to praise the capacities that remain to fallen men, but rather to show, while admitting them, that they fail precisely in those matters which are of ultimate concern. Nor, of course, was he seeking to enquire into the various kinds of knowledge and skill required in a governor, but rather to combat the anti-intellectualism not uncommon among sectarians.[78] And in any case, we have already seen general grounds for considering distinctions between celestial and terrestrial, civil and religious, external and internal, as insecurely based in Calvin's theology. In the passage cited, for example, 'heavenly things' includes 'the rule of ordering life in accordance with the will of God', a notion capable of indefinite extension. Even so, Calvin's caveats demonstrate an assumption that governance requires skills and gifts other than those of a competent familiarity with Scripture. When it suited his purpose, however, he could write off examples of prudent conduct as merely that 'carnal sagacity' usual amongst 'politic men'.[79] In a published sermon, he referred to 'ma dame la prudence charnelle'.[80]

All this suggests that unless distracted by polemic, Calvin was content to admit that it was one thing to make a law, another to apply it wisely and justly (a view explicit in the *De Clementia Commentary*), and also that more is involved in lawmaking, let alone governing in general, than merely looking up the relevant pattern in Scripture. And if this was what he was taking for granted, it explains why Calvin left a certain latitude and freedom of action to both magistrates and ministers.

The business of magistrates, to sum up, is to enforce both justice and godliness. Even without Scripture, men know (according to Calvin) that the honour of God and the care of religion are the principal duties of government, but without the light of Scripture they know nothing whatever about true religion or the right honour and worship of God. As to external justice and righteousness, its content is to some extent known from natural law, but it is known much more precisely and unmistakably from Scripture. But Calvin did allow that there is a certain gap between the imperatives of Scripture and the knowledge of what is to be done in a particular time and place. And this gap, he thought, must be filled by a godly spirit and prudence.

9

The laws and mores of a Christian commonwealth

It is now time to consider what specific measures and policies Calvin sheltered under the general labels and maxims that served him for his description of the magistrates' office. As we have seen, the connection between principle and practice was not explicated by Calvin. And, to anticipate the results of the investigation, it appears that Calvin entertained a set of perfectly conventional views about the conduct of government and the practices and mores of a well-ordered commonwealth. Indeed, as has been 'discovered' in study after study, almost all the laws and arrangements supposed to be distinctively Genevan and Calvinian prove to have had their parallels elsewhere, amongst Romanists as well as evangelicals, and both contemporaneously and in previous centuries. What was distinctive about Geneva and about Calvin's conception of the laws of a godly commonwealth is neither the content of these laws nor their theocratic orientation, but the rigour and impartiality with which these laws were enforced at Geneva, and the single-mindedness and lack of concession to current practice with which the organization of the church and the practice of pastors and magistrates were directed to its end.

Calvin could of course hardly have been unaware that his opinions on 'moral' matters were in most respects conventional, albeit peculiarly strict and severe, at any rate amongst godly men; but their conventionality or otherwise was an entirely secondary consideration for him. What counted, as far as his official doctrine was concerned, was their conformity with Scripture. On the other hand, he did not see it as any part of the business of a prophet or an evangelical theologian and pastor to reveal novelties: his task was to remind people of what they ought to know already. Had it not been for the exigencies of polemic, he might very well have emphasized the conventionality of his views, and indeed made a virtue of it. As it was, he usually acknowledged such conventionality in a dismissive fashion: 'even profane men know . . .', 'our enemies themselves admit . . .'.

What Calvin expected from magistrates, and what to a not inconsiderable extent he obtained at Geneva, was that they should use the distinctive resources which God had placed at their disposal in order to punish the wicked, uphold and protect the good and prevent the corruption of the weak. Calvin was prepared to acknowledge (what Luther had been at pains to stress) that a range of benefits from the magistrates' actions redounded to the wicked, and in fact to distinguish between the requirements of merely secular association and those of godliness. But the wicked were not his concern or that of his intended audiences, and furthermore he persistently supposed that sound polity and godliness pointed to the same policies. Nor did he dissociate sin and crime in his later years any more than he had done in the *De Clementia Commentary*. In short, his view was that the business of magistrates is to enforce virtue.

That this was indeed his view is obscured only by the fact that he did not think that true righteousness can be enforced. For it was an especial point of emphasis of his theology that not even the most perfect compliance with a body of laws, however complete their conformity with divine law, suffices to make a man righteous, since God regards the heart rather than the outward form of the act. As he sometimes expressed it, secular law and punishment 'do not touch the heart'.[1] This, however, cannot be said to be a particularly felicitous way of stating what he meant, and the doctrine of election and justification by faith and not by any external work seems to be making for confusion. For Calvin not only fully approved the Genevan magistracy's propensity to equip its laws and edicts with sententious preambles and glosses,[2] and took it for granted that it was entirely appropriate to urge on magistrates their duty to see to the piety and virtue of the citizenry by means of laws and directives; he also, on one occasion, contrasted the modern practice of peremptory royal commands with the greater civility of Israelite rulers in giving grounds to their subjects for the laws that they were imposing.[3] The point in all these instances would appear to be precisely to touch hearts, and there seems to be no more reason to deny a capacity to do so to laws and magisterial activity than there is to deny it to persuasive speech, of the virtue of which Calvin was fully convinced.[4] On occasion Calvin expressed himself more cautiously.[5]

The distinction between 'external', or 'civil', and 'true' righteousness, and equally between external and true piety, might be thought conducive to the conclusion that neither virtue nor piety ought to be the concern of governors. It is possible to construe Castellio as saying just that.[6] And the denial that magistrates were entitled to 'force consciences',[7] a denial common amongst evangelicals, tends in the same direction. But this is not what Calvin concluded, as is apparent from his propensity to see divine law as the model for human law. We have seen him concerned to assert that a godly spirit, a spirit of election, ordinarily manifests itself in a willing performance of duties specifiable in detail. The difference between the righteous and the unrighteous and hypocritical lies not in what they respectively do – in a well-ordered commonwealth, non-compliance with duty is a costly and painful alternative to compliance – but in the spirit in which they do it. Consequently the righteous are in no way harmed or inhibited by having virtue commanded as law, the views of the unrighteous on the matter do not have any standing at all, and the weaker brethren are, in Calvin's view, aided in their striving for sanctification by the elimination of stumbling-blocks to godliness of life. And in a sense all the elect are weaker brethren: the striving for sanctification is not crowned with final success in this life. Coercion by magistrates, from this point of view, can be looked on as an aid to sanctification, and Calvin did so look on it.

Since the church's *potestates* do not include coercion (as we have seen, Calvin did not interpret public reprimand and humiliation as coercion), the church is – in principle – permanently debarred from making or enforcing laws. In consequence, the legal establishment of ecclesiastical institutions, especially the pastorate and the Consistory, the expulsion or execution of persistent and impenitent heretics, the chastisement of deriders of the ministry and the Word, of contemners of piety and of those of scandalous immorality of life, diplomatic and military

activity to relieve hard-pressed brethren abroad and to defend
reformation at home, the public mobilization of resources for
ecclesiastical and charitable works such as the payment of
ministers, teachers and officials, and public institutions for the
relief of distress, are all activities which would be either quite
frustrated or severely handicapped without the use by the
magistracy of its particular sorts of powers. Calvin's view, like
that of most of his evangelical and Romanist contemporaries,
was that these were proper, indeed divinely ordained, functions
of magistracy and aids to godliness. Such things cannot, indeed,
make anyone righteous, for only the will of God can do that,
but they are capable of serving as aids to sanctification. Another
parallelism in Calvin's thought seems to be at work here.
Ecclesiastical discipline cannot make men righteous either,
but this in no sense restricts its competence as an agency which
facilitates the task of sanctification.[8] Civil 'discipline' (a term
which Calvin used in this connection)[9] works in precisely the
same way, albeit with different and ultimately inferior implements: being concerned with 'externals', the law and the
magistracy are more easily satisfied.[10]

It follows that it would be erroneous to attribute to Calvin
an interpretation of magistracy as exclusively a repressive and
punitive agency. Repression and punishment of course have
their place: godliness of life does not come naturally, so to
speak, to fallen men. But 'discipline' is not concerned merely
with repression: it is both 'bridle' and 'spur'.[11] Indeed, the
metaphor of a bridle (a favourite with Calvin ever since the
De Clementia Commentary) is itself congenially ambiguous, for a
bridle serves not only to restrain but also to guide. Punishment
can be understood in the same way. Fear, too, can be a road to
righteousness.[12] In a word, and one that Calvin used for this
purpose, the office of magistrates is to participate in *aedificatio*,
though primarily in a ground-clearing capacity. And the final
edition of the *Institution* made this point in its very structure.
Whereas in previous editions Calvin had been obliged to
content himself with leaving the cooperation of ministers and
magistrates in the performance of God's work in the world as a
mere desideratum justified by the divine institution of magistracy, the 1559/60 edition treated both church and government
as 'external media' whereby the grace of God is distributed to
the world, and it dealt with both of them in the same book

(book 4). This was the only edition with whose arrangement Calvin professed himself satisfied.[13]

Here, the doctrine of predestination once again confused everything. It not only involved Calvin in interminable defences of a distinction by comparison with which those of the scholastics seem simple and lucid, namely that between necessity and compulsion, but it also entirely undermined the notion of desert which Calvin nonetheless needed to justify the ways of God to man. On his account, malefactors deserve damnation, but doers of good do not deserve salvation, so that the ways of God on this interpretation remain those of an arbitrary tyrant, a remark which cost Bolsec dear. Ultimately, indeed, the predestinarian doctrine undermined the very concept of human agency, and in a rather peculiar way: it undermined the capacity of the godly for agency, while the wicked seemed to remain capable of it. For while the ungodly have a will, which is their will, and which they do, the godly are God's perfectly serviceable instruments; the more godly they are, the less they are anything but instruments.

But even if Calvin was theologically committed to this account of things, according to which grace is not so much a thing offered as a torrent sweeping all before it, a much less passive and more voluntarist interpretation of man's response to God and to grace is appropriate to the pastoral ministry, the sermon and the exercise of discipline, and equally to the activities of the magistrates. From that perspective, a rather more papist approach is indicated, according to which grace is offered to all, and all are to be urged and encouraged in every way to respond to it, although it is certain that a good many will not. And while (in a theological perspective) God not only holds out his grace, but also determines in advance who will accept it, the pastor knows nothing of the latter: all he can do is to use whatever resources are to hand to persuade people to accept what is offered. And persuasion of course implies agency. No man knew better than Calvin how to value the arts of persuasion, and to some extent he even assigned the business of government to this category. Be that as it may, what magistrates ordain and what they enforce constitutes a kind of invitation to righteousness. That much of what Calvin expected of magistrates consisted in making it impossible or excessively costly or painful to refuse the invitation does not contradict this interpretation: a man must learn to walk (abstain from outward wrong-doing) before he can run (do what is right of his own 'free' will or voluntarily).

None of this alters the fact that Calvin envisaged a division of labour between magistrates and ministers, which he to some degree actualized at Geneva. But it was not one between secular and spiritual matters, between *humanitas* and *pietas*, between teaching and coercing,[14] between moral instruction and legal enforcement, or between outward and true righteousness. Instead, both agencies were to use the distinctive resources committed to them by God for the disciplining of the same congregation or body of inhabitants (the distinction between resident and citizen, whether *bourgeois* or *citoyen*, being from this point of view irrelevant) to obedience to the same body of laws which covered both piety and righteousness. The laws of the Christian commonwealth are here understood as directives concerning the external form which righteousness takes: the true Christian brings to acts having the correct form the correct spirit, whereas the unrighteous conform only externally. Since the profession of Christianity is a condition of residence in the godly polity, and since all Christians are already understood to be committed morally to actions of this form, no resident has any right to complain about the rigour of the laws, or about supposed infringements of his Christian liberty.

It is thus clearly the duty of every Christian commonwealth to aim at exemplary righteousness and piety, as Geneva did. And if every Christian commonwealth were to do its duty, an amelioration of the world would be the result. And this has prompted the suggestion that we are entitled to discern in Calvin a doctrine of progress. Thus, according to Biéler, and (following him but stating the position in more extreme form) Little,[15] there is in Calvin's work a propensity to see in the church theologically, and in his Genevan enterprises an attempt to make the church in fact, an agency for the continuous transformation of the Christian society, a transformation to be accomplished in the last days. We have ourselves noted a continuing emphasis on *aedificatio*, a notion which bears particularly closely on Christ's (universal) church, as that is partially embodied in particular visible churches which Calvin took to be the incipience of the kingship of Christ on earth. The psychic correlate of *aedificatio* is zeal, or 'strenuousness' as it came to be called in connection with, and by, Calvin's puritan disciples, and zeal too we have seen to be central to Calvin's idea of the Christian life. Finally, although the historiographic appropriateness of the perspective is suspect, it is the case that Calvin's followers, like their mentor, were often distinguished by their zeal for mission, and one is tempted to seek a foundation for this in the theology which equipped them with their interpretation of the world and their place in it.

There is no doubt, then, that Calvin attributed a transformative power to the Gospel, and more particularly to its agents, and that he expected such transformation to bear visible fruit in the lives of men. What is in doubt is the propriety of calling this 'the regeneration of society' or 'the creation of a new order' and of seeing it as a cumulative process building up to a climax in the last days.[16] For the latter implies an openendedness in the transformations and a progressive triumph of righteousness in the world, and this is not at all what Calvin imagined. There is nothing whatever in his works to suggest that the church would not always be a beleaguered and persecuted minority until a dramatic and sudden termination of its sufferings in the last days. What is more, the most proximate and perhaps the only vocabulary available in the sixteenth century for anything akin to the later doctrine of progress was millennialism, which was so badly compromised by its Anabaptist associations that Calvin would have no truck with it whatever.[17] Attacks on Anabaptism in its various forms (for Calvin was minded to construe it inclusively) account for much of the material adding to the bulk of the last edition of the *Institution*. And as we have noticed, Calvin did not offer a commentary on Revelation, the only non-historical book of either the New or the Old Testament so excluded.

Calvin did not, of course, deny that there would be a Second Coming of Christ in his glory and a Last Judgement, and the elect do have certitude of the final triumph of Christ's church over Satan, but the only last judgement and last days which in his view were an appropriate subject for the Christian's meditations were the Christian's personal last judgement and his own last days. 'A new heaven and a new earth' is simply not a theme of his theology.[18] As for the transformation wrought by the Gospel and the building up of the church, these Calvin envisaged as the transformation of the Christian's own conduct to bring it into outward and inward conformity with a set of standards perfectly well known already, namely 'the Law', and he explicitly dissociated this from institutional changes in society: the Christian slave is a prompt and obedient slave, but still a slave, the Christian father a stern but just *paterfamilias*, but a *paterfamilias* and a domestic monarch none the less, the Christian subject a reliable and submissive subject still. As to the building up of the church, here Calvin meant primarily the elimination of popery and its relics, and the energetic practice of a highly organized piety.

The changes in the relations between men that the Gospel brings about, therefore, are not principally new laws or new institutions, but an actual conformity to laws mostly already in existence, enforced by institutions of which only the ecclesiastical ones were at all clearly defined or specified as being other than what was in existence already. It was not a new doctrine, and Calvin certainly did not say that it had been unheard-of in previous centuries, that the church had a particular concern for widows, orphans and strangers, for the poor, the defenceless and the down-trodden, or that the labourer was worthy of his hire, or that a man should have the wherewithal, by means of his labour, to feed his family, or that there should be schools for the young, or hospitals for the sick. Nor was it news to anyone that monopolies and artificially induced shortages were a scandal or that fraud and rack-renting were incompatible with Christian profession, and theologians and priests had distinguished for centuries between acceptable and unacceptable levels of interest, and acceptable and unacceptable circumstances in which to demand interest on loans at all.[19] Calvin was much concerned with all these matters in his sermons and commentaries, and in keeping with his prophetic stance he was unstinting in his condemnation of the luxurious, the hardhearted, the idle and those in any way lacking in *humanitas* towards their neighbour. A Christian commonwealth would be one in which such conduct was repressed and in which more men than was usual would actually do what all professed to believe ought to be done. But, as Calvin repeatedly argued, a society of Christians would never be coextensive with any church in the world, still less with any commonwealth.[20] On the contrary, because of the reliable and unfailing propensity of all (including the elect) to fall lamentably short of the standards set for them, there was an equally unfailing need, while the world should last, for a prophetic office and a magistracy to recall men to their duty. The warfare of the church militant (and Calvin was fond of military metaphors, which were *d'ailleurs* conventional enough) was a holding operation, an advance on one front being offset by a set-back on another; God was to be praised for his especial mercy if there were not set-backs on all fronts simultaneously. The only progress of which Calvin cared to speak was the progress of the elect Christian in his sanctification, and sanctification is a progressive evacuation of self and death to the world.[21] Biéler is right to say that the sanctification of the individual does not proceed in isolation,[22] but neither is it dependent on the prior sanctification of the visible church.

We may now return to our distinction between the respective operations of the magistracy and the church within the economy of the Christian commonwealth. The church teaches standards of conduct and the practice of piety; it removes obstacles to righteousness and piety where it can, and institutes arrangements and practices conducive to such piety. In doing so, it necessarily improves the standards of civility and *humanitas* of the congregation.[23] And it punishes breaches of these standards, wherever they are encountered, with its own resources. Geneva was certainly exemplary in this respect: office, standing, wealth were none of them passports to immunity from punishment for failings in piety or for breaches of the law. The ministers, Calvin foremost amongst them, were never laggard in reminding magistrates of their duty, or in doing it themselves, without fear or favour. But the church has no weapons with which to coerce, nor can it simply command magistrates either to create such weapons or to employ them in accordance with ministerial instruction. Its duty in this connection is to urge on the magistracy an ever stricter conformity of positive with divine law, and an ever stricter enforcement of obedience to the law.

But the magistrates' duties are not confined to making and enforcing laws. The only reason of principle why anything which can be determined, commanded, abolished, established, directed, regulated or in some other way attended to by the magistracy should not be done is that it has already been earmarked for the especial attention of the ministry. And even here Calvin was prepared to accept magisterial initiatives *faute de mieux*, although his church was of course designed in such a way as to ensure that such a state of affairs would not occur.[24] There was, then, no inherent limitation in Calvin's thought on the competence of a magistracy, provided it was godly. On the contrary, there were reasons why the activities of a godly magistracy should become ever more wide-ranging, specific and intrusive.[25]

An illustration of this, drawn from what the Genevan Messieurs did at Calvin's prompting and with his full approval,[26] is the Genevan laws governing conspicuous consumption, luxury in dress and 'excessive' ornamentation.[27] To the concern with minutiae native to what was after all a town council, a military high command and a small state (such as building and sanitary regulation,[28] prices, weights and measures, the sale of liquor, furnished lettings and so forth; the provision and keeping in good repair of weapons, the training of the militia, military intelligence; the conduct of foreign policy, taxation, the servicing of the state's debts) Calvin now added the concern with minutiae that derives from the demand that the laws lay down not minimal standards of conduct compatible with civility, but maximal standards of conduct construed as the legal expression of the standards to be expected from Christians.

The Reformation at Geneva (as elsewhere) was concerned from the beginning with improvement of morals, especially sexual morals, and with piety, and breaches of both carried legal penalties. But the magistracy displayed little zeal for legislation concerning ornaments (such as jewelry, hair-fashions and clothing) and conspicuous consumption before 1558. It will be recalled that hostility to clerically enforced discipline and to the French clergy was vocal in the Councils until 1555. For the most part, Messieurs were content to leave it to the ministers to inveigh against such vices from the pulpit. The only items of fashionable wear to attract their attention, and against which Calvin conceived a particular animus, were 'chausses et pourpoints chapplez' (slashed hose and doublets). These had already been banned several times when, in 1547, they again became controversial because the arque-busiers wanted to wear them for their annual shooting-feast. Calvin denounced this demand as being 'en depit de Dieu et de la justice'.[29] In a private letter of the time he made clear that he was particularly concerned about the dissoluteness of the youth of Geneva which was involved in the matter.[30] The law was upheld by the PC, but the prohibitions had to be reaffirmed almost every year until 1557.

In 1558, the ministry launched an initiative to have the whole issue of luxury and excess dealt with by law. Nicholas des Gallars appeared before the PC to denounce what he claimed was an increasing laxity of standards in this respect, citing women as the worst offenders. This was also Calvin's view.[31] The result appears to have been an ordinance, but no record of it remains in the PC minutes or in the Registers of the Venerable Company.[32] A comprehensive ordinance governing such matters was, however, issued in 1560.[33] It went into extraordinary detail about such things as how many rings could be worn, and on what occasions; it banned gold and silver chains, embroideries of all kinds, gilding of hair; it regulated the number of courses at public banquets,[34] and it also consolidated previous ordinances concerning attendance at sermons, the prohibition of blasphemies, gaming and so on, as well as all manner of policing regulations. These edicts were intended to be observed 'for all time'; they were printed. A translation of them was offered by Fills for the edification of his countrymen.[35]

Although these ordinances were detailed, they were evidently not detailed enough: they left open questions like the wearing of bracelets, silver belts and golden ornaments in the hair. In addition, a whole range of new and offensive habits seem to have been imported subsequently from abroad, and in any case these godly laws had often been disregarded. Another large consolidating ordinance was therefore found necessary in 1564 when Calvin was close to death. The preamble preached to all their duty to dress with the modesty befitting Christians, so that God might be better honoured than hitherto. There followed an extremely detailed set of regulations amplifying those of 1560 and consolidating a wealth of other regulations governing conduct which had been made on various other occasions. The new regulations now governed banned materials, styles and ornamentation of garments, permitted and prohibited personal ornamentation, hair-styles, the proper attire of artisans and their families, and so on and so forth.[36] The magistracy's decision about what was to be permitted and what

was not was in the most perfect harmony with Calvin's sentiments: it aimed at permitting what was comely, useful and
decorous, as well as not too expensive; so silver belts and
buckles were permitted, but silver chains, bracelets, collars,
embroidery, necklaces and tiaras were not. Women were
ordered to wear their hair in a style sometimes referred to as
selon la reformation, that is, without bouffon or colouring, and
plaited or tied so as to sit close to the head.

Taking this together with the prohibition of dancing of all
kinds,[37] indecent songs, swearing and blaspheming, all kinds of
gambling, the prohibition of all games on Sundays,[38] the legal
duty to attend sermons on Sundays (and whenever possible on
other days) and to see to the religious instruction of children
and servants, the prohibition of the printing, acquisition or
owning of all unlicensed books,[39] and the banning of popish
objects of every kind, not to mention all the other matters
governed by the criminal laws and edicts, there were very few
matters which were entirely exempt from the solicitude of a
pious magistracy.[40] Of course, no sixteenth-century state,
not even Geneva, had anything like the administrative resources
to ensure compliance with such a welter of regulations, as the
frequent restatement of these regulations, often accompanied
by reprimands about non-compliance, amply demonstrates.
And although legal penalties for infringements, normally in the
shape of fines (at least for lesser offences), were provided for,
these would have been difficult to collect. It seems that at
Geneva the Consistory dealt with first offences of a 'moral' or
doctrinal kind, and that only repeated or very grave infractions
of the law actually came before the PC, perhaps after a denunciation of the impenitent by the Consistory. The latter had no
power to fine, and the legality of this manner of proceeding
over infringement of the laws governing *moeurs* is unclear.
It did however have the advantage, from the point of view of
rigour, that there was a division of labour and cooperation
between ministers and magistrates, without which lesser
infractions might have gone altogether unnoticed. The PC was
the agency legally responsible for enforcing such laws, and
charged as it was with every sort of public business except civil
cases, it could not possibly have dealt with every infringement.

A nineteenth-century misrepresentation, fancying that this
was how Calvin might be demonstrated to be a tyrant, asserted

that there was a system of ecclesiastical spies.[41] This has been convincingly shown to be false, and was in any case exceedingly naive: a much more obvious and effective policing system was in force, namely that of mutual surveillance. A section of the consolidating edict of 1560 reads: '*citoyens, bourgeois* and *habitants* are to keep diligent watch, both by day and by night, each in his own place, on all comings and goings'.[42] This was no more than a restatement of the existing duty, also recognized in other states, of all inhabitants to denounce malefactors, and only such a system could mobilize anything like enough resources for efficient surveillance. The difference between Geneva and other polities was that in Geneva the virtuous were committed to making it work,[43] and that what glimmerings the century had of a respect for privacy were here quite extinguished by the superior duty of ensuring public godliness.

Now Calvin did not claim that the number of rings or the style of garment compatible with Christian modesty were laid down in Scripture. What is more, he did not even desire that there should be laws of the kind of intricacy to which he was driven.[44] But that detail was inescapable, once Christian moderation ceased to be a general standard whose detailed implications were left to the virtue and good sense of the individual. Not surprisingly, given the absence of direct scriptural legitimation and the intrusiveness and fiddling nature of the regulations, Calvin and his lieutenants were driven to finding secular reasons, such as the presumed incompatibility of luxury and general well-being, and the example of the Romans,[45] to support their demands. The magistrates, who shortly afterwards agreed to the demand of Christian moderation that they should be addressed with no more grandiloquent titles than a civic 'treshonorés seigneurs', concurred.[46]

The image (a retroactive projection on to Calvin's theology and conduct of some of the more unlovable characteristics of his posterity) of Calvin as the theologian of the wet blanket, the apotheosis of the kill-joy, is only marginally more just than that of Calvin the blood-thirsty.[47] He did not, as far as is known, initiate or play any part in the most ludicrous venture of this kind, an apparently independent initiative of the magistracy to bar Geneva's hostels to the native Genevans, and to replace them with five 'abbayes', each under the supervision of a senior magistrate, where strict regulations, governing drunkenness, licentious singing, blasphemy and (of course) treasonous talk,[48] were intended to ensure a godliness of conversation. Bibles were to be provided (at the expense of mine host, for the Genevan authorities had little money to disburse on godly ventures) in case pious conversation should flag. The experiment lasted two months.[49] Calvin's verdict is not recorded, which is perhaps equivalent to saying that he thought the project ill-advised.[50]

Though himself abstemious to a degree which would do credit to a Cistercian, he made no virtue or example of it, but on the contrary ridiculed asceticism,[51] and explained his own abstinence as the only way he knew of preventing the migraines to which he was a martyr. And although he had no friends who were not also *commilitones*, and indeed broke off friendships on the grounds of theological differences,[52] he pronounced friendship, conviviality, sociability as the *deliciae* of this-worldly existence; a 'bossot' of old wine was considered and accepted as an appropriate recompense and mark of appreciation for his work on the Genevan edicts of 1543, and in his last illness he would not tolerate the abandonment of the banquet for ministers and magistrates which had become customary as the conclusion of the *grabeau*, or session of mutual criticism; on the contrary he had it held at his house, even though he was too ill to take part. He did indeed consider adversity, exile, poverty and subservience, illness, loss of family and friends and all sorts of suffering as 'exercising' the Christian and hence as capable of yielding good, but this was no more than an orthodox view amongst Christians; and there is only the slightest suspicion that he thought adversity more useful to sanctification, and therefore more to be prized, than prosperity. The view to which he adhered was that the Christian (in the words of Paul) should know both how to abound and how to want, and that he should preserve *moderatio*, self-control and measure.[53]

It is not the case, therefore, that Calvin looked with a censorious eye on all human enjoyment;[54] nor (more to our point) was such an attitude implicit or explicit in his theology; nor do the Genevan laws presuppose such an attitude. Instead we are confronted by another instance of Calvin's unwillingness to distinguish between sin and crime, moral and legal rules. In the righteous, *moderatio* was of course self-discipline, and the righteous man knew how to govern himself. The populace at large, however, could not be trusted to discern or, more important, to adhere to, this standard; it had therefore to be laid down in law, as well as preached by the ministry. Those things that are *mala in se*, such as dancing and indecent songs, were therefore to be banned altogether, for there is no such thing as sinning in moderation. Those things that are good in moderation, were permitted in moderation.

Again, since sin and crime are equally offences against God, it seemed inexcusable to Calvin that any educated man should consider persistent heresy and public blasphemy as different from any other crime. The execution of Servetus in 1553 has perhaps coloured Calvin's posthumous reputation more than any other event of his life. And while the trial, condemnation and execution of this most unlikely of martyrs were the action of a magistracy in other respects hostile in the extreme to Calvin, involving the Consistory not at all and Calvin only as indirect first preferrer of charges and theological expert, there is no question whatever that Calvin approved of every aspect of what was done, except the delays and the manner of the execution.[55] Even that does not establish the coherence between the act and the cast of Calvin's theology. Nonetheless, the coherence is not difficult to discern. The business of the Christian commonwealth is to assist the sanctification of its members. Those who not only resist the call to sanctification, but seek to involve others in their heresy and blasphemy (as Servetus had done, according to Calvin's view),[56] have no place in such a commonwealth. It does not, of course, follow that it is either necessary or expedient that on this account one man should die for the good of the people, and to justify that contention Calvin was driven to finding a peremptory Scriptural imperative (and support from the custom of the nations) and the threat of the wrath of God for unavenged blasphemy, according to a logic which has been examined earlier. It must be said, however, that on Calvin's view of the matter, the only alternatives open were either exile or death;[57] *tertium non datur*.

Again, Calvin's position here is easily misrepresented. Precisely because the Christian commonwealth concerns itself with sanctification and not merely with repression, severity is not called for on all occasions or without qualification. The soul of the heretic or blasphemer[58] is to be considered, as well as the soul of those who might be corrupted by him. The homology between Calvin's ecclesiology and his political thought (which we have frequently had occasion to note) is here once again perfect: just as excommunication, the *ultima ratio* of ecclesiastical discipline, is to be resorted to only when all else has failed, so the death-penalty, the *ultima ratio* of civil discipline, is not to be administered on every possible occasion.[59] It is true that Calvin's hatred of Servetus was such that he spoke of not letting him escape with his life if it were in his power, years before Servetus was rash enough to venture a trip to Geneva.[60] This, however, was not his invariable manner of dealing with those with whom he disagreed,[61] and even if it had been, this would tell us more about Calvin's irascibility than about his conception of godly statecraft.

This brings us to a related aspect of Calvin's concerns, on which it is appropriate to close. Since the public institutions of the Christian polity were constructed for *aedificatio* and not merely for repression, it is only consequent that Calvin should have given much attention to the education of young and old alike. In a sense, the Christian polity is an educational enterprise, although it does not appear that Calvin ever presented it in quite that light. The very notion of education takes on a menacing aspect in the context of the *universitas*, to use Oakeshott's illuminating distinction between *societas* and *universitas*.[62] But just as education must be harnessed to the common enterprise of the Christian polity, so the conception of that enterprise is itself subject to modification by being construed as education, and at least in the context of his discussion of the church, such a line of thought is discernible in Calvin.

The church's main task is to teach. It might seem obvious that the church might therefore be described as a 'school'. On occasion Calvin did so describe it.[63] What is more, some of his master-conceptions have overtly educational connotations: preeminently *disciplina* itself, the first meaning of which is 'teaching', 'instruction', 'training'; and *castigatio* ('chastisement') and the rod (a familiar teaching-aid), as aspects of discipline. However, metaphors drawn from schooling do not dominate Calvin's account of the discipline, the bivalence of repression and correction in the notion being tilted sharply towards the former by Calvin's conception of the office of the church as *jurisdictio*, *gubernatio*, and by his metaphors of ambassadors, imperial agents and messengers exercising a delegated *potestas*. Calvin's metaphors in this connection were somewhat mixed. He spoke in quick succession of the church as a 'mother' and a 'school',[64] and then went on to describe its 'discipline' as a 'fatherly rod',[65] but also (in more equestrian mood) as 'bridle' and as 'spur'.[66] In any case, Calvin tended to construe the teaching office of the church as ideally accurate transcription and transmission of doctrine on the one side, complemented by humble but enthusiastic reception on the other. And when he came in the *Institution* to speak of Scripture as the test and touchstone to be applied to all teaching, he persistently left obscure who was entitled to apply this test, the assumption, however, being that the purveyors of falsehoods were the papists and the applicants of the test the evangelical churches, that is to say ministers and theologians.

Calvin's discussion of this whole topic is persistently conditioned by the polemic against papists and the presupposition of recalcitrant but ignorant congregations; under the circumstances the image of teaching as strict indoctrination by ministers, and learning as willing submission to their teaching authority, is readily intelligible. When not concerned with the reeducation of the ignorant and recalcitrant, Calvin was addressing himself to the education of pupils and students intended for careers in the ministry or the magistracy. These were to acquire an enormous body of knowledge and skills, both in doctrine and in the philological disciplines which Calvin, as a good humanist, considered to be indispensable for a mastery of theology. A large part of such an education was rote-learning, reinforced with public beatings before the whole school, as well as by public praises.[67] But this was not all: for the higher classes, emphasis was placed on composition and disputation. It is difficult to know how much latitude was left to the parties to such disputations; certainly there is no suggestion of the degree of freedom permitted in disputation among scholastics, for Calvin insisted that the public scholars

by turn set out certain positions each month, which are to be neither extravagant (*curieuses*), nor sophistical, nor are they to contain false doctrine . . . Then they are to sustain them publicly in disputation. It shall be permitted to all there to speak. All sophistry, shameless and bold eagerness to corrupt the word of God, and similarly all evil contentiousness and obstinacy, are to be banished.

The points of doctrine are to be treated in godly and religious fashion by all parties to the disputation.[68]

Already bound to subscribe to an enormously detailed *Confession de la Foy* designed to 'close the door to all subterfuges' as a condition of admission to the Academy,[69] students were evidently to be kept on a very tight rein.

But none of this tells us how the education of the already learned is to proceed, nor what follows from Calvin's general theology about the appropriate relationship between an educated congregation and a godly ministry, or amongst the learned themselves. Since the matter was not a current issue, Calvin did not give it any consideration. But there was no reason in principle why a doctrinally well-instructed person should be either a minister or a 'doctor', both of these being clerical estates. Indeed, Calvin's public sermons were designed precisely to raise up an 'instruct people' (to quote More's description of his Utopians). We have also seen that Calvin conceded to magistrates the right to an independent judgement in doctrinal matters. Finally, it may be noted that the Friday *congrégations* were open to laymen. What was objected against Bolsec, a layman (although a former member of a religious order), was not that he had *spoken* at the *congrégation* at which he denounced predestination, but that he had been bold in maintaining a heretical opinion.[70]

Nothing much on Calvin's theoretical position on this subject can be derived from Geneva. For one thing, Calvin's personal dominance and intolerance of criticism were both unrivalled, and this state of affairs was not a theological desideratum. For another, as a centre for recuperation and training for missionaries to France,[71] Geneva was not the place in which to consider the position of the learned layman in the godly commonwealth. But it may be suggested that a quite different and much less one-sided relationship must have prevailed in further education among the learned, and even that the severe restrictions placed by Calvin on the competence of the congregation in matters doctrinal and organizational were equivocal enough to allow room for more freedom of action in a godly congregation. There are, for all that, no grounds for claiming a populist (or, more vacuously, 'democratic') potentiality in Calvin's thought; a *de facto* division of congregations into the godly and the merely outwardly conforming, like the distinction between participants and non-participants in the *classes* in Tudor England, is much more in keeping with the general tenor of his thought. Populist attitudes were to be characteristic of sectarian and not orthodox Calvinists.[72]

10

Unfinished business: a speculative summary and postscript

By 1558 Calvin was an extremely sick man, plagued by migraine, gout, colic, piles, nephritis, the stone and quartan fevers. He feared that he might not live to complete the last *Institution*, which he was composing on his sick-bed. And although he drove himself as hard as ever when not entirely prostrated by illness, his activities were those of a man putting his affairs in order. The *Institution* was now given an arrangement with which Calvin professed himself satisfied; the Genevan Academy, already described in its statutes as a *Université*, was at last established in 1559, complete with its own statutes and Theodore de Bèze (Beza) as its first rector; an expanded version of the *Ordonnances* of 1541 was put on the Genevan statute-books in 1560 and 1561; an ordinance concerning the law and discipline of matrimony was appended; and the laws governing Genevan morals and mores were consolidated. All this had been done by 1561; his last *magnum opus*, the *Harmony of the Last Four Books of Moses*, was not completed until 1563, but Calvin had been working on it for years. In fact, he did not die until 17 May 1564. His last public act was an address to his ministerial colleagues summarizing his life and travails, and impressing on them the need to 'make no changes, no innovation' and to maintain amity and solidarity amongst themselves.[1] Nothing could more aptly epitomize his lifelong concern with the consolidation and defence of such gains as the Reformation had made, and equally nothing could point up better the gloomy pessimism about the way of the world that characterized the last decade of Calvin's life. If his thinking contained a potentiality for a relationship between magistrates and their subjects and ministers and their congregations quite different from the severity, bridling, repression, chastisement and discipline that are so prominent on his pages, such things had to remain *in potentia* rather than *in actu* while Calvin himself was still on hand to deliver definitive verdicts on the content and implications of his theology.

The work of his last years does not suggest that Calvin had any surprises yet to spring on the world. The *Institution* now appeared in an orderly arrangement which, while it followed in outline the Apostles' Creed, in fact concentrated on the theme of man's *duplex cognitio* of God as creator and as redeemer in and through Christ. Sources of this knowledge are the creation and man himself (book 1) and, much more significantly, the revealed Word (books 1 and 2); God the redeemer as appre-hended and lived in faith is discussed in book 3, and the external 'means' or 'aids' to the life of sanctification, the church and civil government, are discussed in book 4. Knowledge (*cognitio, cognoissance*), meaning emphatically not a cerebral or 'historical', still less a speculative, knowledge, but rather a certainty enjoyed and exhibited in the lives of the faithful, had already been a dominant theme of the *Confession de la Foy* of 1536 and the *Catechisme* of 1537. And although Calvin certainly allowed to the unaided faculties of fallen man a part in the *duplex cognitio Dei*, it is noticeable that he was concerned to stress that the knowledge of the Creator to be derived in this way is grossly inferior to what is offered in Scripture (book 1, ch. 6), and that for the knowledge of Christ, God the redeemer, these resources are of no avail whatever. So that while Calvin might well have claimed that he had now stated the doctrine of faith decently and in good order, that order simply allowed a more adequate presentation of themes and emphases evident for twenty years.[2] The increased length of the book is mostly accounted for by the incorporation of earlier attacks on Servetus and his like, which demanded an expansion of the Christo-logical doctrine,[3] on Bolsec and other anti-predestinarians, which necessitated interminable defences of predestination,[4] and expanded discussions of the Lord's Supper to deal with the sacramentarian controversy.[5] The amount of space now devoted to these issues does not demonstrate that they were newly arrived or of increased importance in Calvin's theology, but only that Calvin had been obliged to elaborate what he had previously taken for granted. It cannot be denied, however, that at least in the case of the doctrine of 'double predestination' (that is, to salvation and to perdition), an emphasis at first rendered necessary by theological polemic subsequently enhanced the status of the doctrine as a component of Calvin's theology.

In the same way, the *Ordonnances* of 1560 and 1561 add little that is new to those of 1541. The exception is a provision now included for congregational objection to candidates for the ministry and the eldership, inserted at the express request of the ministers (OS 1, 330). This may be read as partial confirmation of what was said in the previous chapter about the possibility of a less one-sided relationship between ministry and congregation. Provision was also made for the consultation of ministers in the choice of elders (p. 362), and *citoyens* and *bourgeois* were henceforth to be equally eligible for the latter office (p. 363). The marriage ordinance of 1561 (pp. 346–55) embodied twenty years' experience of these matters on the part of the Consistory. Other *Ordonnances* clarified excommunication and the status of the Consistory. But most of this is little more than official recognition of what Calvin had been urging for twenty years.

But while Calvin was thus putting his house into the order in which he wished to leave it, he was confronted by the last, and in some ways the most dispiriting, challenge of his life. The affairs of the Huguenots now reached a crisis. The institution of the Chambre Ardente by Henri II shortly before his death, the uncertainties and intermittent persecutions of the regency of Catherine de' Medici and the Guise family, the Huguenot conspiracy of Amboise of 1560 in which Louis de Condé, one of the princes of the blood, was implicated, the massacre of the Huguenots at Vassy in 1562 and the subsequent outbreak of civil war all marked a turning-point in the life of the French evangelical congregations. From leading a persecuted and covert existence, the Huguenots were now becoming a political and military power out of all proportion to their numbers, in virtue of their concentration by region, the energy of their evangelizing, and their support among the nobility and in the towns. Geneva was at this time inundated by requests for ministers, and the Genevan church responded magnificently: the town and its dependencies were stripped of ministers to satisfy the insatiable demands of the French brethren.[6] Meanwhile, the Genevan presses gushed forth unprecedented quantities of literature to serve the Cause.

Despite all these goings-on, about which Calvin was uniquely well informed, he was so far from addressing himself to the general question of the right of resistance, or even adding to what he had said already, that the occasion did not warrant even a new treatise. And the most minute examination of his letters of the period discloses only, first, that he thought that what needed to be said in point of doctrine had been said already, and second, that he took the practical implications of scriptural doctrine in the present contingency to be entirely clear.[7] This cannot surprise us, for we have already seen that he was given to imagining that scriptural morality did not permit of perplexity or irresolution. His view was that godly private persons had no choice but to obey magistrates, or to disobey them when the honour of God required it, and that they must suffer imprisonment, murders, executions and outrages, whether any official pretext was pleaded or not. As for public persons, Calvin had long since conceded to 'popular magistrates', where the laws of the land established them, an unspecified right to protect the liberties of the people, and he now allowed this right to urban magistrates, local lords, provincial governors, princes of the blood, all within the limits of legality and their civil duty. When the laws prohibited 'la preche' (the significant colloquial term for Calvinist services) in the towns, Calvin counselled submission.[8]

As is well known, Calvin's closest disciples abandoned their master's doctrine of political obedience within a decade of his death; or, more precisely, they worked it out in directions in which Calvin himself had not gone and employed as authoritative materials which Calvin himself never used.[9] This by itself is certainly not enough to establish that Calvin's own doctrine of obedience was out of key with the rest of his theology; they may simply have distorted the master's doctrine. It is also, of course, the case that the Calvinian corpus was not all that the disciples brought to their interpretation of the world, any more than Scripture was all that Calvin brought to his. Nonetheless, the fact that the disciples did reject, or at least substantially alter, Calvin's doctrine of political obedience does suggest that, within the corpus of Calvin's thought, there was a diversity of possibilities, some of which he exploited and others of which he closed off. It is not a question of doctrinal contradictions or incoherences in Calvin's thought: he had good reasons for what he taught. Equally, however, the disciples' interpretation of the polity was also entirely defensible in Calvinian terms. The choice of which of these possibilities to exploit was not dictated by the system of thought itself (it was hardly tight enough to dictate anything of the kind), but by particular judgements about priorities and contingencies.

The topic of political obedience, in view of its centrality to Calvin's political thought, affords a suitable occasion for drawing together the main lines of our account. Here we must abandon all the qualifications and nuances necessary hitherto, for the sake of clarity of outline. The matter may perhaps be represented as follows.

The still centre, the foundation, the uncompromisable requirement of the Christian life for Calvin is the combination of the purity of doctrine and the striving for sanctification. Without the former, the latter is impossible, and without the latter, the former is not truly faith at all but a denatured thing, a misnomer, a *froide speculation*.[10] In the nature of things, the Christian life is of course a life which may be lived under any circumstances whatever, and perhaps a heroic Christian virtue presupposes extreme adversity confronted and overcome. This, however, has never been treated as a reason for Christians to wish for extreme adversity;[11] since even the most godly are weak, the prayer of Christians must be: 'lead us not into temptation', and external helps to compensate for their weakness are devoutly to be wished. Calvin had worked out in very great detail, and with much care and acumen, the character of a Christian polity designed precisely to serve as an aid to sanctification: a polity devoted to the honour and glory of God, to *pietas*, to *aequitas* and to *aedificatio*. Discipline is the means to these ends, and it must be, at least ideally, a two-fold discipline of magistrates and ministers.

Now, an emphasis on purity of doctrine at any price, such as Calvin's, cannot fail to encourage centrifugal tendencies in a church, especially when complemented by the requirement that everyone both be well instructed in doctrine and adhere to it as a matter of conviction and not mere conformity. And separation on the grounds of the need to preserve doctrine pure and undefiled was constitutive of the evangelical revolt from Rome. Therefore, no evangelical church could ever count itself immune from further separations on the same ground. It is readily understandable, therefore, that Calvin should have considered purity of doctrine to be threatened more by schism and by internal and covert enemies of the faith than by any number of external and overt ones. Anabaptists and apostates are a much graver menace than papists, and divisions amongst the custodians of purity of doctrine are graver than either.[12] The most intolerable kind of division is one that hardens into sects.

To counteract the propensity of godly churches to schism and sectarianism, and also to lesser lapses from purity, such as 'frivolous speculations', subtleties and contentiousness, as well as to aid the godly in their striving for sanctification, Calvin (as we have seen) insisted on a clear division between clergy and laity, and mobilized whatever resources were to hand to ensure the prestige, authority and cohesion of the clergy; the alternative, a world divided into as many voluntary congregations as there were believers willing to associate into associations of the like-minded, never even appeared within Calvin's field of vision. But he at no time supposed either that any ministry whatever was utterly reliable in its fidelity to the Word, or that schisms, sects and irreligion could be prevented simply by teaching and a discipline administered by a clergy, however united and orthodox. On the contrary, the resources of the secular magistracy were essential to maintain unity both among the ministers themselves and in the congregation, as well as providing valuable external support for the pursuit of sanctification. And in this connection, an insistence on the duty of private men to political obedience was entirely consequent: such obedience was a precondition of sanctification, and civil government was sacrosanct.

This nexus of considerations, then, provides religious and theological reasons for Calvin's insistence on political obedience. It is for that reason alone more plausible than alternative explanations which attribute the doctrine to merely political prejudices on Calvin's part; such as (for example) the view that Calvin was politically conservative, or that his thought exhibits a 'pathos of order'. It also makes it intelligible why Calvin should have insisted on obedience, even when obedience was inconsistent with the most energetic way of building up the church and furthering reformation, as in France.

However, this reading of the requirements of the Christian life and the dangers to a godly church may now also be seen to rest on certain judgements and assumptions which not every Calvinist was obliged to make. In the first place, Calvin judged that the greatest dangers to the purity of doctrine were schism, heresy and disputes internal to the church, rather than external threats. And he also assumed that if magistrates were themselves protagonists of heresy, this was less serious for the purity of doctrine than schism and sects. But these are contingent judgements: they may not be equally true in all times and all places. And they are more plausible in the context of an established evangelical church (Geneva once more being presupposed in Calvin's general reflections) than in circumstances when the godly are not yet united and organized into churches, and when the main obstacle to their union is hostility and persecution on the part of the magistrates themselves.

Again, the straight-forwardness of the injunction to obey magistrates is deceptive. For what if there is more than one level, so to speak, of magistrates? The problem did not arise in Geneva; but outside Geneva, and especially in territorial states whose political form was monarchy, the injunction to obey magistrates begged two vital questions. First: which magistrates? And second: whom are the magistrates themselves to obey? These matters were of very considerable significance for the godly in France, where the territorial jurisdiction of godly churches and godly magistrates was by no means coextensive with the territory of France or the civil authority. Thus Calvin's reference to *primarii conventus* and popular magistrates in *Institution* 4.20.31 presupposed an answer, but did not address itself, to such traditional questions of jurisprudence and political thought as whether the king is *singulis maior* but *universis minor*, and, if so, whether only with respect to lesser magistrates, or to the totality of his subjects. And again, it presupposed an answer to the question whether the king is beneath or above the law.

Calvin's letters of the time make it clear that he regarded such questions as matters to be resolved by reference to the positive law of the land, that is to say, in the case of the Huguenots, the law of France. In fact his willingness to consider as in any way defensible the somewhat unusual activities of Huguenots during the early sixties rested on the fact that during this time there was a regency, and as Calvin understood it, the positive law of France ('secundum veterem regni morem et scriptas leges')[13] gave to the Estates General and to the princes of the blood the right to compose a regency–council while the Guises were holding the young king captive (according to a story which Calvin and the Huguenots affected to believe). The Edict of January 1561, granting a degree of toleration, was in every sense a god-send from the Huguenot point of view, for, emanating as it did from the highest legal authority in the land, its authority was unproblematic from either the legal or the religious point of view. But the questions which Calvin here left to be resolved by reference to the positive law of the land were, and had always been, as much philo-sophical and moral as they were legal questions, and on Calvin's own showing it was perfectly legitimate to bring scriptural, moral and religious considerations to bear on them, just as Calvin himself had offered religious and moral objections to the claim of kings to be *legibus soluti*. Why then should French custom, even when reinforced by the characteristically Calvinian addition of 'written laws',[14] have such authority with the godly?[15] It appears that Calvin regarded what by the end of the century were distinguished as 'fundamental' (later 'constitutional') laws of any polity as an inviolable datum claiming the obedience of Christians. In the same way, he took for granted the entitlement of any established polity to its territorial integrity and continuance; indeed he could hardly accept one without also accepting the other. Now, in a godly city-state there is indeed no reason for distinguishing between the demands of godliness and the integrity of the state. But it was by no means self-evident that an ungodly kingdom like France could lay the same religious claim to the maintenance of its territorial integrity. And while Calvin certainly provided weighty reasons, prudential, moral and religious, for respecting ancient laws and customs, he provided equally weighty reasons of the same sort why on occasion ancient laws and customs might need to be overturned, their contradictoriness to *pietas*, *aedificatio* and *aequitas* being amongst the foremost of such reasons.

Finally, Calvin took for granted the conventional distinction between private and public persons, and gave it religious significance by differentiating the religious duties before God of these two categories of persons. But since the distinction was in fact a legal one, created by the positive laws of a polity, it once again presupposed the validity and obligatoriness for Christians of whatever positive law they happen to find.

Read in the light of Calvin's distinction between public and private persons, his preoccupation with the need for legality and order and his assumption that *de facto* polities are entitled to their continuance, Scripture did indeed teach the kind of obedience which Calvin sought to impose on his French disciples; but if Scripture was not read in this way, not necessarily. And the views Calvin was presupposing have in themselves nothing whatever to do with evangelical doctrine; they are conventional political views and judgements which achieved religious significance by being integrated into Calvin's theology. Nor were they suited to an entirely seamless integration: they were merely one possible reading of the practical implications of a theology of order and obedience, and their suitability to a godly city-state like Geneva is much more apparent than their suitability to an ungodly territorial state such as France or the Holy Roman Empire.

The stance of the Huguenots as defenders of strict legality and legal propriety, here entirely in accord with the teachings of Calvin, served them well enough in the early 1560s.[16] All the same, it was far from being entirely plausible, nor was it adequate once the king was out of his minority, for it left the question of the duty of obedience to a tyrant who was out of his minority completely untouched. In the meanwhile, it merely preserved Calvin and the Huguenots from facing the fact that from the strictly legal point of view, the whole enterprise of reformation in France was at the very best a skating on the thin ice on the margins of legality, and, more usually, was <u>blatantly illegal.</u> Overt taking over of Roman churches, abolishing the Mass and profaning the Host, persecution of Catholics, conversion of towns into Huguenot fiefs, assassinations, armings, military organization, the establishment of a church apart from the ancient church of France complete in every detail of political and ecclesiastical organization from consistory to national synod, none of these bore the remotest resemblance to a legal way of proceeding. But on the view which adherence to Calvinian orthodoxy forced upon Huguenots, deliberate and blatant illegalities of this sort could not be openly avowed for what they were, that is to say illegalities, for then the Huguenots would have lost the main plank in their platform in the early sixties, which was that they were the partisans of legality, and their opponents the progenitors of illegality and sedition.

An organized, magisterially supervised reformation of France by territories (since a conversion of the whole of France was out of the question) does not seem at all at variance with what Calvin might have approved, and in so far as Calvin did whatever he could to provide the churches with pastors, and approved of the establishment of churches and consistories provided it was with the cooperation of the local magistrates, he may be said to have approved it. His doctrine of obedience and legality on the other hand, taken strictly, could not possibly license it.

Hence, given authentically Calvinian readings of the importance of godly magistrates for Christian discipline, and of Christian discipline for *pietas* and *aedificatio*, given also a truly Calvinian strenuousness and zeal for furthering reformation, it was perfectly reasonable for the Christian, confronted by a magistracy some of whose members (and those the most dignified and powerful) were actively seeking to prevent reformation and either persecuting, or allowing the persecution of, the godly, to chose the objects of his political obedience in accordance with the demands of *pietas*, rather than those of legality. The Christian might thus distinguish between godly and ungodly, and fundamental and other, laws, between lesser[17] or popular magistrates and higher magistrates, Estates General, Parlements and kings, between the rights of 'the people' and the rights of kings. He might find the authorization for laws, polities and governors in consent, in a covenant between the polity and God or the people and kings. And he might treat the defence of Calvinist provinces as more important than the integrity of the kingdom.[18] In short, he might reopen for debate all the scholastic and jurisprudential problems to which Calvin's biblicism had given short shrift. And Calvin's followers in fact did so, once more finding serviceable instruments of the 'Cause' in what Calvin had rejected or emasculated. No doubt these gains were purchased at a price, but then so were the gains of Calvin's position. And Huguenot writings did do justice to the Calvinian desiderata of a godly magistracy, the republican political form, the right of the godly to their liberty, as well as to his qualified hostility to hereditary monarchy, to large states, and to *principes legibus soluti*, all of which had perforce to remain mere velleities in the position which Calvin had adopted.

It is, therefore, no matter for surprise that those who in later years looked back to Calvin as a uniquely favoured expositor of the Word should have ranged in their politics from firebrands to quietists, without consciousness of the least deviation from orthodoxy. Sometimes the same man changed from the one stance to the other in the course of his life. John Milton was following in the footsteps of the master as much when he claimed that presbytery was compatible with any political form, including monarchy, as when he denied that 'any man that knows aught' could deny the justness of executing tyrants, and when he at last asserted the peculiarly divine nature of the republican political form. For Calvin's political thought was not so bonded to his theology that a man might not detach the former without tearing the latter.

Appendix I: Calvin's conversion

An examination of Calvin's conversion is not essential to the argument of this book, but has become a kind of test of academic *virtù* in Calvin studies, and in any case the gap between Calvin the humanist and Calvin the evangelical author of the *Institutio* ought to be filled.

It is perhaps appropriate to begin by distinguishing between the conversion experience itself and the sequence of theological and intellectual positions which terminated in Calvin's emergence as an evangelical. The character of the former, aside from its inherent inexplicability, was itself a principal subject of evangelical faith. Accounts of it can therefore be expected to conform to a predefined pattern, especially when the purpose of such accounts, as in Calvin's case, was primarily didactic rather than autobiographical. As to the latter, since conversion was to evangelicals the direct action of God, the human mediations and stages preceding it were of distinctly secondary interest. We must therefore beware of accepting as history what was at the very least accommodated to a theological pattern. The *fons et origo* of this pattern is ultimately St Paul, but a more immediate source is the *Confessions* of St Augustine. Luther's *Freedom of a Christian* intimates the existence of such a model, and Calvin may be presumed to have been familiar with this work.[1] In any case, Paul was the centre of the evangel for them both.

There are only two apparently autobiographical pieces offered by Calvin himself: a passage in the *Reply to Sadoleto* of 1539 and a brief section of the Preface to the *Commentary on the Psalms* of 1557.[2] The account of the conversion process in both places has certain common features: it is a 'history' of an initial state of obduracy, blindness and superstition, followed by a call at first ignored, resisted and fled from, which in turn was followed by some experience of being mastered, overpowered by God: the dawning of *fides*. The final *terminus ad quem* is the experience of liberation, release and certitude and the life of sanctification, the struggle to conform one's life and conduct to the righteousness gratuitously imputed by God to the soul of his elect. All this finds its parallels in Luther. Beyond this, Calvin's two accounts diverge.

In the *Reply to Sadoleto*, penned in the space of a week according to Beza, a supposititious evangelical answers Sadoleto's charges by rehearsing the speech he would give when called to the Last Judgement.[3] The account is thus explicitly didactic and not autobiographical; on the other hand, precisely because the experience related there is intended to be paradigmatic, it must have been thought by Calvin to apply to himself. No one in the 1530s was born an evangelical, and a conversion was therefore constitutive of being an evangelical.

Now, since the believer knows what form conversion takes, it is impossible not to see the whole process from the point of view of its preordained outcome. It follows that differentiations within the pre-conversion life appear as flattened and insignificant, irrespective of the importance they might have had at the time. Thus the *Reply* attributes to 'the church' of Calvin's youth a monolithic consistency of doctrine, and to himself a correspondingly total acceptance of its 'superstitions', which are simply not borne out by the evidence.[4] This is, of course, not to say that Calvin was fantasizing or lying; only that, as the *Reply* itself bears witness, since the conversion experience was the subject of the evangelical's every meditation and prayer, biography and theology would rapidly become inextricable. In fact Calvin had moved from the Sorbonnist interpretation of 'philosophy', 'theology' and the religious life in general, in which he had been nurtured at La Marche and Montaigu, to that of the humanists, and both orientations were orthodox, except from each other's viewpoint. From Calvin's later perspective, these differences were insignificant.

The initial condition of 'reverence for the church'[5] is seen as one in which despite 'intervals of peace'[6] there is mainly restlessness, even terror, 'which no expiations, no satisfactions could cure',[7] and this condition is said to have been followed by a recognition of the impossibility of 'work-righteousness'.[8] This spiritual state, described in terms which offer parallels to Luther too striking to be overlooked,[9] is succeeded by what in retrospect appears as God offering grace, seeking out the sinner. The agency by which God operates is teachers of a 'far different sort of teaching',[10] and Calvin depicts the sinner at first putting up a stiff resistance, out of stubbornness and 'reverence for the church', until at last 'I let my ears be opened and allowed myself to be taught'.[11] The preachers' message is depicted as consisting largely of an indictment of the papal primacy and a denial that their own teaching constituted a leaving of the church; it was instead an *aedificatio*.[12] Their purpose was 'to lead us back to [the] very source [of Christianity], and, purging it of its dross, to restore it to its purity'.[13]

The 'autobiographical' section of the Preface to the *Commentary on the Psalms*[14] is very short. But despite this, and its personal tone and detail, theological condensing cannot be ruled out, especially since the account was written more than a score of years after the events narrated. Certain details which fall outside the pattern seem to be reliable; for example Calvin's assertion that neither 'theology' (also called 'philosophy', the former being the official, the latter Calvin's own — in this instance derogatory — title for his studies), nor law were his choice of study, but his father's. For the rest, the account not only differs materially from the former, but also brings into play certain additional preoccupations.

Calvin claims to have been 'so strongly devoted to the superstitions of the papacy that nothing less [than an act of God] could draw me from such depths of mire'. This parallels his previous assertions, but also those of Luther,[15] and both seem to be variations on Augustine's theme of the sinner steeped in sins of a more carnal nature, and Paul's 'persecuting the brethren', of neither of which Calvin or Luther could claim to be guilty. Calvin now quite ignored the agencies which 'the providence of God' had employed in the conversion, but there is no reason to doubt the former account, which accurately depicted Calvin as a second generation Lutheran; Luther's own account referred only to Scripture as the medium of faith.[16] And whereas the previous account let through, perhaps involuntarily, the debt Calvin owed to humanist modes of thought in the assertion that evangelical preachers preached a 'return to the fountainhead', a 'clearing away of the dross',[17] none of that now remained, all of it being replaced by the direct agency of God. Similarly, the resistance at first offered to the Word, the terror, the seeking for 'oblivion' of the *Reply*, now show through only in the metaphor 'tamed to teacheableness', which is followed by the obscure assertion that his mind was 'too stubborn for its years', whereas the previous story explained such resistance as only too natural: 'such is the firmness or effrontery with which it is natural to men to persist in the course on which they have once embarked'.[18] God's 'secret rein [or curb — *frenum*]' now takes the form of a *subita conversio*. It has been pointed out by Parker[19] that in the *De Clementia Commentary* Calvin had explained that '*subita* means not only sudden (*repentina*), but also unpremeditated. Indeed, things done extempore are almost always unpremeditated. Accordingly, *subitum* is used to mean unadvised.'[20] Thus *subita conversio* could mean 'an unexpected conversion'. This is subtle, but in the *De Clementia Commentary* Calvin was explaining an unusual meaning of *subitus*, hence the need for a special note. (His phrase there was also ambiguous, since it is not clear whether 'not only ... but also' means 'both', or 'either/or'.) I do not see why Calvin should here have been using the term in its unusual rather than its usual meaning. The French has *subite*, which means 'sudden', but of course sudden happenings in their nature tend to be unexpected, and conversion is not something one plans.

The *Reply* had contained no suggestion of suddenness: on the contrary, we hear there of a protracted struggle. The pattern seems to be replacing memory. What is more, the Preface, as Ganoczy has pointed out,[21] runs together *conversio* and vocation to be a minister of the Gospel: the passage begins with the assertion that 'God drew me from obscure and lowly beginnings and conferred on me that most honourable office of herald and minister of the Gospel' (CO 31, 21). It continues with an account of his studies and conversion, 'the secret rein [or curb] of God's providence' (or does this refer to God's wishing him to be a minister?) and a desire to advance, accompanied by a corresponding neglect of his other studies. Since Calvin never found enough hours in the day to do all that he felt he ought to do, and even blamed himself for indolence (*sub specie aeternitatis*, it must be supposed), we need not take this 'neglect of other studies' too literally, nor need it refer to his law studies: it might equally well refer to 'philosophy' or to Greek. But, he continued, although himself only a *tiro*, a novice in godly doctrine, 'before a year had slipped by, anybody who longed for a purer doctrine kept coming to learn from me' (CO 31, 22). We have no independent evidence at all of Calvin's being besieged by anxious seekers after truth; the reference to 'a year' need not be taken literally (as Parker has pointed out); and in any case there is nothing to say which year this is. At any rate, Calvin claims that he 'began to seek some hiding-place and way to withdraw from the people' (*ibid.*). But without success, for 'God so led me and caused me to twist and turn by various changes [of circumstance] that he never left me at peace in any place, until, in spite of my natural disposition, he brought me into the light' (*ibid.*). Here Calvin seems to be saying that it was the desire to shun publicity and enjoy a private station that caused him to leave France and to 'depart into Germany, in order that, hidden away in some obscure corner, I might in tranquillity enjoy things long denied me' (*ibid.*). Beza's *Vita*, however, gives quite another reason for Calvin's leaving France and one tallying well with independent evidence: 'in order to live more peaceably and according to his conscience'.[22] Calvin appears, then, to have run together his conversion and his vocation to the ministry; in retrospect, the two things could be seen as part and parcel of the same calling. At one time this may not have been clear: Calvin was devastated by his expulsion from Geneva in 1538, possibly because he interpreted it as evidence that he had no vocation to the ministry; otherwise he might have welcomed the expulsion as a merciful release, given his addiction to privacy and scholarship.[23] He may even at one time have reproached himself for not remaining in France and risking the martyr's crown; in later years he continued to be sensitive to the charge that it was easy for him to counsel patience in the face of persecution, sitting safe in Geneva.[24] Memories of past travails of conscience about what to do may account for the lack of clarity of the account, but apart from the conflation of conversion and vocation, all else is conjectural.

Our independent evidence does not permit us to date his conversion any more precisely than does Calvin's own account. He fled Paris, but not France, after Nicholas Cop's Rectoral Sermon on All Saints' Day 1533 had brought down the wrath of the Sorbonne on Cop and all associated with him. It is quite possible that Calvin either wrote the Sermon himself or took part in its composition: of the two extant manuscripts, Calvin's, while incomplete, is both earlier and better than Cop's.[25] But the Sorbonne's verdict that the Sermon is 'Lutheran' is not inescapable; even if it is radically scriptural and anti-scholastic, it also includes an invocation of the Virgin. We know that Calvin resigned his benefices in April 1534, but have no information about his intentions. Calvin visited Lefevre d'Etaples at the court of Marguerite of Navarre in 1534, but we do not know what they discussed. A meeting with Servetus, which Servetus failed to keep, was arranged in 1534,[26] but we do not know what Calvin and Servetus knew of each other that made a meeting seem a profitable enterprise. All we can say with complete confidence is that by the time of the persecution following the Affair of the Placards (against the Mass),[27] Calvin thought it advisable to leave France for the reformed city of Basel. But Basel tolerated a wide diversity of opinions,[28] so even the choice of this place of exile does not permit us to say precisely what views Calvin now held.

One further, equally ambiguous piece of evidence must be introduced here, partly because it bears on the dating of Calvin's conversion, and partly because it concerns us elsewhere. At some time in 1534[29] Calvin completed the first draft of a book later to bear the title *Psychopannychia*. The doctrine against which the work was directed, as abhorrent to most Reformers[30] as it was to the Fifth Lateran Council and to Leo X, who condemned it in 1513, held that the soul dies with the body, to be revitalized at the Last Judgement. The version of the doctrine condemned by Rome was one which attracted Italian Averroist philosophers, but it was quite widespread amongst the spirituals and Anabaptists of what Williams has called the 'Radical Reformation'.[31] Curiously, Luther, alone amongst the orthodox Reformers, espoused soul-sleep; he seems to have found it congenial in that it was another nail in the coffin he had prepared for the invocation of the saints, the doctrine of purgatory and all the malpractices which in his view depended upon it.[32] In the version we now have, which was revised at least once subsequently to the first draft,[33] Calvin's piece was directed against 'the Anabaptists',[34] but it is entirely unclear why Calvin should have thought it worth his while to attack this particular doctrine, which, even if it was not at all uncommon amongst Anabaptists and spirituals, was of primary importance to scarcely any of them.[35] In any case, while there is evidence of Calvin's encountering certain spirituals, especially A. Pocquet and his followers, at the court of Marguerite of Navarre,[36] there is no evidence of 'thousands' being misled by them into this heresy, still less of the existence of thousands of French Anabaptists, despite Calvin's claims in the Preface; nor is there anything to say that the doctrine of soul-sleep was the main preoccupation of Pocquet. In the light of Calvin's later polemics against Anabaptism, it is tempting to think that it was the polemics against Anabaptism that induced Calvin to contribute something, but even in the form in which we have it *Psychopannychia* makes no reference whatever to political matters, despite the fact that in Anabaptist thought soul-sleep and millennialist expectations were often closely associated. The only explanation that Calvin offered for ploughing this admittedly stony ground was that 'when divine truth is openly (*ex professo*) attacked, we must not tolerate the adulteration of one single iota of it';[37] but this was in the second, Basel Preface of 1536. In short, he was more concerned to show that the doctrine was unscriptural and erroneous, as might have been expected given its source,[38] than to demonstrate that any specific evil flowed from entertaining it; but then, the fact that some doctrine which he considered true was being denied was always for Calvin sufficient reason to insist on it all the more strongly. He submitted the manuscript to Capito (at what date is not entirely clear, for Capito's reply is undated, though generally taken to be of 1534),[39] but the latter counselled against publication on the grounds that it might alienate Luther, and give prominence to a doctrine of which people would otherwise have remained in ignorance. There is no reason why Calvin should have known of Luther's espousal of the doctrine; it did not figure in any of Luther's most prominent writings.[40] If he did know, it is just possible that the work was begun while Calvin was still a Romanist:[41] lumping together Luther and the Anabaptists would have been a highly serviceable tactic from that point of view. The extant text still mentions that a certain John, bishop of Rome, had been forced to recant the doctrine by the Theological Faculty of Paris (not usually an authority that Calvin cared to enlist),[42] and contains a reference to 'the same things [having been] handed down to us by tradition'[43] (again not something it was Calvin's later practice to cite with approval). The fact that the existing text consists entirely of scriptural exegesis could be the result of subsequent editing, which might also explain the utter shapelessness of the work: it is surely the worst organized thing Calvin ever wrote.[44]

As has already been remarked, *Psychopannychia* contains no reflections whatever of a political sort, and while it certainly exhibits a profound aversion to schisms and sects,[45] the burden of its argument is not that soul-sleep is a schismatic, but that it is an unscriptural, doctrine. Its only interest from our point of view here is that it demonstrates that by 1534 Calvin was thoroughly at home in scriptural learning, a kind of knowledge that is not acquired overnight and which was not in the least in evidence in the *De Clementia Commentary*. On the other hand, the latter work in no way called for an exhibition of such learning, even if Calvin was already possessed of it. That his studies were taking an increasingly scriptural direction by 1534 is not in doubt in any case: the commencing of his Greek studies under Volmar dates from about 1530.[46]

In summary, then, we cannot say when Calvin's conversion took place or what kind of an experience it was. What we can say, however, is that doctrinally Calvin's spiritual history followed a clearly defined path, from scholasticism via humanism to an outright Lutheran position, and that the mediacy of humanism was crucial. Each step along the path, which was trodden by a great many others,[47] was marked by a sloughing off (not as complete as Calvin supposed) of a part of his intellectual inheritance: first of scholastic theology and philosophy, then of pagan philosophy, the vacuum being filled in each case by a more intensive preoccupation with Scripture, and particularly St Paul. The mediacy of Lutherans, to which the *Reply to Sadoleto* still alluded, was also important. That the process did not seem like this in Calvin's retrospect has been explained by reference to the 'sudden' conversion, a break which to Calvin seemed so dramatic that his preconversion state appeared as one of undifferentiated wandering in darkness. The fact that Calvin, unlike Luther, could not assign a precise date to his conversion, suggests perhaps that the *conversio*, the turning around, was more evident in retrospect than it had been at the time.

Appendix II: Predestination

It may be thought odd that predestination has been mentioned only in passing. The explanation for the neglect is (a) that Calvin nowhere used predestination as a starting-point or underpinning either for his political thought or for his ecclesiology, as far as the visible church is concerned, and (b) that its place in the economy of Calvin's theology is not nearly as important as the number of pages he devoted to the topic might suggest. A discussion of predestination in all its aspects would require another book and another author; here we are concerned with it solely in its relationship, or lack of it, to Calvin's political thought.

We have seen that predestination rated barely a mention in the first edition of the *Institution*, but that a separate article was devoted to it in the 1537 *Catechisme*. In the 1539 *Institution*, a very substantial chapter 'Concerning predestination and the providence of God' appeared; it was lodged, for no obvious reason, between another new chapter on the relationship between the Old and the New Testament and a chapter on prayer. In the 1559 edition, the chapter was split up: predestination was allotted to book 3, chs 21–4, providence to book 1, chs 16–17, and the lines which had linked the two themes were suppressed.[1] We shall return to the significance of this in a moment. In addition, Calvin wrote two treatises on the subject,[2] and also several pamphlets between 1557 and 1562 directed at Castellio, notable chiefly for their unbridled vituperativeness, and constituting perhaps the least glorious episode in Calvin's literary career.[3] Finally, in 1562, Calvin published the transcript of a *congrégation* originally held in 1551.[4]

The sheer volume of these writings by itself indicates only the difficulty and controversial nature of the subject, and the expansive habits of sixteenth-century polemic. Nonetheless, Calvin deliberately chose this exposed ground, especially by insisting on both reprobation and election, and the hostility and interminable controversy he incurred were entirely predictable.

The first expansion of the doctrine, then, occurred between 1536 and 1539. It does not appear that Calvin was merely taking part in a controversy which was already under way. However, Melanchthon's 1535 edition of his *Loci Communes* unquestionably marked a departure from his position on predestination and free will in 1521[5] and from Luther's *De Servo Arbitrio*, and Calvin may well have seen in this a reason for reaffirming evangelical orthodoxy against a new incursion of human traditions. That this danger to the purity of doctrine should come from Melanchthon, whom Calvin always held in high regard, would have made an articulation of what he had previously simply taken for granted all the more urgent. At any rate, the new emphasis on predestination can hardly be ascribed[6] to the fact that between 1536 and 1539 Calvin was occupying himself intensively with Romans, where that doctrine figures prominently, for the first edition of the *Institution* already contains more references to Romans than to any other book of either the Old or the New Testament.

It is correct to say that Calvin presented the doctrine of predestination in the *Institution* (though not in the *De Aeterna Dei Predestinatione*) as an answer to the question: Why is the Word not preached to all men, and why, of those to whom it is preached, do so many either pay no attention, or hear for a time and then relapse? (3.21.1).[7] This has been taken by Wendel and others to mean that Calvin took his point of departure from fact and experience, not from any speculative idea, and that it was practical, pastoral and ecclesiological considerations which moved him to insist on the doctrine.[8] This is not persuasive. Calvin presented his doctrine, as has been said, as an answer to a question in two parts. First: Why has the Word of God not been preached to the greatest part of mankind, who are accordingly reprobated? Calvin had already argued that the knowledge of natural law is enough to damn them in their consciences, and therefore did not require predestination to answer the only question which experience posed, that is, the fact (of history and contemporary life) that most of mankind had never heard the Word. Second: Why, of those who hear the Word, do only a few persevere in faith? This is not an item of knowledge vouchsafed by experience, for we are not entitled to infer from experience whether any one or any number of individuals are elect or reprobated: Judas, chosen by Christ himself, was reprobated, whereas the thief on the cross and St Paul, the erstwhile persecutor of the brethren, were numbered amongst the elect. In short, predestination answers theologically a problem which arises theologically and explains out of revelation a fact known only from revelation.[9]

As for the pastoral and ecclesiological considerations which are said to have weighed with Calvin, these again seem doubtful. In view of the ineradicable ignorance of mere mortals concerning who is elect and who not, predestination can yield no principle of pastoral practice or ecclesiastical organization, and Calvin nowhere attempted to elicit one. In 1559 he expressly forbade attempts to coerce belief which treated an unwillingness to hear as evidence of reprobation (3.23.14). Ministers and elders must proceed as if there were no predestination; must proceed indeed as if everyone had a free choice whether to accept or reject the offer of salvation in the Word. He endorsed St Augustine's sentiment that in view of our ignorance of the state of other people's souls, 'we ought to be so minded as to wish all men to be saved'.[10] A presumption of election, the 'judgement of charity', is indicated in dealings between professed Christians, and the forensic judgements required in the exercise of the discipline do not presuppose verdicts about the reprobate status of even those excommunicated, even if, as a matter of practice, Calvin seems to have been fairly confident about his judgement of those who opposed him.

This is not to say that Calvin thought that the doctrine of predestination has no consequences for the life of the Christian, or that he was at a loss about what use and edification was to be drawn from it. On the contrary, he mentioned several ways in which the doctrine is beneficial to those who hear it in the right spirit.[11] But in the light of the cloud of scandals and doubts which the doctrine occasioned, the pastoral benefits to be derived from insisting on it were (to say the least) ambiguous. It was indeed precisely considerations of this kind which weighed with Melanchthon, Bullinger and the Zurich ministers and others[12] in wishing to see the doctrine (in Calvin's words) 'buried'. Pastoral considerations certainly governed the way in which Calvin *defended* the doctrine, but this means no more than that having once determined that the doctrine was indispensable, Calvin had no choice but to try to neutralize the fearful theological and pastoral difficulties the doctrine spawned.

Rather more significant than Calvin's preamble about those who hear and those who do not is his presentation of predestination as a middle way between total suppression and unrestrained speculation.[13] The latter course, as will be seen, is encouraged by the doctrine itself. The former was excluded for Calvin by the nature of the subject-matter itself. And here Calvin unfolded his decisive argument. Scripture teaches nothing but what is necessary and beneficial for us to know. Scripture teaches predestination. Therefore predestination is necessary and beneficial for us to know (3.21.3). The force of this argument ought to be apparent. It was now not even necessary, strictly speaking, for Calvin to be able to demonstrate what uses and benefits redound to us from hearing the doctrine. That Scripture teaches predestination is by itself sufficient reason why the evangelical pastor and theologian should go and do likewise. He is to teach (as Calvin thought he taught) no more than is contained in Scripture, but also no less. Seemingly harmful effects and damaging implications of predestination can therefore count for nothing and are merely apparent: to the pure all things are pure. In short, on his view, predestination was bound to be beneficial in its pastoral consequences, because it was true.

If Calvin had got up this doctrine of the scriptural truth, the whole scriptural truth and nothing but the truth merely in order to justify his teaching this particular doctrine, we might have grounds for looking for esoteric or remote reasons for his doing so. But he always held a whole-Gospel view; he adhered to it even to the extent of trying to find a theological rationale for the endless genealogies in which the Old Testament in particular delights, and even the most apparently unedifying episodes of the Old Testament were made to yield an edifying message. Therefore, if Calvin thought that Scripture taught predestination, he had no choice but to teach it in his turn. The only question is whether his reading of Scripture is in any way idiosyncratic in sixteenth-century evangelical terms. And it is not, at least as far as election is concerned. Scripture, and especially St Paul, certainly does teach predestination. Equally, however, Scripture presupposes what in the sixteenth century would have been understood as free will: it takes it for granted that human beings have choices to make, that they can make choices, and that the choices they make are their choices, for which they are responsible, that choosing the good merits reward and choosing evil deserves punishments, and that God is righteous and judges men according to their deserts.[14] Scripture, then, seems to affirm both free choice and predestination,[15] and the task of theologians since the time of the Church Fathers has been to try to determine what view should be held on this score.

Calvin rejected scholastic treatments of predestination, whether these were Thomist attempts to reconcile human responsibility and divine omnipotence and justice or nominalist ones. To the latter he objected that they implied a God who is *exlex* and whose mere will is law, to the former that they denied providence and were guilty of Pelagianism. In particular, he rejected any attempt to restrict predestination to God's foreknowledge, as opposed to his preordination of the fate of each individual from eternity (3.21.5; 3.22.1), as also any attempt to distinguish between God's will and God's permission (3.23.8). He seems to have thought that he did not need to choose between attenuating human choice and responsibility on the one side or predestination on the other. The falsity of this supposition is apparent from the way in which he misrepresented what nominalists actually thought,[16] a convenient misrepresentation which enabled him to postulate a purely factitious difference between his position and one perfectly familiar amongst nominalists. The problem for the predestinarian, and hence for Calvin, is that of avoiding the conclusion that history is simply the unrolling of a stage play, the scenario, script and parts of which have all been predetermined before the beginning of time.[17] An attendant problem is that of avoiding making God the author of evil, a tyrant whose mere will is law, and who punishes the 'villains' in the cosmic stage play with real punishments, simply for performing their allotted parts. And Calvin's repeated assertions that he rejected all these implications in no way prove that he had in fact succeeded in avoiding them, but merely that he wished to succeed. This is not, of course, to say that the espousal of free will at the expense of predestination carries no theological problems of its own in its train; it is merely to say that these were the problems attendant on Calvin's and the early Reformers' choice. But given his and their reading of the Scriptures through Pauline spectacles, they had little choice but to teach as they did.

Otten is certainly right in saying that one of the functions of predestination in Calvin's theology was as the most radical way of rejecting any doctrine of work-holiness.[18] And in so far as he took the doctrine as being a logical entailment of any other doctrine, rather than as one independently delivered in Scripture, it was an entailment of the doctrine of justification by faith, whose exposition preceded that of predestination in all the versions of the *Institution*, albeit at some distance.[19] The significance of this is that predestination was therefore not treated as a metaphysical inference from the nature of God. It might be thought, for example, that Calvin's reason for espousing predestination was that he inferred it directly from God's omnipotence, and that he thought God's omnipotence would be compromised if human free will were conceded. And while there is evidence of Calvin arguing in this way,[20] it is not the way he normally argued in the *Institution*. Indeed, in the 1559 edition Calvin separated the discussions of providence and predestination entirely, although too much should not be made of this: the separation necessitated much duplication, and the dissevering of discussions could not destroy the conceptual link, especially in view of the fact that for Calvin the universe was created for man, and God's especial providence was for the church.[21]

Thus predestination is not for Calvin a metaphysical inference from God's attributes;[22] it is simply the ultimate, scripturally vouchsafed 'explanation', or more precisely, the final cause of justification and the ultimate specific against any recurrence of work-holiness. Calvin's position much resembles that of Luther in *De Servo Arbitrio*, and like Luther, Calvin claimed to see the doctrine as pointing men towards Christ: it appears in the book of the *Institution* dealing with redemption.[23]

Whether Calvin distinguished sufficiently clearly between what is theologically sound and what is philosophically unexceptionable, and whether he refrained from the habit of spinning out conclusions (*Konsequenztreiberei*, as the Germans untranslatably put it), cannot be discussed here.[24]

In so far as predestination is taken to receive its correct elucidation in the context of justification, it is (for the elect) identical with election, and both are testified to in the consciences of believers by their vocation. This is indeed how Calvin wanted the faithful to understand the doctrine; it is in this way that predestination is said to point to Christ, and it is in this way that it could be described as a 'comforting doctrine' (3.24.4), a claim which in any other context would be a cruel mockery of the anguish experienced by evangelical consciences. It is for this reason, too, that Calvin thought there was no difficulty about identifying the 'use' of preaching predestination: in its connection with justification, the doctrine conduces to humility and gratitude for God's mercy (3.21.1; 3.23.12), and is a preservative against pride (3.21.5, 1559); in connection with the Christian's vocation, it is a source of comfort and assurance (3.24.4–6, 17), provided it is prudently and fittingly taught; and in both respects, the doctrine 'illustrates' God's glory (3.21.3; 3.24.12).

However, but for the explicit scriptural warrant for the doctrine, this account of the 'use' of preaching it could not be persuasive even on Calvin's own showing. For while it is certainly true that knowledge of the doctrine teaches humility, it does so simply in virtue of its reference back to the doctrine of justification by faith. Both doctrines absolutely exclude any cooperation between God and man in the work of salvation, or any sort of work-holiness. But whereas justification by faith highlights God's mercy, predestination points instead to God's power.[25] In as far as predestination means election, it is indeed an instance of God's mercy. But Calvin insisted that reprobation was the direct, deliberate and parallel implication of election: to elect is to reprobate (3.23.1, 1559; and CO 8, 270, *mutua relatio*). The grounds for God's distinguishing between the elect and the reprobate are indeed said to be just grounds, but they are necessarily unintelligible to men; God's righteousness, humanly speaking, is thus indistinguishable from his power. It is noteworthy that on several occasions when Calvin claims that predestination 'illustrates' (that is, makes to shine forth) God's glory, it is reprobation he is speaking about, not election:[26] the reason is that both reprobation and election, but particu-

larly reprobation, exemplify God's unsubordinatedness to
anything humanly conceivable, his freedom from anything
except his own will; the suggestion of arbitrariness cannot be
eliminated, however much Calvin denied it.[27] The answer to
the question why God consigns the overwhelmingly large part
of the special objects of his creation, namely mankind, to
eternal torments would seem to be: Where were you when I
created the world? – an answer in terms of God's power.

Thus in so far as the teaching of predestination reduces
Christians to due humility, it does nothing which is not already
done by the doctrine of justification by faith, a doctrine which,
what is more, does not put the stumbling-block of reprobation
in the way of submission to God's will; justification by faith and
God's omnipotence between them are quite enough to satisfy
the requirement that men be humbled.

As for this being a comforting doctrine – a claim which Calvin
was obliged to make because mere humbling might equally be
grounds for despair or licentiousness of life – Calvin's exposition
itself belies this claim. It will be recalled that it was one of the
main headings of Luther's indictments of the Romanist doctrine
of salvation that the latter conduced to restlessness and despair,
in contrast to the placid confidence inspired by the true
evangelical doctrine.[28] Evangelical *fides* was indeed assurance,
con-*fide*nce. And equally it was one of Calvin's criticisms of the
Council of Trent's doctrine of faith that it denied that anyone
could be assured of salvation while he lived.[29] For the evangelical, the promises of God through Christ and the personal
experience of vocation between them permitted a certitude of
salvation. But while this doctrine was reassuring enough in the
first flush of evangelical conversional vigour, there had been
time enough for evangelicals to experience doubts about their
election. Calvin had no intention of qualifying the original
doctrine of certitude in any way, but the consequence of his
teaching was that he simply perpetuated the doubts that were
de facto being experienced.

His teaching, in so far as the taunts of enemies did not
require him to amplify, was that vocation is our knowledge of
our incorporation in Christ. There is no certitude of salvation
except through Christ, and those who experience any doubts
are told to see their salvation in Christ as in a mirror (3.24.5).
But in this way predestination is a comforting doctrine only to

those already assured of their adoption or incorporation in Christ. But who can be assured of that? Those who have been called (3.24.1, from 1543). But it remains the case that all continue to be plagued with anxiety concerning their elect status.[30] To make matters worse, many seem even to themselves to have been called, only to fall away again after a time (3.24.7). And leaving aside the scriptural passages according to which God wishes all men to be saved (3.24.15–16), it follows that human perception of calling is inherently faulty. For the only sort of calling that reliably testifies to election is a calling joined with perseverance in faith,[31] and this in the nature of things can only be recognized by those who know themselves to be dying.

It should be noted here that it was once again not experience or pastoral considerations which posed the problem with which Calvin was dealing. He was confronting scriptural evidence to the effect that some who for a time seemed to be, and thought themselves to be, of the elect had subsequently fallen away. To handle this difficulty, Calvin insisted that there was a qualitative difference between true certitude of salvation enjoyed by the elect, and mere 'carnal security', which deceived the reprobate, lulling them, so to speak, into a false sense of security.[32] From the standpoint of what is experientially known to the Christian, it is impossible to judge of another's election or reprobation, and neither apparent righteousness nor apparent reprobation raises any difficulty which requires explanation.

However, from the standpoint of the individual assailed by fear and trembling about his salvation, this is no answer at all: he has now to determine whether what he experiences, if he experiences it, is true certitude of salvation or merely carnal security. He has further to determine whether such doubts and travail of conscience (Luther's *Anfechtungen*) as assail him are merely temptations of the devil or evidence of reprobation. And it is impossible to derive from Calvin any criteria immune to distortion by wishful thinking or moroseness of spirit (such as Dr Johnson's) whereby an individual might be assured that he is or is not elect. Calvin simply exhorts to faith in Christ and perseverance in good deeds.

In sum, while the doctrines of providence and justification by faith may fairly be described as comforting doctrines, the same cannot be said of double predestination. It now appears that despite Calvin's animadversions against the papists, the evangelical can be no more assured of his salvation than the papist. It is true that the former is not required to earn his way to heaven by works (not that any Roman theologian of any consequence ever asserted that that was possible or required), but the upshot is simply that there is nothing at all which can provide him with even a modicum of reassurance. For while his 'good works' do not merit a reward, the individual can be very sure that evil works deserve punishment, and the individual inspecting his conscience can be equally sure that his works, take them all in all, are evil. And as far as probabilities are concerned, the probability even amongst nominal Christians would appear to be something between four to one and a hundred to one that any particular individual is amongst those destined for hell-fire.[33]

It may be remarked finally that Calvin's doctrine of reprobation seems to be an instance of precisely that sort of 'metaphysical speculation' which Calvin deplored in the scholastics, and the absence of which from Calvin's theology is applauded by sympathetic exegetes. The decree of reprobation can hardly claim for itself the scriptural evidentness of the decree of election.[34] In any case Calvin repeatedly infers it in the following way: for an omnipotent and omniscient Being to leave someone in the state of damnation, or not to elect him, is indistinguishable from decreeing that he should be reprobated (3.23.1, 3, 6, 7, the last from 1559). The parallel argument, that for an omnipotent and omniscient Being to permit evil is indistinguishable from that Being's willing and indeed being the cause of evil, was of course rejected by Calvin. It seems that Calvin's much proclaimed unwillingness to submit God to measurement by human standards was selective: it was permissible when it suited Calvin's purpose.

In the circumstances, Calvin's extreme vituperativeness towards enemies of the teaching is readily understandable, for anything beyond a bare announcement and a linking of it with justification and vocation at once opened the way to a host of problems. It is noticeable that Calvin systematically treated opposition to the doctrine as opposition to God, even though he was on occasion obliged to admit that some of those who denied it were 'not otherwise bad', a curious way to describe Melanchthon and Bullinger.

The answer to the question why Calvin insisted on the doctrine of double predestination cannot, therefore, be that experience, pastoral considerations or the manifest usefulness of doing so demanded it; on his own showing, the only unequivocal reason for doing so is that Scripture teaches it and the evangelical theologian must therefore do the same: *fiat justitia, ruat coelum*. To ask further why Calvin emphasized predestination amongst all other possible scriptural doctrines is to impute a falsehood. Calvin did not get anywhere near making the doctrine the mainstay of his theology; he eventually even dissociated it, discoursively if not conceptually, from the theme of God's *maiestas*, which undoubtedly was such a mainstay. As Niesel rightly says, predestination is not the central doctrine of Calvin, if by that it is meant that his other doctrines flow from it.[35] And if, as the ultimate revealed ground of the doctrine of justification by faith, this is what other doctrines point to as a subject fit for humble contemplation, it was not double predestination but election that occupied Calvin, and he always found infinitely more to say, and more reason to say it, about justification by faith, than he ever did about predestination.

Finally, in the light of the work of Max Weber, the following question might be posed. Given that the Christian cannot but be in doubt concerning his membership of the elect, he may, despite the illogicality of such a response, seek assurance of salvation by an anxious inspection of his conscience and his works, for it is all he can do. The psychic energies generated by such anxiety might then be released in the form of a righteous zeal. And in view of our interpretation of Calvinian morality as characterized precisely by strenuousness, it might be wondered whether Calvin in any way sought either to generate or to capitalize on such energies.

It should be said first of all that Weber himself insisted (a) that he was treating Calvinism ideal-typically, and (b) that he was speaking not of Calvin's theology but of Calvinism, starting with the epigones.[36] For Calvin, 'the question am I one of the elect? and how can I become certain of this election, was not a problem'.[37] Whether this means that certitude of his own salvation was not a problem, or that general question of certitude was not a problem, it is incorrect. As regards the general question, Calvin treated disquiet, anxiety, doubt, violent temptations (*tentationes*; given the context, this will be

Anfechtungen, rather than more carnal sorts of temptation) as a normal and inescapable feature of the life of faith (3.2.17–18; 3.2.37, added in 1559; cf. also 3.24.4). 'In the course of the present life, it never goes so well with us that we are wholly cured of the disease of unbelief and entirely filled and possessed by faith' (3.2.18). And he offered the assurance that 'faith ultimately triumphs over those difficulties which surround and imperil it'. Naturally, Calvin fully exploited the consciousness of unworthiness and helplessness, fear and trembling: this is saving knowledge for him as for any Christian (3.21.22–3). But these are not doubts and tribulations concerning our election. The remedy for the latter is to look to the promises of God in Christ, the ground of faith, and nowhere else (3.24.4). It is here, too, that we must look for a remedy for the despair which would otherwise be occasioned by our sense of our own unworthiness and vileness (3.2.31–2).

Calvin, *pace* Weber, was therefore well aware of the problem of certainty of election, but, as has been argued already, he had no real answer to it, although he seems not to have been conscious of any insufficiency. What can be said with confidence, as Weber rightly went on to say, is that Calvin rejected the idea that we can infer the election or reprobation of others from their works,[38] and that he also rejected works, although they were the fruits of faith, as marks of election.[39] There is, however, room for an element of doubt as to the last point. For having affirmed once again that man's own efforts can contribute nothing to making him righteous (3.14.6–11, 16–17, largely from 1539), Calvin went on to say that 'the saints quite often strengthen themselves and are comforted by remembering their own innocence and uprightness' (3.14.18). The saints, he argued, do so by turning their eyes solely to God's goodness. 'A conscience so founded, erected and established, is further consolidated by the consideration of works, in so far as these are testimonies of God dwelling and ruling in us', and 'the grace of good works (like all gifts of God) . . . shows that the spirit of adoption has been given to us' (3.14.19; cf. also 3.24.4, added in 1559). Such signs are, however, of value only a *posteriori*, that is on the basis of precedent election and vocation.

Here Calvin is exceedingly anxious that works should not be taken as the reason why we are saved, and the context was the discussion of the scholastic doctrine of salvation and work-righteousness. He was, however, prepared to treat works as evidence of salvation, but even so, he was not here dealing with the doubts of the saints concerning their own election. I suspect that it was the context of opposition to Romanist theologians that once again evoked the stereotyped contrast between evangelical security and Romanist insecurity.[40] There is nothing here which can be taken as encouragement to evangelicals to inspect their works for evidence of their salvation.

Notes

Introduction

1 On this point, see the judicious comments of T. H. L. Parker, *Calvin's New Testament Commentaries* (London, 1971), chapter 1. (Referred to below as CNTC.)

2 Such a view is clearly implied in the practice of many commentators of citing references simply by the volume and page of CO, no other information being vouchsafed to the reader who happens not to have the fifty-nine volumes in question to hand.

1 *The training of a lawgiver*

1 It was not reprinted independently of collected editions of Calvin's writings until 1969.

2 Here I must reluctantly take issue with F. L. Battles's valuable introduction to his translation of the 1536 *Institution* (*Institution of the Christian Religion*, Atlanta, 1975), p. x: 'If . . . [we] view the *Seneca* in the light of the 1536 *Institution* . . .' History is not to be read as witches say their prayers.

3 F. L. Battles and A. M. Hugo (ed. and trans.), *Calvin's Commentary on Seneca's 'De Clementia'* (Leiden, 1969), Introduction, p. 24. All references below are to this edition and its pagination; the edition itself is cross-referenced to the text of the 1532 edition. Even-numbered pages are the Latin text, odd-numbered ones the translation. It will be referred to as *De Clem[entia] Comm[entary]*.

4 T. H. L. Parker, *John Calvin* (London, 1975), p. 159. This is the most authoritative and well-written biography available.

5 My debt to Battles and Hugo in what follows should be apparent. That I dissent from some of their interpretations in no sense detracts from this debt.

6 This was presumably the method of Calvin's revered teacher at Orleans, Pierre de l'Etoile. Cf. Parker, *Calvin*, p. 15: 'In practice [the students'] contact with the *Corpus [Juris Civilis]* was probably at second hand, or rather, third hand, by way of their lecturers' expositions of medieval glosses on the work', especially those of Bartolus.

7 *De Clem. Comm.*, pp. 114/5. To Erasmus he assigned only second place: *ibid.*, pp. 6/7.

8 This is cogently argued by J. G. A. Pocock, 'The Origins of the Study of the Past' in *Comparative Studies in Society and History* 4 (1961–2), pp. 226–32.

9 In a lecture before the visiting Francis I, Alciati asserted the superiority of Roman law over Plato's and Aristotle's more than forty books on morals. Cf. Q. Breen, *John Calvin: A Study in French Humanism* (Hamden, 1968), p. 50.

10 Cf., for example, *Commentary on Acts* II (1554), on Acts 16.21: 'The Roman laws were splendid.' And cf. B. Hall, 'John Calvin, the Jurisconsults and the Jus Civile', in *Studies in Church History* 3 (1966), pp. 202–16.

11 Cf. ch. 6.

12 What remains of Calvin's drafts has been reprinted in CO 10, I, pp. 125–46. Cf. ch. 6.

13 Some comments on this vexed question may be found in Appendix 1.

14 Guillaume Budé, who may be supposed to have known his erstwhile pupil's limitations, wrote his *Institution du Prince* for him in French, a language in which Budé was clearly acutely ill at ease.

15 *De Clem. Comm.*, pp. 354/5: 'Clemency is an inclination of the mind towards leniency in exacting punishment.' He did, however, sometimes use it in a more general sense: *ibid.* pp. 86/7: 'est enim clementia vere humanitas' where he seems to be equating it with *mansuetudo*, 'gentleness'. This seems also to be the sense in which he referred in the Prefatory Letter of the 1536 *Institutio* to the *clementia* of Francis I (OS I, 21).

16 'optimum authorem' (pp. 6/7), rendered as 'best of authors' by Battles and Hugo, might of course mean no more than 'excellent author', which would somewhat lessen the extent of the hyperbole.

17 Seneca was in fact an extremely popular mine for the *bons mots*, *elegantiae* and flowers of speech and wisdom which the age relished. That he should also have found detractors in no way justifies Calvin's claim that there was a 'fixed prejudice' against Seneca (pp. 6/7). On Seneca's popularity, see Battles's and Hugo's Introduction (pp. 41–2); they, however, seem disposed to take Calvin's claims at face value.

18 It strikes me, all the same, that the commentary on the last book or so is mechanical and shows an impatience to get to the end.

19 Battles and Hugo single out particularly Erasmus's *Adagia* and Beroaldus's *De Optimo Statu Libellus*.

20 This explains expressions like Erasmus's *philosophia Christi*. The term was used in Augustine's time; cf. R. A. Markus (ed.), *Augustine* (New York, 1972), p. viii.

21 The evidence is from Beza, *Vita Calvini*, CO 10, I, 126. It is a little too reminiscent of the 'early signs of promise' component in the 'lives of the saints' genre, and may be *ben trovato*. Calvin did function as a director of souls on at least one occasion before he left France (*De Clem. Comm.*, p. 40); he would have been entitled to preach in view of his ecclesiastical status as a clerk in minor orders, although he was never a priest. Cf. Ganoczy, *Le Jeune Calvin, Genèse et Evolution de sa Vocation Réformatrice* (Wiesbaden, 1966), pp. 53–4.

22 Historians of the laws and institutions of France like Jean du Tillet,

Bernard du Haillan and Etienne Pasquier, writing in the second half of the century, were rather more concerned about dates. Biblical chronology is a later preoccupation. Cf. P. Hazard, *The European Mind, 1680–1715* (Harmondsworth, 1964), esp. ch. 2; D. R. Kelley, *The Foundations of Modern Historical Scholarship: Language, Law and History in the French Renaissance* (New York, 1970).

23 Calvin's strictures will be found mainly in his comments on book 2, chs 5 and 7.

24 Battles and Hugo, Introduction, pp. 46–62, provide an excellent account of the various Christian attitudes to Seneca, including those of Erasmus, Budé and Calvin himself.

25 *De Clem. Comm.*, pp. 334/5, and compare the editors' footnotes.

26 Literally: 'he ran in his own field' (*in campo suo currit*).

27 *De Clem. Comm.*, pp. 10/11. My translation agrees with Battles's and Hugo's in considering the praise rather faint, but I read in Calvin's words a side-long glance at the scholastics. For a humanist to praise someone for 'eloquence' was, of course, high praise *per se*.

28 E.g. the introductory comments about the task on which Seneca was engaged (pp. 22/3): 'It is in this round-about way that Seneca insinuates himself into Nero's good graces.'

29 Battles's and Hugo's list of such terms used by Calvin fills one and a half pages, double columns (Introduction, pp. 80–1).

30 Thomas More, *Utopia* in the Yale edition of *The Works of Thomas More*, vol. 4 (New Haven and London, 1965), esp. pp. 98–103. Erasmus's edition of *The Works of L. Annaeus Seneca* (1529) bears the legend: 'most useful both for speaking well and living well' (cited Battles and Hugo, Introduction, p. 32).

31 This point is expanded in chs 3, 4 and 6.

32 *Pace* Battles and Hugo, Introduction, p. 139.

33 It is perhaps relevant to remark that the only part of More's *Utopia* in which he was articulating a genuine perplexity, the 'Dialogue of Counsel' to use Hexter's term, is in the form of a dialogue; the humanist sermon on pride which forms the 'Discourse of Utopia' abandons this form, for here More was only retailing moral reach-me-downs in an arresting manner.

34 Note the expressions 'frivolis argutiis' (*De Clem. Comm.*, pp. 78/9) and 'scholasticis argutiis' (*argutiae*: 'quibbling', pp. 336/7). In a little-noticed discussion of 'the absurdities [of] the Sorbonnists' concerning the 'contemplative life', Calvin attributed their espousal of it to ambition, which in turn begat pride in their own indolence. *Gospel Harmony* (1555), on Luke 10.38–42.

35 Hence his later embarrassment at the labyrinthine subtleties required to defend the doctrine of predestination, and his insistence that the matter itself would be straight-forward, but for the malice of the detractors from this 'necessary' doctrine in confusing it.

36 Pp. 42/3, 146/7; the expression does not occur at either point in Seneca's text.

37 J. G. A. Pocock, *The Ancient Constitution and the Feudal Law* (Cambridge, 1957), chs I–III, is indispensable for understanding customary law,

which in France would be the Salic Law and the *coutumes*. But see also F. Kern, *Kingship and Law in the Middle Ages* (Oxford, 1939).

38 Pp. 270/1; cf. also pp. 68/9, 70/1, 378/9, all to the same effect. A citation of Budé by Calvin is equivalent to an express endorsement of the opinion cited.

39 This ambiguity recurred ten years later in his account of the *jurisdictio* of the church. Cf. p. 114.

40 *Institutes of Justinian*, 1.2.6; Calvin's quotation (in fact a paraphrase) is on pp. 36/7.

41 On this, and on arguments by correspondence, W. H. Greenleaf, *Order, Empiricism and Politics* (London, 1964) chs 1 and 2, is essential reading.

42 Pp. 90/1. Calvin did not at this point allude to Augustine, but he cited the *City of God* seventeen times (p. 415) and he did impute 'the splendid virtues of the pagans' to 'ambition' in a thoroughly Augustinian manner (cf. pp. 94/5 and footnote; but cf. Introduction, p. 132 fn. 5).

43 Pp. 186/7. The subject is mentioned at pp. 34/5, 134/5 and 140/1.

44 Contrast Budé's *Institution du Prince* (1519), reprinted in C. Bontemps, L. P. Raybond and J. P. Brancourt, *Le Prince dans la France des XVIᵉ et XVIIᵉ Siècles* (Paris, 1965), esp. pp. 100–2.

45 See the sources cited below, p. 272 n. 49.

46 Pp. 42/3. The reference is to the *Codex* of Justinian.

47 Pp. 212/13; *ius*, of course, like *droit* and *Recht*, may mean both what is right and what is legal.

48 E.g. pp. 116/17; cf. also pp. 40/1.

49 E.g. pp. 116/17; cf. also pp. 40/1: Seneca's text: 'displays might through terror'. Calvin: 'This is customary in tyrants . . . By their raging they find out how far they can go.' And pp. 146/7: 'How great a plague do you think will come upon the earth if princes, free of the laws, released from all, as they say, reins and restraints (*frenis et repagulis*), would only wish to exercise their power in order to do harm?' The metaphor of *frenum*, 'bridle' or 'rein', was to become Calvin's favourite. It does not occur in Seneca's text at this point, but was used by him in connection with the people's need for restraint. Claude de Seyssel had spoken of 'freins' upon the French king in his *La Grant Monarchie de France* of 1519, but there is no evidence that Calvin had read it.

50 Pp. 320/1. He also took up Seneca's comment that tyrants 'invent devices by which suffering may be varied', adding: 'for it is not enough for tyrants to inflict death, but they are always devising new methods by which those whom they wish ultimately to perish may languish long in pain: in order really to feel themselves dying, as Caligula used to boast'.

51 Pp. 152–5; the discussion of Dionysius (pp. 204/5) is obscure.

52 Unless we choose so to regard his endorsement or espousal of certain expressions such as *pastor* (pp. 86/7), which he himself introduced as a description of the prince, and *pater patriae* (pp. 104/5; 120/1; 236/7 ff.), which occurs in Seneca's text, and on which Calvin offered learned, and apparently approving, disquisitions.

53 'Factious, discordant, unruly: these are the invariable epithets which are applied to the crowd (*multitudo*), and not without reason' (pp. 24/5). Calvin then went on to characterize the crowd (*turba, plebs imperita,*

vulgus, insana multitudo) as 'anxious for novelties', faction-prone, head-strong and 'ready to run riot'.

54 Pp. 302/5. 'Excision' from the commonwealth is to be reserved for the 'incurable': pp. 74/5.

2 The 'Institution': the first version

1 He arrived at the turn of the year 1534/5.
2 The literature refrains from speculation on this choice of name, and so shall I. The anonymous referee from Cambridge University Press points out that 'Lucianus' is an anagram of 'Caluinus'. 'Martianus' defeats me.
3 By authorizing persecutions of 'Lutherans' after the 'Affair of the Placards' of 17 October 1534.
4 On which see Appendix I.
5 The first translation of the *Institution* into English, that of Thomas Norton of 1561, simply retained the word 'institution'. But an English translation and abridgement by Edmund Bunnie and Edward May of 1580 refers to the book as *The Institutes of Christian Religion* and 'M. I. Calvin's Institutions', and so does another abridgement of 1596 by Piscator. In 1636 there appeared *Analysis Paraphrastica Institutionum Theologicarum Joh. Calvini*, and various seventeenth-century Latin editions have the title *Institutionum Christianae Religionis Libri Quattuor*. The nineteenth-century translations of John Allen and H. Beveridge have *Institutes*. (My sources are the British Library and the National Union Catalogues.)
6 Cf. Erasmus, *Institutio Principis Christiani* (1516) and G. Budé, *L'Institution du Prince* (title, not his own, for the published version of 1547). And cf. Luther, *Sermons on the Catechism* (1528), in *Luther's Works* (Philadelphia, 1959), vol. 51, p. 181: '[The Creed] should be an *institutio*, that is to say, instruction for the children and simple Christians . . .' On the other hand, the Italian writer Francesco Patrizi (1412–94) used *Institutio* in two book-titles: *De Institutione Reipublicae*, where it means 'founding', and *De Regno et Regis Institutione*, where it means 'education'. (My source is Q. Skinner, *The Foundations of Modern Political Thought* (Cambridge, 1978), vol. 1, p. 269.)
7 French versions have always simply retained Calvin's own *Institution*, Dutch translations are always entitled *Institutie ofte Onderviisinge*, and German ones have *Unterricht*.
8 *Constitutiones* was the common sixteenth-century term for 'statutes'. Compare the German equivalent of the time, 'Satzungen', which appears to be a translation from the Latin. As regards *instituere*, let us take examples at random from both French and Latin, early and late, public and private writings: letter to P. Daniel, October 1536 (CO 10, II, 64): 'Disputationes . . . instituae fuerant senatus Bernensis decreto . . .'; *Catechisme*, 1537 (OS 1, 416): 'Qu'ilz instituent la vie du peuple par tres bonnes loix . . .'; *Institutio* of 1543 (CO 1, 411): 'nonne Deo et naturae ab Eo institutae repugnemus . . .'; (CO 1, 572): 'de ministeriis, ut sunt a Christo institutis'; (CO 1, 562): 'in sua

[God's] hac institutione [i.e. the ministry] . . .'; (*ibid.*): 'vetera ecclesia . . . divinae institutionis imago'; (CO 1, 578): 'instituere ministros [i.e. 'appoint']'; letter to Neuchâtel, November 1544 (CO 11, 763) concerning ecclesiastical censures: 'Vestrum ergo institutum, quale describitis, sanctum et legitimum esse iudicamus'; *Commentary on Isaiah*, 1552 (CO 36, 38): 'Ceremonias instituit Deus . . .'; *Sermons on Deuteronomy*, 1555 (unpublished transcript, CO 25, 645): 'Quand les Rois, les Princes et Magistratz sont instituez . . .'

9 OS I, 22: 'the fury of certain wicked persons has prevailed so far in your realm'; *ibid.*, p. 35: 'the wicked poison of our calumniators'; *ibid.*, p. 22: 'more through the tyranny of certain Pharisees than with your approval'.

10 OS I, 22. Nor was there any need for something elementary: there was already Guillaume Farel's *Sommaire et Brièfve Declaration . . .* of 1525.

11 Published in 1525, the work was dedicated to Francis I.

12 Battles, *Institution*, pp. xxxii–xxxiii.

13 The letter was reprinted in all subsequent editions of the *Institution*, although Francis I died in 1547. It was thus no more a letter to Francis I than the *Reply to Sadoleto* was a reply to Sadoleto.

14 E.g. OS I, 21: *causam nostram*. The context in which Calvin was using the term was explicitly juridical, at least by analogy: he was claiming to offer a defence of a case which would otherwise go unheard. But the term 'cause' here seems to be well on the way to its modern meaning. The Calvinist derivation of the change in meaning is asserted by Eric Voegelin, *The New Science of Politics* (Chicago and London, 1952), p. 135, noting an observation of Richard Hooker's.

15 There are some valuable observations on the purpose of the *Institution* in CNTC, ch. 1.

16 Cf. Appendix 1. A. Ganoczy, *Le Jeune Calvin*, ch. 2, Article 1, is a comprehensive study of the nature and extent of Calvin's debts.

17 See two letters of 1538 (CO 10, 1, 139) and 1540 (CO 11, 24) and the high praise for Luther in the *Commentary on Isaiah* (both editions, 1552 and 1559) at Isaiah 57.1. Cf. also B. Gerrish, 'John Calvin on Luther', in J. Pelikan (ed.), *Interpreters of Luther* (Philadelphia, 1968), pp. 67–96.

18 Ganozcy, *Le Jeune Calvin*, p. 139.

19 Zwingli's works cited below follow a different order; so do Melanchthon's *Loci Communes* and Bucer's *Enarrationes Perpetuae;* so does Guillaume Farel's *Sommaire et Brièfve Declaration* of 1525.

20 Luther's seminal *Freedom of a Christian* of 1520 does not discuss the church or secular authority in any context. The clue to this omission is the assertion: 'So müssen wir nu gewiss sein, dass die Seele kan allis dings emperen on des Worts gottis, und on das Wort gottis ist yhr mit keynem ding beholfen'. *Von der Freiheit eines Christenmenschen* (WA 7, 22). (All references to Luther are to the Weimar Edition, 'WA'.) His other main writings of that year confine themselves to destructive criticism of the current state of the church, with a view to freeing Christian consciences and, where secular authority takes a hand, Christian persons from bondage to man-made impositions. See: *Von den guten Werken* (*On Good Works*), *An den christlichen Adel deutscher Nation* (*To*

the Christian Nobility of the German Nation), *De Captivitate Babylonica* (*Concerning the Babylonian Captivity of the Church*), and *Von dem Papstthum zu Rom* . . . (*On the Papacy at Rome*).

21 See for example *Von den guten Werken*, 1520 (WA 6, 212, 214); *Von dem Papstthum zu Rom* . . ., 1520 (WA 6, 293, 294, 296, 297); *Auf das überchristliche Buch Bock Emsers Antwart* (*Reply to the Ram Emser's Hyperchristian Book*), 1521 (WA 7, 63); *Wider die himmlischen Propheten* (*Against the Heavenly Prophets*), 1524/5 (WA 18, 63, 66, 136); *Ob Kriegsleute auch im seeligen Stand sein können* (*Whether Soldiers too can be in a State of Grace*), 1526 (WA 19, 625); *Von den Schlüsseln* (*On the Keys*), 1530 (WA 30, II, 437).

22 Melanchthon's *Loci Communes* of 1521 mentioned the church only twice, once to insist that 'ecclesiastical laws do not bind the conscience', the other to say that 'ecclesiastical magistrates' were inferior in authority to, and dependent for their authority on, Scripture. H. Engelland (ed.), *Melanchthons Werke* (Gütersloh, 1952), vol. II, part I, pp. 56–63, 159–60. This should be compared to the extensiveness of his discussion of Christian liberty. Zwingli's *Commentary on True and False Religion* of 1525 merely denied the title of 'church' to the pope and his bishops, and insisted on the rights of the congregations (*peculiares ecclesiae*) to judge doctrine and excommunicate, not troubling to specify who was entitled to act on behalf of these congregations: *De Vera et Falsa Religione* . . . *Commentarius* (Zurich, 1525), esp. pp. 171–94.

23 Note the language of *De Captivitate Babylonica*, esp. WA 6, 512. Practically all the proposals in *An den christlichen Adel* (WA 6, 427–57) concern the banning, ending or abolition of practices and arrangements; no specific new arrangements are enjoined at all. Luther remained reluctant to specify precise arrangements. Cf. *De Instituendis Ministris Ecclesiae* (*On Establishing Ministers of the Church*), 1523 (WA 12, 160–97).

24 E.g. Luther, *De Servo Arbitrio* (WA 18, 606), for a particularly extreme statement. Zwingli, *Commentarius*, p. 60: 'audacter ignaros, vel scienter impios . . .'.

25 At times, Luther thought the demands of Christian liberty satisfied by rectifications of the understanding which might leave external practices little altered. This seems to be his position in *De Captivitate Babylonica* (e.g. WA 6, 507, 524–5, 536–7, 546); *Von dem Papstthum* (WA 6, 321–2); *Eine treue Vermahnung*, 1521 (WA 8, 678–88). *Von den guten Werken* (WA 6, 202–76) seems to adopt this position throughout. The extent to which the external order of the church required recasting only gradually became clear to Luther.

26 This was an ironic consequence of Luther's diagnosis of the papacy as a secular tyranny: all *de facto* powers, irrespective of their title, were owed obedience. *Von dem Papstthum* (WA 6, 321): 'Die weyl wir sehen, das der Bapst ist ubir alle Bischoff in voller gewalt, da hin er on gottichen rad nit ist kummenn, wie wol ichs nit acht, das ausz gnedigem, sondern mehr ausz zornigem rad gotis datzu kummenn sey . . .' In *De Captivitate Babylonica* (WA 6, 536–7), the duty to obey the tyranny of the pope is derived from the duty to turn the other cheek.

27 I here follow B. Moeller, *Imperial Cities and the Reformation* (Philadelphia,

1972), essay with same title. Cf. also R. Walton, *Zwingli's Theocracy* (Toronto, 1967), pp. 76–86.

28 *Von göttlicher und menschlicher Gerechtigkeit, wie die zemen sehind und standind*. In F. Blanke, O. Farner and R. Pfister (eds), *Zwingli, Hauptschriften* (Zurich, 1942), vol. VII, p. 55.

29 G. W. Locher, *Die Zwinglische Reformation im Rahmen der europäischen Kirchengeschichte* (Göttingen and Zurich, 1979), p. 39.

30 *Von der Freiheit eines Christenmenschen* (WA 7, 21).

31 *De Captivitate Babylonica* (WA 6, 507) (concerning communion under both kinds and confession); 536: 'neque Papa neque Episcopus neque ullus hominum habet ius unius syllabae constituendae super Christianum hominem, nisi id fiat eius consensu. Quicquid aliter fit, tyrannico spiritu . . .'; 566; *Von weltlicher Oberkeit* (*On Secular Authority*), 1523 (WA 11, 252–3, 263–5, 268); *De Instituendis Ministris* (WA 12, 180–1, 184, 187–8).

32 *Ob Kriegsleute auch in seeligem Stand sein können* (*Whether Soldiers too can be in a State of Grace*), 1526 (WA 19, 657); *Von weltlicher Oberkeit* (WA 11, 277–8).

33 See especially *De Captivitate Babylonica* (WA 6, 537); *Wider die himmlischen Propheten* (WA 18, 112–113); *De Instituendis Ministris* (WA 12, 189); *Von den guten Werken* (WA 6, 259).

34 *De Instituendis Ministris* (WA 12, 171).

35 *Von dem Papstthum* (WA 6, 296): 'die naturlich, eygentlich, rechte, wesentliche Christenheit stehe ym geiste, unnd in keinem eusserlichenn ding . . .'.

36 *Von dem Papstthum* (WA 6, 300–301). Luther did not usually qualify the term 'church' with any adjective; he seems never to have used the term 'visible church' at all (although he had used the term 'invisible church' as early as the *Dictata* of 1513–15).

37 *An den christlichen Adel* (WA 6, 406–15); *De Captivitate Babylonica*, throughout; *Von dem Papstthum*, throughout, especially WA 6, 287 ('geweltige ubirkeyt'), 300, 321–2; *Von weltlicher Oberkeit* (WA 11, 271); Cf. S. S. Wolin, *Politics and Vision* (London, 1961), ch. 5.

38 *An den christlichen Adel* (WA 6, 408): 'Die wyl dan nu die weltlich gewalt ist gleych mit uns getaufft, hat den selben glauben unnd Evangely, mussen wir sie lassen priester und Bischoff sein, und yr ampt zelen als ein ampt, das da gehore und nutzlich sey der Christenlichen gemeyne.' Compare *Von der Freiheit* (WA 7, 27–8); *De Instituendis Ministris* (WA 12, 181–4, 193–4); *De Captivitate Babylonica* (WA 6, 507).

39 *Das eine christliche Versammlung oder Gemeine Recht und Macht habe, alle Lehre zu urtheilen und Lehrer zu berufen . . .* (*That a Christian Community or Congregation has the Right and Power to Judge All Doctrine, and to Appoint . . . Teachers*, 1523 (WA 11, 408–16). Cf. also *An den christlichen Adel* (WA 6, 407–12).

40 *Von dem Papstthum* (WA 6, 301): 'Die zeichnn, da bey man euszerlich mercken kan, wo die selb kirch in der welt ist, sein die tauff, sacrament und das Evangelium'. *De Instituendis Ministris* (WA 12, 173): 'cum sine verbo nihil constet in Ecclesia et per solum verbum omnia constent'.

41 See the excellent discussion and the quotations and literature cited in W. D. J. Cargill Thompson, 'The "Two Kingdoms" and the "Two Regiments": Some Problems of Luther's *Zwei-Reiche-Lehre*' in his *Studies in the Reformation: Luther to Hooker*, ed. C. W. Dugmore (London, 1980), pp. 42–59.

42 The *locus classicus* is *Von weltlicher Oberkeit*, but see also *Ein Sendbrief von dem harten Büchlein wider die Bauern (Missive about the Harsh Pamphlet against the Peasants)*, 1525 (WA 18, 389–90), and quotations cited in Cargill Thompson, 'The "Two Kingdoms" ', pp. 213–16.

43 *Von weltlicher Oberkeit* (WA 11, 249–50): 'Disse leutt durffen keyns welltlichen schwerdt noch rechts'. *Von der Freiheit* (WA 7, 21–3).

44 An implication of Luther's *theologia crucis*. In his *Von den guten Werken* (WA 6, 259), Luther described the temporal power as 'only a trivial thing in the sight of God' ('gar ein gering ding fur got'), and inferred the duty of not resisting it from its incapacity to harm the soul.

45 *Von den guten Werken* (WA 6, 213–15), where he divided men into four classes and demanded special consideration for the fourth class, the 'weak in faith'. Cf. also his *Preface to the Epistle of St Paul to the Romans*, 1522 (WA *Deutsche Bibel*, 7), on Romans 14. Discussions of 'scandals' and their avoidance were an evangelical commonplace. Cf. Melanchthon, *Loci Communes (Werke*, vol. II, part I), pp. 161 ff.; Zwingli, *Commentarius*, pp. 412–28.

46 In general, Luther's position seems to be that secular government cannot harm the soul, but spiritual government can: *Von den guten Werken* (WA 6, 259); and *De Captivitate Babylonica* (WA 6, 537). But see also *Ermahnung zum Frieden, auf die zwölf Artickel der Bauerschafft . . . (Admonition to Peace, Concerning the Twelve Articles of the Peasantry)*, 1525 (WA 18, 322): 'Wer aber myr das Evangelion weret, der schleusst myr den hymel zu und iagt mich mit gewallt ynn die helle.' And compare *Von weltlicher Oberkeit*, WA 11, 263, lines 8–9, with 262, lines 24–5. There is a suspicion of casual expression about all these assertions.

47 I do not find in Luther's political writings, all of which are *Streitschriften*, any of that care or subtlety over terminology which marks his theological expositions; in the former he never examined his organizing ideas except with a view to making polemical points.

48 WA 11, 262.

49 WA 11, 262–4, 268.

50 WA 11, 267.

51 *Wider die himmlischen Propheten* (WA 18, 136): 'das die eusserlichen stücke sollen und müssen vorgehen. Und die ynnerlichen hernach und durch die eusserlichen komen . . .' The reference is to the 'spoken word of the Gospel'. He had previously in the same work used 'external' in a thoroughly dismissive manner, pp. 66, 120, 122.

52 *Von weltlicher Oberkeit* (WA 11, 264); *Von den guten Werken* (WA 6, 259); *Ermahnung zum Frieden* (WA 18, 309); *Ob Kriegslsute . . .* (WA 19, 636).

53 Cargill Thompson, 'The "Two Kingdoms".' See also H. H. Schrey (ed.), *Reich Gottes und Welt* (Darmstadt, 1969), sections IV and V. This excellent collection unfortunately includes no contribution by Johannes

Heckel, the foremost contributor to the debate, whose interpretation on the two *Reiche* I favour.

54 WA 11, 250: 'Nu aber keyn mensch von natur Christen odder frum ist, sondern altzumal sünder und böse sind, weret yhnen Gott allen durchs gesetz, das sie eusserlich yhr bossheyt mitt wercken nicht thüren noch yhrem muttwillen üben.' Luther does not seem to have adduced his notion of man as *simil justus et peccator* in this connection, but he at times alleviated the extreme other-worldliness of the Christian's unconcern with worldly things.

55 *Sendbrief von dem harten Büchlein* (WA 18, 389); *Von weltlicher Oberkeit* (WA 11, 247, 251, 'law and sword' throughout). *Ob Kriegsleute . . .* (WA 19, 629).

56 In *Ob Kriegsleute . . .* Luther treated all questions of obedience and resistance from the point of view of each individual's having a superior, except the Emperor, against whom Luther elsewhere found it difficult to justify resistance; he did so with the utmost reluctance and only in terms of what he took to be the given legalities of the situation. See Skinner, *Foundations*, vol. II, pp. 194–202. Luther also conceived good government in terms of good princes, as opposed to good laws. *De Captivitate Babylonica* (WA 6, 554); *Von weltlicher Oberkeit* (WA 11, 272); *Von den guten Werken* (WA 6, 260–1); *An den christlichen Adel* (WA 6, 549); *Ob Kriegsleute . . .* (WA 19, 600).

57 *Von weltlicher Oberkeit* (WA 11, 273); *Ermahnung zum Frieden* (WA 18, 293–9).

58 *Von weltlicher Oberkeit* (WA 11, 270–1).

59 Much as Calvin did in the *De Clementia Commentary*. Luther's proposals for reform often included exhortations to the secular authorities to take public morals firmly in hand, especially in the matter of brothels, usury, ostentation in dress, gluttony and drunkenness. *Von den guten Werken* (WA 6, 261–3); *An den christlichen Adel* (WA 6, 465–8).

60 *Wider die himmlischen Propheten* (WA 18, 80–1). The assertion in WA 11, 250 that Christians are 'durch den geyst unnd glawben aller ding genaturt, das sie wol und recht thun mehr denn man sie mit allen gesetzen leren kan' presupposes that laws aim at inculcating a certain level of morality.

61 See the excellent discussion of J. Lecler, *Histoire de la Tolérance* (Aubier, 1955), vol. I, pp. 168–75 and the texts cited there. The concluding paragraph of *Von dem Greuel der Stillmesse, so man den Canon nennet* (*Of the Abomination of the Silent Mass, Called the Canon*), 1525 (WA 18, 36) reads: 'Darumb, lieben Christen, last uns fur solchem grewel fliehen, und der sach eynis werden, das man kan durch ordentliche gewalt dise Gotteslesterung abthun, das wyr nicht frembde sunde auff unsern hals laden, Denn die oeberkeyt schuldig ist, solche offentliche Gottes lesterung zu weren und straffen, leydet sie es aber und sihet zu, wo sie es weren kan, wird doch Gott nicht durch die finger sehen, und mit grewlichem ernst beyde die lesterer, und so dazu verwilligen, straffen . . .'

62 Lecler, *ibid.* Much of Luther's advice on these matters was in private letters.

63 Cf. the memorandum of Luther, Bugenhagen, Melanchthon, and Creutziger of 1536 quoted in Lecler, *Tolérance*, pp. 174–5, and the letter to Spalatin of 11 November 1525, *ibid*. The accent throughout is on the honour of God requiring such repression. The letter to Spalatin asserts a position which Luther had explicitly rejected in *Von weltlicher Oberkeit* (WA 11, 268).

64 *An die Ratsherren aller Städte deutschen Landes, dass sie christliche Schulen aufrichten und halten sollen* (*Exhortation to the Councillors of All the Towns of Germany to Erect and Maintain Christian Schools*), 1524 (WA 15, 27–53). Luther also wished all to be compelled to go to sermons; Lecler, *Tolérance*, pp. 171–2.

65 WA 36, 195 ff.

66 S. Ozment, *The Reformation in the Cities* (New Haven and London, 1975), pp. 121–5; Locher, *Zwinglische Reformation*, chs IX (Zurich) and XIV (Bern).

67 There are some very sensible remarks on this topic in J. W. Allen, *A History of Political Thought in the Sixteenth Century* (reprinted London, 1977), pp. 23–6.

68 H. Schmid, *Zwinglis Lehre von der göttlichen und menschlichen Gerechtigkeit* (Zurich, 1959), esp. pp. 15–17, 210 ff.

69 F. Wendel, *L'Eglise de Strasbourg* (Paris, 1942), *passim*.

70 W. Köhler, *Zürcher Ehegericht und Genfer Konsistorium*, Quellen zur Schweizerischen Reformationsgeschichte 13 (Leipzig, 1942), *passim*, but see particularly the account of the proposals of Conrad Sam at Ulm in 1531, pp. 20 ff. It is arguable that only Luther's increasing despondency about the future of the Reformation prevented him espousing a ministerially enforced discipline. Cf. E. Doumergue, *Jean Calvin. Les Hommes et les Choses de son Temps* (Lausanne, 1899–1927), vol. v, pp. 20, 133–7.

71 There is nothing in Luther to match Zwingli's brusquely republican assertion: 'Sed absint argutiae. Si ergo in impium degeneret pius [Magistratus], impium moveto et pium subroga.' He however recognized (in the next line) that this is not possible with kings, and in that context counselled patience (*De Vera et Falsa Religione*, ch. 27, p. 389). Cf. also Locher, *Zwinglische Reformation*, pp. 167, 171, for their contrasting political attitudes.

72 I am here discounting the claims in the Preface to the *Commentary on the Psalms* about Calvin's being besieged by zealots for godly knowledge (CO 31, 21–2) as immaterial to this point, unsupported and difficult to interpret: they savour of retrospection.

73 Ganoczy (*Le Jeune Calvin*, pp. 130–1) may however be right to stress the 'ecclesiastical sense' that Calvin may have absorbed in the course of an entire youth spent in the proximity of ecclesiastics.

74 A good number of Luther's and Zwingli's writings were in Latin, or were subsequently translated into Latin.

75 Doumergue, *Calvin*, vol. v, pp. 28–9.

76 In the 1525 *Commentarius de Vera et Falsa Religione* (ch. 27, p. 380), Zwingli spoke of 'ecclesiae Christianae vita, quod ad eam pertinet quae videmus . . .' Luther had, however, long been using the term 'invisible

church'; cf. F. E. Cranz, *An Essay on the Development of Luther's Thought on Justice, Law and Society*, Harvard Theological Studies 19 (Cambridge, Mass., 1959), p. 118, citing the *Dictata* of 1513–15.

77 This was also the formulation of the *Augsburg Confession* of 1530, Article 7, quoted in E. G. Léonard, *A History of Protestantism* (London and Edinburgh, 1965), vol. I, p. 176: 'in qua Evangelium pure docetur et recte administrantur sacramenta'.

78 Cf. Köhler, *Zürcher Ehegericht*, part I; F. Wendel, *L'Eglise de Strasbourg*, *passim*, esp. pp. 48–9, 152–61, and the *XVI Articles* of 1533 (*ibid.*, pp. 244–52). Also M. Bucer, *Enarrationes Perpetuae* (1530), where excommunication is described as a 'sanctissimum . . . et saluberrimum Christi institutum' for safeguarding the 'gloria Dei et fratrum salus'; cited Ganoczy, *Le Jeune Calvin*, p. 176.

79 Contrast Melanchthon's 'Libertas est christianismus'; 'sed quin christianismus libertas quaedam est . . .' (*Loci Communes, Werke*, vol. II, part I, pp. 128, 132). Nothing remotely comparable appears in Calvin's writings, although Melanchthon's own formulation is, of course, polemical. Locher (*Zwinglische Reformation*, p. 89) regards Zwingli's *Von der Freiheit der Speisen* (*Concerning the Free Choice of Foods*) of 1522 as Zwingli's first reformational work.

80 It appears attenuated almost beyond recognition (OS I, 210/4.19.28) as a brief polemical point against papists, and not at all (as with Luther) in the context of 'Christian liberty'.

81 Locher, *Zwinglische Reformation*, p. 135: 'Zwinglis prinzipielle reformatorische Methode: erst Predigt und Glaube – dann, als Konsequenz, die Reformation des Gottesdienstes, der Kirche, der Gesellschaft. Darum hat Zwingli die ganze Zeit seiner Wirksamkeit hindurch mit Unzufriedenen zu tun gehabt, denen sein Vorgehen zu langsam war.'

82 E. Choisy, *La Théocratie à Genève au Temps de Calvin* (Geneva, 1897), pp. 108 ff.

83 *Politia*. The term 'organization' was never used in this sense before the later eighteenth century, but here fits Calvin's meaning.

84 See for example OS I, 63/3.15.5.; 103–4/3.20.33; 191/3.5.4; 234/4.8.1; 237/4.8.9; 257/4.10.32. The term is Pauline; e.g. Ephesians 1.18 and 4.11–13, and 1 Corinthians 10.23–4.

85 Wendel, *Calvin*, p. 135 and footnote 77.

86 In OS I, 217 he seems to distinguish them: 'Quanquam scio presbyterium eo loco [1 Timothy 4] a quibusdam accipi, pro coetu seniorum. Sed simplicius, meo judicio, de ministerio intelligetur.'

87 Evangelical linguistic usage on this point appears not to have stabilized for some time. Thus Bucer also used 'Eltisten' ('elders') to mean 'ministers'.

88 A French translation of the *Schleitheim Articles* was widely diffused in western Switzerland. W. Balke, *Calvijn en de Doperse Radikalen* (Amsterdam, 1973), pp. 173–84, 191–7. The positions attacked by Calvin read like a not unfair, but of course exceedingly hostile, version of Article 6; a translation may be found in L. W. Spitz (ed.), *The Protestant Reformation* (Englewood Cliffs, N.J., 1966), pp. 89–96.

89 *Politia*, which here approaches the meaning of 'state'; cf. J. Baur,

Gott, Recht und Weltliches Regiment im Werk Calvins (Bonn, 1965), pp. 98–100.

90 This point is emphasized throughout in Balke, *Calvijn en de Doperse Radikalen.*

91 The justifications of war and capital punishment are plainly directed at them (OS I, 264–6/4.20.10–12); they had also given Luther much difficulty: see *Von weltlicher Oberkeit* (WA 11, esp. 248–61).

92 Luther's position was dangerously close to that of the quietist Anabaptists. Article 6 of the *Schleitheim Articles* reads in part: 'The sword is ordained by God outside the perfection of Christ. It punishes and puts to death the wicked and guards and protects the good . . . In the perfection of Christ, however, only the ban [excommunication] is used.'

93 *Administratio* is a synonym for government, *gubernatio* or *moderatio*, as well as for administration in the modern sense (*Thesaurus Linguae Latinae*, Leipzig, 1900, vol. I). However, it clearly retained its connotation of service or ministry. Thus Erasmus in his *Institutio Principis Christiani*, instancing Matthew 20.25 ('The princes of the Gentiles lord it over them . . . but among you it shall not be so'), writes: 'Quid est autem quod [the Lord] ait . . . nisi non eodem modo fieri convenit inter Christianos? inter quos principatus *administratio* est, non imperium, et regnum beneficium est, non tyrannis.' And even more emphatically: 'Cogitato semper dominium, imperium, regnum, maiestatem, potentiam ethnicorum esse vocabula, non Christianorum; Christianum imperium nihil aliud esse quam *administrationem*, quam beneficentiam, quam custodiam.' (Erasmus, *Opera Omnia*, Amsterdam, 1974, vol. 4–1, p. 159, lines 700–4, and 164, lines 889–91; my italics, punctuation modernized.)

94 *Von weltlicher Oberkeit* (WA 11), e.g. p. 260: 'Schwerd soll keyn Christen für sich und seyne sache fueren noch anruffen, Sondernn für eynen andern mag und soll ers fueren und anruffen . . .'.

95 In contrast to Luther, who thought litigation in a Christian, unselfish spirit would approximate to a 'miracle', although he did not deny absolutely that it might be possible. *Von weltlicher Oberkeit* (WA 11, 261).

96 Contrast Zwingli, *Commentarius de Vera et Falsa Religione*, ch. 27.

97 This is exactly what we encountered in the *De Clementia Commentary*. It is also the attitude of Luther.

98 It had also been all that Luther would allow, with the utmost reluctance: Skinner, *Foundations*, vol. II, pp. 195–206. For Calvin, this exception occasioned far less difficulty, since (unlike Luther) he tended to subordinate princes to laws, and did not personalize authority.

99 Melanchthon in the *Loci Communes* (*Werke*, vol. II, part I, p. 132) had also expressed a preference of this sort, as had Zwingli in *Von göttlicher und menschlicher Grechtigkeit* (*Hauptschriften*, vol. 7, e.g. pp. 55–8).

100 Melanchthon, *Loci Communes*, supra, pp. 46–7, 54; and Zwingli, *Commentarius de Vera et Falsa Religione*, pp. 113–15. Luther impugned its validity, but had referred to it in the same context: *Wider die himmlischen Propheten* (WA 18, 76–7).

101 This is not, although it resembles, the distinction of the *De Clementia*

Commentary between *aequitas* and *summum ius*, which has regard not to the formulation of the law, but to its application to specific circumstances.

102 'for whom it is not lawful [or 'permitted', *non licet*] to meditate anything to do with the disposition of public affairs'. This line quite defeated Beveridge.

103 Contrast the scope left to 'reason' in secular affairs by Luther, for example in the last pages of *Von weltlicher Oberkeit*, and see the writings cited in Cranz, *Essay*, pp. 148–9, although there is no reason to think that Calvin had read the latter.

104 The most detailed attempt to establish this case is G. Gloede, *Theologia Naturalis bei Calvin*, Tübinger Studien zur systematischen Theologie 5 (Stuttgart, 1935). Some reasons for doubting the significance of Calvin's allusions to natural law and reason are given later, cf. pp. 179–84 and sources cited there.

105 However, Ganoczy's contention (*Le Jeune Calvin*, p. 200) that this notion, albeit unexplicated, underpins the frequent references to God's *regnum* and *imperium* and the duty to serve and praise him (e.g. OS I, 101, 105, 108, 121, 145) deserves some attention.

106 Or more precisely, the common evangelical distinction; see, for example, Zwingli, *Von göttlicher und menschlicher Grechtigkeit* (*Hauptschriften*, vol. 7), pp. 35–103.

107 Wolin, *Politics and Vision*, p. 167.

108 See the uncharacteristic lapse in this respect of the admirable Ganoczy (*Le Jeune Calvin*, pp. 252–7), who claims to find certain 'ébauches' of a plan of action, but then weakens this into a reference to a certain spirit and general orientation. Doumergue, *Jean Calvin* (vol. v, p. 25), takes the same view. 'Calvin . . . fut subitement appelé à mettre en pratique la théorie qu'il venait d'exposer au monde chrétien'; 'le programme de son Institution', etc. Cf. also pp. 26–7.

3 The first public ministry

1 Parker, *Calvin*, p. 57. The magistrates presumably put Calvin on probation for a time.

2 Henceforth referred to as *Ordonnances*, following OS, although this was not a title devised by Calvin. All references to the *Confession*, the *Ordonnances* and the *Catechisme* are to OS, volume I.

3 *Politics and Vision*, p. 16.

4 A fuller account of Genevan circumstances is to be found in ch. 6.

5 *Du Contrat Social*, book II, ch. 7.

6 *puissance ne auctorité*: but Calvin used these French terms interchangeably, whereas he distinguished *potestas* and *auctoritas* carefully.

7 *La Saincte Cène*; Calvin (like Zwingli and unlike Luther) scrupulously eschewed *messe*.

8 Contrast Luther's emphasis on the sermon. Compare *Deutsche Messe*, 1526 (WA 19, 78): 'Weyl alles Gottis diensts das grössist und furnempst stück ist Gottis wort predigen und leren.'

9 Despite this term, Luther seems to have been more concerned to safe-

guard the freedom of individual churches to order things as they saw fit, and to insist that such matters did not constitute essentials of faith, than to deny their importance. Cf. his Preface to *Deutsche Messe*, 1526 (WA 19, 72–9). And Luther's contribution to communal singing in churches scarcely needs to be underlined.

10 Thus, rightly, Parker and McNeill, as opposed to Biéler and Wendel, who erroneously make the *Confession* a later document.

11 A former syndic, Jacques Balard, made it plain that his submission to the Reformation was an act of civic loyalty and not a profession of his belief, having previously stated what his beliefs were and undergone or ignored various degrees of harassment. The ministers refused to be satisfied by such a submission; Messieurs, on the other hand, were, and Balard was to remain unmolested and later to resume civic offices, to the end of his days. The episode is recounted in E. W. Monter, *Calvin's Geneva* (London and New York, 1967), pp. 9–11.

12 The various classes of residents at Geneva are explained below, ch. 7.

13 The original procedure envisaged was for a minister and some delegate of Messieurs to go from house to house demanding subscription. This policy was a complete failure and much resented. A subsequent device was to require subscription at public meetings. It does not appear that those determined not to subscribe (for whatever reason) were ever successfully brought to do so or punished for refusal. Cf. Wendel, *Calvin*, pp. 52–3, and E. Choisy, *La Théocratie*, pp. 22–9.

14 I am following OS in calling it *Catechisme*, both because that is what it was intended to be, and in order to avoid confusion with the *Confession de la Foy* discussed above.

15 J. T. McNeill, *The History and Character of Calvinism* (New York, 1967), p. 140.

16 Wendel, *Calvin*, p. 52.

17 Uwe Plath in his excellent *Calvin und Basel in den Jahren 1552–1556* (Basel and Stuttgart, 1974), p. 22, seems disposed to attribute significance to Calvin's experience of Basel's 'Gemeinwesen', but gives only conjectural evidence, namely that the *Articles* bear Basel's imprint and that Calvin there met Bullinger, Viret and Farel, who, it is supposed, must have mentioned ecclesiastical matters. But Bullinger's ideas on the ministry, like Zwingli's before, were different from those of the *Articles*; and in 1539, at any rate, Calvin expressed a low regard for Basel's kind of discipline (cf Köhler, *Zürcher Ehegericht*, p. 508). It is, however, true that the *Registres du Conseil* persist in regarding Farel and not Calvin as the leading minister until 1538, and it may be that at the beginning of his public ministry, Calvin stood *in statu pupillari* to the older man. If so, this relationship had been transformed at the latest by 1538.

18 There was no mention of 'elders', although some arrangement of this sort had been, as we saw, envisaged in the *Ordonnances*.

19 The phrase is Augustine's and had appeared in the *Institution*.

20 Cf. *Institution*, 1536 (OS I, 69).

21 Only a few paragraphs of the *Institution* (OS I, 86–8) were devoted to the subject.

22 OS I, 390; cf. *Institution*, OS I, 94.

23 K. Schwarzwäller, *Theologia Crucis* (Munich, 1970), pp. 46-51.

24 Most recently in the 1535 edition of the *Loci Communes*, with which Calvin was familiar; Wendel, *Calvin*, p. 114.

25 It may be remarked here that Bucer shared these views: Christians are to beware of the pernicious error which regards 'den dienst der Kirchen am wort und sacrament als ein eüsserlich unnoetig ding', and that they are to keep to 'der ordnung meines Herren, der verordnet seiner Kirchen seine ordentlichen diener'. *Von der wahren Seelsorge*, in R. Stupperich (ed.), *Martin Bucers deutsche Schriften*, vol. 7 (Gütersloh and Paris, 1964), p. 111. This work was published in 1538 and in German, but it expressed long-standing views of Bucer, with whom Calvin had been in correspondence since 1535. It is, however, quite possible that Calvin arrived at these views independently.

4   Reconstruction

1 A sort of burgomaster, of whom there were four at any one time, elected annually.

2 The previous syndics and their council, although sympathetic to Farel and Calvin, had also insisted on this in the last month of their administration.

3 *Calvin*, pp. 55-6.

4 J. Kampschulte, *Johannes Calvin: Seine Kirche und sein Staat in Genf* (Leipzig, 1869), vol. I, pp. 13-19 is particularly valuable on Calvin's expulsion and on his and Farel's attempts to get reinstated. Cf. also Choisy, *La Théocratie*, pp. 32-5.

5 *Articuli a Calvino et Farello Propositi*, April 1538 (CO 10, II, 190-2). The articles in question are VI, VII and IX.

6 Calvin had been lecturing on the Pauline Epistles at Geneva in early 1537 and presumably since his arrival. Cf. Parker, *Calvin*, p. 57.

7 There seems never to have been any inclination to invite Farel to return. The aged Courrault had died shortly after his exile.

8 When he did return, it was officially as a sort of loan.

9 The demand is recorded in the *Registres du Conseil* (cited CO 21, 282) and in Beza, *Vita* (CO 21, 131) and Colladon (CO 21, 64).

10 Letter to an unknown recipient, January 1542 (?) (CO 11, 363).

11 This is argued against Doumergue (*Jean Calvin*, vol. V, p. 40) by M. J. Courvoisier, 'Les Catechismes de Genève et de Strasbourg', in *Etudes sur Calvin et le Calvinisme* (Paris, 1935). H. Strohl, 'La Théorie et la Pratique des Quatre Ministères à Strasbourg avant . . . Calvin' in the same volume, as also Wendel, *L'Eglise de Strasbourg*, provide much circumstantial evidence about the arrangements Calvin encountered there. Doumergue himself admits(*Jean Calvin*, p. 22) the importance of Bucer's thought for Calvin; cf. also M. E. Chenevière, *La Pensée Politique de Calvin* (reprinted Geneva, 1970), pp. 221, 256-7, and A. Ganoczy, *Calvin Théologien de l'Eglise et du Ministère* (Paris, 1964), pp. 191-6.

12 A. Autin, *L'Institution Chrétienne* (Paris, 1929), p. 88.

13 I am working from the French text of 1541, ed. J. Pannier, 4 vols (Paris, 1936–9), compared with the variorum text in CO 1.

14 This Preface (translated by H. Beveridge in *Institutes*, vol. 1, p. 21) also makes clear Calvin's purpose that the *Institution* should be the companion to his commentaries.

15 See Appendix 1.

16 R. Stupperich, 'Calvin und die Konfession des Paul Volz' in *Actes du Colloque Calvin à Strasbourg*, Cahiers de la Revue d'Histoire et de Philosophie Religieuses 39 (1965), pp. 17–27, shows that Volz, one of Calvin's most famous converts, was not in any obvious sense an Anabaptist at all.

17 See Appendix 11.

18 In the *Petit Traicté de la Saincte Cène*, written late in 1540, Calvin was insistent: 'Ce n'est pas l'office d'un chascun particulier de juger et discerner, pour admettre ou deschasser qui bon luy semble; veu que ceste prerogative appartient a toute l'Eglise en general, ou bien au Pasteur, avec les Anciens qu'il doit avoir pour luy assister au gouvernement de l'Eglise.' F. M. Higman (ed.), *Jean Calvin, Three French Treatises* (London, 1970), p. 115.

19 OS 1, 373.

20 At the end of the chapter, after introducing his notion of 'vocation' (equivalent to *statio*) Calvin spoke of God's wrath, as opposed to the philosophers' approval, for the private man who lays hands on a tyrant (CO 1, 1152).

21 OS 1, 88–9.

22 This sounds like an allusion to psychopannychism, but it is nothing of the sort. Both before and after 1539 Calvin described the latter doctrine as pernicious and as thrusting souls into hell. It was therefore not something about which evangelicals might safely differ. In the 1543 *Institution* he made it a damning point against the claims of the papacy that pope John XXII had been a psychopannychist (4.7.28, cf. also *Psychopannychia*, CO 5, 171).

23 The exchange took place in 1538. Du Tillet's letters are in CO 10, 11, nos. 99, 139 and 153; Calvin's are nos. 90 and 147 in the same volume.

24 Doumergue, *Jean Calvin*, vol. v, pp. 32–3. Compare *Institution*, 1536 (OS 1, 92).

25 *Institution*, 4.1.4.

26 The history of evangelical opinion on clerical autonomy is too complicated to be rehearsed here. Köhler, *Zürcher Ehegericht und Genfer Konsistorium*, and Wendel, *L'Eglise de Strasbourg*, are highly informative. It seems that Bucer, Luther, Zwingli and Oecolampadius were all persuaded of the necessity of excommunication by the mid-twenties: the question was of an ecclesiastically administered 'Bann' or 'Zucht', and for them (as for Calvin) the problem was the accusation that tyranny was being introduced, as well as the usual antipathies to such an arrangement. Oecolampadius, the Reformer of Basel, seems to have been the one who persuaded Bucer of the need for a relatively autonomous clerical discipline involving elders (subsequently called 'Kirchenpfleger' at Strasbourg, 'Bannherren' at Basel) somewhere

about 1530; Capito eventually came round to the same view about 1532 (Strohl, cited, p. 256, n. 11). Oecolampadius also won over Zwingli, but Zurich was not to be persuaded. (Both Oecolampadius and Zwingli died in 1531.) Much of Calvin's later language about 'discipline' and about the church, as also much of his scriptural proof-material, is already to be found in a speech of Oecolampadius (in Latin) to the 'senate' of Basel in May or June 1530. The speech, and much else bearing on this topic, may be found in E. Stähelin (ed.), *Briefe und Akten zum Leben Oekolampads*, vol. II (Leipzig, 1934). The speech is pp. 448–57; Oecolampadius's winning over of Zwingli is pp. 488–91.

27 Letter 384 (CO 11, 363–4) to an unknown, dated by the CO editors to January 1542.

28 This appears to be an echo of Bucer. Cf. Wendel, *L'Eglise de Strasbourg*, p. 189. In a letter to Farel of September 1541 (CO 11, 281) Calvin recounted that he had told the Petit Conseil that 'non posse consistere ecclesiam, nisi certum regimen constitueretur quale ex verbo Dei nobis praescriptum est et in veteri ecclesia fuit observatum'.

29 Martin Bucer, both in his *Von der Wahren Seelsorge* and in his various *Zuchtordnungen*, confines talk of governing and ruling strictly to the 'obren' and speaks of the office of 'eltisten' or 'hirten' as 'seelsorge'. And in an open letter from the ministers of Zurich to those of Basel, the former (which presumably means Bullinger) wrote: 'Quid opus humilibus ministris illa loquutio: Deus regit ecclesiam visibiliter per ministros? Papae vicariatum ambienti congruentior est. Deus regit suam ecclesiam . . . nos sumus servi, nihil prorsus usurpantes nobis dominii' (CO 12, 472, letter 875, January 1547).

30 Dillenberger, following Reid, translates *elire* as 'elect'; this is quite misleading, since the modern term 'elect' has inseparable connotations of voting, whereas *elire* meant no more than to select or choose; God does not vote in choosing his 'elect'.

31 P. 329. The italicized passage was added by the Council.

32 Bucer in the *Ziegenhainer Zuchtordnung* (for Hesse) seems to have had somewhat different ideas about the 'eltisten'. For one thing, he proposed that they be elected in part from the congregation (*gemeyn*); for another, he particularly wished them to keep a close eye on the preachers ('besonders fleissig auffsehen auf die prediger haben'). See R. Stupperich (ed.), *Martin Bucers deutsche Schriften* (Gütersloh and Paris, 1964), vol. 7, p. 263.

33 It is noteworthy, however, that the elders were not to be chosen from or by the General Assembly of all the citizens. For the Genevan Councils, cf. ch. 6.

34 'Ce n'est pas matiere spirituelle, mais meslee avec la practique.'

35 Kampschulte, *Johannes Calvin*, p. 377.

36 Similarly OS II, 358 and 359.

37 *Commentary on Romans, loc. cit.*

38 Parker, *Calvin*, p. 105.

39 CO 10, II, 352.

40 *Ibid.*, p. 354: 'quod nullum pectus christianum sine horrore etiam auribus haurire possit'.

41 Calvin's letters to Farel had a way of becoming public, sometimes to Calvin's intense irritation. It should not be concluded from this however that Calvin was always averse to the contents of such communications becoming known.

42 CO 10, II, 275, letter 148 to Farel, October 1538.

43 CO 10, II, 437, letter 200 to Farel, December 1539.

44 CO 10, II, 309, letter 156 to Pignaeus, January 1539.

45 CO 10, II, 323, letter 162 to Farel, March 1539.

46 By way of comparison, Luther had never lost a sense of the value of that institution, even if (in keeping with his respect for Christian liberty) he regarded every Christian as a possible confessor. Cf. R. Seeberg, *Lehrbuch der Dogmengeschichte*, vol. 4, part I, pp. 130, 135. The practice Calvin followed was recommended by Matthew Zell and Bucer. Cf. Wendel, *Calvin*, p. 61.

47 Letter 218 to Farel, 1540 (CO 11, 37–42).

48 'ut mihi antea se purgaret, vel certe resipiscentiam promitteret'.

49 Letter 169 to Farel, April 1539 (CO 10, II, 339).

50 J. C. Olin (ed.), *John Calvin and Jacopo Sadoleto: A Reformation Debate. Sadoleto's Letter to the Genevans and Calvin's Reply* (New York, 1966), p. 65.

51 *Ibid.*, p. 64.

52 *Ibid.*, p. 80.

53 *Ibid.*, p. 44.

54 *Ibid.*, p. 46.

55 *Ibid.*, p. 93.

56 *Ibid.*, p. 58.

57 OS II, 335.

58 CO 10, II, 191.

59 CO 1, 545; 4.1.12.

60 CO 1, 1091.

61 Cited in Léonard, *History of Protestantism*, p. 329.

62 CO 10, II, 331, letter 164, March 1539.

5 The 'Institution' of 1543

1 Wendel, *Calvin*, p. 117.

2 The length of the chapter can be gauged from the fact that with some additions it subsequently became chapters 1–12 of book 4 of the final edition of 1559/60.

3 Wendel, *ibid.* P. Wernle's term 'kirchenrechtliche Überarbeitung' (cited in D. Schellong, *Calvins Auslegung der synoptischen Evangelien* (Munich, 1969), p. 101) is much more apposite, but misses the theological and polemical focus of Calvin's account of the church.

4 References throughout are to the final and most readily accessible edition, whenever the wording of 1543 is preserved unchanged.

5 Bucer was in fact to include it. Cf. Wendel, *Calvin*, pp. 300–1.

6 Calvin was briefly side-tracked into the matter of discipline (4.1.15–16) by the fact that, having given his usual minimalist specification of a true visible church, he had to cope with the objection that a church exhibiting these marks might yet be replete with ungodliness. Since it was he that

raised the objection, this is as near to a confession of embarrassment as one could reasonably expect. In editions after 1539, he suppressed a passage expressing violent hostility to the tolerance of the overtly ungodly added in 1539 (CO 1, 550).

7 In 4.7.23, Calvin used the absence of discipline at Rome to prove that there was no bishop and no church there.

8 In the little-changed edition of 1550, where the division of chapters into numbered sections was first introduced.

9 Another instance of the ease with which Calvin moved between conceptions of the ministry and conceptions of the magistracy, more striking because it was (presumably) not deliberate, is the description of the pastoral office as being more necessary to the conservation of the church than the light and warmth of the sun and food and drink are to the preservation of human life (4.3.2). He had employed the same analogy since 1536 to underline the usefulness of civil order (*politia*) (4.20.3).

10 Skinner, *Foundations*, vol. II, p. 192.

11 Or 'the divine teaching': *institutio* is ambiguous throughout the ecclesiological sections, since the Word is our source both for what the Lord has taught and for what he has instituted. I prefer to follow Battles's translation, which preserves the ambiguity, at least for those familiar with sixteenth-century European usage of 'institution'.

12 This seems to be an echo of Tacitus's *arcana imperii*.

13 All these expressions are taken from book 4, ch. 3. The 'imperial' terminology had not appeared before.

14 See *Institution* 4.9 throughout.

15 An observation of Richard Hooker's seems characteristically judicious: 'That which Calvin did for the establishment of his discipline, seemeth more commendable than that which he taught for the countenancing of it established.' *The Laws of Ecclesiastical Polity*, Preface, ch. 2.7.

16 There are, of course, difficulties about what in sixteenth-century terms is and is not a strained interpretation; even sixteenth-century writers could not agree on the 'plain sense' of Scripture, and all evangelical exegesis of the text 'though art Peter and upon this rock' seemed utterly arbitrary to Romanists. But leaving aside matters generally controverted between evangelicals and Romanists, the following seem to me instances of strained and contrived interpretation: 2 Corinthians 4.6 in 4.3.3, which does not demonstrate that ministers should be thought of as 'governing', however highly they are to be esteemed; the distinction between permanent and temporary 'offices' in the church in 4.3.4–5; the interpretation of 1 Corinthians 12.28 and Romans 12.8 as proving the existence in Paul's churches of elders and a senate (i.e. a Consistory) in 4.3.8 and in 4.11.1; ministers as the choice of the whole church in 4.3.15; the irrelevance of the Old Testament high priesthood as a model for the church in 4.6.2; the argument from silence about Ephesians 4.4–5 in 4.6.10; the distinction between Matthew 18.15–18 and Matthew 16.19 in 4.11.1–3; the distinction between secret and public sins and the scriptural procedure in disciplining in 4.12.3.

17 'Quod ut facilius intelligatur, dividamus ecclesiam in duos ordines

praecipuos: clerum scilicet et plebem. Clericos appello usitato nomine qui publico ministerio in ecclesia funguntur.' In 4.4.9 he had objected to the term, and in the French version of 4.12.1 he said that the term 'clercs' was 'commun' but 'impropre'. In 4.4.10 he had used it without any apparent difficulty. The term 'laicus' occurs at 4.15.20.

18 The subordination of country to town was simply assumed: the Reformation is an urban phenomenon.

19 This is the sense in which Bucer had become colloquially known as the 'bishop of Strasbourg'. Wendel, *L'Eglise de Strasbourg*, pp. 95–6.

20 Most of what became book 4, chs 5–7 dates from this period.

21 His short definition of a sacrament (4.19.34) did not, however, include the requirement of universal availability: 'an external ceremony appointed by God to confirm a promise', and neither did the longer definition at 4.12.1. Cf. also A. Ganoczy, *Calvin Théologien*, pp. 321–3, and *Adultero-German Interim*, 1549 (Calvin Translation Society, Tracts, vol. III, p. 291): 'The Laying on of hands by which ministers are consecrated I do not quarrel with them for calling a sacrament.' (Hereafter CTS).

22 Thus he says of St Peter that 'when he writes to the pastors, he does not command them as one having the *imperium* of a superior' (4.6.7), having just spoken of St Peter's office and power. It is perhaps significant that in 4.20.4, when speaking of legitimate civil authority, he used the term *civilis potestas*, and he translated the word in Romans 13.1 as *potestas* (as the Vulgate does); but when he spoke of the misuse of civil power in 4.20.25, he used *imperium*, even though for him the latter could be a neutral technical term in the context of civil government. The remark in 4.7.6, where *jurisdictio* is equated with the right of hearing appeals and is taken for a mark of sovereign authority (*summum imperium*), is (I take it) a comment about the terminology of Roman law and not an attempt to ascribe *imperium* to the church. Sometimes Calvin even felt *potestas* to be not quite the right term to use about the church: 'nec tam potestatem esse quam ministerium' ('n'est pas tant puissance que ministère', 4.11.1), although he normally used it without qualm or reservation.

23 See, for example, Claude de Seyssel, *La Monarchie de France* (first published in 1519), ed. J. Poujol (Paris, 1961): 'Comme l'autorité et puissance du Roi est reglee et refrenee en France par trois freins' (p. 113) and 'puissance absolue' (p. 120). Despite similarities in outlook, and a shared predilection for the metaphor *frein*, I have found no evidence that Calvin had read Seyssel.

24 See 4.11.3, 5 and 16, where Calvin also denies any *imperium* to the church.

25 It had been the subject of intensive discussion since the twelfth century. Cf. D. Wyduckel, *Princeps Legibus Solutus* (Berlin, 1979).

26 Calvin was careful to add in the same section that 'we are not to rush into innovations hastily, or constantly, or for trivial causes' (4.20.30).

27 The criteria of *aedificatio* and *honestas* (4.10.28) were sufficiently general to permit the condemnation of various papist ceremonies to which Calvin's objections seem to have been mainly of an aesthetic sort.

28 At best, Calvin was entitled to say that externals bind the conscience *in a different way* from the way in which essentials bind them, and from the way papists taught: 'It is indeed the duty of a Christian people to observe with a free conscience and without superstition, but also with a pious and ready inclination to obedience whatever has been instituted in accordance with this rule (*canonem*) . . .' (4.20.31).

29 The same point is made again, with 'discipline' substituted for *politia*, in 4.12.1.

30 'Because some people, in their hatred of discipline, recoil from its very name . . .' (4.12.1).

31 To take the example of Geneva: a morals-police which was in some ways extremely strict had been adopted in Calvin's absence, but it was magisterial and not ministerial. The reasons for his recall are not clear, but it was not because his partisans were enthusiasts for a ministerial discipline. It seems that it was rather because they were hostile to Bern, like Calvin, and for a time at any rate saw ministerial discipline as a price worth paying for the restoration of civic morals and morale.

32 It will be recalled that in the *De Clementia Commentary* he had used this metaphor to describe 'laws' in the body politic, and in another part of the *Institution* he had described the ministry in the same way.

33 Cf. ch. 21, subsequently book 3.6–10: 'Of the life of a Christian'.

34 The formulation was modified in the 1559 edition.

35 It covers roughly items (1), (4), (5) and (8) listed above.

36 Items (2), (6) and (7) above.

37 Items (3) and (6). It was a consideration which Calvin was to stress in his defence of the justifiability of the death-penalty for persistent gross heresy.

38 A 1559 addition to 4.20.2 incorporated what Calvin had long been saying in other places about the duty of civil government 'to cherish and protect the outward worship of God, to defend the sound doctrine of piety and the good order and estate of the church (*status ecclesiae*)', but did not mention the civil consequences of excommunication.

39 See the rather confused discussion in 4.12.8.

40 Calvin never, as far as I know, saw it as a problem that in the Consistory's proceedings, the Consistory itself was prosecutor, witness, judge and executioner.

41 Calvin's terminology on this matter was often far from careful. In 4.1.15 he referred to the disgracefulness of tolerating 'pigs and dogs' and 'the wicked'; all these expressions require qualification in the light of 4.1.8. In his dealings with his opponents Calvin seems to have been confident enough about their reprobate status.

42 When Calvin mentioned hypocrites for the only time in this discussion, at 4.1.7, he did not consider this topic at all.

43 In his *Commentary on 2 Corinthians* (1547), at 2 Corinthians 10.4, he described pastors as 'standard-bearers [in the Christian's 'warfare'] marching before the rest'.

44 Cf. Wendel, *Calvin*, p. 170; Imbart de la Tour, *Calvin et l'Institution Chrétienne* (vol. 4 of *Les Origines de la Réforme*, Paris, 1935), pp. 423 ff.

45 The sixteenth-century term 'the example of the best reformed churches'

is relevant here; also Knox's description of Geneva as 'the best school of Christ that ever was on the earth since the time of the apostles'.

46 Here again the question of hypocrisy is not discussed.

47 Since Calvin had expressly referred to discussions among 'philosophers' concerning 'forms of government', *politia* is presumably a reference to Aristotle's popular form of virtuous government, 'democracy' being the corrupt alternative.

48 Calvin's expression leaves unclear whether he meant his readers to infer that monarchy henceforth enjoyed divine approval, or whether Israelitic monarchy was a special providential dispensation, and therefore not a suitable example for imitation.

49 In the light of later discussions (cf. ch. 7), it seems that Calvin had in mind possession of the franchise by at least a part of the citizenry, and a 'government of laws'.

50 Peter 'fatetur sibi cum illis [the apostles] esse societatem, non adversus eos imperium' (4.6.7). The Apostles were 'collegae . . . non domini'.

51 The point is made in passing several times. Against the papacy: 'they leave no jurisdiction on earth to control or restrain their lust . . .' (4.7.19); similarly 4.7.21. In the early church 'ecclesiastical power was not at the disposition of one man, to do with as he pleased (*pro sua libidine*)' (4.11.6).

6   Geneva and Calvin, 1541–64

1 This account does not aim at comprehensiveness. For more detailed descriptions of Geneva in Calvin's time the reader is referred to the following: the best works in English are undoubtedly E. W. Monter, *Studies in Genevan Government* (Geneva, 1964; referred to below as *Studies*), and *Calvin's Geneva* (referred to as *Geneva*); R. M. Kingdon, *Geneva and the Coming of the Wars of Religion in France* (Geneva, 1956); and J. T. McNeill, *Calvinism*. These should be supplemented by CO 21, *Annales Calviniani*, for its wealth of chronological data and extracts from the *Registres du Conseil*, and by J. F. Bergier and R. M. Kingdon (eds), *Registres de la Compagnie des Pasteurs de Genève* (vols I and II, Geneva, 1962 and 1964). Among the older continental works those of Kampschulte and Choisy already cited are still usable, and Doumergue, *Jean Calvin*, vols V and VI is a mine of citations, although its interpretations are questionable throughout. W. Köhler, *Zürcher Ehegericht* is excellent, and E. Rivoire and V. van Berchem, *Sources du Droit du Canton de Genève*, Sammlung Schweizerischer Rechtsquellen, vols II and III (Aarau, 1920–30) is invaluable. Also useful, if treated with caution, is E. Pfisterer, *Calvins Wirken in Genf* (2nd ed., Neukirchen, 1957). One wishes there were more studies of the standard of thoughtfulness and scholarship of U. Plath, *Calvin und Basel*, already cited. More specialized studies are cited in the notes.

2 Calvin did not entrust the printing of any of his editions of the *Institution* or his Commentaries to a Genevan-based printer until 1545 (French *Institution*), 1550 (Latin *Institution*) and 1547 (French *Commentary on 1 Corinthians*) respectively.

3 Monter, *Studies*, pp. 79–83.

4 Most notably Jerome Bolsec, after his expulsion in 1551 for open dissent from the doctrine of predestination, and the refugees of the defeated Perrinist faction after 1555.

5 Rivoire and van Berchem, *Sources*, show that the edicts concerning this were constantly being reasserted: vol. II, p. 345 (12.2.1538), p. 348 (22.2.1539), p. 532 (10.3.1550); vol. III, pp. 39–40 (16.2.1557), p. 106 (15.3.1560). This may mean that the edicts were being disregarded.

6 E.g.: the proposals for reformation at Wittenberg presented to the Elector Frederick in December 1521, which listed the abolition of endowments and requiem masses, the institution of the chalice for laymen, the closing of taverns where illegal drunkenness occurred, the closing of whorehouses and the punishment of their proprietors. Cited Ozment, *Reformation*, p. 143.

7 Rivoire and van Berchem, *Sources*, vol. II, pp. 347–8, *Cryes* of 22.2.1539; the licensing of printing, p. 352 (9.5.1539) and again p. 354 (19.9.1539), where a concern for 'l'honneur et laz [*sic*] gloyre de Dieu' is asserted; also compulsory attendance at sermons, p. 354.

8 Köhler, *Zürcher Ehegericht*, p. 540 for the decision of Council of 5.4.1541.

9 Monter, *Geneva*, esp. pp. 65–9, and *Studies*, p. 91.

10 Doumergue, *Jean Calvin*, vol. VI, *passim*, making allowances for his hostility to all the enemies of his hero.

11 L. Fulpius, *Les Institutions Politiques de Genève* (Geneva, 1965), p. 17.

12 Williston Walker, *John Calvin, the Organizer of Reformed Protestantism* (New York, 1910), p. 166. The other councils date from the fourteenth century.

13 R. Fills, *The Lawes and Statutes of Geneva . . .* (London, 1562), p. 20 *recto*. Fill(e)s and his translation are discussed in note 83 below.

14 *Lawes*, p. 23 *recto*. Fills is reproducing in translation the Edicts of 1543.

15 Fulpius, *Institutions Politiques*, describes it as 'moribund'. It appears to have met on occasion: cf. Choisy, *Théocratie*, p. 166; F. de Bonivard, *Advis et Devis sur l'Ancienne et Nouvelle Police de Geneve* (1555), in *Mémoires et Documents publiés par la Société d'Histoire et d'Archéologie de Genève* 5 (1845), p. 387.

16 Fills, *Lawes*, p. 33 *recto*.

17 *Ibid.*, p. 30 *recto*.

18 Fulpius, *Institutions Politiques*, pp. 17–18. The main beneficiary of this tendency was the PC.

19 Bonivard, *Advis*, p. 387; cited Monter, *Studies*, p. 86.

20 Ed. P. F. Geisendorf, vol. I, 1549–60 (Geneva, 1957).

21 The Genevan practice was to wear swords at elections, as a badge of citizenship. But if there was such a prohibition it was totally disregarded, and the Perrinist attempt to prohibit French refugees from wearing swords in public was considered an outrage. Choisy, *Théocratie*, p. 128.

22 Bonivard, *Advis* (quoted in Monter, *Studies*, p. 86) says that 'only *citoyens* can hold office'. This is true if the very well-paid pastoral and teaching offices are not considered 'civic offices', but I find no evidence to suggest that Genevan law made any fine distinctions, and Bonivard seems simply to have ignored the anomalous status of Geneva's doctors

and ministers, who were almost invariably mere *habitants* or at best *bourgeois*.

23 Pfisterer, *Calvins Wirken*, pp. 29–34 argues inconclusively that it was; I find no mention of the *Carolina* throughout Rivoire and van Berchem, *Sources*. Eberhard Schmidt, *Einführung in die Geschichte der deutschen Strafrechtspflege* (3rd ed., Göttingen, 1965), p. 144 states that the *Carolina* did not attain legal force in the Helvetic Confederation, but that it was used by courts all the same, especially at Basel and Schaffhausen. Schmidt's work is an excellent guide to juridical principles and practice at the time; cf. esp. pp. 107–50.

24 Monter, *Studies*, pp. 64–5; J. Bohatec, *Calvin und das Recht* (Graz, 1934), ch. I.

25 The legal adviser to Geneva, Germain Colladon, would hardly have known German. Two legal opinions cited by Choisy, *Théocratie*, mention Deuteronomy and *constitutions imperiales* in the same breath, but it is unclear whether the latter refers to Roman law or to the laws of the Holy Roman Empire: case of Gentilis (p. 196) and Gruet, where the 'law of God and men' is cited (p. 94).

26 Pfisterer, *Calvins Wirken*, p. 33.

27 Monter, *Studies*, pp. 69–75, which contains the memorable if tasteless pun that 'Battonat was feeling the strain', not surprisingly after several sessions with the strappado.

28 On this point and for citations from the *Registres du Conseil* only, see the egregious work by O. Pfister, *Calvins Eingreifen in die Hexen- und Hexer-Prozesse von Peney* (Zurich, 1947). The quality of the argument in this book makes one look with favour on his arch-enemy, E. Pfisterer.

29 Choisy, *Théocratie*, pp. 94, 180.

30 This was, I believe, the usual state of things throughout Europe until the late eighteenth century, although France had its galleys and Britain its colonies; one forgets just how innovative was More's suggestion of hard labour as an alternative to the death-penalty.

31 *Calvins Wirken*, pp. 149–50. By way of comparison, Basel's population at this time is estimated at 15,000–16,000 (Plath, *Calvin und Basel*, p. 18, n. 1); Bern's with its Oberland at about 75,000 (Monter, *Geneva*, p. 1), of whom 4000 to 5000 were inhabitants of the city itself.

32 Monter, *Geneva*, p. 1.

33 Pfisterer, *Calvins Wirken*, pp. 46–9, drawing on J. B. Galiffe and A. Roget.

34 In a sermon of 1562, Calvin protested about the cruelty of the enemies of the faith, who had gone so far as to 'invent kinds of death never customary before' (SC I, 497). This recalls a remark in the *De Clem. Comm.* about tyrants, pp. 318/19. For some interesting figures, see E. W. Monter, 'Crime and Punishment in Calvin's Geneva, 1562', in *Archiv für Reformationsgeschichte* 64 (1973).

35 Rivoire and van Berchem, *Sources*, vol. II, p. 362 (20.10.1540 decision of the Conseil General).

36 Machiavelli, *Discorsi*, book I, chs VII and VIII.

37 Monter, *Geneva*, p. 8. Rivoire and van Berchem, *Sources*, vol. III, p. 107 (1560).

38 Doumergue, *Jean Calvin*, vol. V, pp. 173–5.

39 Choisy, *Théocratie*, p. 75.

40 He was accused at various times of slandering his colleagues, practising usury and ill-treating his wife. The magistrates protected him for years. Cf. Parker, *Calvin*, p. 111 and n. 28.

41 Calvin cited a French proverb to the effect that 'la maison est comme une retraicte [sanctuary] a ung chacun' in an unpublished sermon on 2 Samuel: SC I, 95 (1562).

42 *Defensio Orthodoxae Fidei de Sacra Trinitate* (against Servetus), 1554 (CO 8, 416). Referred to below as *Defensio*.

43 P. E. Hughes (ed.), *Registers of the Pastors of Geneva in the Time of Calvin* (Grand Rapids, 1966), pp. 16–17.

44 Cf. p. 113.

45 Choisy, *Théocratie*, p. 125, quoting the *Registres* for 9.11.1555, where the PC pronounced 'ledit livre d'Institution estre bien et sainctement faict et sa doctrine estre saincte doctrine de Dieu, et que l'on le [Calvin] tient pour bon et vray ministre de ceste cité, et que des icy al'avenir, personne ne soit ausé ['be so presumptuous as to', a common formulation in Genevan edicts, which tend to the sanctimonious] parler contre ledit livre ny contre ladite doctrine . . .'.

46 The fate of C. B. Macpherson's attempt to prove the presence of un-recognized, or at any rate unarticulated, assumptions in Hobbes' *Leviathan* does not inspire excessive confidence in the possibility of its being done even with self-consciously systematic political thought, unless the author is still available to be asked.

47 The best discussion of the matter is that of M. E. Chenevière, *La Pensée Politique de Calvin*, pp. 206–21. The PC seems to have called on Calvin's services because he was learned in the law and efficient at getting things done (both qualities in rather short supply at Geneva) and not because of his theological prowess.

48 E.g. *Commentary on Deuteronomy*, 1562; The *Commentary on Isaiah*, first edition 1551, seems to be based on *leçons;* see Parker, CNTC, p. 20, Calvin's Dedication to the revised edition of 1559 (CO 13, 669) and des Gallars's Preface of 1570, CO 36 (unpaginated).

49 Compare for example CO 8, 471: 'principes . . . in fidei dissipatione cessabunt?' with the French version: 'Seront-ils oisifs et tiendront-ilz les bras croisez?' (*Defensio*, 1554) and generally Calvin's mastery of the French vocabulary of abuse with the nerveless Latin equivalents.

50 Thus Calvin insisted that Luke wrote Acts and that Moses personally wrote the first five books of the Old Testament, even though he was, according to Calvin, reporting a tradition passed down to him through the patriarchs. I do not know why Calvin should have insisted on Moses' or Luke's authorship: he thought Mark, Hebrews, 2 Peter and James authoritative, but not necessarily by the authors to whom they are usually attributed. Cf. E. Dowey, *The Knowledge of God in Calvin's Theology* (repr. New York and London, 1965), pp. 90–121.

51 *Sermons on Deuteronomy*, e.g. CO 26, 134–6; CO 27, 82, 88–91, 237.

52 It is clear that, for example at Easter 1538 and 1548, Calvin expressed himself with manly frankness on topics of current concern. Cf. Choisy, *Théocratie*, pp. 34 and 102.

53 The *Commentary on Romans* of 1539 came first in time and importance. The collected commentaries on Paul's letters appeared in both Latin and French in 1548.

54 Parker, CNTC, pp. 77–8 offers a cogent theological reason for the omission, except that he makes it rather difficult to explain why Calvin concerned himself so deeply and constantly with the incomplete revelation of the Old Testament. I should be disposed to stress Calvin's antipathy to millennialism, as tainted with Anabaptism.

55 He had lectured on Isaiah in 1549/50, and was to offer three hundred and forty-two weekday sermons on this text between 1556 and 1558; the attendance and response for this marathon are not recorded.

56 Introduction to the *Gospel Harmony*, CO 45, 2.

57 A revised edition was published in 1559; it was dedicated to Elizabeth of England.

58 They were published in the form of a 'harmony', prefaced by a reprint of the *Commentary on Genesis*, in 1563, as *Mosis Libri V . . . Genesis seorsum, Reliqui Quatuor in Formam Harmoniae Digesti.*

59 The sermons on 1 Samuel were published in a Latin translation in 1604, those on 2 Samuel not until 1961 in the SC.

60 The evidence before 1549, when sermons were recorded in shorthand and clean copies made from the shorthand, is erratic and scanty.

61 See SC 1, Introduction by H. Rückert, pp. vii–viii.

62 More precisely, attendance at one of Geneva's churches was compulsory; a Genevan therefore did not have to hear Calvin.

63 Parker, *Calvin*, p. 91.

64 D. Schellong, *Calvins Auslegung*, p. 165.

65 There is little change in this respect between the humanist Calvin and the evangelical commentator. Cf. p. 10.

66 Strictly speaking, Calvin did not see the relationship between the Old Testament and the New as a problem at all, and the chapters of the *Institution* devoted to that topic are simply an attempt to demolish various (primarily Anabaptist) suggestions which would have made it into a problem. Schellong, *Calvins Auslegung*, p. 208.

67 *Sermons on Deuteronomy* (CO 25, 610): 'que nous ayons les aureilles batues de ce que nous devrions avoir compris en un mois . . .'; cf. also SC 1, 99.

68 *Commentary on Isaiah*, Preface.

69 *Ibid.*

70 *Commentary on Isaiah*, 1551 and 1559 (CTS, p. xxvii).

71 See *Commentary on Isaiah*, at 57.1, where Calvin saw a particular instance of God's favour in taking Luther from the world before these debacles.

72 E.g. letter 1381, June 1550 (CO 13, 594–5), reproaching Melanchthon for his over-generous interpretation of *adiaphora*.

73 For instance, the *Defensio* (1554), which included a justification of the execution of heresiarchs, was prompted by the Servetus affair, just as the *De Aeterna Dei Predestinatione* two years earlier had been prompted by the trial and expulsion of Jerome Bolsec for his denial of the doctrine of predestination.

74 E.g. *Excuse de Jehan Calvin, à Messieurs les Nicodemites* (1544), *De Scandalis* (1550), *Quatre Sermons* (1552).

75 E.g. *Brieve Instruction pour armer tous bons fideles contre les erreurs de la secte commune des Anabaptistes* (1544). *Contre la Secte . . . des Libertins* (1545).

76 *Advertissement contre l'Astrologie qu'on appelle indiciaire* (1549).

77 A late example is the *Response a un Certain Hollandois* (1562), once again urging the necessity of avoiding the pollutions of the papists, which was prompted by the submission by a Dutch church of a certain book for Calvin's opinion.

78 Although it cannot be demonstrated that Calvin thought every word of the Bible literally inspired or 'dictated' by God to his *amanuenses* or *notaires* (these are his own expressions), he appears never to have used the possible difference between the Word and the words to explain any of the repetitions, compositional anomalies and textual problems of the Old Testament; he did, however, frequently use the idea that where what Scripture says cannot be literally true, it is the result of an 'accommodation' by God of his Word to the capacities of his hearers. Cf. Dowey, *The Knowledge of God*, pp. 90–121, and Preface to the second printing, and Parker, *Calvin*, pp. 59, 76–7.

79 A systematic discussion of this question by an evangelical is not to be encountered, it seems, until Hooker's *Laws of Ecclesiastical Polity*.

80 Anti-Machiavellianism was a *topos* of Huguenot polemic in the 1570s. The classic of this literature is Innocent Gentillet's *Anti-Machiavel*, published in Geneva in 1576.

81 Barth's and Niesel's assertion that the 1559 addition to 4.20.1 about 'flatterers of princes' is an allusion to Machiavelli's *Prince*, published in a French translation by G. Cappel in 1553, is purely conjectural and highly unlikely (OS v, 457, n. 10). For the same assertion, equally unsupported, cf. Wendel, *Calvin*, p. 30.

82 'Status reipublicae bene constitutus'; *Commentary on Isaiah*, 3.4 (CO 36, 82).

83 Next to nothing is known of the author, who is listed as 'Filles (Robert), fl. 1562' in the British Museum Catalogue, but as 'Fills' in the work cited, in DNB, and in the National Union Catalogue. No Fils, Fills or Filles appears in the Genevan *Livre des Habitants*, vol. 1, but 'Un Anglois' named 'Robert Fillet' was received as *habitant* on 29 November 1557, along with Eduard Cant, William Colle, Thomas Bentam and Jehan Mans Field (*sic*), and, given the unusualness of the name, this looks to be the same person. Filles explicitly identified himself as having been at Geneva (p. 4 *recto*). The dedication of the book was to 'Robert Duddeley, Master of the Queen's horse', shortly thereafter to become 'the Puritan Earl' of Leicester. The translation is 'worde for worde' (p. 5 *recto*) and highly accurate. There is no mention of Calvin from one end of the book to the other.

84 *Ibid.*, p. iii *recto*.

85 *Ibid.*, p. iii *verso*.

7 The civil order of a Christian commonwealth

1 Rivoire and van Berchem, *Sources*, vol. III, p. 100; 'que la jurisdiction temporelle soit distinguee d'avec la spirituelle . . .'.

2 There seem to be no reliable figures for membership and actual attendance, although Calvin himself was assiduous. There were twelve lay members and the urban pastors (at least six of them) were members *ex officio*; not so the ministers of the foreign congregations or the country parishes. The importance of the lay majority should, however, not be overestimated: what counted was authoritativeness, for the Consistory did not vote; in any case, it need not be assumed that all the lay elders attended all of the time. Fills, *Lawes*, p. 33 *verso*, cites regulations for fining members of even the PC for non-attendance at council meetings.

3 H. Baron in his seminal *Calvins Staatsanschauung und das Konfessionelle Zeitalter, Historische Zeitschrift*, Beiheft 1–3 (1924), ch. 3 and *passim*, asserts an increasing hostility to monarchy in Calvin's writings. But sermons not available to Baron, some of them contemporary with the ones he cited (see especially E. Mühlhaupt, *Der Psalter auf der Kanzel Calvins*, Neukirchen, 1959, and *Sermons on 2 Samuel*, SC 1), contain nothing as sustained as the anti-monarchical sentiments of the *Sermons on 1 Samuel*.

4 This addition to 4.20.8 left untouched a 1536 formulation in the previous section: 'The [form of government] which is least pleasing to men is singled out for honour above all the others, that is to say the sovereignty (*seigneurie et domination, potestas*) of one'; this is the passage in which Calvin, in keeping with his usual antipathy to merely human reasoning and sentiment, had seen it as a point in favour of monarchy that the judgement of heroic and more excellent minds in Antiquity disrelished it.

5 Even in the 1543 addendum to 4.20.8, Calvin added the 'confirmation of the Lord himself' (as exhibited in the order he established for·the Israelites) to 'experience'; the habitual ambiguity about the relative importance of 'experience' or human reasoning in general and the will of the Lord therefore remains.

6 3.19.15 (from 1536).

7 In an addendum of 1543 to this section, Calvin made clear that it was the dangers of Christian liberty misunderstood that were mainly on his mind, despite the generality of the formulation. D. Little, *Religion, Order and Law* (Oxford, 1970), part II, ch. 3, is therefore ill advised to make so much of this distinction.

8 In his letters about organization to ministerial colleagues, Calvin sometimes used prudential arguments to the exclusion of all others; cf. letter 547, May 1544 (CO 11, 707) and letter 1294, October 1549 (CO 13, 133).

9 The French version of 1541 (ed. Pannier, vol. IV, pp. 206–7), which included a brief explanation of the three pure forms, has: 'it is just as easy' for aristocracy to degenerate into an 'iniquitous domination (*domination inique*)'; the Latin from 1543 has: 'it is hardly more difficult'

for such a form to collapse into a 'faction of a few'. The reader should be warned against the Beveridge translation of this whole section.

10 Even this was unclear: Beza and Peter Martyr went to France to negotiate with Catherine de' Medici at the Colloquy of Poissy in September 1561.

11 *Supplex Admonitio ad Caesarem Carolum Quintum*, 1543.

12 Most of the letters concerning these episodes are in CO 18. Particularly revealing: letters 3207 (May 1560); 3202, a very 'Machiavellian' letter advocating ruthless measures against the Guise; 3314, 3315 (December 1560 to January 1561); 3317 (January 1561); 3332 (February 1561); 3347 (August 1561).

13 More, *Utopia*, pp. 56/7: 'From the prince, as from a never failing spring, flows a stream of all that is good and evil over the whole people.' Calvin chose rather to stress the possible evils: 'as there is no disease more injurious than that which spreads from the head to the whole body, so there is no evil more destructive in a commonwealth than a wicked and depraved prince'. (*Commentary on Isaiah*, 1551 and 1559, at Isaiah 1.23). And cf. n. 74 for his use of the river metaphor.

14 In 1555, Bern forbade its subjects' attendance at *ceremonies calvinistes*; Choisy, *Théocratie*, p. 171.

15 Plath, *Calvin und Basel*, p. 27 and *passim*. For Joris, see J. M. Stayer, *Anabaptists and the Sword* (Lawrence, Kansas, 1972), pp. 267–8, 289–90, 294–5, 298–301.

16 *Sermons on Deuteronomy* for 21 and 22 May 1555 (CO 26, 134); this was four days after the Perrinist putsch.

17 *Commentary on Acts*, II (1554) at 16.31; 17.8–9; 19.29–40. Calvin was working on the second volume of *Acts* between 1552 and 1553; Parker, *CNTC*, pp. 24–5.

18 *Sermons on Deuteronomy* (CO 25, 644): 'hurler avec les loups'.

19 *Commentary on Acts*, II, at 19.35–40: 'homines politici'.

20 E.g. SC I, 396.

21 *Sermons on Deuteronomy* (CO 25, 642), and cf. *Sermons on I Samuel* (SC I, 396 and 489).

22 Rivoire and van Berchem, *Sources*, vol. III, p. 10.

23 E.g. the parts of the *Gospel Harmony* (CTS, vol. III), where Calvin might have made much of the crowd's part in the suffering of Christ, but chose rather to dwell on the misdeeds of priests and magistrates. Cf. the comments on Matthew 29.59 (p. 283); Matthew 27, 20 (p. 283); Matthew 27.24 (p. 287). There are exceptions, e.g. pp. 281–2. His hostility to the 'crowd' seems to have been at its height in the *Commentaries on Acts* of 1552 and 1554. Even here he was inclined to blame magistrates, e.g. 5.8 and 17; 16.31; 17.8–9; 19.29–34. The dates coincide with Calvin's time of troubles.

24 CO 25, 635.

25 CO 27, 457; *estat* here comes close to the modern term 'state', which seems to derive from expressions like *status reipublicae*, *estat public*.

26 CO 27, 410–11.

27 CO 27, 457: 'fretillent leurs esprits pour rien innover'.

28 CO 29, 544. These sermons are extant only in a Latin translation not published in Calvin's lifetime. No importance can therefore be attached to the specific words used in it. H. Rückert's exemplary edition of the *Sermons on 2 Samuel* shows that on occasion it was impossible for the stenographers to establish a clean text. Generally, however, their skill was remarkable, and I have no doubt of the utter fidelity of the *Sermons on 1 Samuel* to Calvin's sense and probably his words.

29 CO 29, 535.

30 CO 29, 555. Compare the exegesis of this passage in *Institution*, 4.20.26 (all editions).

31 'ad fovendam mediocrem statum'; my translation is a little free, but it is at any rate better than Pringle's 'mediocrity'. *Harmony of Moses* (CTS, vol. III, p. 154).

32 CO 24, 697, on Deuteronomy 15.1. The context is the treatment of debtors.

33 The term is that of Marsiglio of Padua, *Defensor Pacis* (1324), ed. A. Gewirth (New York, 1956), vol. II, discourse I, chs 12 and 13.

34 However, the 1560 amplification and revision of the ecclesiastical ordinances included an express provision for congregational objection to proposed candidates for the ministry, and for new selection if one were found unworthy. The preamble to these provisions refers to complaints by the ministers that current practice meant that 'le peuple et tout le corps de l'eglise ont esté fraudez de leur liberté'. Text in OS II, 330.

35 'Besides, although there are various forms of magistracy, there is no difference between them in this respect, that they are all to be taken by us as ordained by God (*pro Dei ordinibus*)' (4.20.7).

36 Although sermons remained unpublished, it does not follow that Calvin's views expressed in them were unknown outside Geneva. It was precisely the Compagnie des Pauvres Estrangers which paid the copyists who took down the sermons, and which had the custody of the transcripts. Cf. CO 25, 579–91 (*Notice Littéraire*).

37 In 4.20.8 (1559), where aristocracy is said to be best, not in itself, but because of the vices and defects of kings, and 4.20.22 (1559), where he explicitly distinguishes the 'men' from the '*ordo*'.

38 *Commentary on Genesis*, 49.8 (CO 23, 597): 'perfectum regiminis statum'.

39 *Commentary on 1 Timothy*, 2.2.

40 CO 30, 675 (on 1 Samuel 29): 'Nemo tam insignis autoritatis rex est quin secreta quadam subjectione sese salutantibus aulicis submittat.'

41 *Commentary on Isaiah*, at 32.2; same expression in *Sermons on 1 Samuel* (CO 29, 557); 'eyes and ears', described as a common saying, in *Institution*, 4.20.23.

42 *Sermons on 2 Samuel* (SC I, 55).

43 *Sermons on 1 Samuel* (CO 29, 557, and cf. CO 30, 675).

44 *Commentary on Isaiah*, 32.1.

45 Or a *moderator*. In a discussion of the point (*Institution*, 4.6.8, from 1543) in the context of ecclesiastical primacy, Calvin described this as demanded by 'nature' and by the human mind itself for every sort of

coetus, citing the example of senates, benches of judges, *collegia* and *societates*.

46 Or just possibly 'counsel'; *conseil* can mean either, but the translation given seems more likely.

47 *Sermons on 2 Samuel* (SC 1, 72).

48 J. H. Hexter, *More's Utopia: The Biography of an Idea* (New York, 1965), part 3.

49 The first part of More's *Utopia* is largely devoted to the question. Machiavelli, *Il Principe*, chs 22–3 is characteristically idiosyncratic and to the point. Sir Thomas Elyot, *The Book named the Governor*, book 2, ch. 14 and book 3, chs 28–30; Guillaume Budé, *L'Institution du Prince*, *passim*; Thomas Starkey, *Dialogue between Reginald Pole and Thomas Lupset*, Early English Text Society, Extra Series 12 and 32 (London, 1871 and 1878, reprinted New York, 1975), pp. 162–70 all have discussions bearing on the point. So does Balthasar Castiglione's *The Courtier*, trans. G. Bull (Harmondsworth, 1967), pp. 124–33. So of course does Erasmus, *Institutio Principis Christiani*, in *Opera Omnia*, vol. 4.1, pp. 155–6 and 175–82, 'de adulatione vitanda'; and Seyssel, *La Monarchie de France*, section II, chs 3–9.

50 *Commentary on Genesis*, 49.10.

51 *Commentary on Isaiah*, 32.1; Calvin's term *proceres* is nicely ambiguous between aristocracy of rank and birth. And in the *Harmony* commentary on Exodus 18.20–1, Calvin added the point that virtue, rather than title or wealth, is the first requirement in a 'judge', i.e. a governor (CO 24, 188).

52 E.g. *Gospel Harmony* (CTS, vol. II, p. 222). Cf. *Institution*, 4.12.7, from 1543: '[Great kings] never hear anything in their courts but mere flattery . . .' and 4.20.32 (1559): 'flattering courtiers'. *Sermons on 2 Samuel* (SC 1, 302): 'les grans de ce monde ont toujours leur flatteurs. . .'; *Gospel Harmony* (CO 45, 753), on Luke 23.11: 'raro in aulis regum haberi iustum Deo honorem'.

53 *Sermons on Deuteronomy* (CO 27, 410).

54 *Commentary on Genesis*, 50.4. The image of golden chains was also employed by More, but may have been a commonplace.

55 *Gospel Harmony* (CTS, vol. II, p. 282).

56 The exegesis of this difficult line is of some importance, given its location early in 4.20.1, and given also the fact that another reference to flatterers was added to the last section of the chapter in the same edition. Barth's and Niesel's claim that there is an allusion to Machiavelli here (OS V, 457, n. 10) is gratuitous. *Sinceritas fidei* is obscure; it means something like 'the purity', 'the integrity of the faith'; taken together with 'zeal for godliness (*pietas*)' in the next line, it suggests that Calvin's preoccupation is with the maintenance of pure evangelical doctrine, endangered on the one side by 'insane and barbarous men' (cf. 4.20.5) who concede too little or nothing at all to civil authority, on the other side by those who concede too much, accommodating true doctrine to what princes wish to hear. I do not think it far-fetched to see here a covert reference to the state-church propensities of evangelicals, as well as a more general condemnation of flatterers.

57 A. B. Ferguson, *The Articulate Citizen and the English Renaissance* (Durham, N.C., 1965). The only reference to More in Calvin's writings is bitterly hostile, and presumably libellous (*Commentary on Isaiah*, at 22.17); Luther's verdict was more circumspect: *Tischreden* (WA 3, 688; 4, 437). A letter from Calvin's revered Budé prefaced editions of More's *Utopia*.

58 Cf. especially *The Praise of Folly.*

59 *Sermons on Deuteronomy* (CO 27, 479).

60 *Sermons on 2 Samuel* (SC I, 250).

61 *Commentary on Genesis*, 12.17; CO 23, 186–7: 'voluntarium sibi modestiae legem imponere'.

62 Dedication of the 1563 edition of the *Harmony of Moses*, translated CTC version of *Commentary on Genesis*, p. xxx: 'Since the pleasures of a court corrupt even your servants, how much more dangerous are the snares laid for great princes, who so abound in all luxuries, that it is a wonder if they do not quite dissolve in lasciviousness.'

63 Cf. above, p. 124, for previous alterations in 1543.

64 'Sibi moderari'. Calvin was very fond of this word and its substantive *moderatio*, which normally mean to govern, government, but express strongly the notion of the imposition of restraint. Cf. also the same passage for the combination of liberty and *moderatio*.

65 4.20.8, addition of 1559.

66 *Ibid.*

67 *Harmony of Moses* (CO 24, 369).

68 *Gospel Harmony* (CTS, vol. III, p. 276).

69 *Sermons on 1 Samuel* (CO 29, 553). And see Calvin's comments about the 'apes who nowadays rule at the courts of kings and princes', in Mühlhaupt, *Psalter*, p. 50.

70 *Sermons on 1 Samuel* (CO 29, 553).

71 *Sermons on 2 Samuel* (SC I, 625).

72 SC I, 102.

73 SC I, 119.

74 *Sermons on 1 Samuel* (CO 29, 556).

75 CO 29, 350.

76 CO 29, 550.

77 *Sermons on 2 Samuel* (SC I, 298): 'Courage, qu'on ait des autres . . .'.

78 SC I, 102.

79 *Commentary on Isaiah* (1551 and 1559). I have compared the French version of 1552 (British Library, 3166 e.2), p. 249, with the Latin of 1559 (CO 36), and the CTS translation. The comment is on Isaiah, at 19.4. There seem to have been no changes between 1551 and 1559.

80 *Ibid.* He simply wrote off world monarchy as *absurdissimum; Institution*, 4.6.9, from 1543. Same expression in *Sermons on 1 Samuel* (CO 29, 601).

81 CO 29, 556. It will be recalled that this is a Latin translation of Calvin's sermons; 'monarchae' may therefore simply translate 'roys'.

82 *Commentary on Genesis*, at 10.11.

83 *De Civitate Dei*, book 4, ch. 4.

84 CO 27, 459: 'ou les loix ont leur cours . . .'. 'Judges' is used in the Old Testament sense. To the same effect CO 29, 554, 636.

85 CO 29, 556.

86 CO 29, 553.

87 CO 38, 322; cf. also CO 39, 4; CO 43, 253 (Jonas); CO 44, 431 (Malachi).

88 The term is Pocock's, *Ancient Constitution.*

89 More precisely, where the relationship between the prince and the laws had been a persistent problem for commentators since the twelfth century; Wyduckel, *Princeps Legibus Solutus.*

90 *Von der Freiheit eines Christenmenschen.*

91 *Sermons on Deuteronomy.* It will be recalled that these are precisely the sermons in which we found the most unqualified assertions of the subjection of magistrates to the law (of the land, it must be supposed). It is perhaps of some interest to note in this connection that the Favre–Perrin–Sept faction had changed Genevan law in two ways to which Calvin was opposed. They had banned *habitants* from having any weapons apart from swords, and required even those to be kept at home, and they had changed the regulations governing the election of members of the PC by the Deux Cents in the sense of giving the Deux Cents a larger number of candidates (24 instead of 16) from whom to choose.

92 Compare *Utopia*, pp. 58/9: 'as if it would be a dangerous thing to be found with more wisdom on any point than our forefathers'.

93 CO 27, 567–8: 'quant aux loix humaines, l'ancienneté doit estre honoree'. The passage is cited *in extenso* in A. Biéler, *La Pensée Economique et Sociale de Calvin* (Geneva, 1959), pp. 383–4.

94 This is well illustrated in another passage from the Deuteronomy catena (CO 27, 567): 'Qu'on se tienne donc aux loix anciennes le plus qu'il sera possible . . .'. He then went on to condemn those who 'alleguent ainsi la liberté pour avoir changement chacun jour . . .'.

95 See my 'Fundamental Law and the Constitution in Sixteenth-Century France', in R. Schnur (ed.), *Die Rolle der Juristen im frühmodernen Staat* (forthcoming), and n. 111 below.

96 CO 27, 567.

97 *Ibid.*

98 On Matthew 19.7, CTS vol. II, p. 382 (CO 45, 429), my italics.

99 Vol. I, at 6.2.

100 *Commentary on Genesis*, at 12.5, about slavery.

101 Calvin on occasion used *dominare* neutrally (compare the German *herrschen* and *Herrschaft*), but that would make no sense here. In any case, there is an echo here of Christ's words: 'The rulers of the Gentiles lord it over them.'

102 *Commentary on Genesis*, at 10.8 (CO 23, 159). For 'rough equality', cf. above, n. 31.

103 I.e. sure or fixed, but Calvin may have meant 'some'.

104 CO 24, 369.

105 Cf. p. 113. This disposes of J. Baur's suggestion that Calvin used *potentia* and *auctoritas* interchangeably (*Gott, Recht und Weltliches Regiment*, p. 10); he did do so occasionally.

106 *Commentary on Genesis*, at 41.40.

107 *Ibid.*

108 M. Walzer, *The Revolution of the Saints* (Harvard, 1965, repr. New York, 1976) discerns such a tendency in later puritanism: 'In human society, as among the angels, God's sovereignty destroyed the old hierarchy of degree' (p. 166).

109 *Institution*, all editions, 4.20.31.

110 Chenevière, *Pensée Politique*, p. 305, citing CO 39, 158.

111 It was precisely men in close touch with Calvin while he lived, such as de Bèze (Beza, Calvin's hand-picked successor at Geneva) and his long-standing correspondents and sometime visitors Hotman and du Plessis-Mornay, who justified Huguenot resistance. Cf. M. P. Thompson and H. M. Höpfl, 'The History of Contract as a Motif in Political Thought', *American Historical Review* 84/4 (1979), and my 'Fundamental Law and the Constitution'.

112 Chenevière, *Pensée Politique*, pp. 167–73, has (as usual) some very sane observations on the subject.

113 He regarded hereditary monarchy as incompatible with liberty: *Lectures on Twelve Minor Prophets*, 1559 (CO 43, 374) at Micah 5.5: 'Ubi etiam reges nascuntur haereditario jure, hoc non videtur consentaneum esse libertati.'

8   Political morality in the thought of Calvin

1 'ad civilem justitiam mores nostros formare'.

2 *Institution*, all editions, 4.20.2.

3 *Ibid.* Both these clauses and the foregoing are extremely laconic in formulation. Beveridge and Battles try to match Calvin's concision; I have abandoned the attempt, because there is no way of rendering either *mores* or *status* by a single modern word. The English equivalent for *pietas* is 'godliness'; cf. T. Norton's translation of 1561, fol. 150 *verso*.

4 4.20.9. This addition appears in the only edition of the *Institution* subsequent to the trials of Bolsec, Servetus and Gentilis. But cf. also the *Commentary on 1 Timothy* (1548) at 2.2, where Calvin cites 'a quiet and peaceable life', conservation of godliness (*piété*) and decency (*l'honnesteté*) as the fruits of a well-ordered rule.

5 An undated reply to a request for a verdict on usury, reprinted in OS I, 391–6, offers some illuminating evidence of this attitude.

6 A very large number of examples of this view are to be found throughout Calvin's writings. E.g. *Confession de la Foy*, 1536 (OS I, 419), 'que ne debvons avoir aultre reigle de bien vivre et justement [que] sa saincte loy'; *Catechisme*, 1537 (OS I, 383), 'une tresparfaicte reigle de toute justice'; Preface to the *Commentary on Isaiah*, 1551 and 1559 (CTS, p. xxvii), 'perpetuam regulam ecclesiae'; at 8.20, 'the rule of a good and happy life'; at 33.11, 'the most perfect rule of life'; *Gospel Harmony* (CTS, vol. III, p. 56), to the same effect. Also *Sermons on Deuteronomy*, 1555 (CO 29, 309–10); *De Occulta Dei Providentia*, 1558 (CO 9, 312); *Harmony of Moses* (CTS, vol. II, p. 155; vol. III, p. 6).

7 *Gospel Harmony* (CTS, vol. II, p. 394) on Matthew 19.17: 'We have no right to deny that the keeping of the law is righteousness, so that any

man who kept it perfectly – if there were such a man – would obtain life for himself.'

8 This seems to be implied in Eric Voegelin's description of the *Institution* as a 'koranic' book; *The New Science of Politics*, pp. 138–9.

9 The *Harmony of the Last Four Books of Moses* (1563) divided its exposition of the Decalogue into (1) various statements of the commandments; (2) 'ceremonial supplements'; and (3) 'judicial' or 'civil' supplements. The third category of imperatives was sometimes taken to be still in force (when it suited Calvin), as over the punishment of heretics and adulterers, but was usually taken to be peculiar to the Israelite commonwealth. But the second category, which dealt in figures, types and teaching by indirection, was deemed entirely superseded. It included such matters as the sacrificing of animals, ritual ablutions, clean and unclean foods and other pollutions, priestly dress, and also the reuse of buildings and objects previously devoted to idolatry. It was therefore just as well that 'ceremonial supplements' were abolished, otherwise evangelicals would have had to find new pulpits.

10 *Response a un Certain Hollandois lequel sous ombre de faire les Chrestiens tout spirituels leur permet de polluer leur corps en toutes idolatries*, 1562 (CO 9, 581–628).

11 The contrast with the papists was, of course, purely factitious.

12 *Gospel Harmony* (CTS, vol. II, pp. 382–3); *Institution*, 4.11.3 (from 1543).

13 The sacramentarian controversy between evangelicals, and the duty to avoid the pollutions of the papists.

14 It should be made clear that my discussion here has nothing to do with the so-called 'syllogismus practicus', attributed to Calvin, whereby election may be inferred from conduct.

15 *Defensio* (CO 8, 475); *Harmony of Moses*, at Deuteronomy 13.5 (CTS, vol. II, p. 73).

16 *Commentary on Genesis*, at 22.1–7.

17 *Sermons on Deuteronomy* (CO 27, 250): 'Que nous devons mettre sous pied toutes affections de nature quand il est question de son honneur . . .'

18 Letter 3150, speculatively dated late 1559, but more likely to be some years later (CO 17, 710, n. 1).

19 E.g. *Defensio Orthodoxae Fidei de Trinitate*, 1554, throughout, but especially CO 8, 470.

20 I take it that at least an important section of those whom Calvin described as 'Libertines' were antinomians. Antinomianism was so antipathetic to Calvin that he could not understand it except as a form of madness, as the title of his pamphlet makes clear: *Contre la Secte Phantastique et Furieuse des Libertins, qui se nomment Spirituelz*, 1545 (CO 7, 164). He interpreted them as simply using Christian liberty as an excuse for carnal licence (cf. CO 7, 165, 170, 174, 206, 211). For the rest, their scriptural exegesis was treated as either frivolity, allegories or vain speculation (e.g. CO 7, 164, 166, 'strange language'; 167, 174, 175, Scripture made a 'nose of wax').

21 Especially at Basel, for which see the admirable treatment of U. Plath, *Calvin und Basel*.

22 For the worsening relations between Calvinists and Lutherans, cf. *Ultima Admonitio ad Westphal*, 1557.

23 *Institution*, all editions, 4.20.16.

24 The distinction is somewhat crudely made in *Sermons on Deuteronomy* (CO 25, 645): 'Quand les Rois, les Princes et Magistratz sont instituez, Dieu leur donne quant et quant l'authorité de faire des loix . . . Mais tant y a, qu'encores les loix civilles, elles sont faites par les hommes . . .'

25 (Where not otherwise identified, all the references which follow are to Calvin's commentaries.) 1 Corinthians 7.37; Ephesians 5.31; 1 Timothy 2 and 5.8; *Sermons on Deuteronomy*, CO 26, 311 (published section); Genesis 24.3.

26 Genesis, 26.10; 38.24.

27 1 Timothy 5.8.

28 Genesis 21.8.

29 Genesis 27.11.

30 *Harmony of Moses* (CTS, vol. III, p. 52); *Sermons on 2 Samuel*, SC 1, 263 (unpublished).

31 1 Corinthians 9.1.

32 *Harmony of Moses* (CTS, vol. I, p. 137).

33 *Harmony of Moses* (CTS, vol. III, p. 45).

34 *Harmony of Moses* (CTS, vol. II, p. 221).

35 Genesis 29.27; *Harmony of Moses* (CTS, vol. III, p. 98); *Gospel Harmony* (CTS, vol. II, p. 22).

36 *Harmony of Moses* (CTS, vol. III, p. 20); *Sermons on Deuteronomy*, CO 26, 323 (published section).

37 Genesis 26.10; *Harmony of Moses* (CTS, vol. III, p. 77).

38 Genesis 12.15; Ephesians 6.1.

39 1 Corinthians 5; cf. CO 49, 379–80.

40 Genesis 41.38.

41 *Harmony of Moses* (CTS, vol. III, p. 18).

42 *Harmony of Moses* (CTS, vol. II, p. 73).

43 *Sermons on Deuteronomy*, CO 27, 444 (unpublished section).

44 1 Timothy 2.

45 *Harmony of Moses*; cf. CO 24, 662.

46 CO 24, 603.

47 *Harmony of Moses* (CTS, vol. II, p. 196); *Sermons on Deuteronomy*, CO 27, 415; Ephesians 6.1.

48 *Harmony of Moses* (CTS, section on 'The use of the Law', vol. III, p. 196); Genesis 29.14.

49 See the extensive comments on Romans, at 2.14–15; also *Contre la Secte des Libertins*, CO 7, 202.

50 'lex scripta', 2.8.1, from 1539.

51 Calvin never denied that pagans could produce a facsimile of righteousness, an 'external righteousness'; cf. *Institution*, 2.3.3; also *Commentary on Isaiah*, 53.11 and *Commentary on Genesis*, 4.20.

52 *Institution*, 2.2.22 (from 1539); *Commentary on Romans*, 2.15; *Commentary on Genesis*, 38.24; *Congregation sur l'Election Eternelle*, 1562, but dating from 1551 (CO 8, 99, 110).

53 *Calumniae Nebulonis . . . De Occulta Dei Providentia*, 1558 (CO 9, 312),

where Calvin himself brought up the justice of God 'qui innoxios foetus a matrum uberibus avulsos in aeternam mortem praecipitat', as a counter to Castellio's claim that no one can be condemned by God unless because of some crime.

54 *Sermons on 1 Samuel* (CO 29, 330); *Sermons on Deuteronomy* (CO 27, 411–12).

55 *Sermons on 2 Samuel* (SC 1, 279); *Sermons on 1 Samuel* (CO 29, 529–30). Both unpublished.

56 Choisy, *Théocratie*, p. 102. Since he cites no source, the story may be *ben trovato*.

57 Servetus had previously been condemned and burnt in effigy at Vienne.

58 *Defensio* (CO 8, 474).

59 *Calvins Wirken*, pp. 51–2.

60 *Sermons on Deuteronomy* (CO 26, 341), published section.

61 CO 26, 342, 'couverture'. See also *Commentary on 1 Corinthians*, at 7.5–6; *Commentary on Genesis*, at 4.1: 'congressum viris cum uxore, rem per se pudendam . . .'; *Harmony of Moses* (CO 24, 312): 'coetus . . . turpis est ac pudendus . . .'. The reader is, however, invited to consider that the Council of Trent managed to recommend *both* daily communion *and* abstinence from intercourse for at least three days before communion. J. Donovan (ed.), *Catechism of the Council of Trent* (Dublin and London, 1829), part II, ch. 4, qu. 69 and part II, ch. 8, qu. 34.

62 *Harmony of Moses* (CTS, vol. III, p. 77), commenting on the *lex Julia de adulteribus coercendis* of Augustus, in connection with Deuteronomy 22.22.

63 CO 23, 499. Calvin was commenting on Genesis 38.24.

64 *Calvin's Commentary on St John*, trans. T. H. L. Parker (Edinburgh, 1959), vol. I, p. 209: 'He did not wish to undertake anything not belonging to his office . . .' Calvin himself was evidently unembarrassed by this exegesis, for he introduced it *proprio motu* in the *Defensio* (CO 8, 463) and also immediately after the passage on Genesis 38.24, quoted above.

65 Choisy, *Théocratie*, p. 10, has some remarks on the subject which are still usable. Biéler, *Pensée de Calvin*, pp. 124–42 also deserves consideration, but despite his unequivocal honesty, he confuses apologetics and historical explanation.

66 Those who, like Bohatec (*Calvins Lehre von Staat und Kirche*, Breslau, 1937, p. 68), stress that Calvin described the relationship between rulers and ruled as one of *mutua obligatio* (which he did), ought also to stress that mutual obligation is a consequence of the duty of both parties to God, and that Calvin nowhere uses contractual vocabulary in this connection: mutual obligations need not be contractual ones.

67 'It is not for the people to constitute princes. For it belongs to God alone to change governments as he pleases' (CO 39, 158). The context is that of a people bound by oath to a prince subsequently vanquished by a 'foreign enemy'; according to Calvin, that people is now morally obliged to obey the latter. Students of Hobbes may wish to consider this passage.

68 *Institution*, 4.3.13, 4.4.10; both from 1543.

69 Discussed on pp. 197–9.

70 W. J. Bouwsma, 'The Two Faces of Humanism', in H. O. Oberman and

T. A. Brady (eds), *Itinerarium Italicum*, Studies in Medieval and Reformation Thought xiv (Leiden, 1975), pp. 3–60 suggests a theoretical context for Calvin's attitude in his Renaissance Augustinianism.

71 *Institution*, 4.20.9: 'My exposition is intended not so much for the instruction of magistrates themselves . . .' (all editions).

72 E.g. Dedication to Protector Somerset of *Commentaries on 1 and 2 Timothy*.

73 E.g. *Commentary on Isaiah*, at 3.14 and 22.22.

74 *Commentary on Genesis*, at 4.20.

75 *Commentary on 1 Corinthians*, at 1.19–22.

76 *Ibid.*

77 *Commentary on 1 Corinthians*, at 12.8. Cf. also *Commentary on Isaiah*, at 19.12.

78 Compare *Commentary on 1 Corinthians*, at 12.1: 'Certain fanatics furiously rage against all the liberal arts and sciences.' The instance of book-burning in Acts 19.18 received no applause from Calvin, who interpreted it as a purely private act, appropriate in the circumstances.

79 *Commentary on Acts* ii, at 19.35–40. In the discussion of Acts 5.34–9, Calvin denied that Gamaliel was a man of prudence, but then went on to argue about what godliness would have required of him. The passage ('regarded as an oracle by many') was a favourite text for freedom of discussion in doctrinal matters; Calvin treated it as if the author of Acts were inviting us to deplore Gamaliel's attitude.

80 *Que Doit Faire un Homme Fidele entre les Papistes*, 1543 (CO 6, 570).

9   *The laws and mores of a Christian commonwealth*

1 *Defensio* (CO 8, 470).

2 Fills, *Lawes*, p. 67 *recto* and *verso*, quotes an ordinance which demanded that all go to sermons, 'live holily and peaceably', obedient to the laws, and which forbade 'all blasphemie, dispisings of God and his ministers, dishonest words, vaine songes, dronkenes, dissolutions, exces, arrogancie and insolencie, playes or games' etc., 'to the ende that the honour of God may be mayntayned and advanced and his wrathe turned from us . . .'. Similar expressions abound in the statutes of Geneva.

3 *Commentary on the Psalms* (CO 37, 450).

4 In the *Commentary on 1 Corinthians*, at 1.12, he expressly defended eloquence as one of the 'praeclara Dei dona' (CO 49, 320–1). Cf. also *Defensio* (CO 8, 469).

5 Cf. especially the discussion in *Gospel Harmony* (CTS, vol. ii, p. 382), on Matthew 19.7.

6 E.g. the passages cited by Calvin in *Calumniae Nebulonis*, 1558 (CO 9, 312).

7 In the *Defensio*, Calvin implicitly admitted this, when he claimed that that was not the purpose of the execution of heretics (CO 8, 470). Cf. Bucer, *Von der Wahren Seelsorge* (*Deutsche Schriften*, vol. 7), pp. 149–50. Bucer there recognized the problem of hypocrites (*Heuchler*).

8 *Commentary on 1 Timothy*, 1548, at 2.9–15: 'godly teachers are to govern (*moderare*) men's consciences'.

9 *Ibid.*, at 2.2: 'It is not enough for [magistrates] to restrain injustice by

giving to each his own and by maintaining peace, if they are not also zealous to promote religion and regulate morals by wholesome discipline . . .' Cf. also *Institution*, 4.12.1 (from 1543).

10 In the *Sermons on Deuteronomy* (CO 27, 665), he answered the question 'why are laws not at all perfect?' by saying that 'in them, one has regard to what is possible. One does not make laws in order to say, "it would be good to act like this", but "this is how men can live together".'

11 E.g. *Institution*, 4.12.1 (from 1543): *fraenum* and *stimulus*, as well as 'fatherly rod'.

12 *Defensio* (CO 8, 470): 'I omit Augustine's sage and true objection that it is useful that the unwilling . . . be drawn, so that having undergone punishment they accede willingly.' And *Gospel Harmony* (CTS, vol. II, p. 173) on Luke 14.23 ('Compel them to enter'): 'I do not disapprove of the use which Augustine frequently made of this passage . . . Although faith is voluntary, yet we see that such methods are useful for subduing the obstinacy of those who will not yield until they are compelled.'

13 Epistle of August 1559, prefixed to the *Institution*: 'Etsi autem laboris tunc impensi me non poenitebat, nunquam tamen mihi satisfecit, donec in hunc ordinem qui nunc proponitur, digestum fuit.' Translation in H. Beveridge, *Institutes*, p. 24.

14 In the *Defensio* (CO 8, 471), Calvin used the episode in Acts 5.1–5 concerning Ananias and Sapphira to assert: 'Ergo verbi ministris licuit corporali poena coercere impios.' However, this was not mentioned in the *Commentary on Acts* I (1552) at that place, and I do not know what to make of it.

15 Little, *Religion, Order and Law*, esp. pp. 62–80. Biéler, *Pensée de Calvin*, ch. I, especially section 2, and ch. III, section 2.iii.3.

16 Biéler, *Pensée de Calvin*, ch. II, section 2.iii.1–3, and cf. pp. 263 and 268; Little, *Religion, Order and Law*, pp. 49, 53; but note the qualification at p. 77.

17 In his commentaries, Calvin systematically ignored, attenuated or explained away as referring to the life-history of individuals, the favourite texts of the millennarians, E.g. *Commentary on 1 Corinthians*, 2.6, 3.15, 6.2, 7.29, 10.3–11, 15.25; *Commentary on 1 Timothy*, 4.1; *Commentary on 2 Timothy*, 3.1; *Commentary on Isaiah*, 2.2, 2.4, 11.6, 34.13, 35.1; *Commentary on Acts* II, 19.21.

18 H. Quistorp, *Calvin's Doctrine of the Last Things* (London, 1955), esp. p. 193.

19 Extensive citations from the Calvinian corpus on all these topics are to be found in Biéler, *Pensée de Calvin*. The author's commentary is not always borne out by the citations, but the wealth of the latter compensates for this.

20 E.g. especially *Institution*, 4.20.1–2; *Brieve Instruction contre les Anabaptistes* (CO 7, 66): 'Ne nous abusons pas donc, d'imaginer une Eglise parfaicte en ce monde.' Cf. also his rejection of common property in *Contre la Secte des Libertins* (CO 7, 214–18).

21 Compare his definition of *aedificatio* in *Commentary on Acts* I, at 9.31.

22 *Pensée de Calvin*, p. 27; his peculiarly French usage of the term 'individualiste' is here profoundly unhelpful.

23 *Institution*, 4.11.1 (1543 onwards).
24 Cf. ch. 4.
25 In the *Sermons on Deuteronomy* (CO 27, 642), Calvin said that 'Juges et gens de justice' are not merely to act when appealed to, 'mais il faut qu'ils s'enquirent soigneusement; encores que nul ne parle ni les solicite, d'eux-mesmes et de leur mouvement propre ils doivent estre vigilans de s'enquerir . . .'.
26 These illustrations therefore conform to our criteria set out above, p. 140.
27 The fullest and most reliable account is still M. L. de Gallatin, 'Les Ordonnances Somptuaires à Genève au XVIᵉ Siècle', in *Mémoires et Documents Publiés par la Société d'Histoire et Archéologie de Genève* 36 (1938). E. Pfisterer, *Calvins Wirken*, especially pp. 64–85, is useful, but to be treated with caution.
28 Genevan edicts repeatedly reasserted the civic duty of cleaning streets and privies.
29 De Gallatin, 'Ordonnances Somptuaires', p. 206.
30 *Ibid.*
31 *Commentary on 1 Timothy*, 2.9–15.
32 Rivoire and van Berchem, *Sources*, vol. III, p. 86.
33 *Ibid.*, pp. 103 ff.
34 The first casualties of this law were the Lieutenant de la Justice and his assessors, who permitted themselves thirteen courses instead of twelve; Pfisterer, *Calvins Wirken*, p. 83.
35 Fills, *Lawes*, pp. 76 *recto* – 77 *verso*.
36 Text in Rivoire and van Berchem, *Sources*, vol. III, pp. 103 ff. A summary of it is to be found in Gallatin, pp. 215–17.
37 *Sources*, vol. II, pp. 480 (1546), 530 (1549).
38 *Sources*, vol. III, pp. 129–30 (1562); this seems to have escaped Pfisterer, *Calvins Wirken*, p. 67.
39 *Sources*, e.g. vol. II, p. 352 (1539, during Calvin's absence); vol. III, pp. 29, 37, 52, 87, 125, 127.
40 At Calvin's prompting, Messieurs passed an ordinance governing what were and what were not suitable Christian names for Genevans. The episode is recounted in Doumergue, *Jean Calvin*, vol. 5, p. 107.
41 Cited in ch. 6.
42 *Sources*, vol. III, p. 107.
43 The logic of such a system of mutual surveillance is explored in More's *Utopia*, 'Discourse of Utopia'.
44 See especially a sermon published in 1563, but delivered in 1554 to the *congrégation* or *concio* (CO 53, 199).
45 De Gallatin, p. 213, quoting the speech by des Gallars. Cf. the text of Calvin cited in n. 59 below.
46 *Arret* of 13.7.1562, in *Sources*, vol. III, p. 131.
47 Chenevière's observations on this subject are apt: *Pensée Politique*, pp. 277–81. See also Pfisterer, pp. 73–81.
48 *Sources*, vol. II, pp. 477–80.
49 *Cries* of 29.4.1546, in *Sources*, vol. II, p. 477, abrogated 22.6.1546 by the Deux Cents.

50 He did, however, express the view that a large number of inns was evidence of a neglect of hospitality. *Commentary on Genesis*, at 18.2.

51 *Institution*, 3.19.7.

52 Notably with du Tillet, and with the Seigneur de Falais, who spoke up for Bolsec, his personal physician.

53 E.g. *Institution*, 3.19.9.

54 There are some apt citations of opinions to this effect in Pfisterer, *Calvins Wirken*, pp. 64, 68, 73. Contrast *Institution*, 3.10.2, from 1539.

55 Parker, *Calvin*, p. 122, and letters to Farel of 20.8.1553 (CO 14, 590) and 26.10.1553 (CO 14, 656).

56 Cf. *Defensio* (CO 8), *passim*, where Servetus is described as a heretic, an apostate, 'impius', of 'indomita . . . contumacia' and guilty of detestable blasphemies.

57 Another alternative, that of long-term imprisonment, was ruled out by the absence of facilities (already noted) and by the rather casual attitude of the time to prison visiting, which would have permitted the spreading of Servetus's 'poison'.

58 Calvin insisted that only grave heresy merited the death-penalty. *Defensio* (CO 8, 477): 'Ergo ut in aliis omnibus peccatis laudabilis sit clementia, severe impietatem, quae Dei cultum evertit, sanctis iudicibus ulcisci necesse est', to avert God's wrath.

59 The correspondence is noted in F. L. Battles, 'Against Luxury and Licence in Geneva', *Interpretation* 19 (1965), pp. 182–202, where an extensive fragment of Calvin's from 1546 or 1547 (CO 10, 1, 203–6) is translated.

60 In a letter to Farel of 1546, reported by Bolsec in a vitriolic diatribe which *inter alia* accused Calvin of sodomy and adulteries. The letter was found, and appears in CO 12, 283; for an abridgement of Bolsec's diatribe, see H. Bordier, *Bolsec Rajeuni* (Libourne, 1880), pp. 26–33.

61 For example Castellio, an erstwhile 'doctor' at Geneva, who, despite attacks on the ministry and a doctrinal disagreement with Calvin, left Geneva with a good reference from the ministry.

62 M. Oakeshott, *On Human Conduct* (Oxford, 1975), ch. III.

63 *Institution*, 1559, 4.1.4: 'And our weakness does not allow us to leave this school, until we have run the whole course of our lives as pupils.'

64 *Ibid.*

65 4.12.1, 5 and 6: *castigare, castigatio*.

66 4.12.1 (from 1543).

67 The *Loix Concernant l'Ordre des Escoles* of 1559 are to be found in OS 1, 364–79. They are very detailed concerning both organization and syllabuses, and deserve careful study.

68 *Loix* (OS 1, 374).

69 *Ibid.*

70 *Actes du Procès de Bolsec* (CO 8, 145–247). Numerous laymen were present at the *congrégation* in question.

71 Kingdon, *Geneva, passim*.

72 The rather unsatisfactory literature on this topic is surveyed by H. Vahle, 'Calvinismus und Demokratie im Spiegel der Forschung', in *Archiv für Reformationsgeschichte* 66 (1975), pp. 182–212.

10 Unfinished business: a speculative summary and postscript

1 Text from the Register of the Venerable Company in CO 34, 412–13; translation in Parker, *Calvin*, pp. 153–5. The same chords were struck in the Preface to the 1559 *Institution*.

2 I here follow Dowey, *The Knowledge of God in Calvin's Theology*.

3 Substantial additions are to be found in book 2, chs 6, 9, 12, 13, 14–17. Servetus is frequently mentioned and abused by name.

4 Additional sections on this theme are to be found in book 3, chs 21–4. Calvin also expended book 3, ch. 11, on a refutation of the former Lutheran, Andreas Osiander.

5 There were substantial changes and additions to book 4, ch. 17.

6 R. Kingdon, *Geneva and the Coming of the Wars of Religion in France* should be consulted for the entire episode.

7 J. Bohatec, *Calvin und das Recht*, ch. III. The extensive correspondence of this period is in CO 17–20.

8 See letters 3185 and 3188, 1560 (CO 18).

9 In particular, contractual vocabulary, an assertion of the rights of the people, natural right and liberty, the argument that the king is subject to law (sometimes 'fundamental law') and that tyrannous conduct by kings releases subjects from their obedience, the right of self-defence, the duty to preserve the covenant with God.

10 *Institution*, 1.12.1 (from 1550).

11 Milton, finding himself unable to praise a 'fugitive and cloistered virtue, unexercised and unbreathed, that never sallies out and sees her adversary', and demanding the freedom of unlicensed printing so that virtue may be exercised, may be regarded as adumbrating this line of thought, compatibly with his conception of virtue as 'strenuous'. Milton, *Areopagitica*, in *Prose Writings* (rev. ed., London, 1958), p. 158.

12 E.g. *Commentary on Acts* II, at 15.1: 'Although we naturally dread the cross and persecution of any sort, yet greater danger comes from internal divisions . . . There is nothing which damages the Gospel more than internal discords, for they not only discourage weak consciences, but provide the ungodly with the opportunity to speak evil of it.' As we have seen, an addition to the *Institution* of 1559 (4.20.1) speaks of 'flatterers of princes' and 'demented, barbarous men' as the main threats to the purity of doctrine.

13 CO 18, 82.

14 The emphasis on written laws is distinctively Calvin's. The pamphlets in the service of the Prince de Condé and of Bourbon generally confine themselves to 'les loix et constitutions anciennes', 'les anciennes loix', 'loix et coustumes'. Cf. *Mémoires de Condé* (Paris and London, 1743), e.g. vol. II, pp. 354, 438–9, 530; vol. III, pp. 251, 259, 406, 594–5; vol. IV, pp. 18, 34, 57, 62, 527. References to the Edict of January 1561 are, naturally, extremely frequent.

15 Bohatec, *Calvin und das Recht*, p. 177, aptly summarizes: 'Auch jetzt bleibt Calvin unbeugsamer Sachverwalter des positiven Rechts.'

16 Cf V. de Caprariis, *Propaganda e pensiero politico in Francia durante le Guerre di Religione* (Naples, 1959).

17 The choice of this term by Beza had, in his earlier writings, the effect of making the condition of 'inferior' magistrates analogous to that of private persons. Cf. R. M. Kingdon (ed.), *Theodore de Bèze, Du Droit des Magistrats* (Geneva, 1970), annexe 2, p. 74, an excerpt from the 'Confession de la Foy' of late 1558: 'Quant aux particuliers, d'avec lesquels ne different rien ou bien peu les Magistrats inferieurs . . .'; these are not to offer resistance, unlike the Electors of the Holy Roman Empire or the Estates of most kingdoms.

18 Excerpt in J. H. Franklin (ed.), *Constitutionalism and Resistance* (New York, 1969), pp. 151–4, from the *Vindiciae contra Tyrannos*, 1579, Second Question, 'May a part of the kingdom resist?'

Appendix I: Calvin's conversion

1 A. Ganoczy, *Le Jeune Calvin*, p. 137.

2 Both have recently been submitted to careful, but inconclusive analysis: Ganoczy, *Le Jeune Calvin*; P. Sprenger, *Das Rätsel um die Bekehrung Calvins* (Neukirchen, 1960); F. L. Battles's Introduction to his edition of the *Institution of the Christian Religion* of 1536 (Atlanta, 1975), pp. xvi–xxvii; Parker, *Calvin*, pp. 162–5.

3 The Latin text of the *Reply* is in CO 5, 385–416; the relevant passages are on pp. 411–13. A translation of and commentary on both Calvin's *Reply* and Sadoleto's letter, which provoked it, appear in Olin, *A Reformation Debate*. The relevant passages are on pp. 87–90.

4 Ganoczy, *Le Jeune Calvin*, provides ample evidence about the divisions within the church, especially the French church; it was simply not possible to say which doctrines were orthodox. In Germany, the matter was decided by governments.

5 Olin, *Debate*, p. 88.

6 *Ibid.*

7 *Ibid.*

8 P. 87.

9 Cf. places cited below.

10 Olin, p. 88.

11 *Ibid.*

12 Pp. 89–90.

13 P. 88.

14 CO 31, 21–4; both Latin and French versions are given in parallel. A translation appears in Parker, *Calvin*, p. 163.

15 Compare Preface to *Von der Freiheit* (WA 54, 179): 'ebrium, submersum in dogmatibus papae . . .'; 'Tantus eram Saulus' (*pace* Parker). Cf. also p. 184: 'Haesi tenaciter . . .', and pp. 185–7. In the next century, the pattern had become standardized and people were evangelicals by birth, not by deliberate decision; this produced real difficulties, for not all were able to produce instances of preconversion depravity to match those of Saul. Richard Baxter was reduced to confessing to having scrumped apples as a boy. Evidently he needed to find *something*. R. Baxter, *Autobiography* (London and New York, 1931), p. 5.

16 *Supra* (WA 54, 185–7).
17 Olin, *Debate*, p. 88.
18 *Ibid.*
19 *Ibid.*, pp. 163–4.
20 *Ibid.*, pp. 56–7.
21 Cf. Ganoczy, *Le Jeune Calvin*, p. 180.
22 CO 21, 30. Beza's account is, admittedly, highly inaccurate, but the revised *Vita* assigned the same reason (CO 21, 57). Colladon's *Vita* is more specific: 'ob schedas quasdam adversus missam per urbem sparsas . . . secedere ex Gallia statuit' (CO 21, 124).
23 J. Kampschulte, *Johannes Calvin.*
24 E.g. letter 3379 (1.5.1561) to the church at Aix (CO 18, 436–7), where Calvin attempts to deal with the accusation 'qu'estans loin des coups et a repos, nous soyons plus hardis a vous exhorter a patience, d'autant que le mal ne nous touche point . . .'.
25 Latin text in OS I, 4–10; translation in Battles, *Institution*, appendix III. For a discussion of the manuscripts, cf. J. Rott, 'Documents Strasbourgeois Concernant Calvin', in *Regards Contemporains sur Jean Calvin*, Actes du Colloque Calvin à Strasbourg, 1964 (Paris, 1965), pp. 28–9.
26 Parker, *Calvin*, p. 30.
27 Text in Battles, *Institution*, appendix I.
28 U. Plath, *Calvin und Basel*, pp. 17–22.
29 This is the date of the first Preface, from Orleans.
30 Bullinger had already written a book against it. Cf. N. T. Burns, *Christian Mortalism from Tyndale to Milton* (Cambridge, Mass., 1972), p. 20. Zwingli considered it an Anabaptist heresy; cf. G. H. Williams, *The Radical Reformation* (Philadelphia, 1962), p. 106.
31 Williams, *Radical Reformation*, p. xxvi: 'in their intense eschatological convictions, some of the Spiritualists, many Anabaptists, and almost all of the Evangelical Rationalists adhered to the doctrine of the sleep or the death of the soul prior to the resurrection'.
32 Burns, *Mortalism*, pp. 27–32.
33 Williams, *Radical Reformation*, p. 583.
34 *Psychopannychia*, in *Calvin's Tracts* (CTS, vol. III, pp. 415, 417, 490). Mostly Calvin referred to his opponents as 'they'.
35 Williams, *Radical Reformation*, index references to 'psychopannychism'.
36 *Contre la Secte Phantastique et Furieuse des Libertins qui se Nomment Spirituelz*, 1545 (CO 7, 226–241); cf. also reference to Quintinists (*ibid.*, pp. 167–73).
37 *Psychopannychia* (CTS, vol. III, p. 418).
38 'now again stirred up by some dregs of Anabaptists', *Psychopannychia*, p. 415.
39 CO 10, II, 45 dates it at 1533.
40 Williams, *Radical Reformation*, p. 584: 'this surely was not the doctrine that would have been the distinguishing mark of Luther's French followers'.
41 *Ibid.*, p. 583.
42 *Psychopannychia*, p. 415 (Orleans Preface).
43 *Ibid.*, p. 468.

44 Further to this, on p. 436 we read: 'Not to omit the reprobate . . .' but the reprobate are not mentioned again until p. 450.
45 *Ibid.*, pp. 415, 418, 490.
46 Parker, *Calvin*, p. 21.
47 G. W. Locher, *Die Zwinglische Reformation*, p. 122: 'Der Weg des Humanisten Zwingli aber vom Bibeltheologen zum Reformator weist Ähnlichkeiten mit demjenigen Calvins auf, soweit er uns erkennbar ist.' However, I would stress the mediacy of Volmar (or Wolmar, the *nom de plume* of the Swiss Melchior Rot) in Calvin's conversion in contrast to Zwingli's claim to independence of Luther, which like Locher I am disposed to accept.

Appendix II: Predestination

1 Cf. J. Pannier (ed.), *Institution*, vol. III, p. 57. The linking paragraph originally followed 3.21.1., first paragraph: 'what they ought to hold concerning election and predestination', which until 1559 was explicitly said to involve a discussion both of election and reprobation and of providence. Cf. also the deletion of the reference to predestination from 1.17.12, first line, as compared with Pannier, *Institution*, vol. III, p. 127.
2 *Defensio Sanae et Orthodoxae Doctrinae de Servitute et Liberatione Humani Arbitrii*, 1543 and *De Aeterna Dei Praedestinatione*, 1552.
3 *Brevis Responsio . . . ad Diluendas Nebulonis Cuisdam Calumniae*, 1557; *Calumniae Nebulonis Cuisdam . . .*, 1558; *Response a Certaines Calomnies et Blasphèmes . . .*, 1562. Musculus complained of the abusiveness of the *Responsio*; cf. CO 9, xxxi. On the tone of these tracts, see the comments of H. Otten, *Prädestination in Calvins Theologischer Lehre* (1938; repr. Neukirchen-Vluyn, 1968), p. 25.
4 *Congrégation . . . sur l'Election Eternelle*, 1562 (CO 8, 93 ff.). This seems to be the record of a *congrégation* held eleven years earlier, evidently to demonstrate pastoral solidarity after the Bolsec affair, which had produced a most disappointing lack of support from other pastoral colleges.
5 In the first (1521) edition of the *Loci Communes*, Melanchthon had simply affirmed predestination and denied free will. (Cf. *Melanchthons Werke*, vol. II, part I, pp. 8–17). By 1535 he was evidently perturbed at the thought that God might be being made the author of sin. He therefore readmitted contingency and free will. To compare the 1539 German translation by Justus Jonas (Wittenberg), with the 1559 edition in *Werke*, variations of which appear in footnotes to the 1535 edition (referred to in brackets below), see: xxxi *recto* (228–9) for Melanchthon's worries that predestination might make God the author of sin; xxxiii *recto* (234) for his worries about the moral effects of something like a *Stoicum fatum* being introduced into Christian doctrine; xxxi *verso* (229) for contingency conceded; xxxiv *verso* (238) for free will; clii *recto* (597) for *tentatio* occasioned if divine providence is restricted to a few.
6 As it is by Wendel, *Calvin*, p. 269.
7 All references to the *Institution*, where not otherwise indicated, are to the 1539 edition.

8 Wendel, *Calvin*, pp. 264, 266, 269. Otten, *Prädestination*, p. 41: 'in direkter Beantwortung der von der Erfahrung gestellten Frage nach dem Ursprung und der Bedeutung der Verschiedenheit der Menschen gegenüber der Botschaft des Evangeliums'. Cf. also pp. 28–9, 78.

9 This of course in no way detracts from the importance of the doctrine: all the things most needful for man to know, in Calvin's view, are known only from revelation. It is, however, the case that Calvin alluded to both experience and revelation as indicating that all are not saved. E.g. *Congrégation sur l'Election Eternelle* (CO 8, 93, 94, 98, 99).

10 3.23.14, from 1559, but repeating what Calvin had said concerning the 'judgement of charity' in 1536. (OS 1, 89, transposed in 1543 to 4.1.8, where we also find Augustine's point: 'many sheep are without and many wolves are within'. The thought of sheep without seems not to have informed Calvin's conduct.)

11 E.g. 3.21.1 (from 1559), 3.21.3. And cf. *De Aeterna Dei Praedestinatione* (CO 8, 260: 'This is not, as some erroneously think, a matter of futile or thorny speculation . . . rather is it a solid argument, entirely suited to pious use.' Cf. also p. 264.

12 Compare the dispiriting replies the Geneva ministers got in reply to their request for support during the Bolsec affair: CO 8, 229–31 for the reply of the Zurich ministers, and see Bullinger to Calvin, a few days later, in CO 14, 214–15: 'nam mihi crede plures offendi tuis Institutionibus de Praedestinatione', and Calvin complaining to Farel about Zurich's attitude, CO 14, 218. Equally negative were Basel (CO 8, 236) and Bern (CO 8, 239–40). None of these endorsed reprobation, or the teaching of the *Institutio* which had been implicitly asked for in the letter of the Genevan ministers (CO 8, 207).

13 See 3.21.4. This presentation of his doctrine as a middle way between two extremes was perhaps an attempt on Calvin's part to demonstrate that he was not a fanatic bent on disturbing the peace.

14 I here follow H. J. McSorley, *Luthers Lehre von dem unfreien Willen* (Munich, 1967), pp. 36–59. Since I can as readily understand why a theologian should feel the need to affirm predestination as to deny it, I am (it seems) debarred from understanding Luther's *De Servo Arbitrio* on Schwarzwäller's account. Cf. K. Schwarzwäller, *Sibboleth* (Munich, 1969), p. 106.

15 Sometimes in the same pericope, e.g. Ecclesiasticus 15.14–20 (admittedly apocryphal in the evangelical view); cf. *Institution*, 2.5.18, 3.15.8. See also Jeremiah 21.8 ff.; Deuteronomy 30.29.

16 Wendel, *Calvin*, pp. 127–9, about 3.23.2.

17 I owe this metaphor to Schwarzwäller, *Theologia Crucis*, p. 51.

18 Otten, *Prädestination*, p. 18.

19 In the 1559 edition, justification is discussed in book 2. Problems about free will and responsibility, the origin of evil, necessity versus compulsion, salvation as a free gift, had all to be treated in that context.

20 An addition of 1559 makes precisely this point: 3.23.7. And in the *Responsio* Calvin claimed that Castellio's position 'est abrogare Deo summum imperium' (CO 9, 259).

21 See 1.16.3 and 6 for the view that God's governance of everything in

the world has man as its especial object. Like predestination, God's providence makes free will impossible (1.16.6); it also conduces to confidence in believers (1.16.3) and solaces them (1.17.6 and 7); it divides into a 'general' and a 'special' providence (1.16.4–5) as does vocation (3.24.8). It raises the same problems about God's will being tyrannical, about God as *exlex* (1.17.2) and about human responsibility (1.17.3, 5). Some uncancelled references to providence from the 1539 edition remained in the chapters on predestination later on (3.23.8, 9). In CO 8, 349, Calvin speaks of 'providence' when one might have expected him to say 'predestination'.

22 Wendel, *Calvin*, p. 269.

23 'Christ is the mirror in which we must, and without self-deception may, contemplate our own election' (3.24.5).

24 Distinction taken from Schwarzwäller, *Theologia Crucis*, p. 51. Although 'election in Christ' is almost Calvin's standard formula, I cannot help but feel that in most of the discussion Christ rather recedes from view behind God's free determination with regard to every individual.

25 The ambiguity here is nicely captured in the concluding lines of Calvin's discussion of the subject (3.14.17, added in 1559). Calvin encourages us to 'tremble with Paul at so deep a mystery' and to exclaim (again with Paul) against those who object to the doctrine of reprobation: 'Who are you, O man, to argue with God?' Trembling and human inferiority clearly refer to God's power, not his mercy. Calvin then added: 'They who measure divine justice by the standard of human justice are acting perversely.' Here the emphasis is on God's justice rather than his power, but again not on his mercy.

26 E.g. 3.22.11, 3.23.6 and 8, 3.24.12. And cf. CO 8, 294.

27 Compare his insistence that he was not attributing a *potestas absoluta* to God (e.g. at 3.23.2, from 1559, 1.17.2, and CO 8, 361) with his assertion that God willed the fall of Adam (3.23.4, CO 8, 314), that reprobation is God's will (3.22.11, 3.23.1), that God's will has no cause (3.23.2), and that God does whatever he pleases (3.23.7 from 1559), the good pleasure of his will (3.23.10).

28 Luther, *Von den guten Werken* (WA 6, 204–10, esp. 207).

29 *Acts of the Council of Trent. With an Antidote*, 1547 (CTS Tracts vol. III, p. 125): 'They [the papists] rob consciences of a calm, placid confidence', and p. 126: 'They are ignorant of the whole nature of faith who mingle doubt with it.' Similar criticisms of the papist doctrine had already been made in the 1539 *Institution*, 3.2.38–40.

30 This point is scantly regarded in the discussion of predestination (3.24.6), no doubt because Calvin had already given it a great deal of attention in the context of his definition of faith as a 'sure and firm persuasion', a 'firm assurance' (3.2.15), boldness, *fiducia*, *indubita salutis expectatio*, *securitas salutis* (3.2.16), *certitudo salutis* (3.2.17), *salutis fiducia* (3.2.40), all of which contrast strongly with the experience of doubt, anxiety and tribulation familiar to evangelicals (3.2.17–18).

31 3.24.6 and 7, where Calvin denies that those who seemed to be Christ's and then fell away again ever 'cleaved to Christ with the heartfelt trust in which the certainty of election has been established for us'. Aside

from being pure conjecture, this is scarcely reassuring for those who do not enjoy a quiet reliance or simple confidence. Cf. also 3.2.40.

32 The distinction also appears in the *Antidote to the Council of Trent* (CTS Tracts, vol. III), e.g. p. 137, where 'carnal arrogance' is contrasted with 'assurance of faith' or 'security', or on p. 125, where the vain confidence of heretics is contrasted with the 'calm, placid confidence' of the godly. In the *Institution*, at 3.24.7, 'simplex securitas' is contrasted with a 'supina ac soluta carnis securitas'.

33 Calvin's numbers here must be read, I suppose, like the biblical 'seventy times seven'. Is it of any consequence that in 1539, Calvin reckoned that twenty out of a hundred hearers of the Word receive it with a ready obedience of faith (3.24.12), whereas by 1559 it had become one in a hundred (1.5.8, 3.20.14) or scarcely that (1.4.1)?

34 The entire edifice of scriptural demonstration of reprobation rests on Romans 9.18–23, and Jacob and Esau, as interpreted by St Paul in the same chapter; there is no text in Genesis for Paul's 'Jacob have I loved, but Esau have I hated' (Romans 9.13), and the Jacob and Esau story would not qualify as a *locus* independently of Paul's interpretation.

35 W. Niesel, *The Theology of Calvin*, trans. H. Knight (London, 1956), p. 166.

36 M. Weber, *Die Protestantische Ethik*, ed. J. Winckelmann (2nd ed., Munich and Hamburg, 1969), vol. I, p. 195, n. 7.

37 Weber, *Protestantische Ethik*, p. 127.

38 *Ibid.*

39 *Ibid.*, p. 206, n. 43, citing 3.2.37 and 38.

40 3.14.14 ff.

Bibliography

PRIMARY SOURCES

CALVIN'S WORKS

Editions of the Institution

A comprehensive bibliography of editions, translations and abridgements of the *Institution* may be found in J. T. McNeill (ed.) and F. L. Battles (trans.), *Institutes of the Christian Religion*, Library of Christian Classics, vols 20 and 21 (Philadelphia, 1960), vol. 21, pp. 1527–30. Only readily accessible editions and translations, or those used in the book, are cited below.

Variorum editions
Barth, P. and Niesel, W. (eds) *Joannis Calvini Opera Selecta*, 5 vols (Munich, 1926–36), vols III–V. (A variorum of all editions, referred to throughout as OS.)
Baum, W., Cunitz, E. and Reuss, E. (eds), *Joannis Calvini Opera Quae Supersunt Omnia*, 59 vols (Brunswick, 1863–1900), vol. 1. (Variorum of the 1539–54 editions, referred to throughout as CO. The secondary literature sometimes quotes this edition according to its numbering in the *Corpus Reformatorum* series in which it appears. References in my text are to the CO numbering. The CR number of any volume is CO plus 28; thus e.g. CO 1 is CR 29.)
McNeill, J. T. (ed.) and Battles, F. L. (trans.), *Institutes of the Christian Religion*, cited above. (Variorum translation of all editions.)

1536 edition
OS 1 (Latin) and CO 1 (Latin).
Battles, F. L. (trans.), *Institution of the Christian Religion* (Atlanta, 1975).

1541 edition
Pannier, J. (ed.), *Institution de la Religion Chrestienne*, 4 vols (Paris, 1936–9)

1559 edition
CO 2.
Tholuck, A. (ed.), *Institutio Christianae Religionis*, 2 vols (Edinburgh, 1874).

1560 edition (French)
Benoit, J. (ed.), *Institution de la Religion Chrétienne*, 5 vols (Paris, 1957–61).
CO 3–4.

Norton, T. (trans.), *Institution of the Christian Religion* (London, 1561) (the first translation into English).
Beveridge, H. (trans.), *Institutes of the Christian Religion*, 2 vols, Calvin Translation Society (Edinburgh, 1845, frequently reprinted).

Commentary on Seneca's 'De Clementia', 1532

Battles, F. L. and Hugo, A. M. (ed. and trans.), *Calvin's Commentary on Seneca's 'De Clementia'* (Leiden, 1969).

Reply to Sadoleto, 1539

Olin, J. C. (ed.), *John Calvin and Jacopo Sadoleto: A Reformation Debate. Sadoleto's Letter to the Genevans and Calvin's Reply* (New York, 1966).

Tracts, pamphlets and treatises other than the Commentaries

CO 5–10, 1; OS 1 and 11.
Beveridge, H. (trans.), *Calvin's Tracts*, 3 vols, Calvin Translation Society (Edinburgh, 1844–51, repr. Grand Rapids, Michigan, 1958).
Higman, F. M. (ed.), *Jean Calvin: Three French Treatises* (London, 1970).
Reid, J. K. S. (ed.), *Calvin's Theological Treatises*, Library of Christian Classics, XXII (London, 1954). (Despite its title, this volume also contains several of Calvin's organizational writings.)

Commentaries

Calvin's Commentaries, Calvin Translation Society, various translators, 47 vols (Edinburgh, 1843–59).
Torrance, D. W. and Torrance, T. F. (eds), *Calvin's Commentaries* (New Testament) (Edinburgh and London, 1959–).
CO 22–59 contains most of Calvin's commentaries and sermons. Previously unpublished sermons are being published in the *Supplementa Calviniana* (Neukirchen, 1961–).

Letters to and from Calvin and related letters

CO 10, 11, – 20.

Selections and individual works in translations readily available

Dillenberger, J. (ed.), *Calvin. Selections from his Writings* (Garden City, New York, 1971).

McNeill, J. T. (ed.), *Calvin on the Christian Faith* (Indianapolis and New York, 1957).

McNeill, J. T. (ed.), *Calvin on God and Political Duty* (Indianapolis and New York, 1956).

OTHER PRIMARY SOURCES

Baxter, R., *Autobiography* (London and New York, 1931).

Bèze (Beza), Th. de, *Du Droit des Magistrats*, ed. R. M. Kingdon (Geneva, 1970).
   Vie de Calvin, CO 21, 20–52
   Vita Calvini, CO 21, 121–72
   Vita Calvini (by N. Colladon but appeared under Beza's name), CO 21, 53–118.

Bonivard, F. de, *Advis et Devis de l'Ancienne et Nouvelle Police de Geneve*, 1555, *Mémoires et Documents publiés par la Société d'Histoire et d'Archéologie de Genève* 5 (1845).

Briefe und Akten zum Leben Oekolampads, ed. E. Stähelin, vol. II (Leipzig, 1935).

Bucer, M., *Von der Wahren Seelsorge*, 1538, in R. Stupperich (ed.), *Martin Bucers deutsche Schriften*, vol. 7 (Gütersloh and Paris, 1964).
   Ziegenhainer Zuchtordnung, in *Deutsche Schriften*, vol. 7.

Budé, G., *L'Institution du Prince*, 1519, in C. Bontemps, L. P. Raybond and J. P. Brancourt, *Le Prince dans la France des XVIe et XVIIe Siècles* (Paris, 1965).

Castiglione, B., *The Book of the Courtier*, 1528, trans. G. Bull (Harmondsworth, 1967).

Elyot, Sir T., *The Book named the Governor*, 1531, ed. S. E. Lehmberg (London, 1962).

Erasmus, D., *Institutio Principis Christiani*, 1516, in *Opera Omnia Desiderii Erasmi Roterodami*, vol. 4.1, ed. O. Erding (Amsterdam, 1974).

Farel, G., *Sommaire et Brièfve Declaration*, 1525, facsimile ed. (Paris, 1935).

Fills (or Filles), R., *The Lawes and Statutes of Geneva*, 1562 (London, 1562).

Livre des Habitants de Genève, ed. P. J. Geisendorf, 2 vols, vol. 1: *1549–1560* (Geneva, 1957).

Luther, M. (cited according to the Weimar Edition (WA), Weimar, 1883–   ),
   Von der Freiheit eines Christenmenschen (*The Freedom of a Christian*), 1520 (WA 7).
   An den christlichen Adel deutscher Nation, von des christlichen Standes Besserung (*To the Christian Nobility of the German Nation*), 1520 (WA 6).
   De Captivitate Babylonica Ecclesiae Praeludium (*Concerning the Babylonian Captivity of the Church*), 1520 (WA 6).
   Von den guten Werken (*On Good Works*), 1520 (WA 6).

Von dem Papstthum zu Rom, wider den hochberühmten Romanisten zu Leipzig (*On the Papacy at Rome*), 1520 (WA 6).

Auf das überchristliche Buch Bock Emsers Antwort (*Answer to the Hyperchristian Book of the Ram Emser*), 1521 (WA 7).

Eine treue Vermahnung zu allen Christen, sich zu hüten vor Aufruhr und Empörung (*A Faithful Admonition to all Christians to Avoid Rebellion*), 1522 (WA 8).

Preface to the Epistle of St Paul to the Romans, 1522, in WA Deutsche Bibel, 7.

De Instituendis Ministris Ecclesiae (*On Establishing Ministers of the Church*), 1523 (WA 12).

Von weltlicher Oberkeit, wie weit man ihr Gehorsam schuldig sei (*On Secular Authority*), 1523 (WA 11).

Das eine Christliche Versammlung oder Gemeine Recht und Macht habe, alle Lehre zu urtheilen und Lehrer zu berufen, ein und ab zu setzen, Grund und Ursach aus der Schrift (*That a Christian Community or Congregation has the Right and Power to Judge all Doctrine, and to Appoint and Dismiss Teachers*), 1523 (WA 11).

An die Ratsherren aller Städte deutschen Landes, dass sie christliche Schulen aufrichten und halten sollen (*Exhortation to the Councillors of all the Towns of Germany to Erect and Maintain Christian Schools*), 1524 (WA 15).

Wider die himmlischen Propheten (*Against the Heavenly Prophets*), 1524/5 (two parts, WA 18).

Ermahnung zum Frieden, auf die zwölf Artikel der Bauerschaft in Schwaben (*Admonition to Peace, Concerning the Twelve Articles of the Swabian Peasantry*), 1525 (WA 18).

Wider die räuberischen und mörderischen Rotten der Bauern (*Against the Thieving and Murdering Hordes of Peasants*), 1525 (WA 18).

Ein Sendbrief von dem harten Büchlein wider die Bauern (*Missive about the Harsh Pamphlet against the Peasants*), 1525 (WA 18).

Von dem Greuel der Stillmesse, so man Canon nennet (*On the Abomination of the Silent Mass, called the Canon*), 1525 (WA 18).

De Servo Arbitrio (*Concerning the Enslaved Will*), 1525 (WA 18).

Ob Kriegsleute auch im seeligen Stand sein können (*Whether Soldiers too can be in a State of Grace*), 1526 (WA 19).

Von den Schlüsseln (*On the Keys*), 1530 (WA 30, 11).

Machiavelli, N., *The Prince* and *The Discourses*, ed. M. Lerner (New York, 1950).

Marsiglio of Padua, *Defensor Pacis*, ed. A. Gewirth, 2 vols (New York, 1956).

Melanchthon, P., *Loci Communes*, 1521, in H. Engelland (ed.), *Melanchthons Werke*, vol. 11, part 1 (Gütersloh, 1952).

Loci Communes, German translation by Justus Jonas (Wittenberg, 1539).

Loci Communes, 1559 in *Melanchthons Werke*, vol. 11, parts 1 and 11 (variants printed in footnotes to the 1535 edition).

More, T., *Utopia*, 1516, in E. Surtz and J. H. Hexter (eds.), Yale edition of *The Works of Thomas More*, vol. 4 (New Haven and London, 1965).

Registres de la Compagnie des Pasteurs de Genève au Temps de Calvin, ed. R. M. Kingdon, 2 vols (Geneva, 1962–4).

Seyssel, Claude de, *La Monarchie de France*, 1519, ed. J. Poujol (Paris, 1961).

Sources du Droit du Canton de Genève, ed. E. Rivoire and V. van Berchem, Sammlung Schweizerischer Rechtsquellen ɪɪ and ɪɪɪ (Aarau, 1920–30).
Starkey, T., *Dialogue between Reginald Pole and Thomas Lupset*, Early English Text Society, Extra Series 12 and 32 (London, 1871 and 1878, repr. New York, 1975).
Zwingli, U., *De Vera et Falsa Religione . . . Commentarius*, 1525 (Zurich,1525). *Von Göttlicher und Menschlicher Grechtigkeit, wie die zemen sehind und standind*, in F. Blanke, O. Farner and R. Pfister (eds), *Zwingli, Hauptschriften*, vol. 7 (Zurich, 1942).

SECONDARY WORKS

Allen, J. W., *A History of Political Thought in the Sixteenth Century* (1928, repr· London, 1977).
Autin, A., *L'Institution Chrétienne* (Paris, 1929).
Balke, W., *Calvijn en de Doperse Radikalen* (Amsterdam, 1973).
Baron, H., *Calvins Staatsanschauung und das konfessionelle Zeitalter*, Historische *Zeitschrift*, Beihefte 1–3 (1924).
Battles, F. L., 'Against Luxury and Licence in Geneva', in *Interpretation* 19 (1965), 182–202.
Baur, J., *Gott, Recht und Weltliches Regiment im Werk Calvins* (Bonn, 1965).
Beyerhaus, G., *Studien zur Staatsanschauung Calvins* (Berlin, 1910).
Biéler, A., *La Pensée Economique et Sociale de Calvin* (Geneva, 1959).
Bohatec, J., *Calvin und das Recht* (Graz, 1934).
Calvins Lehre von Staat und Kirche (Breslau, 1937).
Bordier, H., *Bolsec Rajeuni* (Libourne, 1880).
Bouwsma, W. J., 'The Two Faces of Humanism', in H. O. Oberman and T. A. Brady (eds), *Itinerarium Italicum*, Studies in Medieval and Reformation Thought xɪv (Leiden, 1975), 3–60.
Breen, Q., *John Calvin: A Study in French Humanism* (Hamden, 1968).
Burns, N. T., *Christian Mortalism from Tyndale to Milton* (Cambridge, Mass., 1972).
Caprariis, V. de, *Propaganda e Pensiero Politico in Francia durante le Guerre di Religione* (Naples, 1959).
Cargill Thompson, W. D. J., 'The "Two Kingdoms" and the "Two Regiments": Some Problems of Luther's *Zwei-Reiche-Lehre*,' in *Studies in the Reformation: Luther to Hooker*, ed. C. W. Dugmore (London, 1980), 42–59.
Chenevière, M. E., *La Pensée Politique de Calvin* (1937, repr. Geneva, 1970).
Choisy, E., *La Théocratie à Genève au Temps de Calvin* (Geneva, 1897).
Courvoisier, M. J., 'Les Catéchismes de Genève et de Strasbourg', in *Etudes sur Calvin et le Calvinisme* (Paris, 1935), 105–21.
Cranz, F. E., *An Essay on the Development of Luther's Thought on Justice, Law and Society*, Harvard Theological Studies 19 (Cambridge, Mass., 1959).
Davies, R. E., *The Problem of Authority in the Continental Reformers* (London, 1946).
Doumergue, E., *Jean Calvin. Les Hommes et les Choses de son Temps*, 7 vols (Lausanne and Neuilly, 1899–1927).

Dowey, E., *The Knowledge of God in Calvin's Theology* (repr. New York and London, 1965).

Duffield, G. (ed.), *John Calvin*, Courtenay Studies in Reformation Theology 1 (Abingdon, 1966).

Ferguson, A. B., *The Articulate Citizen and the English Renaissance* (Durham, N. C., 1965).

Franklin, J. H., *Constitutionalism and Resistance* (New York, 1969).

Fulpius, L., *Les Institutions Politiques de Genève* (Geneva, 1965).

Gallatin, M. L. de, 'Les Ordonnances Somptuaires à Genève au XVIᵉ Siècle', in *Mémoires et Documents Publiés par la Société d'Histoire et d'Archéologie de Genève*, 36, (1938).

Ganoczy, A., *Calvin: Théologien de l'Eglise et du Ministère* (Paris, 1964).

Le Jeune Calvin. Genèse et Evolution de sa Vocation Réformatrice (Wiesbaden, 1966).

Gerrish, B., 'John Calvin on Luther', in J. Pelikan (ed.), *Interpreters of Luther* (Philadelphia, 1968), 67–96.

Gloede, G., *Theologia Naturalis bei Calvin*, Tübinger Studien zur Systematischen Theologie 5 (Stuttgart, 1935).

Greenleaf, W. H., *Order, Empiricism and Politics* (London, 1964).

Hall, B., 'John Calvin, the Jurisconsults and the Jus Civile', in *Studies in Church History* 3 (1966), 202–16.

Hazard, P., *The European Mind, 1680–1715*, trans. J. Lewis May (Harmondsworth, 1964).

Hexter, J. H., *More's Utopia: the Biography of an Idea* (New York, 1965).

Höpfl, H. M., 'Fundamental Law and the Constitution in Sixteenth-Century France', in R. Schnur (ed.), *Die Rolle der Juristen im frühmodernen Staat* (forthcoming).

Imbart de la Tour, P., *Calvin et l'Institution Chrétienne*, vol. 4 of *Les Origines de la Réforme* (Paris, 1935).

Kampschulte, J., *Johannes Calvin: Seine Kirche und sein Staat in Genf* (Leipzig, 1869).

Kelley, D. R., *The Foundations of Modern Historical Scholarship: Language, Law and History in the French Renaissance* (New York, 1970).

Kern, F., *Kingship and Law in the Middle Ages*, trans. S. B. Chrimes (Oxford, 1939).

Kingdon, R. M., *Geneva and the Coming of the Wars of Religion in France* (Geneva, 1956).

Köhler, W., *Zürcher Ehegericht und Genfer Konsistorium*, Quellen zur Schweizerischen Reformationsgeschichte 13 (Leipzig, 1942).

Lecler, J., *Histoire de la Tolérance*, 2 vols (Aubier, 1955).

Léonard, E. G., *A History of Protestantism*, ed. H. H. Rowley, 2 vols (London and Edinburgh, 1965).

Little, D., *Religion, Order and Law* (Oxford, 1970).

Locher, G. W., *Die Zwinglische Reformation im Rahmen der europäischen Kirchengeschichte* (Göttingen and Zurich, 1979).

McNeill, J. T., *The History and Character of Calvinism* (New York, 1967).

McSorley, H. J., *Luthers Lehre von dem unfreien Willen* (Munich, 1967).

Markus, R. A. (ed.), *Augustine* (New York, 1972).

Saeculum: History and Society in the Theology of St Augustine (Cambridge, 1970).

Moeller, B., *Imperial Cities and the Reformation*, trans. H. C. Midelfort and M. U. Edwards (Philadelphia, 1972).

Moltmann, J. (ed.), *Calvin-Studien, 1959* (Neukirchen, 1960).

Monter, E. W., *Studies in Genevan Government* (Geneva, 1964).

Calvin's Geneva (London and New York, 1967).

'Crime and Punishment in Calvin's Geneva', *Archiv für Reformationsgeschichte* 64 (1973), 281–7.

Mueller, W. A., *Church and State in Luther and Calvin* (Nashville, Tennessee, 1954).

Mülhaupt, E., *Der Psalter auf der Kanzel Calvins* (Neukirchen, 1959).

Niesel, W., *The Theology of Calvin*, trans. H. Knight (London, 1956).

Oakeshott, M., *On Human Conduct* (Oxford, 1975).

Otten, H., *Prädestination in Calvins Theologischer Lehre* (1938, repr. Neukirchen-Vluyn, 1968).

Ozment, S., *The Reformation in the Cities* (New Haven and London, 1975).

Parker, T. H. L., *Calvin's New Testament Commentaries* (London, 1971).

John Calvin (London, 1975).

Pfister, O., *Calvins Eingreifen in die Hexen- und Hexer-Prozesse von Peney* (Zurich, 1947).

Pfisterer, E., *Calvins Wirken in Genf* (2nd ed., Neukirchen, 1957).

Plath, U., *Calvin und Basel in den Jahren 1552–1556* (Basel and Stuttgart, 1974).

Pocock, J. G. A., *The Ancient Constitution and the Feudal Law* (Cambridge, 1957).

'The Origins of the Study of the Past', in *Comparative Studies in Society and History* 4(1961–2), 209–46.

Potter, G. R., *Zwingli* (Cambridge, 1976).

Quistorp, H., *Calvin's Doctrine of the Last Things* (London, 1955).

Rott, J., 'Documents Strasbourgeois Concernant Calvin', in *Regards Contemporains sur Jean Calvin, Actes du Colloque Calvin à Strasbourg, 1964* (Paris, 1965).

Schellong, D., *Calvins Auslegung der synoptischen Evangelien* (Munich, 1969).

Schmid, H., *Zwinglis Lehre von der göttlichen und menschlichen Gerechtigkeit* (Zurich, 1959).

Schmidt, E., *Einführung in die Geschichte der deutschen Strafrechtspflege* (3rd ed., Göttingen, 1965).

Schrey, H. H. (ed.), *Reich Gottes und Welt: Die Lehre Luthers von den zwei Reichen* (Darmstadt, 1969).

Schwarzwäller, K., *Sibboleth* (Munich, 1969).

Theologia Crucis (Munich, 1970).

Seeberg, R., *Lehrbuch der Dogmengeschichte*, vol. 4 (Leipzig, 1917).

Skinner, Q., *The Foundations of Modern Political Thought*, 2 vols (Cambridge, 1978).

Spitz, L. W. (ed.), *The Protestant Reformation* (Englewood Cliffs, N.J., 1966).

Sprenger, P., *Das Rätsel um die Bekehrung Calvins* (Neukirchen, 1960).

Stadtland, T., *Rechtfertigung und Heiligung bei Calvin* (Neukirchen-Vluyn, 1972).

Stayer, J. M., *Anabaptists and the Sword* (Lawrence, Kansas, 1972).

Strohl, H., 'La Théorie et la Pratique des Quatre Ministères à Strasbourg avant l'Arrivée de Calvin' in *Etudes sur Calvin et le Calvinisme*, 123–44.

Stupperich, R., 'Calvin und die Konfession des Paul Volz', in *Actes du Colloque Calvin à Strasbourg*, Cahiers de la Revue d'Histoire et de Philosophie Religieuses 39 (1965), 17–27.

Thompson, M. and Höpfl, H. M., 'The History of Contract as a Motif in Political Thought', in *American Historical Review* 84/4 (1979), 919–44.

Vahle, H., 'Calvinismus und Demokratie im Spiegel der Forschung', in *Archiv für Reformationsgeschichte* 66 (1975), 182–212.

Voegelin, E., *The New Science of Politics* (Chicago and London, 1952).

Walker, W., *John Calvin, the Organizer of Reformed Protestantism* (New York, 1910).

Wallace, R. S., *Calvin's Doctrine of the Christian Life* (Edinburgh, 1959).

Walton, R., *Zwingli's Theocracy* (Toronto, 1967).

Walzer, M., *The Revolution of the Saints* (1965, repr. New York, 1976).

Weber, M., *Die Protestantische Ethik*, ed. J. Winckelmann, 2 vols (2nd ed., Munich and Hamburg, 1969).

Wendel, F., *L'Eglise de Strasbourg* (Paris, 1942).

Calvin. The Origins and Development of his Religious Thought, trans. P. Mairet (London, 1965).

Williams, G. H., *The Radical Reformation* (Philadelphia, 1962).

Wolin, S. S., *Politics and Vision* (London, 1961).

Wyduckel, D., *Princeps Legibus Solutus* (Berlin, 1979).

Index

adiaphora (things indifferent or inessential), 83, 85–6, 108
administratio, 46–7, 105, 253 n. 93, 261 n. 22
adultery, 180, 182–4, 278 nn. 62, 63, 64
aedificatio (building up), 37, 39, 41, 63, 64, 75, 88, 101, 108, 112, 114, 116, 191, 193, 194, 203, 211, 252 n. 84, 261 n. 27, 280 n. 21
aequitas, 13–14, 50, 172, 179, 183, 211, 253 n. 101
Alciati, A., 6, 242 n. 9
Anabaptists, 27, 31, 34, 44–5, 47, 50, 52, 54, 58, 60, 80–1, 85–6, 146, 172, 187, 194, 224–5, 257 n. 16, 280 n. 17, 285 nn. 31, 38; see also millennialism, Schleitheim Articles
anti-Machiavellianism, 268 nn. 80, 81
antinomianism, 23, 175, 276 n. 20
argutia (quibbles), 13, 38, 243 n. 34
aristocracy, 97, 124, 153–5, 171, 272 n. 51; see also forms of government
Articles Proposed by Calvin and Farel, 77, 100
auctoritas, 95, 139, 165, 169, 254 n. 6; see also potestas
Augsburg Confession, 98, 111, 252 n. 77
Augustine, St, 15, 98, 219, 221, 229, 255 n. 19, 280 n. 12, 287 n. 10

Basel, 9, 19, 32, 224, 255 n. 17, 257 n. 26, 276 n. 21
Battles, F. L., 241 nn. 2, 3
Bern, 77, 125, 129–30, 131, 178, 270 n. 14
Beza (de Bèze), Th., 168, 207, 220, 242 n. 21, 270 n. 10, 275 n. 111, 284 n. 17, 285 n. 22
Biéler, A., 3, 193, 196, 280 nn. 19, 22
bishops, 42, 109–10, 112, 123; see also elders

blasphemy, see heresy
Bohatec, J., 3
Bolsec, J., 119, 192, 208, 264 n. 4, 267 n. 73, 282 nn. 52, 60, 70, 287 n. 12
books, 199, 264 n. 7, 279 n. 78
bridle, metaphor of, 191, 204, 244 n. 49, 261 n. 23, 280 n. 11
Bucer, M., 24, 30, 78, 80, 89, 94, 101, 246 n. 19, 252 n. 78, 256 nn. 11, 25, 257 n. 26, 258 nn. 28, 29, 32, 261 n. 19; see also Strasbourg
Budé, G., 6, 14, 52, 242 n. 14, 244 nn. 38, 44, 272 n. 49
Bullinger, 140, 236, 255 n. 17, 258 n. 29, 285 n. 30

Calvin, J., biographical: education, 5, 6, 220; publishes *De Clementia Commentary*, 5; leaves France for Basel, 19, 223, 285 n. 22; writes *Psychopannychia*, see psychopannychism; publishes first *Institution*, 19, *Confession de la Foy*, 22, 56, 65–7, 118, 208, *Catechisme* (1537/8), 22, 56, 67–75, 118, 208; arrives in Geneva, 56; presents *Ordonnances* (*Articles* of 1536), 56, 61–5; compositional habits, 67, 82, 116; expulsion from Geneva, 76–8; at Strasbourg, 78–9, 80, 99–100; publishes *Institution* of 1539, 79; returns to Geneva, 79; presents *Ordonnances* (1541), 90–102, 137; publishes *Institution* of 1543, 97; participates in revision of Genevan civic ordinances, 141, 266 n. 47; protected by law from insult, 266 n. 45; political opponents, 131, 136, 157, 178, 274 n. 91; personal authority, 138–41; health, 207; not kill-joy, 200–1; publishes *Institution* of 1559/60,

299

Cambridge Studies in the History and Theory of Politics

Editors: Maurice Cowling, G. R. Elton, E. Kedourie, J. R. Pole, J. G. A. Pocock and Walter Ullmann

A series in two parts, studies and original texts. The studies are original works on political history and political philosophy while the texts are modern, critical editions of major texts in political thought. The titles include:

TEXTS

Does one side need to be 'wrong'?